Montana Place Names
from Alzada to Zortman

D1602440

Montana Place Names
from Alzada to Zortman

Rich Aarstad
Ellie Arguimbau
Ellen Baumler
Charlene Porsild
Brian Shovers

Montana Historical Society Press
Helena, Montana

FRONT COVER PHOTO: Beartooth Highway, fifth level—Rock Creek Gorge, F. W. Byerly, photographer, Montana Historical Society Photograph Archives, Helena (color added)

EPIGRAPH: Richard Hugo, "Driving Montana," from *Selected Poems* (New York: Norton, 1979), 100–101. Used with permission of Ripley Hugo.

QUOTE P. XIII: Kim Robert Stafford, "There Are No Names but Stories," from *Places & Stories* (Pittsburgh: Carnegie Mellon University Press, 1987), 11.

QUOTE P. XIV: *Fort Benton (Mont.) River Press,* June 4, 1890, from Joseph Kinsey Howard, *Montana Margins: A State Anthology* (New Haven, Conn., 1946), 446.

COVER AND BOOK DESIGN BY Kathryn Fehlig, Helena, Montana

TYPESET IN Adobe Garamond

PRINTED IN Canada by Friesens

This book has been financed in part with federal funds from the National Park Service, U.S. Department of the Interior, administered by the State Historic Preservation Office of the Montana Historical Society. This program receives federal financial assistance for identification and protection of historic properties. Under Title VI of the Civil Rights Act of 1964 and Section 504 of the Rehabilitation Act of 1973, and the Age Discrimination Act of 1975, the U.S. Department of the Interior prohibits discrimination on the basis of race, color, national origin, age, or disability in its federally assisted programs.

Copyright © 2009 by Montana Historical Society Press, P.O. Box 201201, Helena, Montana 59620-1201. All rights reserved.

Distributed by The Globe Pequot Press, 246 Goose Lane, Guilford, Connecticut 06437 (800) 243-0495

09 10 11 12 13 14 15 16   10 9 8 7 6 5 4 3 2

ISBN-10: 0-9759196-1-X

ISBN-13: 978-0-9759196-1-3

Library of Congress Cataloging-in-Publication Data

Montana place names from Alzada to Zortman / by Rich Aarstad . . . [et al.].
    p. cm.
Includes bibliographical references and index.
ISBN-13: 978-0-9759196-1-3
ISBN-10: 0-9759196-1-X
1. Names, Geographical—Montana. 2. Montana—History, Local.
        I. Aarstad, Rich.
F729.M66 2007
978.6—dc22
2006103183

To all those namers of places—tribal peoples and those who followed—with a special appreciation for the work of Roberta Carkeek Cheney, who documented many Montana places now gone

Funding for the publication of this book was provided in part by a National Park Service Preserve America grant.

Driving Montana

The day is a woman who loves you. Open.
Deer drink close to the road and magpies
spray from your car. Miles from any town
your radio comes in strong, unlikely
Mozart from Belgrade, rock and roll
from Butte. Whatever the next number,
you want to hear it. Never has your Buick
found this forward a gear. Even
the tuna salad in Reedpoint is good.

Towns arrive ahead of imagined schedule.
Absarokee at one. Or arrive so late—
Silesia at nine—you recreate the day.
Where did you stop along the road
and have fun? Was there a runaway horse?
Did you park at that house, the one
alone in a void of grain, white with green
trim and red fence, where you know you lived
once? You remembered the ringing creek,
the soft brown forms of far off bison.
You must have stayed hours, then drove on.
In the motel you know you'd never seen it before.

Tomorrow will open again, the sky wide
as the mouth of a wild girl, friable
clouds you lose yourself to. You are lost
in miles of land without people, without
one fear of being found, in the dash
of rabbits, soar of antelope, swirl
merge and clatter of streams.

—Richard Hugo, *Selected Poems*

Contents

Preface

THIS PROJECT BEGAN AND ENDED at one of my favorite places in Montana: the reference desk at the Montana Historical Society in Helena, when I was director of the Research Center. Like so many great ideas, this one began in a conversation between friends: Brian Shovers and I were stumped about the origin of the name of a mountain peak. Though Roberta Carkeek Cheney's *Names on the Face of Montana,* first published in 1971 and updated in 1983, has been the standard source, we lamented the absence of a comprehensive reference on Montana's place names and natural features. One of our patrons calmly pointed out that if there was ever a team to write that book, we were it.

And so the gauntlet had been thrown. "You know Charlene, that's not a bad idea," Brian said.

"Sure, we have all the resources within twenty feet of this reference desk," I replied.

But we both had many competing demands for our time (not the least of which was answering patrons' questions about the origin of obscure place names), and so the idea languished. After several more months and many place name searches later, I again brought up the idea and asked Brian if he would coauthor the book with me.

As we talked about what such a book would look like, it quickly became apparent that the scope of the project was too large for the two of us, so we turned to the talented people we worked with every day. Archivist and avid outdoorswoman Ellie Arguimbau was the logical choice to help Brian research the naming origins of Montana's natural features and industrial sites. Historian and Libby native Rich Aarstad seemed similarly suited to help me research the names of Treasure State towns. I'll never know if any of them would have said no if I hadn't been their boss, but they all gave the appearance of great enthusiasm from the start.

All we were missing was someone to help us with historic sites. Historian Ellen Baumler didn't actually work in the Research Center, so I had to coax and cajole a little harder, and eventually she said yes. Since Ellen had researched hundreds of

Montana sites listed in the National Register of Historic Places, she had much to contribute.

This team of five met beside the reference desk every Friday morning for two years. I looked forward to those meetings. They were part group therapy when we got bogged down with other work and needed encouragement to keep going, and part strategizing sessions on how to shape the growing mountain of data into a book. But most of all they were opportunities to share the weird, off-color, sad, crazy, mundane, and funny tidbits that make Montana history so rich.

Along the way we were fortunate enough to have the assistance of Carroll College student Lindsay Thompson for a full semester, and she helped research many of the towns. Our other colleagues within the Montana Historical Society assisted when we were stuck.

We also sought and received aid from the staff at the Montana State Library. Butte native Jim Hill and his amazing staff at the Natural Resource Information Service, especially Sibyl Govan and Gerry Daumiller, built the database into which we entered all our findings and assisted us in many ways as we compiled hundreds of thousands of pieces of information. I'm sure they thought we were crazy (I know they thought we were computer idiots), but I hope the results will show them that their patience was well placed. And we owe a special thank you to the late Dave Walter of the Montana Historical Society, Don Spritzer of the Missoula Public Library, and Jon Axline and Art Jacobsen at the Montana Department of Transportation, all of whom contributed their vast knowledge of Montana history to our endeavor.

Ultimately, this project was completed because of the assistance we received from a wide variety of Montanans across the state. Time and again, they responded to our phone calls, e-mails, and letters, patiently correcting "those people up in Helena" who had it all wrong. We called museums, coffee shops, local libraries, and schools, from the Yaak to the Crow Indian Reservation. We asked old friends, slight acquaintances, and total strangers to help us, and they all did. When we had completed a rough draft of the entries, we sent them to folks in all fifty-six counties and seven Indian reservations. We received comments, edits, and suggestions from almost every single person. We were awed. We were surprised. We were humbled. And we were so glad we had asked.

We apologize and accept responsibility for any remaining errors and omissions.

—*Charlene Porsild, Ph.D.*
Albuquerque, New Mexico

Introduction

MONTANA—THE ORIGIN OF THE TERRITORY'S (AND STATE'S) NAME IS SIMPLE. Montaña means "mountain" in Spanish. The primary advocate for naming the new territory Montana was Ohio congressman James M. Ashley, who, during debates on the subject, pointed to a place of the same name near Pikes Peak in Colorado Territory. Ashley, a friend of Montana's first territorial governor, Sidney Edgerton, prevailed against suggestions such as Jefferson and Shoshone. On May 26, 1864, President Abraham Lincoln signed the bill creating Montana Territory.

The names assigned to geographic features and inhabited places are among the most enduring legacies of Montana's past. As long as humans have been in this region, they have been naming places, and with each wave of settlement, other people renamed those same places. Although the past century and a half have brought enormous changes to the way people live on the land, some of the oldest place names have persisted. Were C. P. Higgins to return to the site of his sawmill along the Clark Fork River today, he would be disoriented by the interstate highway and box stores, but Missoula's name would be familiar—it derives from a word used by the Salish, some of the first people to call this part of western Montana home.

Many other familiar Montana place names also originated with the area's native inhabitants. These names often tell a story about something that happened there. In "There Are No Names but Stories," poet Kim Robert Stafford describes this phenomenon:

> When the anthropologist asked the Kwakiutl
> for a map of their coast, they told him
> stories: Here? *Salmon gather.* Here?
> *Sea Otter camps.* Here *seal sleep.*
> Here we say *body covered with mouths.*
>
> How can a place have a name? A man,
> a woman may have a name, but they die.
> We are a story until we die.
> Then our names are dangerous.
> A place is a story happening many times.

From the early nineteenth century on, explorers and surveyors marked names on their maps. Captains Meriwether Lewis and William Clark were among the earliest mapmakers; they arrived in present-day Montana in 1805. David Thompson of the North West Company followed shortly thereafter, and Father Pierre-Jean De Smet, a Jesuit missionary, was here in the 1840s. Geographic features came to dominate early maps, and the designations assigned to these by early Euro-Americans are often linked to familiar plants and animals: the Bitterroot Mountains, Bears Paw Mountains, Musselshell River, and Grasshopper Glacier. In some instances, the explorers' names describe the color or form of a prominent feature, such as Yellowstone River, Heart Butte, or Sphinx Mountain.

The first towns appear on the map the first territorial legislature commissioned from Walter W. DeLacy, and in just over half a century, Montana sprouted hundreds of new names. Many are associated with an early resident or a dominant economic activity, such as Bozeman (for John Bozeman), Philipsburg (for Philip Deidesheimer, the first superintendent of the St. Louis & Montana Mining Company), Billings (for Frederick Billings of the Northern Pacific Railroad), Colstrip (named for its association with strip-mining coal), and Rocker (for the placer-mining device).

Some town names grew from local legend. The June 4, 1890, edition of Fort Benton's *River Press* describes the origin of Big Sandy's name:

> The town and creek of Big Sandy take their name from "Big Sandy" Lane, who was formerly a mule skinner on the old freight road out of Fort Benton. . . . The legend is that Big Sandy came to the creek one evening with a train of time freight due at Fort Assinniboine the next day. . . . It had been raining hard all day and the wheels were often clogged with gumbo, but Sandy had such a persuasive way of addressing the mules that good headway was made until the creek was reached. Here he found the banks so treacherous and the water so swollen that after much shouting and rattling of chains, he found it impossible to cross. Sandy then began cursing his luck, the weather, and the mules so vehemently that in a short time the creek dried up, and he crossed on dry land, reaching his destination in time to save the garrison from starvation.

With the homestead boom of the early twentieth century, tens of thousands of people poured into Montana seeking cheap land. The new towns that sprang up were often named by the railroads for their employees. Other names, such as Sumatra and Malta, were plucked from a world globe. Between 1900 and 1918, Montana's population more than tripled, but drought during the 1920s and 1930s prompted a mass exodus and the demise of many communities. Since that time, hundreds of other towns across the state have disappeared, reflecting a shift in the state's economy from mining, lumbering, and farming to a service economy in which much larger farms and ranches are served by regional commercial centers.

This guidebook explores the name origins of nearly 1,300 Montana towns and cities, Indian reservations, geographic features, and historic sites. Entries document the names we currently know and, whenever possible, previous names. The authors focused on names that have persisted over time and excluded those long gone. Thus, only those that appear on the 2002–2003 Montana Department of Transportation (MDT) highway map are included here (and since that map is modified from year to year, not all of these names are now on the state highway map). As much as possible, names that appear for railroads, mining companies, and other businesses and for state and federal agencies are correct for the time period discussed in the entry.

In addition, this book identifies more than one hundred historic sites listed in the National Register of Historic Places (National Register) or designated National Historic Landmarks (NHLs). These sites range from military forts to missions, from churches to archaeological sites, and from bridges and dams to ranches, homesteads, tourist lodges, and inns. However, only a portion of Montana's many hundreds of National Register–listed properties are included here.

The spellings used in this book are those designated by the U.S. Board on Geographic Names (except in the case of names that begin with Saint, which are abbreviated St. here). In some cases, the names used in the book may differ from those on the highway map.

Elevations included in each entry are from three sources—the 2002 version of National Elevation Dataset (NED), the MDT highway map, and the 2004 version of the Geographic Names Information System (GNIS). The elevation of mountain peaks came from the U.S. Geological Survey (USGS).

The history of Montana is full of intriguing stories. And not all of those stories are represented here. A project of this scope is necessarily a work in progress, and we are always discovering new information about Montana and its special places. We have tried to be as accurate and comprehensive as possible in creating this guide. However, some mistakes may have slipped in. Please send any suggestions for subsequent editions of this book to Montana Place Names, Montana Historical Society, P.O. Box 201201, Helena, MT 59620-1201.

Montana's Tribes

MONTANA IS TODAY HOME TO TWELVE TRIBAL GROUPS—Assiniboine, Blackfeet, Chippewa, Cree, Crow, Gros Ventre, Kootenai, Little Shell Band of Chippewa, Northern Cheyenne, Pend d'Oreille, Salish, and Sioux. A thirteenth group, the Métis, although not formally recognized as a tribe by state or federal government, share the cultural traditions of both their native and European forbearers. Historically, the Lemhi Shoshone and the Nez Perce both lived in and seasonally visited the region that would become Montana.

To understand the story of Montana place names, it is important to appreciate that the tribal groups who lived here and the names by which these peoples were known changed over time. Often the names that came to be used by English speakers were not the ones used by the people themselves, but a mistranslation or name used by another group. Some tribes were given the name their neighboring enemies called them. The word *Sioux* is a Chippewa slur. Cheyenne means "unintelligible speakers" in Dakota Sioux. The Gros Ventre, Shoshone, and Flathead all received those names due to misinterpretation of the iconography of their sign language names. The "Children of the Large-beaked Bird," the Raven Tribe, mislabeled as Crow, speak of themselves as Apsaalooke. And the origins of some English names, including Nez Perce and Blackfeet, are still mysterious.

Complicating the situation is the fact that native groups have been grouped together for bureaucratic convenience and separated from family and tribal relatives by national and reservation boundaries. For example, there are no Flathead Indians—the native residents of the Flathead Indian Reservation, today members of the Confederated Salish and Kootenai Tribes, are Salish and Pend d'Oreille (who are geographically distinct branches of the same cultural and linguistic group) and the Kootenai—who are not related; the Montana Kootenai (the K´tanaxa band) are affiliated with a Kootenai band in Idaho and five bands in British Columbia. Similarly, the Montana Blackfeet (the Southern Piegan, or Pikuni) are the southern portion of the much larger Blackfoot Confederacy whose other members reside in Alberta. The Assiniboines are divided between two Montana reservations (Fort

Belknap and Fort Peck) and live with tribes (the Gros Ventre and Sioux) with whom they shared no affiliation until the U.S. government assigned them to live together. A far larger group of Assiniboine live in Canada where they are called the Stoneys.

The turbulent events of the late nineteenth century and early twentieth century were the catalyst for the creation of reservations. The federal government made strategic decisions regarding the location of these reservations. For example, the federal government assigned the Cheyennes who fled north from the Oklahoma Cheyenne reservation after the Indian wars to a new reservation in Montana rather than allow them to join their allies the Sioux in the Dakotas. This group of Cheyennes became known as the Northern Cheyennes, and their Oklahoma relatives as the Southern Cheyennes. Similarly, the federal government assigned the Sioux returning from Sitting Bull's Canadian encampment in the 1880s to the Fort Peck Reservation rather than permitting them to rejoin their Sioux relations on the troubled reserves of the Dakotas. In 1916, Montana's "landless Indians" were fused into the Chippewa-Cree of Rocky Boy's Reservation. Although sharing historical and cultural affiliations, the inhabitants of Rocky Boy's were Chippewa, Cree, and Métis people excluded from earlier treaty and reservation making. The Litte Shell Chippewa continue to fight for federal recognition.

The table on the following pages provides a summary of the names by which Montana's native groups have been and are currently known.

George Oberst
Former Curator of Ethnology
Montana Historical Society

Montana Reservations

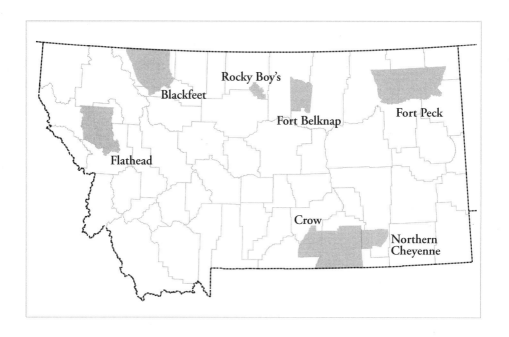

Tribes Living in Montana Past and Present

Name in Popular Use	Historical Names/Misnomer(s)
Arikara	Rees
Assiniboine	Assiniboin
Blackfeet (Southern Piegan)	
Chippewa	Salteaux, Ojibway (Canada)
Cree	Kristenaux
Crow	
Gros Ventre	Atsina, Minnetarres of Fort de Prairie
Kootenai	Flathead, Kutenai
Lemhi Shoshone	Snake
Little Shell Band of Chippewa	Landless Indians
Métis	Red River half-breeds
Nez Perce	
Northern Cheyenne	Cheyenne
Pend d'Oreille	Flathead
Salish	Flathead
Sioux (western division, Lakota; eastern division, Dakota)	

Montana Reservation	Name Used by Tribe
Fort Berthold (North Dakota)	
Fort Belknap, Fort Peck	Nakoda
Blackfeet	Pikuni (Southern Piegan)
Rocky Boy's	Anishanabe
Rocky Boy's	Ne hiyawak
Crow	Apsaalooke
Fort Belknap	A´aninin
Flathead	K´tanaxa Band of 'Aqɫsmaknik
Western Shoshone and Shoshone-Bannock on Fort Hall Reservation, Idaho	Newe
none, not federally recognized tribe	Anishanabe
none, not federally recognized tribe	Métis
Lapwai (Idaho)	Nee-Me-Poo
Northern Cheyenne	Tsetsėhesta´hese
Flathead	Qłispé
Flathead	Seliš
Fort Peck	Sioux; various band names

Sources

THE MONTANA HISTORICAL SOCIETY (MHS) RESEARCH CENTER is the largest repository of Montana history anywhere. The archives contains primary sources in the form of diaries, reminiscences, and other materials, from manuscript collections and oral histories, to business and state government records. Secondary sources in the library collection include such materials as newspapers, books, maps, pamphlets, and vertical files containing newspaper clippings and articles. The Photograph Archives cares for more than four hundred thousand images.

The authors tapped many different kinds of materials to discover the story of the naming of Montana. Foremost among them was Roberta Carkeek Cheney's *Names on the Face of Montana: The Story of Montana's Place Names* (1971; rev. ed., Missoula, Mont., 1983). Cheney's seminal work became the springboard for research and, in some instances, was the only source available. A close second was *Montana Post Offices and Postmasters,* by Dennis J. Lutz and the Montana Chapter No. 1 National Association of Postmasters of the United States (Rochester, Minn., 1986). Lutz's work helped the authors determine whether a community actually developed or if a place existed only as a post office, as well as when towns' names changed. *The Journals of the Lewis and Clark Expedition,* edited by Gary Moulton (Lincoln, Nebr., 1983–2001) proved their worth again and again, supplying the authors with not only the names the Corps of Discovery applied to Montana geographic features but, in some instances, also the Native American names for rivers and streams and a host of other colorful and not-so-colorful place names. Donald B. Roberts's *Encyclopedia of Western Railroad History* (Caldwell, Idaho, 1986–98) proved useful for determining the names of railroads, branch lines, and spur lines. The card file of geographic place names, compiled by the Society's first professional librarian, Laura E. Howey, in the early 1900s, also provided a bounty of information.

In searching the origins of place names, the authors consulted numerous other sources as well. The MHS library has the most complete collection of Montana local histories in existence, and these histories proved to be terrific sources. Invaluable sources for information about communities built along the rail routes include the R. L. Polk and Company's *Minnesota, North Dakota and South Dakota and Montana Gazetteer and Business Directory* (St. Paul., Minn., 1890–1900s) and the Great Northern Railway Company's *The Origin of Station Names in Montana* (n.p., 1937). For geographic names, the authors used a number of sources, but especially the twenty-volume Montana Geographic series (Helena, Mont., 1980s–1990s). The USFS Northern Division's *Early Days in the Forest Service* (Missoula, Mont., 1944–65) provided information about the naming of quite a few features in the national forests, as did "Origin of Geographic Names: Montana National Forests," a typescript in the library's collection, and J. P. Rowe's *The Origin of Some Montana Place Names* (Missoula, Mont., n.d.).

The State Historic Preservation Office, a program of the Montana Historical Society, has other rich resources on Montana's historic places. The Montana Antiquities Database housed there contains information on historic and archaeological sites, previously conducted cultural resource inventories, National Register sites, and other information. In addition, each place listed in the National Register has its own file, arranged by county and easily accessible to the public. Much of the information on the National Register sites in this book came from these files. Montana's National Register of Historic Places sign program provides plaques with interpretive text to owners of Register-listed places, and these sign texts were the basis for many of the historic place names entries.

Of equal importance to the research were a number of Internet resources, including the following:

• The U.S. Geological Survey's Geographic Names Information System (GNIS), http://geonames.usgs.gov, the federal standard for geographic nomenclature, provided names, locations, elevations, and other information.

• The Montana Historical Society's journal, *Montana The Magazine of Western History,* supplied information about many facets of the state's history. A searchable index is available at http://www.his.state.mt.us/pub/magazine/ReferenceIndex.asp. The full text of the magazine is available through the academic database JSTOR.

• The Montana Natural Resource Information System website, http://nris. mt.gov/interactive.html, helped determine the exact location of geographic features as well as Montana cities and towns.

• The Montana Department of Commerce Census and Economic Information Center website, http://ceic.mt.gov/historicalpopdata.asp, provided decennial population numbers for incorporated cities and towns.

• The Montana Department of Environmental Quality Abandoned Mine Program website, http://deq.mt.gov/abandonedmines/hist_nar.asp, not only provided information on significant mining operations across the state but, in some instances, also included historical information regarding those communities that developed as a result of mining.

• The Montana Railroad History website, http://www.montanarailroadhistory. info, proved a very useful resource listing the origins of Great Northern Railway Company station names.

• The U.S. Bureau of Reclamation's website provided useful information on dams at http://www.usbr.gov/dataweb/dams/index.html.

• The Montana National Register of Historic Places website, http:// nationalregisterofhistoricplaces.com/MT/state.html, provided information on all properties in Montana listed in the National Register.

• Also very useful was the Bureau of Land Management/Government Land Office (GLO) website. Many small towns, creeks, and reservoirs (especially in eastern Montana) were named for the family that homesteaded the adjacent land. The GLO records provided the family's full name and when they proved up on the homestead. See http://www.glorecords.blm.gov.

All photographs used in this book are from the MHS Photograph Archives unless otherwise credited. Those with H numbers are from the MHS Haynes Foundation Collection.

How to Use This Book

Montana Place Names consists of two basic parts. The first section, the bulk of the book, contains alphabetically arranged descriptions of more than 1,200 places scattered across Montana. This substantial section is followed by a smaller section containing a map of the state broken into 24 individual sections to allow a closer focus on specific areas. The book is designed to be used in various ways—forward (alphabetically, from text to map), backward (numerically, from map to text), and a little bit of both (browsing between the two sections).

Here is an example to get you started. This is the name line from a typical place name description:

Paradise Valley **841** *map 20 B-2*

In this example, Paradise Valley is the place name being discussed, **841** is the locator number (each place name has a unique locator number), and *map 20 B-2* is the map directional, which includes both a map number and a grid letter and number.

To use the book alphabetically, you might look up in the text a name you are curious about (much like using a dictionary), read the accompanying description, and then use the locator number and map directional to find the place's location on the map. In the example above, you would see that the Paradise Valley's unique locator number is 841 and that its map directional is 20 B-2. You would turn to the map section at the back of the book, find map 20, and trace B-2 from the grid along the edge of the map to find the Paradise Valley. More detailed instructions about how to use the map and a map of the entire state appear on the first three pages of the map section.

Or you may want to take a map-to-text, or numerical, approach. Perhaps you are interested in a particular geographic region and would like to visit or learn about what sites it contains. To continue with the above example, for the Paradise Valley you would turn to the individual map section containing that geographic region and take note of the locator numbers scattered across the area, all representing specific sites and features in the region. Say you first chose 841, the locator for Paradise Valley itself. Turning to the Site Listing/Index at the back of this book, you would find 841 in the numerical list, note the name Paradise Valley, and turn to its description in the text alphabetically. After reading this description, you might return to the same geographic region on the map to choose other sites to read about in the same manner.

A third option is to browse at will, moving from text to map and from map to text (as described above) and following wherever your curiosity leads.

Here are a few more details about the site descriptions themselves. Elevations are shown at the end of the descriptions for discrete locations (e.g., towns and cities, mountain peaks, lakes). For obvious reasons, descriptions of places that are spread over a wider area (e.g., creeks, rivers, parks, counties, mountain ranges) do not contain elevations. Also, many descriptions show a location at the end, usually a county (or two, if the place straddles a county line) but sometimes a park. Any county names used for locations are current rather than historic.

Many descriptions include proper names and terms from native languages. You will encounter place names and general terms presented differently. General terms appear in lowercase and are italicized, with their accompanying English translations in quotation marks—for example, *aotaqpkdl*, meaning "skunk on a log." Place names are set without italics or quotation marks and the first letter of the name is capitalized—for example, Aotaqpkdl'gyl, meaning "Skunk on a log river."

Some descriptions use common abbreviations (including some shortened railroad names) without accompanying definitions. These abbreviations are listed with their full forms in the list of abbreviations following this section. If you encounter an unfamiliar abbreviation while reading, please refer to this list.

Finally, this book is meant to be a general guide to locations. For more specific directions, refer to a current edition of the *DeLorme Montana Atlas & Gazetteer* or ask for directions in nearby communities. If you want to learn more about a specific place, we recommend the resources described in the introduction.

List of Abbreviations

Anaconda Company . . . . Anaconda Mining Company (1891); Anaconda Copper Mining Company (ACMC, mid-1895); Standard Oil's Amalgamated Copper Company purchases ACMC and becomes its holding company (1899); Amalgamated becomes the Anaconda Copper Mining Company (ACM) (1915); name change to The Anaconda Company (1955); ARCO (Atlantic Richfield) buys ACM and creates its Anaconda Minerals Division (1977); Dennis Washington's Montana Resources, Inc. buys out ARCO's mining properties (1986)

BIA . . . . Bureau of Indian Affairs

BLM . . . . Bureau of Land Management

CCC . . . . Civilian Conservation Corps

EPA . . . . U.S. Environmental Protection Agency

ft . . . . foot or feet (measurement)

kW. . . . . kilowatt(s)

Milwaukee Road . . . . Chicago, Milwaukee & St. Paul Railway (before 1928); Chicago, Milwaukee, St. Paul & Pacific Railroad (after 1928)

MT . . . . Montana state highway (e.g., MT 10A)

mW . . . . megawatt(s)

Northern Pacific. . . . . Northern Pacific Railroad (until 1893); Northern Pacific Railway (after 1893)

National Register . . . . National Register of Historic Places

NHL . . . . National Historic Landmark

NHP . . . . National Historic Park

NHS . . . . National Historic Site

NPS . . . . National Park Service

NRA . . . . National Recreation Area

NWR. . . . . National Wildlife Refuge

U.S. . . . . United States

US . . . . U.S. federal highway (e.g., US 212)

USFS . . . . U.S. Forest Service

USFWS . . . . U.S. Fish and Wildlife Service

USGS. . . . . U.S. Geological Survey

WMA. . . . . Wildlife Management Area

WPA . . . . Works Progress Administration

Montana Place Names
from Alzada to Zortman

Ashland, c. 1910
Detail, L. A. Huffman, photographer, MHS 981-997

Absaroka-Beartooth Wilderness 941
map 20 C-4

In 1978, Congress designated 1.2 million acres of rugged terrain within these 2 mountain ranges as wilderness. This south-central Montana wilderness area contains Montana's highest summit, Granite Peak (12,799 ft.), and 29 other peaks over 12,000 feet.

Absaroka Range and Yellowstone River viewed from a train window

Herman Schnitzmeyer, photographer, MHS 940-029

Absaroka Range 890 *map 20 C-3*

The name of this impressive range of high mountains forming the eastern boundary of Yellowstone National Park and extending 150 miles south into Wyoming is derived from the Hidatsa name for the Crow people; it means "children of the large-beaked bird." The range is divided from the Beartooth Mountains to the east by the Boulder River.

Absarokee 936 *map 21 B-2*

A corruption of Apsaalooke, the name Absarokee refers to the Crows, or "children of the large-beaked bird." In local parlance, it is pronounced "Ab-SOR-kee." For a time, Crow Agency was located about 3 miles south of here, but when the agency moved to a site near Hardin in 1882 and the federal government opened this area

to homesteading, Absarokee grew into a thriving supply and service community. The town's spelling differs from that of the nearby Absaroka Range supposedly because the poor penmanship of an early settler resulted in the final "a" being mistaken for "ee." Absarokee's Cobblestone School is listed in the National Register. Elevation: 4,039 ft. Location: Stillwater County

Ackley Lake State Park 719 *map 12 C-4*

Ackley Lake is a reservoir that was created by an earthen dam constructed in 1938 on Jean Acly's 40-acre natural pond using $65,000 from the federal Public Works Administration and the Montana State Water Conservation Board. The lake's name was intentionally spelled "Ackley." Ackley Lake became part of the state park system in 1960. The park covers 160 acres and provides 23 campsites. In 1962, water from Ackley Lake irrigated more than 1,600 acres. Elevation: 4,317 ft. Location: Judith Basin County

Acton 970 *map 21 A-4*

Acton began as a stop on the Great Northern Railway's Billings and Northern branch line at the turn of the nineteenth century and was named for a railroad employee who lived there. By 1910, with the establishment of a post office, it had become a supply center for outlying ranches and farms. Elevation: 3,803 ft. Location: Yellowstone County

Adair General Mercantile Historic District 45 *map 2 B-1*

Remote wilderness where a man could live by his own rules drew Bill Adair to northwestern Montana in 1904. He and his wife, Jessie, built a log mercantile on the east side of the North Fork of the Flathead River, supplying goods to settlers in the sparsely populated area. When the creation of Glacier National Park in 1910 eliminated homesteading on the east side of the river, Adair chose a spot on the other side, filed a land claim in 1912, and built a cabin of square-notched, unhewn logs. Adair's holdings, maintained with Jessie's help until her death, and later that of second wife, Emma, reflected a self-sufficient lifestyle. From 1913 to 1920, Adair's was the only general store in the North Fork region and was a favored spot for social events. The property is listed in the National Register. Elevation: 3,526 ft. Location: Flathead County

Agawam 268 *map 3 D-3*

Named by a Milwaukee Road official for the Massachusetts town and river, this small town was platted by the railroad in 1912. The homestead settlement boasted a lumberyard, store, livery, and other businesses even prior to the railroad's arrival in 1917. Elevation: 3,803 ft. Location: Teton County

Alberton 202 *map 9 B-4*

Alberton was named for Albert Earling, president of the Chicago, Milwaukee & St. Paul Railway. Originally a small agricultural settlement, the fledgling town became a railroad division point when the railroad came through in 1908. The economic stimulus provided by this dis-

tinction ended with the electrification of the Milwaukee Road in 1916, when the machine shops moved to Deer Lodge, arresting Alberton's growth at its peak. The depot, however, continued to serve the town for the next 6 decades. After the Milwaukee Road declared bankruptcy in 1977, salvage crews pulled up the tracks, boarded up the depot, and abandoned Alberton. Rehabilitation grants turned the railyards into a city park and refurbished the 1908 depot, which is listed in the National Register along with Bestwick's Market and the Alberton School. Elevation: 3,071 ft. Location: Mineral County

Alder 711 *map 19 C-2*

Alder takes its name from Alder Creek (named by Henry Edgar in 1863), the site of the second major gold discovery in Montana. The Northern Pacific Railway founded the town of Alder in 1902 as the terminus of its Gaylord & Ruby Valley branch line. The town also served as headquarters of the Conrey Placer Mining Company until 1922, when the dredging company ceased operations. During the 1960s, Cyprus Industrial Minerals built a talc-processing and shipping hub at Alder. In the 1980s, Ruby Garnet, Inc. began extracting industrial garnets from the placer-gold gravels along Alder Creek. Elevation: 5,123 ft. Location: Madison County

Alberton, c. 1910
MHS 940-268

Alder Gulch 715 *map 19 C-3*

In 1863, Bill Fairweather, Henry Edgar, and Barney Hughes found gold in Alder Gulch, precipitating Montana's second gold rush. The gulch was named for the alder bushes that grew along the creek. Communities in the gulch included Virginia City, Nevada City, Adobetown, Central City, Highland, Junction, and Summit. Virginia City and Nevada City and the shortline railroad linking them are now popular tourist attractions. Location: Madison County

Alhambra 501 *map 11 D-3*

The community of Alhambra grew slowly, helped by the construction of 7 coke kilns to process the gold and silver ore mined nearby. The hot springs here did not flourish as a commercial venture until the arrival of the Montana Central Railway, which connected Helena and Butte in 1888. Judge Wilson Redding developed Alhambra Hot Springs (a misspelling of Alhama, the renowned Spanish spa), after purchasing the springs from Sylvenius Dustin in 1888. Alhambra Hot Springs Resort operated until a fire destroyed the hotel in 1959. Elevation: 4,267 ft. Location: Jefferson County

Alice Creek 331 *map 11 B-2*

This creek took its name from Alice Cox, a sister of William Cox, who homesteaded at nearby Flesher Pass. The USFS trail east of the creek climbs to Lewis and Clark Pass, traversed by Capt. Meriwether Lewis and his men in July 1806. Location: Lewis and Clark County

Alpine 960 *map 21 C-1*

John Branger Sr. settled in the Beartooth Mountains because they reminded him of his native Switzerland. He built a cabin for his family near East Rosebud Lake in 1913. The establishment of the post office in 1914 inspired Branger to name the place

Alpine. Elevation: 6,237 ft. Location: Carbon County

Alzada 1250 *map 24 C-3*

Alzada began as a telegraph station on the Little Missouri River between Fort Keogh in Montana Territory and Fort Meade in Dakota Territory in 1877. The community that grew there was named Stoneville in 1880 for Lewis M. Stone, the first settler and proprietor of the saloon. Stoneville officially became Alzada on July 16, 1885, to honor local pioneer Laura Alzada Shelden. Elevation: 3,444 ft. Location: Carter County

Amsterdam 714 *map 20 A-1*

Originally called Walrath for farmer A. J. Walrath, Amsterdam was established in 1911 by the Northern Pacific Railway on a branch line between Manhattan and Anceney. The railroad changed the name to Amsterdam because of the large number of Dutch settlers who had moved to the area in the 1890s to grow malting barley to supply the Manhattan Malting Company. These Dutch settlers were closely associated with the Presbyterian Church in Montana, and later the Christian Reformed Church. Elevation: 4,455 ft. Location: Gallatin County

Anaconda 439 *map 10 E-4*

Anaconda is the creation of Copper King Marcus Daly, who financed the construction of a smelter on nearby Warm Springs Creek to process copper ore from the Butte mines. In June 1883, Daly filed a town plat for "Copperopolis," but that name already graced a mining town in Meagher County. Instead, Daly named the town for his Anaconda Mine. The Anaconda Company expanded smelting capacity over time, and by 1919 the Washoe Reduction Works could boast that its 585-foot smokestack was the tallest masonry structure in the world and that the smelter-refining complex constituted the world's largest nonferrous processing plant. In 1980, Atlantic Richfield Company closed the smelter, bringing an end to almost a century of mineral processing. The Commercial, Goosetown, Old Works, West Side, and Butte, Anaconda & Pacific Railway historic districts are listed in the National Register, along with Anaconda's Art Deco–style Club Moderne, Deer Lodge County Courthouse, Washoe Theatre, and City Hall. Elevation: 5,246 ft. Location: Deer Lodge County

Anaconda-Pintler Scenic Highway 374
map 10 E-4

In 1978, the Montana State Highway Commission designated as a scenic route the Pintler Road, which passes through the Flint Creek Valley and Philipsburg, the Georgetown Lake area, and the smelting town of Anaconda. The name Pintler is derived from early homesteaders Charles and Katie Pintler, who built a cabin north of Wisdom in 1885. The Anaconda-Pintler Scenic Highway follows MT 1 from Drummond through Philipsburg and over the Flint Creek divide into Anaconda.

Anaconda-Pintler Wilderness 441
map 10 E-3

Established by the 1964 Wilderness Act, the Anaconda-Pintler Wilderness, just west of Anaconda, spans 158,615 acres. The name is derived from the town and its copper mining company and from Charles and Katie Pintler, homesteaders who in 1885 settled along Pintler Creek between the Big Hole National Battlefield and Wisdom.

Anaconda Range 420 *map 10 E-3*

The Anaconda Range stretches along the Continental Divide for 40 miles, encompassing forests, meadows, and alpine peaks.

This mountain range takes its name from the nearby town of Anaconda, founded by Marcus Daly in 1883. The Anaconda-Pintler Wilderness lies within the range.

Anaconda Smoke Stack State Park 455
map 10 E-4

Heralded as the tallest freestanding masonry structure in the world when it was completed in May 1919, the Washoe Stack measures 585 feet in height and 60 feet across at the top. The towering brick chimney is all that remains of the massive Washoe Reduction Works, constructed in 1918 in a record 144 days. At the height of production during World War II, the smelter produced more than 25 million pounds of copper per month and employed about 2,500 men. After the smelter's closure in 1980, citizens of Anaconda organized to "Save the Stack," and in 1986 it was designated a state park. Environmental cleanup continues on the site. A viewing stand alongside the highway provides information about this engineering wonder. Elevation: 5,759 ft. Location: Deer Lodge County

Washoe Reduction Works,
Anaconda Company, Anaconda, 1936
MHS PAc 82-62

Angela 1107 *map 15 C-2*

Angela got its start when Ann and John Garvin opened a combination post office and store in 1913. The business was moved to this spot on MT 59 between Miles City and Jordan in 1931. When the building burned in 1953, loyal neighbors banded together to construct a new one. The origin of the name is not known. Elevation: 2,920 ft. Location: Rosebud County

Antelope 1179 *map 8 B-2*

Named for the nearby creek, Antelope began as a tiny community along the Great Northern Railway's Bainville to Scobey branch line in 1910. That year, John and Richard Grayson built a hardware store next to the Antelope Creek Lutheran Church. A post office, bank, lumberyard, and saloon soon followed. The community thrived during its first decade, adding general mercantiles, a butcher shop, a concrete plant, restaurants, and other businesses to serve the region's growing homesteader population. Over the years, however, better roads to the south siphoned off business, and the "Biggest Little City in Eastern Montana" sank into decline. Elevation: 2,044 ft. Location: Sheridan County

Apgar 70 *map 2 B-2*

This town, the mountains, and the campground in the southwestern corner of Glacier National Park all take their name from Milo and Diane Apgar, who arrived in 1892 from Minnesota with their 2 sons and built the first cabin at the foot of Lake McDonald. On this same site, Milo's sons, Harvey and Esli, built the Apgar Log Cabin Resort in the mid-1890s to provide services for the many tourists arriving at West Glacier on the Great Northern Railway. In 1908, Harvey Apgar filed a homestead claim and received the patent to his father's original property. In 1914, he platted a 52-lot subdivision and sold one of the first lots to cowboy artist Charlie Russell. Fire destroyed the original Apgar cabin, and in 1957 the NPS removed the second. Elevation: 3,168 ft. Location: Glacier National Park

Apgar Mountains 63 *map 2 B-2*

A small range on the southwestern edge of Glacier National Park, the Apgar Mountains are noted for abundant crops of huckleberries and for grizzly bears. The range was named for the Apgar family—Milo, Diane, Harvey, and Esli—who homesteaded along the shore of Lake McDonald. Later, Harvey Apgar and his wife, Jessie, rented "tourist camps" to park visitors, and Jessie acted as postmaster at the town of Apgar.

Archer 1148 *map 8 B-1*

Archer was born when the Great Northern Railway's Bainville to Scobey branch line was completed in 1914. The town takes its name from William Archer, who homesteaded nearby. As a railroad town, Archer soon had a depot, a section house, and 2 grain elevators. At one time, it bragged of having the largest covered lumberyard in northeastern Montana. By 1970, Archer had a population of one; years of drought and economic depression had slowly drained the life out of the town. Elevation: 2,066 ft. Location: Sheridan County

Archie Bray Foundation for the Ceramic Arts 451 *map 11 D-3*

Englishman C. C. Thurston established a brickyard at this site in 1883. One of his employees was Charles Bray, a fellow Britisher who had served an apprenticeship in brick making before leaving England. In 1885, Nicholas Kessler, a longtime Helena brewer and brick maker, bought the brickworks from Thurston and placed Bray in charge. Bray expanded manufacturing to include sewer pipes, tiles, flowerpots, and decorative bricks. By 1900, the Kessler Brick and Sewer Pipe Works was one of

Montana's leading brick and tile manufacturers. In 1905, Kessler merged with brick maker Jacob Switzer to form the Western Clay Manufacturing Company. Bray remained manager, brought sons Archie and Raymond into the business, and eventually came to own it. On his father's death in 1931, Archie became company president. A ceramics engineer, Archie was a creative, talented man and a lover of fine art who envisioned a pottery on the brickyard grounds. With the enthusiastic help of friends, the dream came to fruition in 1951. Although Bray died in 1953, his foundation survived the 1960 closure of Western Clay and in 1984 purchased the abandoned brickyard buildings and kilns. Today the Archie Bray Foundation for the Ceramic Arts is internationally acclaimed. The historic Western Clay Manufacturing Company is listed in the National Register. Elevation: 3,926 ft. Location: Lewis and Clark County

Argenta 648 map 18 B-4

Argenta, a ghost town originally named Montana City, takes its name from the French word *argentin*, meaning "silvery." Founded in 1865, Montana City was one of the first mining communities in the Blue Wing Mining District in southwestern Montana. By 1868, it boasted 1,500 residents, several hotels and saloons, and the St. Louis & Montana Mining Company smelter (the first in the territory), built in 1866 to process silver, gold, and copper. The town was renamed Argenta in 1866 by the territorial legislature to reflect the rich silver mines in the area. Production from the Argenta mines totaled $1.5 million by 1930, when operations ceased. Elevation: 6,134 ft. Location: Beaverhead County

Arlee 201 map 10 B-2

Arlee was named after the Salish leader Arlee. In October 1873, he moved a small group of his people from the Bitterroot Valley, which was designated a "conditional reservation" in the 1855 Hellgate Treaty, to the Jocko Agency (later Flathead Indian Agency) located a few miles north of the current town of Arlee. This forced move stemmed from the efforts of a congressional delegation led by future president James Garfield to negotiate Salish removal from the Bitterroot Valley. The town of Arlee gained importance in 1883 when the Northern Pacific Railroad established a depot there. Two years later, the post office opened its doors in Arlee. Another notable event occurred in 1898 when the first (now annual) Fourth of July powwow was held at Arlee. Elevation: 3,097 ft. Location: Lake County

Armells Creek (Fergus) 834 map 13 A-3

Armells Creek is named for fur trapper Augustin Hamell (roughly pronounced "Ar-mell") of the American Fur Company, who came upriver from an Arikara village near the Knife River to Fort Union in the 1820s. Hamell operated several trading posts along the Missouri River from the 1820s to the 1840s. The Blackfeet called this creek Et-tsis-ki-ots-op, meaning "It fell on them," in reference to an incident in which several women digging for red clay died in a cave-in. The creek's source is on Judith Peak in the Judith Mountains northeast of Lewistown. It flows into the Missouri River in the Charles M. Russell National Wildlife Refuge.

Armells Creek (Rosebud) 1089 map 15 E-1

Named for fur trapper Michael Immell and referred to by Kit Carson, Jim Bridger, and John Colter as Emmel's Fork of the Yellowstone, this stream over time became known as Armells Creek. In 1859, Capt. William F. Raynolds, leader of the Raynolds Expedition, which conducted a topographical survey of the Yellowstone area, reported in his journal that the area along the creek was "literally black with buffalo."

Armington 519 *map 12 A-2*

Sheep rancher J. T. "Doc" Armington established the town of Armington on his property in 1888, building the first home for himself. The town was on the line of the Neihart branch of the Montana Central Railway, and it served as a freighting depot to supply the mining camps of the Little Belt Mountains and the farmers and ranchers of the Highwood and Judith Basin areas. Andrew Voight owned and operated a brick and stucco plant at Armington that furnished bricks to the Anaconda Company in Anaconda and Great Falls. Armington's bright future, however, faded with the establishment of the coal-mining community of Belt 2 miles down the road. Elevation: 3,563 ft. Location: Cascade County

Arrow Creek 654 *map 5 E-1*

Arrow Creek flows into the Missouri River below Eagle Buttes in Chouteau County. Indians referred to it as "Arrow creek" long before the arrival of Lewis and Clark, who called it the Slaughter River. Capt. Meriwether Lewis noted in his May 29, 1805, journal entry: "Today we passed on the Stard. Side the remains of a vast many mangled carcases of Buffalow which had been driven over a precipice of 120 feet by the Indians and perished; the water appeared to have washed away a part of this immence pile of slaughter and still there remained the fragments of at least a hundred carcases they created the most horrid stench." A short distance above this site, the expedition camped opposite a "bold running river 40 yards wide"; this campsite is listed in the National Register. By the 1880s, trader Joseph Kipp and others had adopted the creek's indigenous name. Location: Chouteau and Judith Basin counties.

Ashland 1158 *map 23 B-2*

The town began as a Northern Pacific Railroad tie-manufacturing camp in 1881, named Straders after its first postmaster. Soon a trading post, saloon, hotel, church, and school were built. In 1886, the community took the name Ashland for the Wisconsin home of trading post operator Sam O'Connell. In 1900, residents moved the town 6 miles to its present location at the confluence of the Tongue River and Otter Creek, to be outside the boundaries of the Northern Cheyenne Indian Reservation. Elevation: 2,920 ft. Location: Rosebud County

Ashley Lake 52 *map 1 C-4*

Ashley Lake is named for Flathead Valley pioneer Joe Ashley, an experienced trapper in the employ of Angus McDonald and the Hudson's Bay Company, who arrived in the valley in 1857. In 1897, area farmers organized the Ashley Lake Irrigating Company and constructed a diversion dam along Ashley Creek, creating the lake. By 1909, the Ashley Irrigation District was irrigating more than 1,600 acres, making dairy farming possible in the western Flathead Valley. Elevation: 3,950 ft. Location: Flathead County

Ashuelot 342 *map 11 A-3*

Established around 1919 as a station stop on the Milwaukee Road, this town was named Ashuelot, after the New England town and river. Elevation: 3,724 ft. Location: Cascade County

Augusta 289 *map 11 A-2*

Augusta takes its name from Augusta Hogan, daughter of homesteader J. D. Hogan. The post office, established in 1884, predated the town's incorporation by 10 years. Augusta thrived until April 4, 1901, when a huge fire ripped through the town. By 1914, Augusta had recovered, but the completion of a Great Northern Railway's branch line to Gilman 2 miles away briefly challenged the town. Augusta, however, reclaimed its status with the extension of the rail line to the town in the late 1920s. Today Augusta is the gateway to the Scapegoat and the Bob Marshall wilderness areas, which encompass more than 1 million acres of the Rocky Mountains. Elevation: 4,068 ft. Location: Lewis and Clark County

Austin 414 *map 11 C-2*
This town began in the 1870s as a placer-mining camp called Greenhorn Gulch. In 1883, the Northern Pacific Railroad established a flag station here named Butler. In 1901, the town changed its name to Austin for James W. Austin, an early miner. Mining continued in the vicinity until the 1930s. Elevation: 4,752 ft. Location: Lewis and Clark County

Avon 379 *map 11 C-1*
John Mullan commented on the Little Blackfoot Valley's fertile soil while surveying the valley for the Isaac I. Stevens railroad survey in the early 1850s, but as the Avon Get Together Club put it: "It was not [Mullan's] report of good soil . . . that attracted settlers to the area, but . . . the magic cry of 'Gold!'" Gold discoveries in Ophir, Snowshoe, and Washington gulches brought a flood of miners to the area between 1865 and 1866. As the inevitable cycle of boom and bust played out, homesteaders began arriving in the valley. Among them was Bill Cramer, a member of the advance survey crew for the Northern Pacific Railroad who had been smitten by the Little Blackfoot Valley when he passed through the area in 1882. Cramer returned to the valley in 1884 and started the settlement of Avon, serving as the town's first postmaster. The first train over the Continental Divide brought 4 barrels of whiskey and Cra-

mer's wife—a celebratory beginning for the new town. Avon became a supply and shipping point for ranchers, homesteaders, and miners. Elevation: 4,692 ft. Location: Powell County

Axolotl Lakes 755 *map 19 C-3*
Axolotl is an Aztec word meaning "play in the water," and it refers to a larval salamander first observed near Mexico City, which is 6 to 10 inches long and never known to mature beyond the larval stage. These rare amphibians have historically been found in several small lakes south of Virginia City. Elevation: 7,305 ft. Location: Madison County

Beartooth Highway, fifth level, Rock Creek Gorge, 1939
F. W. Byerly, photographer, MHS

Babb 131 *map 2 B-3*

Established in 1905 as a post office, the town of Babb was named for Cyrus C. Babb, the engineer in charge of surveying the U.S. Reclamation Service's St. Mary Irrigation Canal, which siphoned water from the St. Mary River into the Milk River and was one of the first Bureau of Reclamation projects in the nation. Elevation: 4,524 ft. Location: Glacier County

Badger Creek (Glacier) 210 *map 3 C-2*

In June 1875, the Commissioner of Indian Affairs authorized construction of a new Blackfeet agency 50 miles north of the original agency, along the banks of Badger Creek (one of several creeks in Montana named for this fur-bearing mammal). This site southeast of Browning is only a few miles from the place where Capt. Meriwether Lewis and his party had skirmished with and killed 2 Blackfeet warriors 69 years earlier. Location: Glacier and Pondera counties.

Bainville 1203 *map 8 D-3*

Charles Bain, a northeastern Montana entrepreneur, established a post office 3 miles southwest of here in 1904. The following year, residents moved the town to its present location to provide better access to the Great Northern Railway. Bainville became a railroad division point with the construction of a branch line to Scobey in 1911. When Bainville incorporated in 1918, it had 5 hotels, 2 grain elevators, and more than 400 residents. Elevation: 1,974 ft. Location: Roosevelt County

Bair Reservoir 680 *map 12 D-3*

Built in 1939 by the State Water Conservation Board, the Bair Reservoir is located on the North Fork of the Musselshell River, adjacent to the town of Checkerboard. It was named in honor of Charles M. Bair, who came to Montana in 1883 as a North-

ern Pacific Railroad conductor. In 1890, Bair established a sheep ranch on the Musselshell River that became one of the largest in the state. His home at Martinsdale is now a private museum and holds collections of fine furniture, artwork, and Native American artifacts acquired by Charles and his daughters, Alberta and Marguerite, in their world travels. Elevation: 5,329 ft. Location: Meagher County

Baker 1233 *map 16 D-3*

The Milwaukee Road established Baker, the future county seat of Fallon County, on the shores of the lake it had created to supply water for its locomotives. Originally named Lorraine, the town was renamed in honor of engineer A. G. Baker in 1908. Thanks to a successful Milwaukee Land Company campaign to attract homesteaders to the area, Baker served a growing community of dryland farmers. In 1912, oil and natural gas deposits were discovered near Baker. By 1920, Baker had more than 1,000 residents, and the population rose steadily until 1970, when it peaked at a little over 2,500. It has been slowly dwindling ever since, though commercial gas wells are still numerous in the area. Elevation: 2,937 ft. Location: Fallon County

Ballantine 1021 *map 22 A-1*

In 1896, the Burlington & Missouri River Railroad established Ballantine as a station, named for homesteader E. P. Ballantine. By 1907, the Chicago, Burlington & Quincy Railroad had taken over rail operations, and the town had a post office to serve the growing number of area homesteaders. At its height in the early 1910s, the town boasted a bank, 3 general stores, a hotel, and even a cheese factory. Elevation: 2,995 ft. Location: Yellowstone County

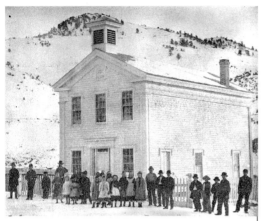

Bannack school and Masonic Hall, c. 1875
H. W. Brown, photographer, MHS PAc 94-11.4

Bannack State Park and NHL 666
map 18 C-4

Montana's first boomtown, Bannack sprang up in the summer of 1862 when John White and company discovered gold in nearby Grasshopper Creek. Its name is a corruption of that of the Bannock tribe affiliated with the Shoshones. By fall 1862, Bannack had a population of 500 and at its peak may have numbered as many as 5,000. Bannack, however, was already in decline when Territorial Governor Sidney Edgerton chose it as the territorial capital in mid-1864. The seat of territorial government moved to Virginia City early in 1865, but upon the creation of Beaverhead County that same year, Bannack was named its county seat. By 1880, Bannack's population stood at only 232; the county seat moved to Dillon the following year. Although only a few residents remained, small-scale gold mining continued until 1954, when the State of Montana acquired most of the town and designated it a state park. Bannack Historic District became a NHL in 1961. Bannack's significant buildings include the 1875 Beaverhead County Courthouse (Meade Hotel), the 1862 jail (the first in the territory), the 1877 Methodist Church, and an unusual combination Masonic Hall and schoolhouse built

in 1874. Visitors can wander inside the many empty buildings and visit the historic cemetery. There are campgrounds and a visitor center. Each year, in the third week of July, Bannack Days celebrates the town's colorful history. Elevation: 5,763 ft. Location: Beaverhead County

Basin 498 *map 11 D-2*

The origin of the name Basin is not known. Although miners found gold deposits in the area along Cataract Creek as early as 1862, the town didn't exist until the 1880s, when John Allport discovered gold at the mouth of Basin Creek. In 1888, the Montana Central Railway connected Basin to the smelter at Wickes. The following year, a stage line from Boulder began serving the town, and William Nichols of Butte platted the townsite. Mining investors Samuel Hauser, Marcus Daly, William A. Clark, and others figured prominently in Basin's development. Elevation: 5,354 ft. Location: Jefferson County

Basin Creek Reservoir 557 *map 19 A-1*

By the 1880s, mining pollution had made Butte's water undrinkable. Because there was no potable surface water closer to town, in 1893 Butte Water Company manager Eugene Carroll engineered the construction of the Basin Creek Reservoir 13 miles south of Butte. It was the first in a series of water projects designed to slake the thirst of the booming mining metropolis. The masonry dam rose 100 feet above bedrock, capturing millions of gallons of pure mountain water. Redwood pipes funneled water from the reservoir into town for use in Butte's mines, mills, homes, and businesses. Elevation: 5,863 ft. Location: Silver Bow County

Battle Creek 722 *map 5 C-2*

This Battle Creek originates in the Cypress Hills of Canada, flows south across the international border, and travels another 115 miles to empty into the Milk River near Fort Belknap, in Blaine County. The origin of the name is unknown.

Bean Lake 302 *map 11 A-2*
Bean Lake was named for the Bean family, who established early homesteads in the area. The first to settle here were Joseph and Rachel Bean, who built a house on the east shore of the lake in the 1880s. Their sons Earnest, Olie, and Walter ranched in the area into the twentieth century. For many years, the Bean family stocked the lake with fish. In the 1960s, they sold the lake to the Montana Fish and Game Dept. The lake now has a campground and fishing access. Elevation: 4,559 ft. Location: Lewis and Clark County

Bear Paw Battlefield—Nez Perce NHP 717 *map 5 C-2*
On September 30, 1877, Col. Nelson Miles struck the Bears Paw Mountains camp of Chief Joseph, where more than 400 Nez Perces had stopped to rest on their 1,600-mile flight from Idaho to Canada. After a brief fight and a 6-day siege (during which many Nez Perces slipped over the border), the Nez Perce surrendered. Joseph was incarcerated in a military prison in the Dry Tortugas, while other Nez Perces were sent to Oklahoma Territory and Kansas, where hundreds died of malnutrition and starvation. "Chief Joseph Battleground of Bear's Paw" was designated a NHL in 1988. Elevation: 3,019 ft. Location: Blaine County

Bearcreek 1009 *map 21 C-2*
Bearcreek owes its existence to area coal mining that began in the 1890s to supply coal for the Northern Pacific Railroad and the Anaconda Company. The town was platted and incorporated after the arrival of the Montana, Wyoming & Southern Railroad in 1906, and it grew rapidly as American and foreign-born workers moved there, drawn by the promise of steady work. By 1917, the mines around Bearcreek were employing 1,200 men. With the trend toward natural gas for heating and diesel locomotives, however, the demand for coal fell sharply, and Bearcreek's production was in decline by the late 1940s. After the 1953 closure of the railroad between Bridger and Bearcreek, the town's population dwindled. Today Bearcreek is again growing thanks to its proximity to Red Lodge. With its diverse ethnic composition, Bearcreek traditionally celebrated Christmas twice, on December 25 and January 6, the Greek Orthodox Church holiday. Elevation: 4,556 ft. Location: Carbon County

Bears Paw Mountains 685 *map 5 D-2*
The Bears Paw Mountains extend in a 45-mile arc between the Missouri River and Rocky Boy's Indian Reservation south of Havre. Native oral history ties the name to a lone hunter in search of deer to feed his clan. He killed a deer but, while returning to the prairie, encountered a bear. The bear held the hunter to the ground, and the hunter appealed to the Great Spirit to release him. The Great Spirit filled the heavens with lightning and thunder, striking the bear dead and severing its paw to release the hunter. Looking at Box Elder Butte, you can see the paw, and Centennial Mountain to the south resembles a reclining bear. Chief Joseph of the Nez Perce surrendered to Col. Nelson Miles in the foothills of the Bears Paw Mountains in October 1877. Locals refer to the range as the Bearpaws.

Beartooth Highway 995 *map 21 C-2*
In 1925, F. E. Thieme and B. F. Kitt surveyed a route for a possible highway between Red Lodge and Cooke City. Now designated US 212, the scenic highway was built as part of the 1931 Park Approach Road Act as a new access road to Yellowstone

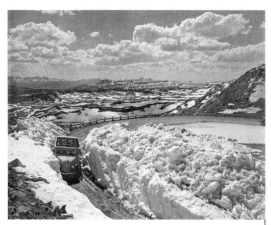

Beartooth Highway in spring, c. 1939
F. W. Byerly, photographer, MHS

National Park. Even though initial engineering surveys found fault with the high alpine route, Red Lodge's Dr. J. C. F. Siegfried, the most vocal advocate for the road, prevailed. Crews began construction in summer 1931 and completed the road in 1936.

Beartooth Mountains 932 *map 20 C-4*

The Beartooth Mountains include 29 summits over 12,000 feet, making this the highest mountain range in Montana; the Beartooth Plateau rises to over 10,000 feet and includes hundreds of alpine lakes. Originally known as the Snowy Range and the Granite Range, the current name, Beartooth, did not come into use until 1908, when the Beartooth National Forest was carved out of the Yellowstone Forest Preserve. Granite Peak is Montana's highest, at 12,799 feet. The Crow name Na piet say refers to the sharp "bear's tooth" promontory on the east side of Beartooth Mountain.

Beaver Creek (Phillips) 865 *map 6 E-1*

In the 1880s, cattle baron Robert Coburn established his Circle C Ranch along a creek in Phillips County. Coburn named

the creek for the fur-bearing animal that lived along its banks. This area is part of the traditional home of the Assiniboines.

Beaver Creek (Wibaux) 1228 *map 16 B-4*

The major drainage in Wibaux County, Beaver Creek eventually flows into the Little Missouri River across the state line in North Dakota. Named by trappers for the numerous beavers in its waters, the creek was vital to both the fur trade and, later, ranching and farming.

Beaverhead County 688 *map 18 B-4*

The territorial legislature established Beaverhead County as one of Montana's original counties on February 2, 1865, naming it after the prominent local landmark Beaverhead Rock. The southwestern Montana county was the site of the earliest gold mining activity in Montana as well as early cattle ranching. William Orr and Philip Poindexter registered the first brand in Montana Territory, the Square and Compass, for their large cattle ranch southeast of Dillon. In 1911, Beaverhead County annexed a portion of Madison County, becoming the largest county in the state. The original county seat was Bannack; in 1881, the county government moved to Dillon.

Beaverhead Mountains 716 *map 18 D-3*

This southern extension of the Bitterroot Range, running 165 miles between Lost Trail Pass and Monida Pass, forms the state line between Montana and Idaho. It is named after Beaverhead Rock, a Jefferson River landmark. When traveling through the area on August 8, 1805, Sacagawea recognized this rock, which her Shoshone tribe called the "Beaver's head." While the name originates with the Shoshones, trappers later applied it to the mountain range and river.

Beaverhead River 644 *map 19 B-2*

In early August 1805, Capt. Meriwether Lewis referred to the stretch of river south of the confluence of Horse Prairie Creek and the Red Rock River as the Jefferson River. By the 1860s, the maps of the territory had adopted Beaverhead, a name commonly used by early fur trappers, for this same stretch of water.

Beaverhead Rock, near Dillon
MHS 941-016

Beaverhead Rock 665 *map 19 B-2*

This huge rock resembles a beaver's head above water, swimming west. When the Lewis and Clark Expedition reached the area on August 8, 1805, Sacagawea knew the landmark. Lewis wrote: "The Indian woman recognized the point of a high plain to our right which she informed us was not very distant from the summer retreat of her nation on a river beyond the mountains which runs to the west. this hill she says her nation calls the beaver's head from a conceived resemblance of its figure to the head of that animal. she assures us that we shall either find her people on this river or on the river immediately west of its source." This episode was an important milestone because the expedition desperately needed the Shoshones' horses. Today Beaverhead Rock is an undeveloped state park, with no direct access. Elevation: 5,193 ft. Location: Madison County

Beaverton 968 *map 6 C-3*

Named for Beaver Creek, which flows past the town, Beaverton was established in about 1888 as a station on the St. Paul, Minneapolis & Manitoba Railway. From 1908 on, it had a post office, and in 1910, O. S. Cutting opened a general store. At the height of the town's prosperity, in 1916, there were 3 general stores and a blacksmith shop, barber, livery stable, lumberyard, grain elevator, and hotel. With the drought of the 1920s and '30s, the town's population declined rapidly and the busi-

nesses closed. The post office closed in the early 1940s. Elevation: 2,171 ft. Location: Valley County

Beehive 918 *map 21 B-1*

Named for Beehive Rock just north of town, Beehive acquired a post office in 1910. It later became a small community with a hotel and grocery store. Over the years, dude ranches, including the P Lazy B Ranch, owned by Bill Parkhill, and the J Bar 4 Ranch, owned by Bill Pafford, operated near here. Elevation: 4,630 ft. Location: Stillwater County

Belfry 1022 *map 21 C-3*

Belfry is one of 3 communities created by the construction of the Yellowstone Park Railroad. The railroad company platted the community in 1905, and the tracks reached town a year later. Belfry, named for Pennsylvania investor Dr. William Belfry, became a shipping point for Clarks Fork Valley farmers and ranchers. When the railroad went into receivership in 1909, reorganization led to the incorporation of the Montana, Wyoming & Southern Railroad, which operated until 1953. Elevation: 3,860 ft. Location: Carbon County

Belgrade 726 *map 20 A-1*

Belgrade's founder, Thomas B. Quaw, arrived in the Gallatin valley from Wisconsin in 1882. The Northern Pacific Railroad completed its line in 1883, and within 10 years, Belgrade (promoted as the "Princess of the Prairies") claimed to be the largest grain-receiving area between Seattle and St. Paul, due in part to the building of the Belgrade Grain and Produce Company by Quaw and William O. Tracy, and investment by both T. C. Power and Nelson Story in grain storage and elevator construction by 1891. Stories vary as to the origin of the town's name, but most certainly the name is linked to Belgrade, Yugoslavia. Quaw's version of the story ties it to Serbian financiers who invested in the Northern Pacific and accompanied Henry Villard to the golden spike ceremony in 1883. The Bozeman regional airport at Belgrade began as a 1940s federal investment to develop Belgrade Field. Today Belgrade is a rapidly growing bedroom community for Bozeman. Elevation: 4,458 ft. Location: Gallatin County

Belgrade Airway Radio Station 662
map 19 A-4

In 1935, Northwest Airways received federal approval to provide Montana with east-west airmail service. Thereafter, the U.S. Dept. of Commerce constructed the Belgrade Airway Radio Station to house the radio and ground-to-air systems used by the Minneapolis-Spokane-Seattle airmail pilots on the route. As part of a system of stations spaced approximately 200 miles apart, the Belgrade station provided services critical to the development of civil aviation. In 1953, Gallatin County moved the Belgrade radio station to Pogreba Field at Three Forks. The station now serves as the Three Forks Airport terminal. Listed in the National Register, it is one of 2 such stations left in Montana. Elevation: 4,084 ft. Location: Gallatin County

Belknap 66 *map 1 E-2*

Belknap began in 1881 as Enterprise. It grew into a railroad town when the Northern Pacific Railroad established a section house, depot, and water tank there in 1882. The railroad renamed the town Belknap to honor Robert L. Belknap, treasurer of the Northern Pacific, in 1879. The town was laid out in 1884 and expanded with the boom that accompanied the nearby Coeur d'Alene gold rush. The Belknap Trail, one of 2 main trails into the Coeur d'Alene Mining District from Montana Territory, began at Belknap and ran north along Big Beaver Creek, then west over the Continental Divide into Idaho. Elevation: 2,395 ft. Location: Sanders County

Bell Street Bridge 1196 *map 16 B-2*

The Northern Pacific Railroad platted the Glendive townsite in 1882. Situated in the arid Montana badlands where the railroad first meets the Yellowstone River, the town was an ideal supply and distribution center, but it looked to ranchers and farmers on the river's opposite side for economic support. After close to a decade of debate over the need for better access to the area across the river, in 1895 Dawson County replaced the dangerous, antiquated ferry crossing with the first bridge at Glendive. The bridge provided stockmen and farmers direct access to the railroad and made stagecoach travel to points northwest more reliable. Rebuilt in 1899 after a flood and ice jam washed out the bridge, it served the area until the present bridge, the Bell Street Bridge, was constructed between 1924 and 1926. The bridge consists of 6 riveted Warren through-trusses, characterized by the W configuration made by the diagonal members of the structure's trusses. At 1,352 feet in length, the Bell Street Bridge, listed in the National Register, is one of the longest of its kind in Montana. Elevation: 2,043 ft. Location: Dawson County

Belle Creek 1240 *map 24 C-1*

In 1967, Sam Gary and his partners discovered oil in what became known as the Bell Creek Oil Fields. In May of the following year, Gary platted a townsite he named Bell Creek after the oil fields. The town changed its name to Belle Creek in 1969. Although the oil wells played out, the field has more recently been the site of coalbed methane development. Elevation: 3,574 ft. Location: Powder River County

Belly River 94 *map 2 A-3*

Sometime in the 1920s, Dr. George Ruhle named the Belly River after a translation of the Blackfeet word Mokowanisz (or Moo-coo-wans), which refers to the bison's digestive system. The Moo-coo-wans name first appeared on the Arrowsmith map of 1802. David Thompson named the river Bull Head in 1814. The river drains the northeast corner of Glacier National Park and flows into Canada.

Belt 515 *map 12 A-2*

Belt is named for the mountain range and creek, which themselves take their names from a nearby butte with a prominent dark band. The Blackfeet were the first to note that the dark strata looked like a belt, or girdle. In the late 1870s, John K. and Mattie Castner built a cabin here at the site of Montana's first coal mine. John developed the mine, and he and John Millard platted the town, originally called Castner, in 1885. Between 1891 and 1893, Belt provided coal for the large smelting operation in Great Falls. National Register–listed properties include the Commercial Historic District and the Belt jail. Elevation: 3,568 ft. Location: Cascade County

Belt Creek 477 *map 12 A-2*

Capt. William Clark originally named this stream Portage Creek because it joins the Missouri River at the start of the rapids leading up to the Great Falls. By the time the Isaac I. Stevens railroad survey passed through the area in the mid-1850s, it was known as Belt Mountain Creek. Belt Creek flows through the silver-mining district at Neihart, through Sluice Boxes State Park, and on to the coal-mining town of Belt. Location: Cascade County

Belton Chalet 77 *map 2 C-2*

Constructed in 1910–11, the Belton Chalet was the first of the Great Northern Railway's 5 sprawling hotels built to serve Glacier National Park. The main hotel and several cottages take their names from the community of Belton, established in 1892 and renamed West Glacier in 1949. The chalet's architecture is a unique example of a Swiss theme in "America's Alps" and draws on the Chalet and Western Rustic styles to create architecture that harmonizes with the park's natural landscape. The decline of rail travel in the mid-nineteenth century led to closure of the hotel for nearly 50 years. Restoration, which began in 1997 under private owners, has been completed. The Belton Chalet is part of the Great Northern Railway Buildings NHL. Elevation: 3,248 ft. Location: Flathead County

Benchland 698 *map 12 B-4*

Early settlers named Benchland for its location on a plateau or flat plain, commonly called a "bench." Homesteaders began arriving in the area in 1904 in anticipation of the Great Northern Railway's branch line between Great Falls and Lewistown, but the largest infusion of settlers occurred after trains reached the town in 1909. Montana State College at Bozeman started an experimental farm station 5 miles southeast of Benchland in 1909, and the threshing rigs and grain binders that dotted the landscape each year during the harvest underscored Benchland's agricultural potential. During the 1910s, the Industrial Workers of the World tried unsuccessfully to organize area harvest workers. The town's population reached 200 in 1915 but has declined over time. The town is still dominated by several large grain elevators. Elevation: 4,337 ft. Location: Judith Basin County

Benteen 1093 *map 22 B-3*
Benteen originated as a station on the Chicago, Burlington & Quincy Railroad, named after Capt. Frederick Benteen of the 7th U.S. Cavalry, who participated in the June 25–26, 1876, fight at Little Bighorn. The town of Benteen is known to the Crows as Isbaatawuaxape, or "Fallen bell," so called because the bell that was once used to call Crow cowboys employed by the federal government fell from its brace. Elevation: 3,220 ft. Location: Big Horn County

Benton Lake National Wildlife Refuge 401 *map 4 E-1*
Established in 1929 by an executive order of President Herbert Hoover, the Benton Lake NWR, originally 12,235 acres of marsh and wetlands, has long been an important migratory stopover and nesting area for waterfowl and shorebirds, with as many as 100,000 ducks and 40,000 snow geese seen historically during the spring and fall migrations. In 1961, the USFWS hired the refuge's first staff, who were directed to pump water from Muddy Creek (approximately 20 miles away) into 6 separate ponds to provide nesting habitat for ducks. In the 1970s, employees planted adjacent croplands in wheatgrass and alfalfa. Today there are permanent protective easements on 86,000 acres surrounding the refuge. There is also a fall hunting season on geese and ducks. Elevation: 3,619 ft. Location: Cascade County

Berkeley Pit 524 *map 11 E-1*
In July 1955, the Anaconda Company began operations at the Berkeley Pit, named for an underground copper mine on the Butte Hill. By the 1970s, the pit had become the largest truck-operated open-pit copper mine in the United States. In the early 1980s, a fleet of 200-ton trucks carried as much as 50,000 tons of low-grade copper ore to the concentrator each day. In 1982, however, the Atlantic Richfield Company (ARCO), Anaconda's successor, shut down the extensive network of underground pumps, flooding abandoned underground mines and eventually filling the Berkeley Pit with acidic water. In search of an answer to the intractable problem of what to do about the ever-rising water (in 2007 it was 800 feet deep), ARCO constructed a large lime precipitation plant to deacidify the mine drainage water, which enters the pit at a rate of 8 million gallons a day. Elevation: 5,240 ft. Location: Silver Bow County

Berkeley Pit, Butte, c. 1963
MHS PAc 94-78.4

Biddle 1229 *map 24 C-1*

When a new post office was established to serve the Little Powder River region in 1919, the new postmaster, Charles Scofield, was asked to come up with 3 names for it. S. P. F. Biddle, the name of Scofield's former employer and the former owner of the large Cross Ranch, was chosen. Elevation: 3,332 ft. Location: Powder River County

Big Arm 122 *map 2 E-1*

Prior to 1910, the major bay, or "arm," on the southwest shore of Flathead Lake was home to the Kootenais, who referred to the area as "big arm." After the opening of the Flathead Indian Reservation to non-Indian settlement in 1910, homesteaders came to the area to farm and log. Big Arm State Park, just north of town, is today a popular place for camping, fishing, sailing, and boating. Elevation: 2,938 ft. Location: Lake County

Big Baldy Mountain 621 *map 12 C-3*

The highest peak in the Little Belt Mountains, Big Baldy takes its name from its domelike shape and the absence of trees. The peak, composed of a type of igneous rock called Barker porphyry, forms the eastern perimeter of the Neihart Mining District. Elevation: 9,183 ft. Location: Judith Basin County

Big Belt Mountains 548 *map 11 C-4*

The Big Belt Mountains east of Canyon Ferry Lake run for 80 miles. The Big Belts are composed of the oldest sedimentary rocks in central Montana, deposited more than 1 billion years ago during the Precambrian period, when the entire area was covered by a vast inland sea. The map created by the Isaac I. Stevens 1853 railroad survey refers to the Big Belts as the Girdle Mountains, a nod to their distinctive banding, which he called a "girdle," or belt. During the 1860s, significant gold discoveries were made here in Confederate Gulch.

Big Dry Creek 1073 *map 15 A-2*

The name Big Dry Creek is attributed to Lewis and Clark, who on May 6, 1805, found a riverbed hundreds of yards wide without a drop of water between its banks. Open-range cattle ranches, such as Frederick and William Niedringhaus's N Bar N Ranch, grazed stock along Big Dry Creek and throughout this area east of Jordan known as the "Big Dry," until the severe winter of 1886–87 put an end to open-range grazing there. Location: Garfield County

Big Hole National Battlefield 497 *map 18 A-2*

The serene landscape of this national battlefield belies the carnage that took place here during the Battle of the Big Hole in 1877. The conflict began when the federal government tried to enforce its demand that the Nez Perce people leave their Idaho and Oregon homeland, and some 750 Nez Perces fled across the border into Montana. In the predawn hours of August 9, 1877, soldiers and volunteers under Col. John Gibbon attacked a sleeping camp in the Big Hole Valley, slaughtering scores of men, women, and children. The warriors rallied a counterattack, driving the soldiers and their entourage to a nearby hill. The Nez Perces held the soldiers until the next day, while the camp buried its dead, then fled again. Gibbon also lost some 30 men. The Nez Perces continued to stay ahead of the troops until Chief Joseph's legendary surrender in October near the Canadian border. The Big Hole Battlefield encompasses 655 acres and includes interpretation of the battle and a museum. Each year on August 9, a commemorative event marks the anniversary of the Battle of the Big Hole. "Hole" refers to the rounded feature, or basin, that eons ago was a riverbed. Elevation: 6,291 ft. Location: Beaverhead County

Big Hole River 641 *map 19 B-2*

The headwaters of the Big Hole River, named the Wisdom River by Lewis and Clark, are in the Beaverhead Mountains. The river's 75-mile-long valley, the Big Hole Basin, bounded on the west by the Beaverhead Range and on the north by the Anaconda Range, was occupied over time by the Salish, Shoshone, and Nez Perce. The Salish called the basin La-im-tse-la-lik, "Place of ground squirrel"; settlers later referred to it as "Land of 10,000 Haystacks." The Big Hole Basin is historically important for many reasons: as the site of Capt. William Clark's camp in July 1806; as the location of an overland route for Hudson's Bay Company trapper Alexander Ross in 1824; as a route for prospectors headed to the rich placer gravels near Bannack in the 1860s; and as the trail followed by the Nez Perce in their flight from the Battle of the Big Hole in 1877.

Big Horn County 1092 *map 22 A-3*

Big Horn County was one of the 9 original counties established by the Montana territorial legislature in February 1865. Defined as all the territory not included in any of the other counties, it encompassed the entire eastern third of the territory. For administrative purposes, since there were no large towns in the region, it was attached to Gallatin County. Over the years, portions of the county were broken off to form new counties. In 1877, Big Horn County became known as Custer County. However, today's Big Horn County, consisting primarily of the Crow Indian Reservation, was established in 1913, with Hardin as the county seat.

Big Mountain 49 *map 2 B-1*

This mountain in the Whitefish Range is home to Whitefish Mountain Resort, formerly Big Mountain Ski Resort. Skiers first began using Big Mountain in 1935, and in 1938 members of the Whitefish Hell-Roaring Ski Club talked the USFS into constructing a 2-mile road into a cabin the club had constructed. The ski resort has grown from a small chalet built in 1949 and serving about 6,000 skiers a season to a 4,500-acre all-season resort serving hundreds of thousands of visitors every year. Elevation: 6,817 ft. Location: Flathead County

Big Porcupine Creek 1086 *map 15 D-1*

The name for this creek that flows into the Yellowstone River just west of Forsyth is derived from the Crow name, A-pat-e-ashi, meaning "Big porcupine." Location: Rosebud County

Big Sandy 576 *map 4 D-4*

At one time the site of a saloon that served Missouri River freighters, the community of Big Sandy is named for nearby Big Sandy Creek. The town began in 1887 with the arrival of the St. Paul, Minneapolis & Manitoba Railway (later the Great Northern Railway). By early 1900, Cornelius J. McNamara and Thomas A. Marlow, owners of the McNamara Cattle Company, had opened the town's first store. Homesteaders began arriving in Big Sandy in 1909, and an influx continued for a decade. Several stories explain the creek's name. The most colorful involves a muleskinner, "Big Sandy" Lane, who arrived one day near the present townsite and, to his dismay, discovered the creek at flood stage. He cursed the uncooperative weather, his bad luck, and the flooded creek crossing so fluently that the offending stream dried up immediately and he was able to cross. Elevation: 2,700 ft. Location: Chouteau County

Big Sky 797 *map 20 C-1*

This year-round resort community on the West Fork of the Gallatin River owes its existence to the Big Sky Corporation, which began constructing a resort on the Crail Ranch at the base of Lone Mountain in 1971; ski lifts opened in 1973. Chet Huntley, Montana native and former television news broadcaster, served as the corporation's board chairman and handled most of the land negotiations. The name Big Sky is derived from A. B. Guthrie's popular 1947 novel that chronicles a fur trapper's adventures in the region. Elevation: 7,179 ft. Location: Gallatin County

Big Spring and Big Spring Creek 737
map 13 B-1

Ranked as one of the largest springs in the United States, Big Spring south of Lewistown bubbles at a rate of 63,000 gallons per minute, or 90 million gallons a day, and forms the headwaters of Big Spring Creek. The spring constitutes Lewistown's municipal water supply; there is no need to treat the water, which has been tested at 99.9 percent purity. The water is also bottled for commercial sale. Location: Fergus County

Big Springs Fish Hatchery 791 *map 13 B-2*

The largest cold-water facility operated by Montana Fish, Wildlife & Parks, the Big Springs Fish Hatchery until 2004 produced 2–3 million fish per year. Operations started in 1922 when the Lewistown Rod and Gun Club raised $1,200 to construct a hatchery along Big Spring Creek. In 1959, the Montana Fish and Game Dept. built the Lower Hatchery. In December 2003, however, the department found high PCB levels in soils downstream from the hatchery, dispersed from paint used on the raceways in the 1960s. A large-scale cleanup of the blue-ribbon trout stream began in 2004, curtailing fish production at the hatchery. Elevation: 4,034 ft. Location: Fergus County

Big Timber 862 *map 20 A-4*

Taking its name from the cottonwood trees along Big Timber Creek, Big Timber became the county seat of Sweet Grass

County in 1895. Originally a stage stop known as Dornix, Big Timber grew into a major wool-shipping depot with the coming of the Northern Pacific Railroad in 1883. On March 13, 1908, a spark from a passing locomotive set fire to the Northern Pacific stockyards. High winds carried flaming embers and started multiple fires. The Livingston fire department arrived by special train to save the community, but half of Big Timber's commercial houses and a third of its homes went up in flames. The Grand Hotel, listed in the National Register, survived. Elevation: 4,091 ft. Location: Sweet Grass County

Big Timber Creek 861 *map 20 A-4*

This creek on the eastern flank of the Crazy Mountains derives its name from a group of very large cottonwood trees that stood at the creek's confluence with the Yellowstone River. Capt. William Clark described this spot as "Rivers Across" when the expedition passed by on July 18, 1806. In the 1920s, the Van Cleve family bought a ranch in Big Timber Canyon and renamed it the Lazy K Bar Ranch, which they have operated as a dude ranch ever since. Location: Sweet Grass County

Bigfork 110 *map 2 D-2*

The name Bigfork is derived from the Salish name for the area. There are reports of a homestead and orchard immediately north of Bigfork as early as 1885. Evcrit L. Sliter set out 500 apple, cherry, plum, and pear trees in 1892 on Flathead Lake's east shore. In 1902, he platted the Bigfork townsite at the mouth of the Swan River. The east shore has since become a major cherry-growing area. Wayfarers State Park lies just south of town. Elevation: 2,998 ft. Location: Flathead County

Bighorn 1046 *map 14 E-3*

In 1807, Manuel Lisa built a trading post at the mouth of the Bighorn River; William H. Ashley built Fort Van Buren at the same spot in 1822. In 1863, James Stuart and Samuel Hauser platted a townsite called Big Horn City at the mouth of the Big Horn River. About 1888, the Northern Pacific Railroad established Bighorn as a station. The community briefly had a post office between 1903 and 1905. By 1930, only 25 residents remained; today nothing is left of the town. Elevation: 2,702 ft. Location: Treasure County

Bighorn Canyon NRA 1069 *map 22 C-2*

Congress established the Bighorn Canyon NRA in October 1966 after completion of Yellowtail Dam on the Bighorn River. Bighorn Lake stretches some 60 miles; 55 miles of the lake are in the canyon. Afterbay Lake below the dam features good trout fishing and birding. Location: Big Horn County

Bighorn Ditch 1068 *map 22 B-2*

Beginning in 1892, 50 Crow laborers and their horse teams worked under contractor William F. Graves to build the ditch, which irrigated 35,000 acres. The Crows were at this time in transition, adapting to an agrarian lifestyle on the reservation, and the project, completed in 1904, was conceived as a way to provide the laborers instruction in construction techniques. The Bighorn Ditch is listed in the National Register. Elevation: 3,210 ft. Location: Big Horn County

Bighorn Mountains 1087 *map 22 C-2*

The Bighorns lie primarily in Wyoming but penetrate southern Montana near Fort Smith. The highest point is Cloud Peak (located in Wyoming), at over 13,000 feet. The Bighorns, or 'Iisaxpu'aahchee Isawaxaawu'ua', remain sacred to the Crow people, and the namesake mountain sheep feature prominently in Crow oral history. In one story, a young boy fell during a hunting foray into the Bighorns but was rescued by a band of 7 sacred bighorn rams led by Big Metal, whose horns and hooves were made of brilliant steel. The boy took the name Big Metal and warned his people never to change the name of the Bighorn River if they wished the Apsaalooke people to survive.

Bighorn River 1044 *map 14 E-3*

François Larocque named the Bighorn River for the bighorn sheep he saw along its banks when he traveled up the Yellowstone River in 1805. Capt. William Clark mapped the mouth of the river in 1806. The Crows called the river It' Saxpúatahch eeaashisee

Billings, 1909
F. J. Bandholtz, photographer, MHS 941-121

for the native sheep. The river flows north for 225 miles, from the Wind River Canyon in Wyoming into the Yellowstone River near the town of Bighorn.

Billings 1003 *map 21 A-4*

The town of Billings was founded in 1882 and named for Frederick Billings, former president of the Northern Pacific Railroad. The population grew dramatically in its first few years, changing the small river town into a bustling metropolis of several thousand. Livestock shipping dominated in the early years, but the local economy diversified with a sugar beet plant built in the 1910s and its first oil refinery in 1923. Subsequent refineries appeared on the east edge of town and in nearby Laurel. Billings prospered after World War II, thanks to area oil refineries, highway construction, and railroads, and during the oil, gas, and coal boom of the 1970s. Today Billings is the largest city in Montana. The Billings Townsite Historic District, the Moss Mansion, and Boothill Cemetery are among the sites listed in the National Register. Lake Elmo State Park lies on the city's east side. Elevation: 3,123 ft. Location: Yellowstone County

Birch Creek 234 *map 3 C-2*

Birch Creek was the site of Capt. Meriwether Lewis and his party's fight with several members of the Blackfeet tribe in 1806. Lewis named it Battle Creek for the encounter. In April 1874, Congress established Birch Creek as the southeast boundary of the Blackfeet Indian Reservation. In June 1964, heavy rain falling on top of melting snow caused a 100-year flood that destroyed the Swift Dam on Birch Creek and caused heavy loss of life and property on the reservation. Location: Pondera County

Birch Creek CCC Camp 626 *map 18 B-4*

Construction on this CCC camp began in April 1935. Some 200 workers, many from the East Coast, worked at Camp Birch Creek, named for its proximity to Birch Creek. Under the direction of the USFS, the camp emphasized educational programs and provided classes in a variety of subjects. Young CCC men were employed at Camp Birch Creek until 1941. The site is one of the few that remain of 61 CCC camps in Montana. The University of Montana–Western in nearby Dillon now leases this facility in the Beaverhead-Deerlodge National Forest. Elevation: 6,501 ft. Location: Beaverhead County

Billings, 1909
F. J. Bandholtz, photographer, MHS 941-121

Birdtail Butte 349 *map 11 A-3*

Named for its bird tail–like appearance by the Stevens survey crew in the 1850s, this igneous intrusion is visible for miles around. The Mullan Road, a key transportation corridor between the Missouri River at Fort Benton and Walla Walla, Washington, had stage stations every 10 miles, including one near Birdtail Divide just north of St. Peter's Mission, established there in 1866. Elevation: 5,028 ft. Location: Cascade County

Birney 1157 *map 23 C-2*

Situated just outside the boundaries of the Northern Cheyenne Indian Reservation on the banks of the Tongue River, Birney was named for an early trader who annually bought furs from the Northern Cheyennes. The town, never more than a few businesses and a post office, served the surrounding ranch community beginning about 1886. In the 1950s, Birney began billing itself as "the heart of dude ranch country." Elevation: 3,125 ft. Location: Rosebud County

Bitterroot Mountains 354 *map 10 E-1*

The river, valley, and mountain range all derive their names from *Lewisia rediviva*, an important food plant for Native Americans. The Bitterroot Valley Salish gathered the pungent root in early summer, and they referred to the valley and mountains as Spet-lum, "Place of the bitterroot." Capt. Meriwether Lewis gathered bitterroot to be classified and later named; the Montana legislature designated it the Montana state flower in 1894. On June 30, 1806, Capt. William Clark descended the Bitterroot Range, which the expedition had crossed on the way to the Pacific the previous autumn. He wrote in his journal, "Leaveing those tremendous montanes behind us—in passing of which we have experiensed Cold and hunger of which I shall ever remember."

Bitterroot River 224 *map 10 C-2*

The Salish word for the Bitterroot River was In-shi-ttogh-tae-tkhu, "Willow river." Alexander Ross noted in 1842 that the Salish called it Spet-lum, "Place of the bitterroot," for this important edible root. The Jesuit priests named it St. Mary's River. By the time of Isaac I. Stevens' survey in December 1853, the names Bitter Root River and St. Mary's River were used interchangeably. The West Fork and East Fork flow into the main stem of the Bitterroot River at the southern end of Ravalli County.

Black Eagle 424 *map 12 A-1*

When Capt. Meriwether Lewis arrived at the Great Falls of the Missouri River on June 14, 1805, he noted 5 cataracts, the uppermost distinguished by a "black" (probably a golden or immature bald) eagle's nest: "Below this fall at a little distance a beautiful island well timbered is situated about the middle of the river. In this island on a cottonwood tree an eagle has placed her nest; a more inaccessible spot I believe she could not have found; for neither man nor beast dare pass those gulfs which separate her little domain from the shores." The Hidatsas had told Lewis about this nest, which still occupied the island as late as 1860. This spot became known as Black Eagle. It is near where the Boston & Montana Consolidated Copper and Silver Mining Company began construction of its reduction works on the north side of the Missouri River in 1891. With the completion of the smelter, immigrant workers constructed the small communities of Little Milwaukee and Little Chicago—the names suggesting the industrialization of the area. The Anaconda Company took over control of the Boston & Montana smelter in 1910. When August Cor established the post office in his store in 1917, the name was changed from Little Chicago to Black Eagle. Towering 506 feet over the community, the smelter's smokestack dominated the skyline until its demolition on September 18, 1982. According to Black Eagle residents: "The stack symbolized job security, progress, and optimism. Later, for many refinery workers, it symbolized callousness and frustration. All of those emotions are part of our history too" (from *In the Shadow of the Big Stack*). Elevation: 3,393 ft. Location: Cascade County

Black Eagle Dam 429   *map 12 A-1*

The Great Falls Water Power & Townsite Company built the Black Eagle Dam at Black Eagle Falls in 1890–91 to provide power for the smelter being built by the Boston & Montana Consolidated Copper and Silver Mining Company. Constructed of wood cribs filled with rock and concrete, the dam was damaged by a 1908 flood but was rebuilt. In 1926, a concrete dam 50 feet downstream replaced the original wooden dam. Elevation: 3,259 ft. Location: Cascade County

Blackfeet Indian Reservation 188
map 3 B-2

The 1855 Lame Bull Treaty with the Blackfoot Nation, negotiated by Isaac I. Stevens, confined the Blackfeet to the land north of the Missouri and east of the Continental Divide, and established an agency to distribute annuity goods. A series of treaties and executive orders between 1873 and 1895 reduced the size of the reservation, shrinking the Blackfeet territory 6 times through land cessions, purchases, and allotments. Today the reservation's economy is largely based on tourism, drawing on visitation to nearby Glacier National Park. Ranching, a spring-water bottling plant, and other enterprises also contribute to the economic base. The reservation encompasses about 1.5 million acres of land, an area larger than Rhode Island, and is governed by the Blackfeet Tribal Business Council.

Blackfoot 183   *map 3 B-1*

Joseph Kipp established a store here in 1889, but the town of Blackfoot came into existence when the Great Northern Railway selected it as a division point in 1893. From the corrals at Blackfoot, ranchers shipped tens of thousands of cattle to the stockyards of Chicago. An oral history collected by the WPA's Montana Federal Writers' Project tells how the Blackfeet people got their name. During a time of widespread starvation, an elder gave a young hunter strong medicine for his feet that made the hunter so swift he caught up with a herd of buffalo fleeing over a burned prairie and shot them with his arrows. The harvest fed all his people. The hunter was thereafter named Blackfoot for his black moccasins, and all his descendants became known as the Blackfeet. Elevation: 4,161 ft. Location: Glacier County

Blackfoot City 368   *map 11 C-1*

Blackfoot City was an early placer gold–mining town that began on Ophir Creek in 1865. Named for the nearby Blackfoot River (early residents mistakenly thought the site was the river's headwaters), the town during its first year boasted 7 mercantiles, 2 doctors, 2 blacksmiths, a carpenter-coffin maker, a Chinese laundry, and several whiskey dealers. Because of confusion with the town of Blackfoot in what

Blackfeet (Piegan) camp on St. Mary Lake, 1916

Roland W. Reed, photographer, MHS 955-521

is now Glacier County, Blackfoot City's name was changed to Ophir Creek in 1896, but locals continued to refer to their community as Blackfoot City. As with most boomtowns, Blackfoot City's demise was almost as rapid as its inception. Today the remnants of a few log cabins are all that remain of the once-famous camp. Elevation: 5,434 ft. Location: Powell County

Blackfoot River 235 *map 10 B-3*

Named for the Blackfeet tribe, this river was first known as the Big Blackfoot Fork and then the Big Blackfoot River. It flows into the Clark Fork River at Bonner. The word *Big* was later dropped, but many people still refer to it as the Big Blackfoot to differentiate it from the Little Blackfoot River, which flows into the Clark Fork River at Garrison. The Salish name for the river, Cokalihishkit, translates as "River of the road to the buffalo." The river was made famous by Norman Maclean's *A River Runs Through It*. The movie of the same name, however, was filmed on the Gallatin and Yellowstone rivers.

Blacktail Mountains 736 *map 19 C-1*

This small range of relatively barren summits is located southeast of Dillon. It provided a base for sheep operations during the early twentieth century.

Blaine County 753 *map 5 B-3*

Proponents who first suggested the creation of Blaine County to the Montana legislature in 1893 selected the name in honor of James G. Blaine, an 1884 presidential candidate who had recently died. The proposal went before the legislature twice more before finally succeeding in 1912. Although selection of the county seat was a topic of intense controversy, voters chose Chinook, in the extreme western part of the county, largely because of pressure from B. D. Phillips, who, 3 years later, convinced the legislature

to break off the eastern half of the county to form Phillips County.

Blodgett Creek and Canyon 311 *map 10 D-1*

The creek and canyon are named for an early resident of the Bitterroot Valley, Joseph Blodgett, who settled near the mouth of the creek in the 1860s and volunteered with Gen. John Gibbon at the Battle of the Big Hole in August 1877. Location: Ravalli County

Blood Creek 939 *map 14 B-2*

Blood Creek is named for the red color of its water, though some locals believe the name is derived from a battle between settlers and Native Americans that resulted in blood spilling into the creek. Several homesteads were established along the creek during the 1920s, and the Blood Creek School (known for a time as the Rice School, for teacher Dorothy Rice) operated from 1917 until 1935 and again briefly between 1940 and 1942. Many homesteads along this creek north of Winnett reverted to the General Land Office during the Great Depression. Location: Garfield County

Bloomfield 1171 *map 16 A-1*

Originally named Adams, this town was once part of an Amish community. In 1907, residents changed the name to Bloomfield in honor of the Nebraska home town of J. Berton and Dave Crockett, brothers who had homesteaded near here in 1905. They were soon joined by other Bloomfield families—so many, in fact, that in 1910 the Northern Pacific Railway offered a special excursion rate of $20 for a round trip from Bloomfield to Glendive. Elevation: 2,613 ft. Location: Dawson County

Bob Marshall Wilderness 207 *map 2 E-4*

The "Bob" is named in honor of forester, conservationist, and author Robert Marshall. Born in New York City, Marshall grew up in a wealthy, philanthropic family. He traveled the country and worked for several years as a USFS employee in Montana, where he spent days hiking in the South Fork of the Flathead River area, occasionally covering more than 50 miles in a day. An outspoken advocate for wilderness protection, in 1935 he became one of the founders of the Wilderness Society. In 1940, shortly after his death, the USFS set aside the South Fork, Sun River and Pentagon primitive areas, later designated the Bob Marshall Wilderness by the Wilderness Act of 1964. Today the Bob Marshall Wilderness Complex also includes the Scapegoat and Great Bear wilderness areas.

Bonner 240 *map 10 B-2*

In 1881, the Northern Pacific Railroad contracted with Eddy, Hammond & Company (in which Edward L. Bonner was a partner) for supplies needed to build the railroad between the Thompson and Blackfoot rivers. Recognizing the timber potential of the region, Bonner and his partners joined with 2 others to create the Montana Improvement Company, which built a sawmill in Bonner in 1886. In 1898, the Anaconda Company bought the lumber mill, built housing, and operated a company store at Bonner. It owned Bonner until 1972, when the U.S. Plywood Company bought the plywood mill, which has since been sold to Champion International and Stimson Lumber Company. Elevation: 3,316 ft. Location: Missoula County

Boulder 528 *map 11 E-3*

Originally called Boulder Valley, this town started as a stage station on the Fort Benton–Virginia City route in the 1860s. The town of Boulder Valley developed in 1862 when prospectors rushed to a new strike on the Boulder River. The Boulder Town Company incorporated 3 years after the first buildings were constructed, and residents chose the name Boulder Valley because of the boulder-lined river that bisects the valley. They shortened the name to Boulder in 1897. The town prospered with the development of mining and agriculture in the valley and received a further economic boost with the arrival of the Montana Central Railway in 1888. It is the county seat of Jefferson County. Elevation: 4,908 ft. Location: Jefferson County

Boulder Hot Springs Hotel 537 *map 11 E-3*

For centuries, native peoples visited the hot springs near present-day Boulder; legend tells that they called this area Peace Valley. In the 1860s, prospector James Riley chanced upon the springs and filed a land and water rights claim. In 1864, he built a crude bathhouse and tavern. When Riley succumbed to smallpox in 1882, new owners built a small, more fashionable hotel, which was remodeled in 1891 in the Queen Anne style. Rechristened the Hotel May for the daughter of the proprietor, it boasted 52 rooms, electricity, facilities for

Saw logs at Bonner mill, 1908
N. A. Forsyth, photographer, MHS

invalids, a resident physician, gymnasium, and various entertainments. Between 1910 and 1913, owner James A. Murray built the present bathhouse, the east wing, and an addition at the west and also remodeled the older building. The grand hotel, newly expanded and refurbished to its present California Mission style, featured raised parapets and a stucco covering. Opulent interior appointments included Tiffany glass lighting, beamed ceilings, and hand-stenciled walls in the Arts and Crafts tradition. Today Boulder Hot Springs is a last vestige of the many large-scale hot springs retreats that provided respite and recreation to early Montanans. Elevation: 4,823 ft. Location: Jefferson County

Boulder Mountains 508 *map 11 E-2*

This range of mountains lies between Butte and Helena, covering an area 50 miles by 32 miles within the Boulder batholith, a granitic intrusion containing some of the world's richest concentrations of minerals. The name of the mountains, river, and valley is derived from the rocky nature of the river.

Boulder River (Jefferson) 624 *map 19 A-3*

The Boulder River, its headwaters in the Boulder Mountains, flows east and south some 60 miles before emptying into the Jefferson River, a tributary of the Missouri River. Its name is derived from the river's rocky character.

Boulder River (Sweet Grass) 863
map 20 A-4

In 1806, Capt. William Clark referred to what was probably the Boulder River as Stinking Cabin Creek, a name supplied to him by the Mandan and Hidatsa. By 1876, it was known as Big Boulder River, thanks to the profusion of large, round stones that fill its channels. A natural bridge and waterfall are located about 25 miles up the river from Big Timber.

Bowman Lake 53 *map 2 A-2*

This lake, named for Fred Bowman, an early rancher who lived along the North Fork of the Flathead River, appeared on a map in 1846 as Lac et Riviere de Point ("Point lake and river," named for Jesuit priest Nicolas Point). The Kootenai name for Bowman Creek means "Big strawberries." Bowman Lake measures 7 miles long, making it one of the longer alpine lakes in Montana. Elevation: 4,034 ft. Location: Glacier National Park

Box Elder 588 *map 4 C-4*

Box Elder was first a stage stop on the Fort Assinniboine–Helena line, then a freight-loading station on the St. Paul, Minneapolis & Manitoba Railway, and finally, in 1887, a town founded by Robert Corcoran, John "Dutch" Henry, Dave Adams, and Clem Sailor, who intended to homestead on the Box Elder Creek flats just west of the Bears Paw Mountains. The first townsite, laid out in 1888, was named Bremer for another early homesteader from Ohio. Over the years, the area proved too dry for most, but the town grew and was eventually renamed Box Elder. After creation of Rocky Boy's Indian Reservation in 1916, the Chippewa-Cree established their tribal headquarters here. Elevation: 2,682 ft. Location: Hill County

Box Elder Creek 1247 *map 24 A-4*

This creek is one of numerous Montana streams named for the box elder tree. It flows out of northeast Carter County and empties into the Little Missouri River. The creek is intermittent for its first 30–40 miles. Location: Carter County

Boyd 981 *map 21 B-3*

Named for homesteader John Boyd, this community was a station on the Rocky Fork branch of the Northern Pacific Railway and prospered when homesteaders first arrived in the area in 1909. When the automobile gained popularity, residents began traveling to Red Lodge and Billings to conduct business, causing the decline and demise of local businesses. Elevation: 4,032 ft. Location: Carbon County

Boyes 1237 *map 24 B-1*

Henry Boyes arrived in Montana from England in 1886 at age 20. Little did he know when he squatted on and later homesteaded a claim on Cow Creek that the nearby town would be named in his honor. The community of Boyes developed with the creation of the post office in 1906 and the town's permanent establishment at the head of Scott Creek in 1910. Supported by farmers and ranchers, Boyes was moved in 1931 to be closer to US 212 between Broadus and Belle Fourche, South Dakota. Every 2 weeks, the community held dances with music played by local residents. Elevation: 3,330 ft. Location: Carter County

Bozeman 764 *map 20 B-1*

While leading wagon trains over the Bozeman Trail to the booming gold camps of Bannack and Virginia City, miner-turned-guide John Bozeman recognized the agricultural potential of the Gallatin Valley. At his direction, William Beall and Daniel Rouse laid out a townsite in 1864. Bozeman soon became a crucial supply center for nearby Fort Ellis and for those heading farther west, and the county seat of Gallatin County. (John Bozeman was killed April 18, 1867, in the Livingston area, allegedly by Blackfeet, although the details of the incident have been disputed over the years.) When designation of Yellowstone National Park brought the promise of renown to the region in 1872, Bozeman already boasted a telegraph line, newspaper, bank, and school. The first building boom along Main Street occurred when the tracks of the Northern Pacific Railroad reached Bozeman in 1883. A decade later, electric streetlights, streetcars, and the grand Bozeman Hotel urbanized the cityscape. The Montana College of Agriculture and Mechanic Arts, later Montana State University, was established by legislative decree in 1893, and the college's presence helped Bozeman prosper as a regional commercial center. Bozeman has 9 districts listed in the National Register and numerous independently listed homes and buildings. In the 2000 census, Gallatin County ranked as one of Montana's fastest-growing counties. Elevation: 4,814 ft. Location: Gallatin County

Queen's float in the Sweet Pea Carnival Parade, Bozeman, November 16, 1909
MHS 940-558

Bozeman Creek 762 *map 20 A-2*

Bozeman Creek is named for John Bozeman, who, with John Jacobs, blazed a route from the Oregon Trail at Fort Sedgwick, Nebraska, northwest through Wyoming to the gold camps near Virginia City, Montana. Bozeman Creek, which flows out of the Gallatin Range, began supplying the city of Bozeman's water in 1917. Location: Gallatin County

Bozeman Pass 792 *map 20 B-2*

Bozeman Pass is named for John Bozeman, the miner-turned-guide who, with John Jacobs, in the early 1860s established the Bozeman Trail, which cuts over Bozeman Pass to enter the Gallatin Valley. (Capt. William Clark used the pass on his return trip in 1806.) In 1883, the Northern Pacific Railroad laid tracks over the pass and, on January 10, 1884, opened the Bozeman Tunnel, a 3,600-foot-long tunnel constructed by 100 men over the course of 2 years. Elevation: 5,760 ft. Location: Gallatin County

Brackett Creek 785 *map 20 A-2*

During the latter half of 1867, the U.S. Army erected a fort just east of Bozeman and named it for Col. Augustus Van Horne Ellis. Two years later, on July 1, 1869, Col. A. G. Brackett and 250 men arrived there, charged with garrisoning the fort. This creek flowing east out of the Bridger Range is named for him. Location: Park County

Brady 303 *map 3 D-3*

Brady is probably named for the Brady brothers of Great Falls. Thomas E. Brady was attorney for the Great Falls & Canada Railway and held extensive agricultural and irrigation interests in Teton County. His brother, Charles A. Brady, was a Great Falls physician. Charles died in February 1908, and Thomas in September 1909. A month after Thomas's death, the Brady Townsite Company incorporated. Brady is now predominantly a grain distribution center. It is the birthplace of actor George Montgomery (1916–2000). Elevation: 3,530 ft. Location: Pondera County

Branham Lakes 693 *map 19 B-3*

The Branham Lakes are named for Thomas Branham, who, along with Jim Jones and James Bradley, built a simple stone arrastra mill there in the 1860s. The 2 small natural lakes were dammed by the Three Creeks Water Company in 1917. Today there is a small USFS campground at the lakes. Elevation: 8,798 ft. Location: Madison County

Bridger 1017 *map 21 C-3*

The Northern Pacific Railway built a branch line through Bridger in 1898, and George "Daddy" Town named the community after his good friend, mountain man Jim Bridger. Supported by ranchers and farmers, Bridger quickly became the second-largest city in Carbon County and continued to grow with the development of coal mining. The townsite was platted in 1902. Elevation: 3,662 ft. Location: Carbon County

Bridger Canyon 766 *map 20 A-2*

In 1856, mountain man Jim Bridger, accompanied by Kit Carson and William F. Drannan, passed through Bridger Canyon, giving the canyon its name. In 1882, cattleman Nelson Story built a flour mill at the mouth of Bridger Canyon to take advantage of the water power provided by Bridger Creek. The mill soon became the largest in Montana. In 1893, the U.S. Commission on Fish and Fisheries built a fish hatchery along Bridger Creek in the canyon, and in 1954 a group of downhill ski enthusiasts organized to build a ski lift and lodge on a slope in Bridger Canyon, the forerunner of Bridger Bowl, a winter recreation area in Gallatin County that today covers hundreds of acres of terrain.

Bridger Creek 895 *map 21 A-1*
One of several Montana creeks named for Jim Bridger, this creek in Sweet Grass County flows into the Yellowstone River just east of the Boulder River. A part owner of the Rocky Mountain Fur Company, Bridger honed his knowledge of the Yellowstone region as a guide for the Raynolds Expedition, which conducted a topographical survey for the U.S. Army in 1859–60. Location: Sweet Grass County

G. A. Trautman's general store and post office, Broadus
MHS 940-306

Bridger Divide 752 *map 20 A-2*
In the nineteenth century, Bridger Divide was known as Flathead Pass, after the Indians of western Montana who were among the tribes to hunt the buffalo plains. In 1859–60, the Raynolds Expedition, accompanied by Jim Bridger, conducted a topographical survey to explore the upper Yellowstone for the U.S. Army. They "entered the [Flathead] pass by a well defined road with evident marks of recent passage of a large band of Indians." It has been known since as the Bridger Divide. Elevation: 6,103 ft. Location: Gallatin County

Bridger Range 732 *map 20 A-1*
The Bridger Range, north of Bozeman, is named for mountain man Jim Bridger, who passed through these mountains in 1856 with Kit Carson and William F. Drannan.

Broadus 1220 *map 23 B-4*
Broadus is named for the Broaddus family who settled in the Powder River area in 1885. A clerical error by postal officials in Washington, D.C., resulted in the changed spelling when the post office was estab-

lished in 1900. In the early years, Broadus was little more than a post office and general store on the G. A. Trautman ranch. In 1920, however, voters selected it as the county seat, and it gradually added houses and businesses. Broadus boomed during the late 1960s with the opening of the Bell Creek Oil Field, and oil and gas production continue to be important to the local economy. Elevation: 3,028 ft. Location: Powder River County

Broadview 933 *map 13 E-3*
Broadview was established about 1908 when the Great Northern Railway's Billings and Northern branch line was built. The town was named by rancher W. X. Sudduth, who wanted to call it Fairview, after his ranch, but a Fairview already existed. Broadview incorporated in 1917. In 1934, almost half the town burned in a devastating fire. Elevation: 3,878 ft. Location: Yellowstone County

Broadwater County 592 *map 12 D-1*
Thanks to intense political effort by Archibald E. Spriggs, a legislator from Meagher County, Broadwater County was

established in 1897 from portions of Jefferson and Meagher counties. U.S. Senator Thomas H. Carter proposed that the new county be named in honor of the recently deceased Charles A. Broadwater, who had located his Diamond R freighting company corrals northwest of Townsend, established the Montana Central Railway, and built the Broadwater Hotel in Helena.

Brockton 1153 *map 8 D-1*

By 1886, the St. Paul, Minneapolis & Manitoba Railway had extended its transcontinental line as far west as Brockton on the Fort Peck Indian Reservation. Here the railroad built a coal chute, water tank, roundhouse, section houses, and water treatment plant. The townsite, however, was not platted until 1909. When the federal government opened the reservation to non-Indian homesteaders in 1913, Brockton boomed, becoming the sixth-largest wheat shipping point in Montana. The town incorporated in 1952. Elevation: 1,985 ft. Location: Roosevelt County

Brockway 1116 *map 15 A-3*

In 1910, 3 Brockway brothers filed on adjoining homesteads along the fertile Redwater River near here. The area was a long way from everywhere, so they established a small trading center on brother James's homestead to provide supplies and other services to their neighbors. By 1913, the settlement's importance to the area justified opening a post office. That same year, the Great Northern Railway announced plans to build a line across central Montana. Anticipating its route, the Brockways platted a new town and relocated their group of buildings to the new townsite. This haphazard set of buildings provided the core of a thriving commercial district that included 20 businesses at the town's height in the late 1910s. The railroad didn't materialize, and Brockway's fortunes faded until the Northern Pacific Railway's

Redwater branch line reached the town in 1928. Brockway's economy boomed by the mid-1930s as it became a major shipping point for livestock and grain. Elevation: 2,597 ft. Location: McCone County

Brooks 771 *map 13 B-2*

In 1879, Henry P. "Governor" Brooks started the first permanent settlement in Fergus County when he established the Horseshoe Bar Ranch for Thomas C. Power on Warm Springs Creek. David Hilger renamed the community Brooks, in honor of the early rancher, when the Milwaukee Road built a station here in 1910. Elevation: 3,961 ft. Location: Fergus County

Browning 176 *map 3 C-1*

Browning (originally Browning Indian Agency) was named in 1885 for Commissioner of Indian Affairs D. M. Browning. Established in 1880, the Blackfeet Agency (Old Agency) in 1895 moved about 15 miles, from Badger Creek north to Browning. The town began as a collection of government buildings, but the community soon expanded to include Joseph Kipp's trading post, followed by several other mercantile operations, churches, and a school. Today Browning is tribal headquarters of the Blackfeet Indian Reservation and the only incorporated town on the reservation. Elevation: 4,376 ft. Location: Glacier County

Browns Lake 292 *map 10 B-4*

Browns Lake is reportedly named for old-timer "Laughing" Brown. Surrounded by open sagebrush grasslands and aspen groves, the lake is part of the Blackfoot Waterfowl Production Area and is frequented by bald eagles, osprey, avocets, Canada geese, sandhill cranes, and numerous other birds. Elevation: 4,293 ft. Location: Powell County

Brusett 1010 *map 14 A-3*

Established on Lone Tree Creek in 1916, Brusett received its name when homesteader Alma Brusett Smith applied to the federal government to open a post office. The town served area ranchers and homesteaders. Elevation: 2,900 ft. Location: Garfield County

Brush Lake State Park 1206 *map 8 B-3*

In 1914, Hans Christian Hansen filed for a homestead at this 60-foot-deep, spring-fed lake named for the chokecherry and buffalo berry lining the shore. He built the Brush Lake Summer Resort, which attracted farm families from miles around during the area's brief summers. Owners Charles Huebner and Albert Morin erected a bar and café in 1919–20; a dance pavilion followed in the 1940s. The State of Montana designated the 280-acre lake a state park in 2005. Elevation: 2,051 ft. Location: Sheridan County

Buffalo 749 *map 13 C-1*

William Shiell, a homesteader on Buffalo Creek, named the post office established here in 1890, Buffalo for the large herds that earlier had roamed the area. Buffalo experienced a period of growth with completion of the Great Northern Railway's Billings and Northern branch line. The railroad platted the new townsite in 1907, and it was rumored that Buffalo might become the railroad's division point. This did not occur, but the town prospered with the homesteading boom until the drought and collapse of the farm economy in the 1920s. Elevation: 4,318 ft. Location: Fergus County

Bull Mountains 977 *map 14 D-1*

The Bull Mountains southeast of Roundup are thought to be named for either the bull pine or the large bull elk present in the mountains in the early days. Elk were common here until the 1880s, when increased hunting and farming depleted the herds. They began to make a comeback in the 1940s and '50s, but their habitat is now threatened by subdivision of land. The Crow tribe called this range Chiilapisa-lachee, "Bull's bluff."

Bull Lake 20 *map 1 C-1*

The area around Bull Lake, traditional territory of the Kootenai and Pend d'Oreille tribes, was ceded by the 1855 Hellgate Treaty and the tribes moved to the Flathead Reservation. Construction of the Great Northern Railway in the 1890s increased logging activity along the Kootenai River. The lake's outlet, Lake Creek, drains into the Kootenai River. Homesteaders settled in the area of Bull Lake in the early twentieth century, and during the early 1920s it became a popular recreation retreat for residents of nearby Troy and Libby. Elevation: 3,642 ft. Location: Lincoln County

Bullhook Creek 636 *map 5 C-1*

Bullhook Creek begins in the northern foothills of the Bears Paw Mountains and flows through the center of Havre. The junction of the creek with the Milk River, originally known as Bull Hook Bottoms, was a popular camping site for the Assiniboine, Gros Ventre, and Cree. When the St. Paul, Minneapolis & Manitoba Railway arrived in the mid-1880s, locals rejected Bull Hook Bottoms as a name for the station and instead chose Havre. Bullhook Creek was dammed for flood control in 1962. Location: Hill County

Burnham 596 *map 5 C-1*

The Great Northern Railway created the Burnham siding in 1887. The railroad advertised the area as prime farming land, producing an influx of homesteaders and establishment of the Burnham post office in 1914. In 1910, the Sprinkle Brothers Sheep

Company of Chinook sheared 125,000 sheep near the siding. Today all that remains is the original school. Elevation: 2,632 ft. Location: Hill County

Burnt Fork of the Bitterroot River 297
map 10 D-2

The name Burnt Fork dates from as early as the 1850s, when Major John Owen filed the first water right in what would become Montana. The upper regions of the creek, in the Sapphire Mountains, had burned in earlier forest fires, hence the creek's name. Samuel M. Caldwell did some placer mining along the creek in 1852, and other miners worked the area in the 1860s, but it never became an important district. At the creek's headwaters is Burnt Fork Lake.

Busby 1115 *map 22 B-4*

Busby, on the Northern Cheyenne Indian Reservation, is named for Sheridan Busby, a homesteader who came to the area in 1895 and established the first post office here in 1904. Trader W. P. Moncure erected the Two Moon Monument at Busby in 1936. This stone pyramid has a locked vault that originally contained artifacts and documents relating to the Battle of the Little Bighorn. Elevation: 3,424 ft. Location: Big Horn County

Butte 525 *map 11 E-2*

Miners named this industrial town, now the Silver Bow County seat, for Big Butte, a nearby landform. It was known as Butte City until the name of the post office officially changed to Butte in 1890. Gold and silver drove the town's population from 40 men and 5 women in 1866 to 14,000 residents by 1885, but it was copper, critical to the electrification of the United States, that gave Butte a 41 percent share of the world copper market and a population estimated at 85,000 by 1916. The city's mineral wealth drew innovative mining technology, capital from the likes of George Hearst and John D. Rockefeller, and 5 railroad lines. Workers came from more than 60 nations to work for the Anaconda Company and its supporting businesses and industries. Open-pit mining began in 1955. In the next few decades, the Berkeley Pit slowly swallowed historic neighborhoods, but spectacular mansions, commercial buildings, and workers' cottages built in the shadows of the tall steel headframes remain to tell Butte's colorful history. Today some mining continues in the Continental Pit. The town is now part of the extended Butte-Anaconda Historic District NHL, created in 2006. Elevation: 5,549 ft. Location: Silver Bow County

Butte-Anaconda Historic District NHL 521 *map 11 E-1*

Looming black steel headframes in Butte and the towering smokestack of the Anaconda Company's Washoe Reduction Works in Anaconda recall the industrial roots of these sister cities, the source of much of the world's copper in the nineteenth and early twentieth centuries. The dangerous work of extracting copper for telegraph wires, telephones, and electrical lines bred solidarity among miners and smelter workers, and Butte became known as the "Gibraltar of Unionism." Two of the nation's most radical unions—the Western Federation of Miners and the Industrial Workers of the World—had their roots here, and clashes between management and labor marked the district, especially after the 1917 Granite Mountain–Speculator Mine fire in Butte, the worst hard-rock mining disaster in the nation's history. Labor unrest and years under martial law followed in Butte, while in Anaconda the company fired agitators and suspected Socialists, devastating the unions. Butte and Anaconda workers reorganized during the New Deal, after the federal government guaranteed the right of workers to unionize. In 2006, the NPS designated Butte, Anaconda, and nearby Walkerville a NHL, one

Butte—the richest hill on earth
MHS PAc 98-57.5

of the largest in the West. It encompasses nearly 10,000 acres, with more than 6,000 contributing resources. Location: Silver Bow and Deer Lodge counties

Buxton 518 *map 19 A-1*

Buxton was a station stop established in 1881 on the Utah & Northern Railway, the first railroad to enter Montana. It was named for J. H. Buxton of New Hampshire, an early gold miner and railroad worker. Elevation: 5,723 ft. Location: Silver Bow County

Bynum 255 *map 3 D-2*

Stephen and Frances Bynum settled on the south bank of Muddy Creek in the early 1880s and quickly established a store and post office, which became known as Old Bynum. The current town of Bynum is half a mile south and east. In 1908, work began on the nearby Bynum Reservoir, developed by the Teton Cooperative Reservoir Company. Elevation: 3,973 ft. Location: Teton County

Bynum Reservoir 249 *map 3 D-2*

Developed in 1907 by the Teton Cooperative Reservoir Company to reclaim 15,000 acres under the Carey Land Act, Bynum Reservoir was named for Stephen and Frances Bynum, who operated a store and the post office on the south bank of Muddy Creek. The company began work on the reservoir in 1908, and the main diversion canal in 1910. In 1925, local farmers created the Bynum Irrigation District, which now irrigates more than 20,000 acres of cropland. Elevation: 4,173 ft. Location: Teton County

Coal Banks Landing, Upper Missouri River, 1880

Detail, F. Jay Haynes, photographer, MHS H-370

Cabinet Mountains 38   *map 1   D-2*

The Cabinet Mountains in northwestern Montana separate the Clark Fork and Kootenai rivers, both tributaries of the Columbia River. Father Pierre-Jean De Smet made reference to the Cabinet Gorge along the Clark Fork, named by early fur traders for the "four compartments" (referring to rock cabinet-like formations) in the river.

Cabinet Mountains Wilderness 32   *map 1   C-2*

A portion of the Cabinet Mountains has been protected as a primitive area since 1935; this 100,000-acre wilderness in northwestern Montana is one of the original areas designated in the Wilderness Act of 1964. Silver and copper mining claims within the wilderness are still being challenged in the courts; an underground copper-silver mine has been proposed within the boundaries of the wilderness area. The Cabinets have a climate more like the Pacific Northwest, and are home to grizzly bears and mountain goats.

Cameron 777   *map 19   C-3*

The Cameron brothers, Addison and James, filed land claims near the settlement of Bear Creek in 1886, under the Desert Land Act. Addison opened a store and post office in the 1890s. When Frank Falbaum purchased the store in 1919, he moved the building 6 miles west to take advantage of the tourist trade on US 287, the route between Ennis and Yellowstone National Park. The residents of Bear Creek expressed their ire by refusing to shop at his store for several years. Ed and Dorothy McAtee purchased land adjacent to the store in 1938 and renovated it, adding a café, a bar, cabins, and a gas station. The McAtee family operated the community's businesses until 1981, when they sold them to the Cameron Group. Elevation: 5,378 ft. Location: Madison County

Camp Disappointment NHL 193   *map 3   B-1*

The Lewis and Clark Expedition's return trip from the Pacific Coast had its share of significant discoveries. Between July 22 and 26, 1806, Capt. Meriwether Lewis and 3 men explored the Marias River to determine the northern boundary of the Louisiana Purchase. They also hoped to find a short portage between the Marias and Saskatchewan rivers that would allow American traders access to some of the western Canadian fur trade. At the northernmost point of this trip, Lewis named a campsite Camp Disappointment because from a high overlook he saw Cut Bank Creek curve southwest toward the Rocky Mountains. He then knew that the boundary of the United States did not extend to 50° north as they had hoped. Camp Disappointment, which has restricted public access, is commemorated with a highway marker and roadside monument on US 2. Elevation: 4,174 ft. Location: Glacier County

Camp Paxson Boy Scout Camp 219
map 10   B-3

In 1924, the USFS granted a permit to the Western Montana Council of Boy Scouts to construct this summer camp, originally a tent camp. A more permanent facility was needed by the late 1930s. The WPA and CCC provided funds and manpower to construct the present camp on Seeley Lake, named for Montana artist Edgar S. Paxson. The rustic log buildings were constructed in 1939 and 1940 under the direction of the USFS. This is the only CCC-constructed youth camp in Montana. Designed to fit the natural landscape, the 20 buildings of saddle-notched native larch demonstrate excellent craftsmanship, made more remarkable because CCC workers were primarily "city boys" trained on the job. The Missoula Children's Theatre has managed the camp since 1995 under a special-use permit from the Lolo National Forest. Elevation: 4,004 ft. Location: Missoula County

Camp Senia Historic District 974
map 21 C-2

As a teenager, Alfred Croonquist guided fishing trips and dreamed of a place where visitors could enjoy Montana's bounty. In 1919, he completed the first building at Camp Senia on the banks of the West Fork of Rock Creek. Camp Senia, named for Alfred's wife, was the first, and is now the only intact survivor of 4 dude ranches and fishing camps in the Beartooth Mountains. Camp Senia's guests paid $45 a week for plenty of good food and a horse. Visitors were instructed to bring "western togs" and hang their "city clothes on the hitching post." With the help of friends, Croonquist added to the camp 19 buildings that reveal sophistication and skill in the use of native materials. Summer of 1929 marked a record-breaking tourist year in the West, but the Great Depression brought an end to dude ranching at Camp Senia in the 1930s. Croonquist, an organizer of the Dude Ranchers Association and an active conservationist, did much to promote and establish tourism in Montana and Carbon County. Today the Rustic-style National Register–listed cabins of lodgepole pine and native river cobble stand as a reminder of Croonquist's foresight. Elevation: 7,780 ft. Location: Carbon County

Campbell Camp No. 4 1061 *map 22 A-2*

Thomas D. Campbell, inspired by the enormous demand for wheat during World War I, founded the Campbell Farming Corporation to raise wheat on the Crow Indian Reservation. Beginning in 1918, Campbell leased more than 30,000 acres on the Crow Reservation and purchased additional acreage near the reservation. A pioneer in industrial agriculture, Campbell went to the Soviet Union during the 1930s to advise the Soviet government on industrial farming methods. The Big Horn County Museum restored Camp No. 4, beginning in 1996, to illustrate life on a large industrial wheat farm. Elevation: 2,903 ft. Location: Big Horn County

Canyon Creek 386 *map 11 C-2*

The town of Canyon Creek at the north end of the Prickly Pear Valley takes its name from a nearby creek that flows through a canyon to the Missouri River. Originally called Georgetown, Canyon Creek changed its name in 1871. The post office at Canyon Creek is one of the oldest continuously operating post offices in Montana. Elevation: 4,339 ft. Location: Lewis and Clark County

Canyon Creek Charcoal Kilns 563
map 18 A-4

These beehive-style charcoal ovens, listed in the National Register, were built to supply charcoal to fuel the smelters at Glendale that processed silver ore from the Hecla Mine to the west. The ovens burned off volatile gases and moisture from lodgepole pine wood to create an almost pure carbon. There were originally 22 ovens. The date of construction is not known, but the nearby settlement of Glendale reached its peak population of 2,000 in 1878. Elevation: 6,488 ft. Location: Beaverhead County

Canyon Ferry 500 *map 11 C-4*

With the discovery of gold in Last Chance Gulch in 1864, prospectors scattered in all directions looking for ore deposits. Gold strikes at French Bar, Cave Gulch, White Gulch, and Confederate Gulch catalyzed development. In 1865, John Oakes established Canyon Ferry at the mouth of Black Rock Canyon to take people and cargo across the Missouri River. The new town quickly became a key point on the stage road from White Sulphur Springs and Diamond City to Helena. J. V. Stafford purchased the ferry from Oakes and later sold it to Court Sheriff, who gave the community a boost by building a stage stop, saloon, hotel, stable, store, and post office. With the construction of the first dam at Canyon Ferry in 1896, the ferry business came to an end, and town residents had to cross the river by boat above the dam until a bridge was completed in 1899. Construction of a second dam backed up the river and wiped out most of the remnants of Canyon Ferry in 1954. Elevation: 3,835 ft. Location: Lewis and Clark County

Canyon Ferry Lake 499 *map 11 D-4*
In 1865, John Oakes established a ferry to cross the Missouri River near the mouth of a deep canyon. The settlement came to be known as Canyon Ferry. In 1896, Samuel Hauser and Thomas Marlow, Helena capitalists, began construction of a dam there to provide hydroelectric power to Helena, creating Lake Sewell above the dam. By mid-century, demands for flood control, irrigation water, and recreation prompted the U.S. Bureau of Reclamation to construct a large concrete dam downstream from the turn-of-the-century dam. When completed in 1954, Canyon Ferry Dam, measuring 173 feet at its base and rising 225 feet, allowed for a maximum generation of 50,000 kW and irrigation of more than 43,000 acres. The dam created Canyon Ferry Lake, a reservoir with a shoreline of 76 miles and a capacity of more than 2 million acre-feet of storage. Construction of the new dam flooded the historic towns of Canyon Ferry and Canton, as well as rich bottomland along the Missouri River, but provided nesting habitat for thousands of white pelicans and cormorants. Elevation: 3,799 ft. Location: Lewis and Clark County

Capitol 1251 *map 24 B-4*
Initially named Capitol Rock, after the prominent landmark to the north, Capitol became a destination for Norwegian immigrants in the 1880s. Farming and ranching were the dominant industries in this area traversed by range riders from the Hash Knife and Turkey Track cattle companies. When a school was created in 1891 in Capitol, ranch children from both

Charcoal kilns, Glendale
MHS PAc 94-78.10

Montana and South Dakota attended since the town was located next to the South Dakota–Montana border. Elevation: 3,181 ft. Location: Carter County

Capitol Rock 1248 *map 24 A-4*
Capitol Rock is a massive white limestone uplift named for its resemblance to the nation's Capitol. In 1976, the USFS designated the rock structure a national natural monument. Elevation: 4,130 ft. Location: Carter County

Carbon County 1013 *map 21 C-3*
The Montana legislature created Carbon County from portions of Park and Yellowstone counties in 1895. The name honors the abundant coal at Bearcreek and at Red Lodge, the county seat. Because of its outdoor recreational opportunities and proximity to the Beartooth Mountains and the northeast entrance to Yellowstone National Park, Carbon County is now a popular tourist destination.

Cardwell 625 *map 19 A-3*

Originally known as Jefferson Island (now the settlement on the opposite bank of the Jefferson River), Cardwell takes its name from Edward Cardwell, area landowner and state senator. The Mayflower Mining Company, which operated a gold and silver mine from the 1890s into the 1930s, helped the town thrive. The Northern Pacific maintained a station in Cardwell from 1890 into the 1970s. Cardwell was on the Yellowstone Trail auto route, and in 1949 Indiana University made it the headquarters of the Indiana University Field Station. Chet Huntley, NBC newscaster, was born in Cardwell in 1912. Elevation: 4,282 ft. Location: Jefferson County

Carlyle 1239 *map 16 C-4*

Arthur C. Knutson, in 1907, became the town's first postmaster. Residents adopted the name of Arthur's son for the town, which has been moved to the west several times over the past century. The area around Carlyle produces large quantities of wheat. Elevation: 3,182 ft. Location: Wibaux County

Carter 463 *map 4 E-2*

Originally called Sidney, this town was renamed Carter in 1905 by the Great Northern Railway to honor the new state's first congressional representative, Thomas H. Carter. After the town was platted in 1909, homesteaders rushed into the area. In 2006, the Burlington Northern Santa Fe Railway announced the expansion of the grain elevator at Carter. Elevation: 3,123 ft. Location: Chouteau County

Carter County 1245 *map 24 B-3*

The Montana legislature separated Carter County from Fallon County in 1917, naming it in honor of U.S. Senator Thomas H. Carter, who had died in 1911. This county in the far southeastern corner of the state is predominantly prairie; Ekalaka is the county seat.

Carter Ferry 480 *map 4 E-2*

Chouteau County established this ferry across the Missouri River in 1917 to provide people living south of the river access to the Great Northern Railway station at Carter. A. H. Stewart built the ferryboat for $850; the county contracted with Sam Denton to operate it. In 1945, the State of Montana replaced the old ferry with a newer, steel-hulled boat that stayed in service until 2004. The ferry still serves local traffic from March to November. Elevation: 2,695 ft. Location: Chouteau County

Cascade 394 *map 11 B-4*

When the Montana Central Railway started building a line on the west side of the Missouri River in 1886, the community of Dodge (named for a railroad official) sprang up to provide services to the railroad workers. A ferry connected Dodge to a settlement across the river that over time was known as Ulidia, Gorham, and St. Clair. In 1887, Dodge residents changed their town's name to Cascade in hopes of becoming the county seat of the new Cascade County. Although Cascade lost its bid, the town secured its future by constructing a bridge over the Missouri River in 1893. Cascade incorporated in 1911. Artist Charlie Russell lived here for a year with his bride, Nancy. Elevation: 3,387 ft. Location: Cascade County

Cascade County 444 *map 12 B-1*

The Montana legislature formed Cascade County from the southwest corner of Chouteau County in 1887, when the arrival of the Montana Central and the St. Paul, Minneapolis & Manitoba railroads guaranteed prosperity to the area. Historically, the economy has been dominated by copper smelting, refining, and fabrication as well as agriculture and the U.S. Air Force. Great Falls is the county seat, and this county, which is named for waterfalls on the Missouri River, is one of the most populous counties in the state.

Castle Mountain 971 *map 21 C-1*

Castle Mountain, on the Beartooth Plateau north of the Beartooth Highway, is the third-highest peak in Montana. Elevation: 12,605 ft. Location: Carbon County

Castle Mountains 671 *map 12 D-2*

The Castle Mountains derive their name from the tall pinnacles of weathered granite that resemble castle battlements when viewed from the Smith River Valley. Rich deposits of lead and silver in the Castles attracted miners during the 1880s, leading to the creation of Castle Town. It supported a population of 2,000 residents, 2 newspapers, a brick kiln, a sawmill, and 14 saloons. Location: Meagher County

Castle Rock Lake 1117 *map 23 A-1*

Castle Rock Lake, a natural lake, is a popular fishing, swimming, nonmotorized boating, and hiking site maintained by Colstrip Parks and Recreation Dept. It is named for a nearby butte that resembles a castle. Elevation: 3,224 ft. Location: Rosebud County

Castle Town 691 *map 12 D-2*

Castle Town derives its name from its location at the base of the Castle Mountains, which resemble the crenellated towers of a medieval castle. Rich deposits of lead and silver brought miners to the area beginning in 1882, and they established mines named Blue Bell, Cumberland, Lamar, Morning Star, and Belle of the Castles. Residents marked the official birthday of Castle Town as April 20, 1887, which celebrated the community's first smelter. As silver prices soared, Castle Town boomed, reaching approximately 2,000 residents. Two more smelters were added, and the future looked bright for the community until Congress repealed the Sherman Silver Purchase Act of 1890. The good times ended when silver prices plummeted and the Panic of 1893 began. By the mid-1890s, most residents had moved on. Today Castle Town exists as a ghost of its former prosperous self. Elevation: 6,011 ft. Location: Meagher County

*Scattered remnants
of Castle*
MHS 940-607

Castner Coal Mine 514 *map 12 A-2*

John K. Castner opened the Castner Mine (also known as the ACM Mine) in Belt in 1877. In 1891, he leased it to P. J. Shields, who, in partnership with Marcus Daly, formed the Castner Coal and Coke Company to provide coal for the Boston & Montana Consolidated Copper and Silver Mining Company smelter in Great Falls. In 1895, the company became the Coal Dept. of the Anaconda Company, and Anaconda built a 600-ton washing plant, 100 coke ovens, and other facilities in Belt. The coke ovens closed in 1903 because Anaconda shifted its coking operations to Cokedale in Park County. The mines closed in 1925. Elevation: 3,677 ft. Location: Cascade County

Castner Falls 415 *map 11 A-4*

In the 1870s, John Castner and Joe Largent filed on homesteads between the Smith and Missouri rivers, and a short-lived post office, Castner, opened there in 1883. Homesteaders trickled into the area during the 1880s and '90s, and farmers established a local of the national Grange farm organization in 1913 and built a community hall. Most of the land around the town of Castner Falls is now planted in wheat; livestock graze on the steep and rocky tracts. Elevation: 3,555 ft. Location: Cascade County

Cat Creek 958 *map 14 B-2*

The name Cat Creek is attributed to an early cowboy who reportedly roped a mountain lion along this creek that flows into the Musselshell River. For years, the creek's location moved about on maps; in 1870, Walter W. DeLacy drew the creek between Blood and Dovetail creeks, as did William Ludlow in 1875. It found its current location in 1900. The 1919 discovery of oil on Cat Creek northwest of Mosby and the construction of a pipeline from the Cat Creek Oil Field marked a radical change for area homesteaders. At the peak

of production in 1922, the 11 wells recovered 3 million barrels of oil. By the 1930s, Continental Oil Company (CONOCO) dominated the oil fields. Another boom in the 1940s lasted until the early 1960s. Location: Petroleum County

Cat Creek (town) 1005 *map 14 B-1*

Oil was discovered along Cat Creek in 1919. The early Cat Creek camp included a community hall and some residences, but nearby Winnett experienced the effects of the boom with new businesses and workers' housing. A brief boom in Cat Creek in the 1940s lasted until the early 1960s. Elevation: 2,907 ft. Location: Petroleum County

Cataract Creek (Glacier) 105 *map 2 B-3*

In 1887, George Bird Grinnell named this creek in Glacier National Park for the many waterfalls along its course, among them Morning Eagle Falls, Walden Falls, Feather Plume Falls, and Hidden Falls.

Cataract Creek (Jefferson) 504 *map 11 E-2*

This Cataract Creek cascades off Old Baldy Mountain in the Boulder Mountains north of Basin. The creek shares its name with an 1862 placer-mining camp along the Boulder River (also known as Old Bar) as well as with a basin and meadows below Old Baldy.

Cataract Mountain 104 *map 2 B-3*

Cataract Mountain rises just east of the Garden Wall in Glacier National Park. It takes its name from Cataract Creek, which flows off the mountain's north face. Elevation: 8,180 ft. Location: Glacier National Park

Cedar Creek 1159 *map 15 C-4*

This creek was originally named Maynadier Creek for Lt. Henry E. Maynadier, who passed through the area in 1859 as part of the Raynolds Expedition that conducted a topographical survey for the U.S. Army. The creek in later years came to be known as Cedar Creek. Location: Prairie County

Cedar Creek Mining District 139 *map 9 B-3*

A placer-gold region discovered in 1869 by French Canadian miner Louis A. Barrette, the Cedar Creek Mining District encompassed Cedar, Quartz, and Trout creeks. It was the locus of considerable gold fever when more than 200 claims were staked within a few months. In 1870, the district boasted a population of more than 1,600 residents, including 50 saloonkeepers. Over the course of the next 65 years, the district produced over $2 million in gold. A large gold dredge (a mechanical device that scoops up and sorts river gravels in the creek) operated on Cedar Creek around 1909. Location: Mineral County

Centennial Mountains 882 *map 19 E-3*

This range, named in 1876 during the U.S. centennial by Rachel Orr, wife of William Orr of the Poindexter and Orr Ranch, runs east-west for 50 miles along the Montana-Idaho state line. The Centennial Valley was the route of the Monida and Yellowstone stagecoach, which transported tourists from the Utah & Northern Railway station at Monida to West Yellowstone. The Centennial Valley is home to the Red Rock Lakes NWR, established in 1935 by the federal government to protect a resident population of endangered trumpeter swans.

Centerville 482 *map 12 A-1*

Centerville derives its name from its position halfway between the nearby coal towns of Stockett and Sand Coulee. It was home to the Stainsby-Latham Coal Mine, developed in 1905, as well as the Lockray Mine, purchased by the Anaconda Company in 1914 to supply fuel to its smelter at Anaconda. Elevation: 3,468 ft. Location: Cascade County

Chalk Buttes 1235 *map 24 A-2*

Named for their crumbly, white sandstone composition, the Chalk Buttes can be seen from both South Dakota and Wyoming. Elevation: 4,143 ft. Location: Carter County

Charles M. Russell House and Studio NHL 425 *map 12 A-1*

Born in St. Louis, Missouri, Charlie Russell came to Montana in 1880 and wrangled cattle for a decade in Montana's Judith Basin, gaining a reputation as a man who could draw good pictures and tell a good story. Russell continued to refine these skills after he quit cowboying. He painted the West as he saw it—romantic, poignant, and changing. The modest white clapboard home in Great Falls where he and his wife, Nancy, lived dates to 1900 and has changed little since the Russells' occupancy. Russell's log cabin studio, built in 1903, sits adjacent.

Charles M. Russell in his studio, Great Falls, 1914
MHS 944-708

The site became a NHL in 1976. Nearby is the C. M. Russell Museum, established in 1953, which displays an impressive collection of Russell's art and artifacts as well as the work of contemporary Montana artists. Elevation: 3,369 ft. Location: Cascade County

Charles M. Russell NWR 997   map 6 E-3
Established in 1963, the Charles M. Russell NWR succeeded the Fort Peck Game Range, formed in 1936 and administered by the Bureau of Biological Survey. The name was selected to honor Charlie Russell, Montana's cowboy artist, whose paintings depict the rugged badlands typical of the refuge. The USFWS now manages the refuge of just over 1 million acres, with the goal of improving habitat and protecting native animals and plants. Location: Garfield County

Charley Creek 1078   map 7 D-2
During the early 1880s, maps referred to Charley Creek as Elk Horn Creek; in 1885, the Burshia family named the creek after their horse Charley, who often strayed there from the ranch. In 1887, Charley FitzGerald, a sheepherder, grazed sheep along the creek, prompting further reference to Charley Creek. Location: Valley County

Charlo 167   map 10 A-1
Originally called Big Flat, the town of Charlo lay on the trail used by freighters traveling between Ronan and the railroad at Dixon. The town underwent a few name changes—Charlotte, Tabor—before finally becoming Charlo in 1918. Tribal members were instrumental in changing the town's name. Charlo was a Salish chief who for decades refused to leave the Salish homeland in the Bitterroot Valley. Charlo eventually settled his people on the Flathead Indian Reservation, and many of them chose allotments in the Big Flat area in 1908. Elevation: 2,936 ft. Location: Lake County

Checkerboard 690   map 12 D-3
This community likely takes its name from Checkerboard Creek, which empties into the North Fork of the Musselshell River just downstream of nearby Bair Reservoir. Checkerboard sits on land that once belonged to the Bair Livestock Company of Martinsdale. An earlier town named Delphine, a supply center for small copper mines in the area, opened a post office at the confluence of the North Fork of the Musselshell River and Checkerboard Creek in 1899 and remained in operation until 1929. Construction of the Bair Reservoir created the new town of Checkerboard. Elevation: 5,219 ft. Location: Meagher County

Cherry Creek 1169   map 16 C-1
One of several Montana creeks with this name, the intermittent Cherry Creek in Prairie County is named for the chokecherries that grow along it. Numerous families homesteaded the area about 1910, but the General Land Office repossessed many of their holdings during the Great Depression. Location: Prairie County

Chester 398   map 4 C-2
The Great Northern Railway began construction of a 50,000-gallon water tank, a windmill, and a section house here in 1891 and added a coal dock in 1900. The first telegraph operator assigned to the new station named it Chester, after his home town in Pennsylvania. Chester applied for and received a post office in 1895, and the town officially incorporated in 1910. By 1912, Chester eclipsed both Havre and Shelby in size and boasted of being the largest town west of Minot, North Dakota. After the creation of Liberty County in 1920, Chester won out over Joplin for the coveted

county seat. The First Episcopal Church and the First State Bank of Chester are listed in the National Register. Elevation: 3,133 ft. Location: Liberty County

Chico Hot Springs 856 *map 20 B-2*

Chico Hot Springs, and the adjacent town of Chico, are said to have been named in about 1866 for a Mexican miner returning to Emigrant Gulch from a trip into what later became Yellowstone National Park. In 1883, the springs opened for public bathing; in 1900, Percie and Bill Knowles built a hotel on the site. The original plunge, built in 1902, consisted of 2 circular pools under a roof. Eight years later, Dr. George Townsend bought the resort and transformed it into a 24-bed hospital, where he performed surgery and provided treatment for polio victims. The facility struggled in the 1930s and '40s, but in the 1950s was again transformed, this time into a dude ranch. Today the hot springs remains a popular resort. Elevation: 5,277 ft. Location: Park County

Chief Joseph Pass 466 *map 18 A-2*

This pass is named for Chief Joseph, the Nez Perce warrior and diplomat who, along with Looking Glass, led his people from their homeland in Idaho over the pass into Montana, with Gen. Oliver O. Howard in pursuit. On August 9, 1877, Chief Joseph and his band repelled an attack by a military contingent in the Big Hole Valley just east of the pass. Chief Joseph and 400 Nez Perces surrendered to Col. Nelson Miles at the Bear Paw Battlefield on October 5, 1877. The date and origin of the naming of the pass are unknown. Elevation: 7,264 ft. Location: Beaverhead County

Chief Joseph, Nez Perce, 1877
O. S. Goff, photographer, MHS H-51

Chief Mountain 109 *map 2 A-3*

Visible from miles away, Chief Mountain is an imposing block of limestone in the Altyn Formation. It was known to the Blackfeet as Niná istuki, "Old chief," and first recorded in 1792 by Peter Fidler, a surveyor for the Hudson's Bay Company. It was identified on maps as King Mountain as early as 1796. The Isaac I. Stevens 1853 railroad survey also recorded Chief Mountain. In 1892, Henry L. Stimson, a future secretary of war and state under 3 presidents, became the first to record ascending the mountain. This landmark has long been revered for its supernatural powers and used as a site for fasting and prayer. In 1992, the Blackfeet tribe limited public access into the area. Elevation: 9,080 ft. Location: Glacier County

Chief Plenty Coups State Park 1027 *map 21 B-4*

Aleek-chea-ahoosh, or "Many achievements," was a fitting name for this influential Crow chief, who was known as Plenty Coups for the 80 feathers he carried on

his coup stick. At age 10, Plenty Coups had a dream that foretold the demise of bison and the Crows' traditional lifestyle. By the 1880s, the decimation of the bison had precipitated irreparable change, and Plenty Coups served his people as a bridge between the old ways and the new. He learned to farm, and in 1888 he chose this spot on the reservation to build a home of square-hewn logs. Completed in 1906, it was the reservation's only 2-story building; in keeping with native custom, the door faces east. Plenty Coups and his wife, Strikes the Iron, executed a deed of trust providing that 40 acres of the farm be "set aside as a park and recreation ground for members of the Crow Tribe of Indians and white people jointly." The U.S. government symbolically accepted this gift at a ceremony in 1928. Plenty Coups died in 1932 at age 84. Big Horn County commissioners and, later, the local Kiwanis, maintained the site until the 1960s, when stewardship passed to the State of Montana. Chief Plenty Coups State Park was created in 1965. The park includes a museum and Plenty Coups' log home, designated a NHL in 1999. Elevation: 4,049 ft. Location: Big Horn County

Child Ranch 490   *map 11   D-3*

Helena mining entrepreneur W. C. Child established this ranch as White Face Farm about 1885, stocking it with some of the first purebred Herefords in Montana Territory. Then came the infamous hard winter of 1886–87 that decimated cattle herds on the open range. When spring arrived, Child determined to make provisions for his livestock in the event of another devastating winter. He built a massive fieldstone barn that held stalls for 500 cattle and could store 350 tons of hay; even today it is Montana's largest barn. Shortly after constructing the barn, Child built the octagonal ranch house. With his permanent residence in Helena, Child used the structure only for entertaining. The

entire second floor was an open ballroom, and guests arrived at the ranch in Child's personal railroad car. This opulence was soon cut short, however. The Panic of 1893 ruined Child financially; he died that same year. As the ranch passed from owner to owner, its buildings deteriorated until the Paul Kleffner family began restoration in 1943. It is now known as the Kleffner Ranch and is listed in the National Register. Elevation: 3,967 ft. Location: Jefferson County

Chinook 706   *map 5   C-2*

Chinook was founded in 1871 by Thomas O'Hanlon of County Clare, Ireland, who arrived at the old Fort Belknap trading post located a mile and a half from the present town. He worked as a post trader and served as Chinook's first postmaster in 1889, the same year the Great Northern Railway arrived. D. R. McGinnis, a newspaperman, suggested naming the community Chinook because of the warm winds called "chinooks" that blew through in the winter. Irrigated agriculture dominated the local economy beginning in 1903 with the approval of the Milk River Irrigation Project, leading to the creation of Blaine County. In 1912, Chinook became the county seat, and the flourishing agriculture eventually led to construction of several sugar beet refineries in the area. Establishment of the Theodore Roosevelt International Highway in 1921 put Chinook on the east-west tourist route to Glacier National Park; this road became US 2 in 1926. Chinook has two 1920s gas stations listed in the National Register: Dave's Texaco and Young Brothers Chevrolet Garage. Elevation: 2,429 ft. Location: Blaine County

Choteau 284   *map 3   E-2*

The town of Choteau was originally a trading post established by A. B. Hamilton in 1873. Six years later, Hamilton and his partner, I. N. Hazlett, built a general mercantile store at the location. In 1883, the town was officially platted, and Hamilton named it Choteau for fur trader Pierre Chouteau Jr. Ten years later, voters selected the town as the county seat for newly created Teton County. The USGS established the spelling of the town as Choteau, and the county and creeks as Chouteau in 1905. Choteau grew rapidly as a market town for the surrounding fertile ranchland, and by the 1920s the Sun River Irrigation Project provided new prospects for agriculture in the valley. Prominent in its early development were brothers Joseph and Julius Hirshberg, who owned the general store and a bank. Julius also served as Choteau's first mayor. Elevation: 3,820 ft. Location: Teton County

Wadsworth family beet farm,
near Chinook, 1928
Ray Bell, photographer, MHS PAc 84-35

Chouteau County 545 *map 4 D-2*

Chouteau County was one of Montana's original counties, formally established by the territorial legislature in February 1865. It encompassed most of north-central Montana and was named for Pierre Jr. and Charles Chouteau, 2 St. Louis fur traders influential in establishing Fort Benton as the shipping point for Montana furs. Chouteau County briefly acquired the northern portion of Deer Lodge County but over the years lost territory to many new counties. Fort Benton, the historic terminus of Missouri River steamboat traffic, is the county seat.

Christina 767 *map 13 A-2*

Christina, on the site of the original Hilger homestead, is named for Christina Fergus Hilger. Daughter of William Fergus, owner of the Box Elder Ranch, Christina was born in Scotland and came to Montana with her parents during the 1870s. In 1884, she married David J. Hilger, and the couple settled on his sheep ranch at Dog Creek (so named for the numerous prairie dog towns along its banks). According to a reminiscence by David Hilger, the fleeing Nez Perces came down Dog Creek and camped in the river bottom at Christina in October 1877. Elevation: 3,577 ft. Location: Fergus County

Churchill 718 *map 20 A-1*

In 1891, the West Gallatin Irrigation Company recruited Dutch settlers to grow malting barley to supply the Manhattan Malting Company. By 1893, the town, originally known as Godfrey, had become the Holland Settlement, and 40 Dutch families made their homes here by 1904. These close-knit settlers associated themselves with the Montana Presbyterian Church but later established a Dutch Reformed Church. In 1911, the settlers named the community for the Christian Reformed church that stood on a hill above town. The Dutch farmers here later grew seed peas and seed potatoes. Elevation: 4,573 ft. Location: Gallatin County

Circle 1121 *map 15 A-4*

Circle takes its name from the circular brand of the Mabry Cattle Company, which in 1884 established its headquarters, the Circle Ranch, on the Redwater River.

Peter Rorvik, the founder of Circle, arrived in the area in 1905. Rorvik opened a store and post office to accommodate area farmers, and the town received an added boost with the influx of homesteaders after 1909. The town moved half a mile in 1914, when the Great Northern Railway created a new station along its branch line from Lewistown to Sidney. Although homesteaders began leaving the area after 1919, Circle persevered. Business picked up with the 1951 discovery of oil southeast of Circle, but this boom lasted only into the 1960s. Elevation: 2,445 ft. Location: McCone County

Citadel Rock 612   *map 4 E-4*

The igneous intrusion known as Citadel Rock is a natural landmark that has long been an inspiration to Missouri River travelers. In 1805, Capt. William Clark used the rock to plot his course and noted it as "a high steep black rock rising from the waters edge." German artist Karl Bodmer painted the prominent rock intrusion in 1833 and called it Cathedral Rock. It is listed in the National Register. Elevation: 2,469 ft. Location: Chouteau County

Clancy 496   *map 11 D-3*

The town of Clancy was founded in 1873 as a gold camp along Clancy Creek and named for prospector William Clancey. That year, Clancey bragged that the town was draining the once-prosperous community of Prickly Pear City—former county seat of Jefferson County—of its population and buildings. Continued silver mining near Clancy Creek accelerated the population shift. In 1879, resident Henry Hill helped establish Montana's first woolen mill near Clancy, as well as a brick plant. The town, however, began to decline in 1890 when placer deposits along the creek played out. Hill would not let the community die. He established a railroad yard on his ranch, which he sold to the Montana Central

Railway in 1896. The railroad built shops, a depot, and a roundhouse at Clancy. In 1902, a winter fire destroyed most of the town's buildings. Over the years, the mines of the Clancy area produced over $3 million in ore. Elevation: 4,235 ft. Location: Jefferson County

Clancy Creek 495   *map 11 D-3*

The headwaters of Clancy Creek flow from the Occidental Plateau in the Boulder Mountains. The creek is named for William Clancey, an early prospector who acquired the moniker of "Judge" while serving in the Nebraska legislature in the 1850s. An investor in the Denver, Colorado, townsite company in 1859, Clancey arrived in Montana about 1864 and prospected widely. He left the state after selling a mine near Radersburg at a handsome profit. Location: Jefferson County

Clark Canyon Dam 713   *map 18 C-4*

The U.S. Bureau of Reclamation completed Clark Canyon Dam, named for Capt. William Clark, in 1964. It is a rock- and earth-filled dam, 133 feet high, 2,500 feet long, and 36 feet thick. The reservoir created by the dam flooded the town of Armstead and the site of the first encounter between the Lewis and Clark Expedition and the Shoshones at Camp Fortunate. Elevation: 5,542 ft. Location: Beaverhead County

Clark Fork River 29   *map 1 D-1*

Lewis and Clark referred to the Clark Fork River as the Flathead River, and stretches of this Columbia River tributary have been known by a variety of names. During the 1830s, trapper Jim Bridger talked about travel "on the deer lodge River and on to the head of the Flat hed River." In 1833, Warren Ferris of the American Fur Company wrote of crossing the mountain to the "Deer House Plains and following the Arrowstone River from its source down stream." Gold Creek, the site of Montana's first gold strike in 1858, flows into the Clark Fork just east of Drummond. From territorial days until 1920, the Clark Fork was known as the Deer Lodge River from its headwaters to Garrison, and as the Hellgate River below Garrison to Missoula. The Upper Clark Fork Basin, from Butte to Missoula, is the largest Superfund site in the nation because of pollution from Anaconda Company operations in Butte and Anaconda over the past century.

Clarks Fork of the Yellowstone River
989 *map 21 B-4*
Named for Capt. William Clark, the Clarks Fork of the Yellowstone River originates just south of Colter Pass in Montana and then immediately enters Wyoming. From there, it cascades through rugged canyon country before crossing back into Montana just south of Belfry. The Montana portion of the river flows more gently past the towns of Belfry, Bridger, Edgar, and Rockvale before emptying into the Yellowstone River at Laurel.

Clarks Lookout State Park **687** *map 19 C-1*
Capt. William Clark climbed a high point of limestone rock projecting above the dense cottonwoods and willows along the Beaverhead River, took compass readings, and sketched a map of the Beaverhead Valley. Clarks Lookout is one of the few places where one can stand exactly where an expedition member stood. A trail leads to the site, locally known as Lover's Leap. Elevation: 5,071 ft. Location: Beaverhead County

Clearwater River **259** *map 10 B-3*
The Clearwater River flows out of Salmon Lake and into the Blackfoot River. The river was named by a local prospector for the clarity of its water, especially in comparison to the Blackfoot at its peak flow. During the early lumbering era, logging companies floated logs down the river during spring runoff.

Cleveland **731** *map 5 D-3*
Postmaster James H. Roberts opened the Cleveland post office in 1893; it remained in operation until 1957. During the homestead era, Cleveland supported a store, hotel, saloon, livery, and school. The Bowes gas field discovered in 1924 just north of town was developed between 1926 and 1935 by the Texas Company. A pipeline connected the gas field to Chinook and Havre to supply natural gas to the Montana Power Company, Montana's major utility company in the twentieth century. Elevation: 3,516 ft. Location: Blaine County

Clinton **264** *map 10 C-2*
When it was established in 1883 as a stage stop and post office on the Mullan Road, Clinton was known as Betters' Station, after settler Austin Betters. Over the years, the community experienced several name changes. The Northern Pacific Railroad named it Wallace in 1885, after Wallace Gulch, the location of several significant gold mines. In 1892, the town became Clinton, for C. L. Clinton, an official of the Northern Pacific Railroad. Although the town's economy historically was based on mining and timber, today Clinton is predominantly a bedroom community of Missoula. Beavertail Hill State Park lies to the east of Clinton. Elevation: 3,474 ft. Location: Missoula County

Clyde Park **778** *map 20 A-2*
Called Sunnyside during the 1870s, Clyde Park attracted Texas cattlemen who trailed cattle into the Shields Valley. The cattle industry helped Clyde Park grow and prosper, and in 1901, 14 years after the establishment of the first post office in

1887, C. A. Arnet and George Kissinger opened a new store. The town incorporated in 1912, 3 years after the Northern Pacific Railway completed its branch line, the Shields River Valley Railway. In 1919, a major fire burned a large portion of the town. According to a USFS informant, residents named the town for local rancher Clyde Durand. An alternative story suggests the town was named for a Clydesdale horse owned by the local Harvey and Tregloan Ranch. Elevation: 4,867 ft. Location: Park County

Coal Banks Landing 570 *map 4 D-4*
Coal Banks Landing was a low-water unloading site, as well as a refueling site, for steamboats headed up the Missouri River to Fort Benton. Steamboats plying the river consumed approximately 30 cords of wood every day, which quickly depleted the available supply of wood. To supplement their fuel, steamers used the low-grade coal dug near Coal Banks. The landing also served as the drop-off point for supplies headed to Fort Assinniboine near Havre. It is the site of an earlier post office called Rerger, known as Camp Otis to the U.S. Army. The landing is now a

BLM recreation site. Elevation: 2,525 ft. Location: Chouteau County

Coalridge 1199 *map 8 B-3*
Eli, Niels, and Ole Hansen started a small coal mine in 1905 to provide fuel for themselves and their neighbors. The following year, George Onstad purchased the Hansen mine and modernized it, but Onstad's mine closed in 1919 due to competition from the nearby Heuth and Farmers Mine. At its peak, not more than 100 people lived in Coalridge. The school district did not have enough funds to provide double desks for all the students, so they improvised extra seating by placing planks on top of empty powder kegs. The grade school closed in 1962 and the post office in 1974. Elevation: 2,178 ft. Location: Sheridan County

Coburg 826 *map 5 C-4*
A once-prosperous stop on the Great Northern Railway, and named for the city in Germany, Coburg is now little more than a sign on a railroad siding. Established about 1890, the town served a growing dryland farm community. In 1920, the town had 132 residents, but by the late 1920s drought had taken its toll. The post office closed in 1936. Elevation: 2,308 ft. Location: Blaine County

Cochrane Dam 446 *map 12 A-1*
Built in 1958, the Cochrane Dam is the last of the 5 hydroelectric dams built by the Montana Power Company on the Missouri River near Great Falls. The dam was named for Harry H. Cochrane, longtime Montana Power Company consulting engineer. By the early 1960s, hydroelectric power

Millers Park, Coal Banks, 1880
F. Jay Haynes, photographer, MHS H-372

constituted approximately one third of the electricity produced in Montana, and large amounts powered the copper smelter and refinery at Black Eagle. Today the River's Edge Trail crosses the dam. Elevation: 3,143 ft. Location: Cascade County

Coffee Creek 673 *map 13 A-1*

Coffee Creek, which flows into Arrow Creek in northwestern Fergus County, derives its name from the stream's brown color and alkaline flavor.

Coffee Creek (town) 651 *map 12 A-4*

Named for the nearby stream, Coffee Creek got its start during the early twentieth century homesteading boom. When the Milwaukee Road established its station here in 1914, businesses relocated along the railroad and the town acquired a post office. Although its population never reached more than 600, Coffee Creek even had its own newspaper, the *Coffee Creek Herald*. Elevation: 3,607 ft. Location: Fergus County

Cohagen 1063 *map 15 B-1*

Harry Harris, Cohagen's first postmaster, bestowed his mother's maiden name on the new post office in 1905. Cohagen enjoyed prosperity as a service and supply town until the 1930s, serving a growing sheep- and cattle-ranching community. Since the 1970s, however, Cohagen has seen a steady decline in population and economic activity. Elevation: 2,722 ft. Location: Garfield County

Collins 313 *map 3 E-4*

Named for Elizabeth Collins, the "Cattle Queen of Montana," Collins was a station on the narrow-gauge Great Falls & Canada Railway. Elizabeth earned her nickname in 1890 by driving a herd of cattle from near Choteau to the railhead at Great Falls, where she negotiated passage to the stockyards for herself. A fellow cowboy proclaimed her "cattle queen of the great West." The town gained a post office in 1891, and in 1902 the Great Northern Railway purchased the line and converted it to standard gauge. By the 1960s, however, the railroad bypassed Collins, and the place remained a town in name only, with the community hall one of the few buildings left standing. Elevation: 3,514 ft. Location: Teton County

Colstrip 1119 *map 23 A-1*

In 1923, the Foley brothers secured the contract to extract coal from lands granted to the Northern Pacific Railroad. While the contract was being finalized, the Northern Pacific built a spur line to a site about 30 miles southwest of Forsyth, appropriately named Colstrip. Over the next 30 years, the Northern Pacific and its operators extracted 44 million tons of coal here. A company town, Colstrip included family housing, a bunkhouse, a mess hall, schools, and a general store, as well as office buildings, warehouses, garages, and machine

Nine hundred-ton shovel at Colstrip, 1930
Ed Kopac, photographer, MHS PAc 81-65

shops. In 1958, Northern Pacific finished replacing its coal-fired engines with diesels. One year later, the Montana Power Company purchased the coal leases, machinery, and townsite from the Northern Pacific, and in 1966 the mines reopened under Western Energy Company, a subsidiary of Montana Power. During the next 20 years, Montana Power built 4 coal-fired power plants here, with a combined capacity of more than 2,000 mW. In 2000, PPL Montana purchased all of Montana Power's generating facilities. Colstrip sits at the center of Montana's coal reserves, some 120 billion tons of coal, constituting one quarter of the nation's coal supply. Elevation: 3,217 ft. Location: Rosebud County

Colter Pass 959 *map 20 C-4*
Colter Pass is named in honor of John Colter, a member of the Lewis and Clark Expedition who returned west in 1807 and traveled into what is now Yellowstone National Park, possibly over the pass that bears his name. Colter's descriptions of the wonders of Yellowstone, though based on fact, were so fantastical that they were given little credence at the time. The area was dubbed "Colter's Hell" by fellow trappers. Elevation: 8,040 ft. Location: Park County

Columbia Falls 65 *map 2 C-1*
Known variously in its early history as Monaco and Columbia, this town takes its present name from its location on the South Fork of the Flathead River, one of the headwaters of the Columbia River, and from its location in the shadow of Columbia Mountain. Although there are no falls on this portion of the river, when James Kennedy applied for a post office in 1891, he was advised that adding "Falls" to the town's name would prevent confusion with Columbus, Montana. One of Columbia Falls's claims to fame is that it is where Montana's first movie, *Where*

Rivers Rise, was filmed in 1921. In 1953, the U.S. Bureau of Reclamation finished the Hungry Horse Dam south of town, and 2 years later the Anaconda Company's aluminum plant opened to make use of low-cost electricity produced at the dam. The town's main industries for many years have been wood products and aluminum production. Elevation: 3,078 ft. Location: Flathead County

Columbus 945 *map 21 B-2*
The earliest reference to the site where Columbus now stands comes from Capt. William Clark, who entered what he called the Rosebud River here in 1806. The first permanent structure was Mithoff and Kaufman's 1865 trading post, known as Eagle's Nest. In 1879, the community moved and became known as Sheep Dip, because the liquor distilled in the gulch north of town tasted more like insecticide than whiskey. In 1882, when the Northern Pacific Railroad arrived, the community moved a little closer to the confluence of the Yellowstone and Stillwater rivers and changed its name to Stillwater. Thus, Columbus is at least the fourth name and location for this community. It was bestowed in 1893 by the Northern Pacific Railroad. In 1900, the builders of the State Capitol in Helena chose Columbus sandstone, quarried near the town, as the primary material for the Capitol's façade. Elevation: 3,585 ft. Location: Stillwater County

Comertown 1192 *map 8 A-3*
Spurred by the construction of the Minneapolis, St. Paul & Sault Ste. Marie Railway through the area in 1913, George Onstad purchased land for a townsite and named it for the previous landowner, W. W. Comer. Postal officials refused the town's initial application for a post office under the name Comer because of the possibility of confusion with Conner, Montana.

Residents settled the issue by submitting Comertown as the new name, and in 1914 Comertown gained a post office. However, a major fire in 1921 and the effects of drought and the Great Depression caused the town's population to dwindle. Comertown's high school closed in 1953, the post office in 1957. The town is listed in the National Register as a historic district, and The Nature Conservancy manages 2,000 acres of native prairie southeast of Comertown. Elevation: 2,272 ft. Location: Sheridan County

Comet 505 *map 11 D-2*
John W. Russell obtained a patent on the Comet Lode in 1874, and a thriving town soon grew up around it. The townsite was laid out in 1876, and a post office opened a year later. By 1911, the Comet Mine had produced around $13 million of silver, lead, zinc, gold, and copper ores. Improved concentrating technologies allowed the Comet Mine to continue producing ore into the 1940s. Comet is now a ghost town. Elevation: 6,375 ft. Location: Jefferson County

Condon 184 *map 10 A-3*
Condon is named for James L. Condon, a Corvallis-area logger and farmer who prospected in the Swan Valley in the late 1800s. Elevation: 3,718 ft. Location: Missoula County

Confederate Gulch 554 *map 11 D-4*
After the 1864 discovery of placer gold here, 1,000 men and women poured into Confederate Gulch, creating the town of Diamond City. The gulch's name is related to the large number of ex-Confederate soldiers and sympathizers among the early residents. By 1871, placer gold had diminished and Diamond City's population collapsed. Elevation: 3,799 ft. Location: Broadwater County

Conner 378 *map 10 E-1*
Aaron Conner and his family arrived in the Bitterroot Valley in the winter of 1882. They spent the winter camped on Whitesell Flat, near where the Conner Wesleyan Church now stands, and Conner filed for a 160-acre homestead on the flat. When his children were grown, he sold the ranch and started a sawmill in Cooper Draw. With the establishment of the post office in 1906, area residents chose the name Conner in honor of the small community's first homesteader. Elevation: 4,022 ft. Location: Ravalli County

Conrad 287 *map 3 D-3*
In 1902, M. S. Darling, an engineer for the Conrad Investment Company, platted the Conrad townsite. Willam G. and Charles E. Conrad owned the Conrad Investment Company, which was responsible for developing much of the land in the area. Situated adjacent to the Great Falls & Canada Railway, Conrad quickly surpassed nearby Pondera; in 1903, Pondera residents moved all their buildings 1 mile west to the new town. The town incorporated in 1908 and expanded during the early homestead era. In 1919, it was named the county seat of the newly established Pondera County. The population declined during the drought years of the 1920s, but with the 1927 discovery of oil in the Pondera Oil Field by E. B. Emrick, the town again prospered. Conrad is now the market town for area farmers. Elevation: 3,517 ft. Location: Pondera County

Conrad Mansion 68 *map 2 C-1*
The Conrad Mansion was the home of pioneer businessman Charles E. Conrad, who, with his brother William, worked for, and later bought out, the profitable Fort Benton I. G. Baker freighting firm. A director of the Kalispell Townsite Company, Conrad chose prominent Spokane architect Kirtland K. Cutter to design this

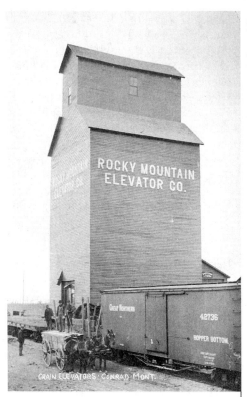

Rocky Mountain Grain Elevator Co., Conrad
MHS PAc 98-36.16

and finest. The mansion, however, had been vacant for 30 years when the U.S. Army Corps of Engineers announced plans to flood the area to create Canyon Ferry Reservoir. Contractors divided the home into 3 sections, transported it across the Missouri River, and brought it to its current location on US 12, where it is now a bed and breakfast. Elevation: 3,844 ft. Location: Broadwater County

Cooke City 955 *map 20 C-4*
Cooke City, at the southern edge of the New World Mining District, is named for Jay Cooke, financier of the Northern Pacific Railroad. Gold mining began in the area in 1870, but the district's isolation and the high cost of transporting coal and processed ore to and from its Republic Smelter limited the profits. Between 1901 and 1923, only $56,000 of minerals were produced, and the population of the fledgling town never exceeded 2,000. Construction of the Beartooth Highway over rugged terrain and a 10,947-foot pass connected Cooke City to Red Lodge in 1936. Cooke City, at the northeast entrance to Yellowstone National Park, is now a destination for winter and summer recreation. Elevation: 7,587 ft. Location: Park County

striking Norman-style home; he moved his extended family into the 23-room mansion in 1895. The sprawling mansion is listed in the National Register and is open for tours during the summer and fall. Elevation: 2,961 ft. Location: Flathead County

Cook Home/Canyon Ferry Mansion
575 *map 11 D-4*
Cattleman A. B. Cook, who began ranching in 1907, dominated the nation's Hereford-breeding industry between 1917 and 1927. A forced dispersal sale of his 2,527 purebred Herefords shortly before his death in 1928 was the nation's largest breeding stock sale on record, grossing more than $450,000. Cook's home, built in 1915 near Canton, was one of Broadwater County's largest

Coolidge 590 *map 18 B-4*
The town of Coolidge owed its existence to the Elkhorn Mine. Its deposits had been discovered in 1873 but not developed until William R. Allen and the Boston & Montana Consolidated Copper and Silver Mining Company acquired the property in 1913. Company president Allen organized the Butte, Wisdom and Pacific Railway (later the Montana Southern Railway) in 1914 and completed the narrow-gauge line between Divide and Coolidge in 1919. Allen named the new town for his friend and colleague Calvin Coolidge, thirtieth president of the United States. The Coolidge mill never ran at full capac-

ity and operated only sporadically after the first few years, but nonetheless, in the 1920s, 600 people lived in Coolidge, which had a company store, school, and post office. In the late 1940s, gold, silver, and copper mining ceased altogether, and the town was abandoned shortly thereafter. The mill stood almost intact until 1975, when salvagers tore down nearly a third of the 2-acre structure, reselling the timbers. Later, the USFS granted a lease to a salvage company to tear down the remainder of the mill, which had become unsafe. Elevation: 7,420 ft. Location: Beaverhead County

Cooney Reservoir 969 *map 21 B-2*
Built in 1937 by the State Water Conservation Board, Cooney Reservoir was named for Governor Frank Cooney (1933–35), an advocate of water conservation and reservoir construction. The site became Cooney State Park in 1965. Montana Fish, Wildlife & Parks stocks the reservoir with rainbow trout and walleye. Elevation: 4,253 ft. Location: Carbon County

Coopers Lake 286 *map 11 B-1*
Locals named this pothole lake for a miner, Charles Cooper. Elevation: 4,490 ft. Location: Powell County

Coram 71 *map 2 C-2*
Coram began as a logging town on the South Fork of the Flathead River in 1905. The community prospered as the timber industry developed, and received a boost with the arrival of the Great Northern Railway. Railroad officials initially named the train station Citadel. In 1914, the community was renamed for James A. Coram, who had arrived in the Kalispell area in 1893 to be a supervisor for the Butte & Montana Commercial Company's logging operations. Coram boomed between 1948 and 1953, during construction of the

nearby Hungry Horse Dam. Elevation: 3,190 ft. Location: Flathead County

Corbin 506 *map 11 D-2*
Corbin, in the Wickes-Corbin Mining District, thrived with the development of silver-lead deposits by the Alta Montana Company and later Samuel T. Hauser's Helena Mining & Reduction Company. The latter company platted Corbin in 1884, named it for early prospector D. C. Corbin, and built a concentrator there to process ore from the Alta Mine, one of Montana's richest silver mines. Corbin and Wickes went into decline when silver prices plummeted in 1893, and again with the closure of rail service between Wickes and Helena in 1900. That did not stop the construction of 2 more smelters at Corbin, one in 1896 and another in 1925, to process the Alta Mine tailings. With the end of mining at Wickes in the 1920s, Corbin became a ghost town. Elevation: 4,764 ft. Location: Jefferson County

Corvallis 310 *map 10 D-1*
Corvallis comes from the Latin for "heart of the valley." The Chaffins, prominent early settlers, had lived briefly in Corvallis, Oregon, and their new community was named Corvallis in 1870. Platted in 1879, Corvallis quickly became the heart of this rich agricultural valley. Elevation: 3,478 ft. Location: Ravalli County

Corwin Springs 876 *map 20 C-2*
In 1909, Dr. F. E. Corwin, a physician formerly employed by Chico Hot Springs and then the Electric Hot Springs Company, built a new 86-room Mission-style hotel and spa, piping 154°F water from nearby La Duke Springs. A bridge across the Yellowstone River made the springs accessible to Northern Pacific Railway passengers headed for Yellowstone National Park. In 1916, fire destroyed the hotel and spa, but

Electric Hot Springs, Corwin, 1914
Jack Ellis Haynes, photographer, MHS H-6593

the pool and bathhouse were rebuilt in the 1920s. In the 1960s, Malcolm Forbes purchased the Eagle's Nest Ranch, adjacent to Corwin Springs. The Church Universal and Triumphant purchased the property in the 1980s. Elevation: 5,135 ft. Location: Park County

Cottonwood Coal Mines 481 *map 12 A-1*
The Cottonwood Coal Company, a subsidiary of the Great Northern Railway, took over the coal mines at Stockett and Sand Coulee to provide coal for the railroad. They did not name the mines but numbered them 1–8. Elevation: 3,702 ft. Location: Cascade County

Cottonwood Reservoir 747 *map 12 E-2*
In 1953, the Montana Dept. of Natural Resources dammed Cottonwood Creek to provide irrigation water to the Shields Valley. The name refers to the trees found along the creek. Elevation: 5,100 ft. Location: Park County

Cow Creek 795 *map 5 E-3*
Cow Creek originates in the Bears Paw Mountains and flows southeast about 40 miles to the Missouri River. On May 26, 1805, when the Lewis and Clark Expedition reached this stream, Meriwether Lewis climbed a hill and "first caught a distant view of the Rock mountains, the object of all our hopes and the reward of all our ambition." He named the stream Windsor Creek, after Pvt. Richard Windsor; it was later named Cow Creek by settlers. The historic Kipp homestead is near the mouth of the creek. Location: Baine County

Cow Island 794 *map 5 E-3*
Cow Island was the head of navigation on the Missouri River during extreme low water. Steamboats offloaded their cargoes

Cow Island camp and landing, 1880
F. Jay Haynes, photographer, MHS H-318

here, which were then freighted by ox team to Fort Benton. In September 1877, Nez Perces crossing the river just above the island had a brief encounter with soldiers who were guarding offloaded freight. Elevation: 2,293 ft. Location: Blaine County

Craig 381 *map 11 B-3*
Craig received its name from homesteaders Warren and Eliza Craig, who staked out a claim and in 1886 built a log cabin on the current townsite. Two years later, a post office was established. The town prospered when the Montana Central Railway built a line through the area and established a station in Craig in 1887. April 14, 1908, brought catastrophe—the failure of Hauser Dam. A 25-foot wall of Missouri River water flooded the town, but remarkably did not take any lives. Elevation: 3,448 ft. Location: Lewis and Clark County

Crail Ranch 804 *map 20 C-1*
Sweeping views of the Spanish Peaks, Madison Range, and Gallatin Canyon made a magnificent setting for Augustus Frank Crail's 960-acre ranch, put together in 1902 by his purchase of 3 homesteads, school lands, and railroad property. Crail, his wife, Sally, and their 3 children settled into a small log cabin while building the main house and established a water-powered

sawmill nearby to mill lumber for private and commercial use. Crail developed and grew a special kind of wheat and raised sheep. By 1934, the Crails' success allowed them to close the sawmill and switch to raising cattle. Most area ranchers who weathered the Great Depression turned to dude ranching, but the Crails continued to run their cattle ranch until 1950. Today the Crail house and cabin, the sole survivors of the once-sprawling complex, are listed in the National Register. The 2 historic dwellings are nestled in the core of the modern community of Big Sky. Elevation: 6,254 ft. Location: Gallatin County

Crane 1214 *map 8 E-3*
Trapper Jimmy Crain and his partner "French Joe" Seymore built a cabin near Fox Creek in 1876. As one of the earliest settlers in the region, "Uncle Jimmy" offered a glowing report on the agricultural potential of the lower Yellowstone Valley that appeared in the *Glendive Times* on December 2, 1881. At the conclusion, he invited interested parties to view firsthand the splendor he described: "If anyone wants to see for himself, he can call at

my place known as Crain's Ranch. I keep a hotel and I will try and treat him well." A bustling place, the Crain Ranch served as a stage stop, hotel, and restaurant and became a general clearinghouse for settlers living in the valley. Crain sold the ranch to John O'Brien in 1888. When the post office opened in 1910, they named it after "Uncle Jimmy" but spelled the name Crane. With the construction of the Northern Pacific Railway's branch line from Glendive to Sidney in 1912, Crane vied with Sidney as the dominant community in the valley. Local lore suggests that unscrupulous businessmen from Sidney purchased the remaining town lots in Crane to retard its economic growth. Elevation: 1,945 ft. Location: Richland County

Crazy Mountains 781   map 12 E-3

The Crazy Mountains, an enormous igneous intrusion in a sea of sedimentary rock, rises north of Big Timber and are a fine example of the "island ranges" that dot Montana. The range reportedly was originally named Crazy Woman Mountains for an early settler separated from her wagon train and left to fend for herself in the rugged terrain.

Crazy Peak 799   map 12 E-4

At age 10, Plenty Coups of the Crow tribe undertook a vision quest atop this peak, the tallest summit in the Crazy Mountains, during which he foresaw the Euro-American invasion and the decline of Native American life. The origin of the name Crazy is uncertain. One story tells of a woman who lost her baby and left the wagon train to wander the mountains, and another invokes an Indian woman who went mad and forever wandered the mountains. Elevation: 11,209 ft. Location: Sweet Grass County

Creedman Coulee NWR 614   map 5 A-1

Congress established this refuge in October 1941 as habitat and breeding ground for migratory birds. The coulee was originally known as Greenman Coulee but became Creedman Coulee when the refuge was established. An earthen dam (now on private property) was built in 1938 by the WPA to provide flow control and irrigation water. The refuge encompasses 80 acres of public land and about 2,650 acres of private easements. Elevation: 2,769 ft. Location: Hill County

Creston 85   map 2 C-2

Named for the home town of Philip Buck, a missionary from Creston, Iowa, this community was established about 1889. The first post office was in the Bucks' home. Elevation: 2,962 ft. Location: Flathead County

Creston National Fish Hatchery 86
map 2 C-2

In 1935, Glacier National Park staff chose the Jessup Mill site in the eastern Flathead Valley for a new fish hatchery. Four years later, 100 men working as part of a WPA grant began construction of 22 concrete ponds, a dam and water system, and a superintendent's house. Beginning in 1944, Glacier National Park transferred ownership to the USFWS. Between 1940 and 1954, the Creston National Hatchery produced millions of Yellowstone cutthroat trout for stocking the waters of Glacier National Park. The facility saw major expansion in 1962, and in 1993 the hatchery began rearing Kokanee salmon for Flathead Lake. Elevation: 2,939 ft. Location: Flathead County

Crimson Bluffs 601   map 11 E-4

While ascending the Missouri River near present-day Townsend on July 24, 1805, Capt. Meriwether Lewis wrote: "Set out

Crow Camp, near Crow Agency, 1895
MHS 955-814

at sunrise; the current very strong; passed a remarkable bluff of a crimson coloured earth on Stard. Intermixed with Stratas of black and brick red slate." The Crimson Bluffs Chapter of the Lewis and Clark Trail Heritage Foundation, in cooperation with the BLM, officially recognized this as a Lewis and Clark Trail landmark on July 27, 2002. Elevation: 3,843 ft. Location: Broadwater County

Cromwell Island 118 *map 7 E-1*
Named for Clarence Cromwell, this privately owned island in Flathead Lake lies just west of Wild Horse Island. Cromwell was a Dixon-area cattle rancher killed by his brother-in-law Frank Masterson on October 19, 1908; a jury found Masterson innocent of the murder, concluding that he was protecting his sister from her drunken husband. Elevation: 3,139 ft. Location: Lake County

Crooked Creek Recreation Area 929 *map 14 A-1*
Crooked Creek, also known as Sacagawea River, flows into the Musselshell River near the UL Bend of the Missouri River. The name Crooked reflects the creek's many meanderings. The recreation area provides a boat ramp and 20 primitive campsites. Elevation: 2,395 ft. Location: Petroleum County

Crow Agency 1083 *map 22 B-3*
The first Crow Agency was established in 1869 about 8 miles east of present-day Livingston. In 1882, the Crows ceded 1.5 million acres of reservation land, and the agency moved to the Stillwater River south of Absarokee. In 1884, the agency moved to its current location on the west bank of the Little Bighorn River. By the end of that year, the Office of Indian Affairs had constructed 11 buildings at Crow Agency, including a school, store, slaughterhouse, carpenter's shop, and blacksmith shop. The Crow people called it Baaxawuaashe,

"Wheat house," for the government flour mill that was the most prominent building in town. Elevation: 3,037 ft. Location: Big Horn County

Crow Creek 618 *map 11 E-4*

Crow Creek is formed by the confluence of Big Tizer and Wilson creeks in the Elkhorn Mountains west of Toston. It flows approximately 37 miles to the Missouri River. The creek is named for the Crow tribe who frequented the area. Ranchers and farmers formed the Crow Creek Irrigation District in 1918, and the U.S. Reclamation Service developed a facility to pump water to nearby ranches through a system of canals. With the creation of Canyon Ferry Lake in 1954, more water became available to Missouri Valley irrigators. The associated Crow Creek Water Ditch is listed in the National Register. Location: Broadwater County

Crow Creek Falls 550 *map 11 D-3*

The name of this lovely 30-foot waterfall in the Elkhorn Mountains is associated with Crow Creek and the Crows who hunted along the Missouri River prior to Euro-American settlement. In the 1920s, a mining claim at the falls was patented, and in the 1980s Robert Lynn began placer mining in the area. When mining ended, Lynn abandoned his equipment, but the site was restored to its original splendor through a cooperative effort by the Helena National Forest and local conservation groups. Elevation: 5,665 ft. Location: Jefferson County

Crow Indian Reservation 1072 *map 22 B-1*

Established in 1869, the Crow Indian Reservation in southeastern Montana is home to the Apsaalooke (Crow) people. Between the Crows' first treaty with the U.S. government in 1851 and the last in 1904, the Crow Indian Reservation shrank from 38.5 million to 2.5 million acres. Today non-Indians own one third of the reservation land. Robert Yellowtail, superintendent of the Crow Indian Reservation from 1933 to 1945, was the first Native American to oversee a reservation for the BIA. Yellowtail opposed damming the Bighorn River, but when it was finally constructed over his protestations, the U.S. Bureau of Reclamation named the dam for Yellowtail. Chief Plenty Coups State Park, the Little Bighorn Battlefield National Monument, Yellowtail Dam, and Little Bighorn Community College are all on the reservation.

Crow Peak 544 *map 11 E-3*

The highest summit in the Elkhorn Mountains, Crow Peak is named for the Crow people who hunted the benches above the Missouri River near present-day Townsend. Elevation: 9,414 ft. Location: Jefferson County

Crown Butte 340 *map 11 3-A*

Crown Butte, an igneous shonkinite intrusion, rises more than 4,000 feet from the valley floor. Both Crown Butte and nearby Square Butte are spectacular examples of laccoliths, remnants of molten magma breaking the surface. On top of the butte is an "eagle catch" whose presence shows evidence of historic Native American use of the butte. The Nature Conservancy purchased the 375 acres of grassland on the butte's top in 1983, opening the area to educational and scientific use and study. Elevation: 4,710 ft. Location: Cascade County

Culbertson 1184 *map 8 C-2*

Culbertson was created in June 1887 with the arrival of the St. Paul, Minneapolis & Manitoba Railway and named after American Fur Company trader Maj. Alexander Culbertson, who in 1839 took over as factor at nearby Fort Union. The ranchers of the 1890s and the homesteaders of the early

1900s helped Culbertson flourish. During the cattle industry boom, 13 saloons lined the 3-block-long main street, providing diversion 24 hours a day for thirsty cowboys. Culbertson served as the shipping point for area ranchers and homesteaders located from East Redwater Creek to the Canadian border. The town did not officially incorporate until September 1909. It has been in 5 different counties—Big Horn, Dawson, Custer, Valley, and, finally, Roosevelt. Elevation: 1,929 ft. Location: Roosevelt County

Cushman 899 *map 13 E-3*

Originally called Olden, Cushman began as a post office and small settlement on David Fratt's ranch in 1880. When the Great Northern Railway's Billings and Northern branch line came through in 1908, the settlement was platted and named Cushman in honor of a local rancher and cowboy. The growing cluster of businesses, including a lumber mill, served a large outlying ranch community, and the community hall became the center of the region's social life. Elevation: 3,548 ft. Location: Golden Valley County

Custer 1040 *map 14 E-3*

Named for Lt. Col. George Armstrong Custer of Little Bighorn battle fame, the Northern Pacific Railroad station established in 1882 was followed by a post office in 1905. A thriving business district, moved in part from the town of Junction north of the Yellowstone River, served area farmers and ranchers. Elevation: 2,742 ft. Location: Yellowstone County

Custer County 1170 *map 15 C-3*

The Montana legislature carved a new county from the former Big Horn County in 1877 and named it in honor of Lt. Col. George Armstrong Custer of Little Bighorn battle fame. Custer County initially encompassed the battlefield and all the land to the territory's eastern boundary, but over the years it lost land to 5 new counties. Today the county surrounds its county seat, Miles City, on both sides of the Yellowstone River.

Cut Bank 221 *map 3 B-2*

Taking its name from Cut Bank Creek, the town of Cut Bank began in 1891 with the arrival of the Great Northern Railway. The railroad made the town a division point and built the Great Northern Hotel to provide room and board for its employees. Many of the town's new arrivals were Japanese railroad workers, some of whom opened businesses here. In 1910, Dan Whetstone, publisher of the local newspaper, petitioned to incorporate Cut Bank. By 1912, homesteaders had fenced and were farming most of the tillable land, which had previously provided open range to large cattle herds. Initially in Teton County, in 1919 Cut Bank became the county seat of the newly created Glacier County. Elevation: 3,772 ft. Location: Glacier County

Cut Bank Creek 236 *map 3 C-2*

The name of Cut Bank Creek is a translation of the Blackfeet name Ponakixi, "River that cuts into the white clay banks." The creek flows from Glacier National Park and joins the Two Medicine River to form the Marias River. Location: Glacier County

Funeral at Beaverhead County Courthouse, Dillon, c. 1885

Detail, MHS 946-748

Dagmar 1201 *map 8 B-3*

In the Danish newspaper *Dannevirke*, Danish-born evangelist Emil Ferdinand Madsen stated his intention to establish a new community in the West; any Dane wishing to join him could meet in the Union Depot in St. Paul, Minnesota, on October 2, 1906. When the 7 men who showed up journeyed west, they discovered that the land Madsen had chosen near Williston, North Dakota, had been taken, so they pushed on to Montana and claimed the site 7 miles west of the state line that would become the town of Dagmar, named for a thirteenth-century queen of Denmark. The next spring, Madsen and others returned with their families to establish a Danish colony, the center of which was always the Dagmar Evangelical Lutheran Church. Elevation: 2,034 ft. Location: Sheridan County

Dailey Lake 855 *map 20 C-2*

Dailey Lake, as well as the nearby Northern Pacific Railroad branch line maintenance station of Dailey, are named for Ebenezer and Catherine Dailey and their sons, Samuel, Andrew, and Isaac, who established the Lake Ranch there in the 1860s. Ebenezer, Samuel, and Andrew all proved up on homesteads in the immediate vicinity of the lake. The family continued to operate the ranch until Andrew's death in 1928. There is a fishing access with camping at the lake. Elevation: 5,241 ft. Location: Park County

Daleview 1135 *map 8 A-1*

The area around Daleview was once a haunt for outlaws and cattle rustlers who could hide in the badlands and breaks along Big Muddy Creek. Daleview owes its development to the nearby lignite coal deposits. It was originally called Ranous, but with the completion of the Minneapolis, St. Paul & Sault Ste. Marie Railway through town in 1913, it was changed to Daleview. Elevation: 2,161 ft. Location: Sheridan County

Daly Mansion/Riverside 314 *map 10 D-1*

Riverside served as the summer residence of Margaret Daly, widow of copper magnate Marcus Daly, from its completion in 1910 until her death in 1941. Marcus Daly began buying Bitterroot Valley land in 1887 and eventually owned 28,000 acres. After his death in 1900, Mrs. Daly built Riverside, so named for its location along the Bitterroot River. This home is a unique Montana example of the early-twentieth-century Revival styles used by successful capitalists to display their wealth. Because the Panic of 1893 destroyed many mining-based

Baseball game, Dagmar, 1920
Detail, MHS 946-674

Daly Mansion/Riverside, 1941–42
Richard Averill Smith, photographer, MHS 955-287

fortunes here, and because out-of-state investors financed later mining ventures, grand homes were a thing of Montana's past by the time Mrs. Daly constructed Riverside. Missoula architect A. J. Gibson designed the house. Comparatively restrained for mansions of this period, the Georgian Revival home features a monumental classical portico, symmetrical façade, hipped roof, and balustraded roof deck. Its 24,000 square feet and 56 rooms include 25 bedrooms, 15 bathrooms, 3 dining rooms, 7 fireplaces, cut glass or brass knobs on the doors, and 13 bells to summon servants. Today the home's appearance is virtually unchanged from that of 1910. The mansion, now owned by the State of Montana and listed in the National Register, is open for tours Memorial Day to Labor Day and at special times during the Christmas season. Elevation: 3,544 ft. Location: Ravalli County

Danaher Creek 217 map 10 A-4

Danaher Creek is named for Thomas Danaher, a forest ranger and homesteader who settled in the wilds of the Swan Range in the late 1890s. Location: Powell and Lewis and Clark Counties

Daniels County 1099
map 7 B-4

Daniels County was founded in 1920 from portions of Sheridan and Valley counties, in northeastern Montana. It is named for Mansfield Daniels, a local rancher. Daniels, in turn, named the county seat Scobey for his good friend Maj. Charles Richardson Anderson Scobey.

Danvers 720 map 13 B-1

First called Warwick, this town began as a station on the Milwaukee Road in 1913. The earliest businesses were a hotel, restaurant, real estate office, lumber and grain operation, and grain elevator. In 1914, the town was renamed Danvers, after a Massachusetts town, by railroad employee C. W. Goodnow. Elevation: 3,556 ft. Location: Fergus County

Darby 357 map 10 E-1

Residents of Darby recognize 1889 as the official year their settlement became a town. The previous year, residents had submitted an application to the federal Post Office Dept. under the community name Harrison, after the newly elected president, Benjamin Harrison. However, since there already was a Harrison, Montana, post office officials named the new town after James W. Darby, who had signed the application. Darby served as the terminal point for the Northern Pacific's Bitterroot Valley branch line. Elevation: 3,882 ft. Location: Ravalli County

Dawson County 1180 map 16 B-1

Dawson County was formed in 1869 from the northern half of the original Big Horn County. The new county was named for Maj. Andrew Dawson, who managed the Fort Benton trading post for the American Fur Company from 1856 to 1864. The legislature chose Fort Peck as the county seat but attached the county to Chouteau County for legislative representation. Over the years, Dawson County lost territory, which formed all of the counties now in northeastern Montana. Glendive, an important station along the Northern Pacific Railway, is the modern county seat.

Dayton 114 *map 2 D-1*

The town of Dayton did not begin at its present location on the west shore of Flathead Lake. The town was originally 2 miles farther inland, on the road to Lake Mary Ronan, but with the opening of the Flathead Indian Reservation to homesteading in 1910, some residents realized that a town on the lakeshore would draw more business. The post office moved as well, prompting the old town of Dayton to petition and change its name to Proctor. During the homesteading era, the community of Dayton bustled. During its peak, Cornelius Vanderbilt, the famous railroad baron, stayed in the Dayton Hotel, calling it "one of only four really comfortable places between New York and Seattle." The town's industrial base included logging, which continues to this day. The Dayton Presbyterian Church was the first Protestant church established on the Flathead Indian Reservation. Today Dayton thrives as a good launch for sailing on Flathead Lake or visiting Wild Horse Island, a primitive park managed by Montana Fish, Wildlife & Parks that protects wild horses, bighorn sheep, deer, bald eagles, and osprey. Dayton is also the home of Montana's first bonded winery, the Mission Mountain Winery. Elevation: 2,910 ft. Location: Lake County

De Borgia 127 *map 9 A-2*

Father Pierre-Jean De Smet named the nearby river St. Regis De Borgia in 1841 after Saint Regis DeBorgia, a Catholic mis-

sionary. John Mullan traversed the area while constructing the Mullan Road. Settlement of the town of De Borgia, named for the river (St. Regis), was sometime in the 1890s. The year 1900 proved to be defining for De Borgia, with the platting of the townsite, the arrival of the Northern Pacific Railway's Wallace branch line, and the opening of the post office. A lumber mill, established by Edward Donlan and Ben W. Henderson, opened in 1904 and operated until 1928. An added bonus between 1907 and 1910 was the construction of the Milwaukee Road through the area, which paralleled the Northern Pacific's line. De Borgia was almost completely destroyed during the epic forest fires that swept through parts of western Montana in 1910. The fire blazed through the town, burning 60 buildings. As the economic fortunes of De Borgia dwindled in the 1920s, the population also began to decline, from 1,000 in 1910 to less than 300 two decades later. Elevation: 3,056 ft. Location: Mineral County

Deadmans Basin Reservoir 859 *map 13 D-2*

Legend has it that in the 1860s a horse wrangler in the area was strung up by a local vigilance committee after several different brands were discovered in his herd. The Deadmans Basin Reservoir covers 2,000 acres, impounding 57,000 acre-feet of Musselshell River water. In 1934, Governor Frank Cooney was on hand to initiate excavation of the 12-mile intake canal, inaugurating one of the first projects of the State Water Conservation Board. It was completed in 7 years, with monies from the WPA totaling over $1.2 million. Elevation: 3,889 ft. Location: Wheatland County

Dean 927 *map 21 B-1*

Orlando E. Haskin settled on the Crow Indian Reservation about 1886. After considerable dispute with the Crow agent, he was allowed "squatter's" rights, property rights acquired by occupation of the land over a period of years. In 1896, Haskin left Montana. When he returned in 1902, he and his wife, Bessie, established a dairy farm and opened the Dean post office, named by Orlando's daughter Helen for her playmate Dean Harris. Elevation: 5,232 ft. Location: Stillwater County

Dearborn River 380 *map 11 B-3*
Lewis and Clark named the Dearborn River for Henry Dearborn, Thomas Jefferson's secretary of war. The stream flows out of the Scapegoat Mountains and empties into the Missouri River near Craig.

Decker 1150 *map 23 C-1*
Two stories tell how Decker received its name. According to one, federal postal officials assigned the name in 1893. Another attributes the name to Charlie Decker, who lived in the area as a sometime prospector and trader. In the late 1930s, the State Water Conservation Board constructed the Tongue River Dam, creating a reservoir just north of Decker to supply irrigation water to local farmers and ranchers. In the early 1980s, the Decker coal mines began supplying fuel for midwestern power plants. Elevation: 3,542 ft. Location: Big Horn County

Decker Mines 1152 *map 23 C-1*
Decker Coal Company operations include coal-crushing, handling, storage, and loading facilities. Each of the 4 silos holds 16,500 tons of coal, and a loading facility can load a train with 10,000 tons of coal in approximately 2 hours. Since the mines opened in 1982, the company has sold more than 250 million tons of coal, shipping some 10 million tons per year to the Midwest's power generation market. Elevation: 3,468 ft. Location: Big Horn County

Deep Creek 594 *map 11 E-4*
Deep Creek is the largest drainage on the west slope of the Big Belt Mountains. The Flathead Trail that crosses the drainage was used extensively by Native Americans. Prospectors explored the area, but it never developed into a major mining area. Grass Mountain Ski Area operated south of US 12 between Townsend and White Sulphur Springs during the 1950s and 1960s. Location: Broadwater County

Deer Lodge 406 *map 11 D-1*
The area around Deer Lodge has a long history of use by Native Americans, French Canadian fur trappers, and others. The local Shoshones called the site It Soo'-Ke-En Car'-Ne, "Lodge of the white-tailed deer"; trappers translated the name as La Loge du Chevreuil, and English-speaking settlers translated the French as Deer Lodge (so named because of the salt lick at the base of the Warm Springs Mound that attracted hundreds of deer). The area had previously been known as Spanish Fork, Cottonwood, La Barge City, and Idaho City. When Montana Territory was formed out of portions of Idaho Territory, the Deer Lodge Town Company

Montana State Prison, inside yard, Deer Lodge, 1940s
MHS 950-030

hired cartographer Walter W. DeLacy to plat the new town under its present name. Deer Lodge is the home of the Montana State Prison, county seat of Powell County, and site of the NPS's historic Grant-Kohrs Ranch, one of Montana's earliest and longest-operating ranches. The historic Montana Territorial and State Prison, in use until 1979, is now a museum and listed in the National Register. Elevation: 4,570 ft. Location: Powell County

Deer Lodge County 442 *map 10 E-4*
The name Deer Lodge comes from the Native American name for the area, It Soo'-Ke-En Car'-Ne, "Lodge of the white-tailed deer." The 1865 legislature established the county's boundaries as a narrow north-south strip west of the Continental Divide, from the Canadian border to the northern edge of Beaverhead County, with Silver Bow as the county seat. In a series of complicated boundary changes, Deer Lodge County lost territory to Lewis and Clark, Flathead, Powell, Granite, and Silver Bow counties. Anaconda is the county seat as well as the historic center of Anaconda Company copper smelting.

Dell 786 *map 19 D-1*
Named for its location in a small valley, Dell sits by the Red Rock River and was founded as a station stop on the newly completed Utah & Northern Railway, which reached Butte in 1881. It was the center of a community of sheep ranches that developed between 1890 and 1920 in the Sheep Creek Valley. Elevation: 6,008 ft. Location: Beaverhead County

Delmoe Lake 551 *map 11 E-2*
Delmoe Lake is named for Aquilane "Tom" Delmoe, a native of Switzerland who arrived in Montana in 1865 from Nevada. After several years of mining, Tom established the first dairy in Butte. Around

1890, he moved to Pipestone Hot Springs, just east of Pipestone Pass, where he spent the rest of his life. He died in 1920. The lake has a campground and is accessible by a gravel road. Elevation: 6,095 ft. Location: Jefferson County

Dempsey 413 *map 11 D-1*
Robert Dempsey established a ranch on Dempsey Creek that served as a board-inghouse for miners traveling to and from Cottonwood (later Deer Lodge) in 1862. He named the nearby stream and community after himself. Rumor circulated that Dempsey was a member of the infamous Plummer Gang and aided road agents with fresh horses and supplies. The suspicions were never proved. Elevation: 4,887 ft. Location: Powell County

Denton 681 *map 12 A-4*
H. F. Dent arrived in this area in 1880 and established a post office called Denton in 1888, named after the Missouri county where he had previously lived. Cattle, horse, and sheep ranches developed here in the late nineteenth century, making way for homesteaders who began arriving in 1906. When the Milwaukee Road completed its track between Great Falls and Lewistown in 1913, Denton's grain elevators immediately saw service, with trains sometimes 4 deep and stretching into a line a quarter mile long. Elevation: 3,597 ft. Location: Fergus County

Devils Slide 877 *map 20 C-2*
Artist Thomas Moran, a member of Ferdinand V. Hayden's 1871 Yellowstone Expedition, named the Devils Slide on Cinnabar Mountain for a devil's-face-shaped rock he painted when he climbed up onto the ridge above the slide. Geological forces, which folded the sedimentary rock into large curves and eroded the surface, created the dramatic cliff of red sandstone in the

Yellowstone River valley about 65 million years ago, in the Cretaceous period. Elevation: 6,412 ft. Location: Park County.

Devon 322 *map 3 C-4*

In 1909, Norwegian farmer Halvor Gardner donated a portion of his homestead to create the town of Devon, originally known as Concord. The source of the name is unclear, but the Great Northern Railway named dozens of towns along the High Line after European towns, and there is a County Devon in southern England. In 1909, the Gardners opened the People's Store to serve the thriving new town, whose population peaked at 300 during the next decade. Elevation: 3,112 ft. Location: Toole County

Dewey 539 *map 18 A-4*

Dewey was founded in 1872 when Joseph Vipond built a road through the Pioneer Mountains from the Quartz Hill Mining District. The town is named for miner D. S. Dewey, the town's first resident. By 1885, Dewey had 3 stamp mills, several charcoal kilns, a hotel, a saloon, and a slaughterhouse. Elevation: 5,490 ft. Location: Beaverhead County

Diamond City 553 *map 11 D-4*

On a 200-mile journey from Fort Benton to Helena in November 1864, four ex-Confederate soldiers—Jack Thompson, Washington Baker, John Wells (Wooly Johnson), and Pomp Dennis—discovered gold at their campsite near the Missouri River at the mouth of a steep canyon in the Big Belt Mountains. A boomtown soon grew up nearby. According to legend, Diamond City was named for the pattern of trails that came together in Confederate Gulch, where the original gold claims were filed. Three years after its birth, the town was home to a population of 5,000 and briefly was the seat of Meagher County.

Diamond City cemetery, 1968
MHS 946-742

By 1908, it was almost completely deserted, and today all that remains are the earthen outlines of the now-gone buildings. Elevation: 4,820 ft. Location: Broadwater County

Dickey Lake 27 *map 1 B-4*

Dickey Lake may have been named for Thomas E. Dickey, an Episcopal minister who founded Christ Church in Kalispell in 1891. He and sons Charles, Jack, Henry, and Ellis lived in Kalispell for many years and were active in public affairs. There is a campground on the north end of the lake. Elevation: 3,108 ft. Location: Lincoln County

Dillon 692 *map 19 C-1*

Dillon, the Beaverhead County seat, is named for Sidney Dillon, president of the Utah & Northern Railway, a branch of the Union Pacific Railroad, which was the first railroad into Montana in 1881. Dillon was created when a small syndicate of businessmen, including B. F. White, purchased Richard Deacon's 480-acre ranch for $10,500 on September 13, 1880. The town incorporated in 1885, and it has served as a ranching supply center from that time forward. The State Normal School, now listed in the National Register, opened for classes here in 1897 specifically to train teachers. The college is now known as the University of Montana–Western. Elevation: 5,101 ft. Location: Beaverhead County

Divide 558   *map 19 A-1*
Established as a station stop on the Utah & Northern Railway in 1873, this community is named for its proximity to the Continental Divide. Elevation: 5,389 ft. Location: Silver Bow County

Dixon 173   *map 10 A-1*
This town is named for Joseph M. Dixon, a prominent Montana political figure who served the state as both U.S. senator and governor. He was instrumental in opening the Flathead Indian Reservation to homesteading in 1910. In the 1910s, Dixon consisted of a Northern Pacific Railway station and section house, a hotel, a mercantile, 2 grain elevators, a lumberyard, McQuarrie's lumber mill, and Drake's Mine. The Dixon Indian Agency of the Flathead Indian Reservation helped stabilize the local economy over time. The town sits adjacent to the lower Flathead River near the National Bison Range. Elevation: 2,524 ft. Location: Sanders County

Dodson 860   *map 6 C-1*
Dodson, located on the Milk River, takes its name from a Great Northern Railway engineer, Thomas Henry Dodson. The town of Dodson first appeared in the early 1890s as a saloon, store, and post office to serve a growing ranch community. Dodson blossomed in 1909 when settlers moved in to take advantage of the Milk River Irrigation Project after completion of the Dodson Dam, built in 1910 by the U.S. Reclamation Service. The town endured through World War I and the Great Depression but started to decline with the onset of World War II. Today large ranches and farms support its economy. Elevation: 2,287 ft. Location: Phillips County

Dooley 1183   *map 8 A-2*
Named for W. D. Dooley, rancher, banker, and owner of the 4–4 brand, this town sprang up in 1913 along the Minneapolis, St. Paul & Sault Ste. Marie Railway. The first baby born here was a little girl christened Dooliette. The town soon had 40 buildings; its electricity, available from evening until midnight, was provided by kerosene-powered generator. Ten minutes before the stroke of midnight, the lights would flash, signaling residents that the lights would soon go out. Dooley suffered a series of natural disasters—fires, tornado, and infestations of armyworms, grasshoppers, and Mormon crickets—that wreaked havoc on local agriculture. Because of its close proximity to the Canadian border, Dooley became known for bootlegging activities during the 1920s. Although its population peaked at 400 residents, Dooley is now one of Montana's many agricultural ghost towns. Elevation: 2,462 ft. Location: Sheridan County

Drumlummon Mine 395   *map 11 C-2*
Placer silver and gold were mined in the 1860s along Silver Creek. Then, in 1876, Thomas Cruse discovered rich, deep veins of silver and gold and he named his mine the Drumlummon Mine, after his parish in County Cavan, Ireland. He sold the mine to a British syndicate in 1882 and became an instant millionaire and subsequent philanthropist. Cruse dedicated part of his fortune to constructing a new cathedral in Helena in the early 1900s. The Montana Company Ltd. expanded the mine, building several stamp mills and a new cyanide plant in 1896 at Marysville. The mine, operating under several different companies and names over the years, produced more than $15 million in gold,

Northern Pacific Railroad bridge, Marysville, Drumlummon Mine on left, 1887
MHS 949-185

making it one of Montana's richest gold mines. The big stamp mill burned in 1971. Elevation: 5,846 ft. Location: Lewis and Clark County

Drummond 316 *map 10 C-4*

John Edwards settled opposite the mouth of Flint Creek along the Clark Fork River in 1866. By 1873, a small community, Edwardsville, had grown up on his ranch. The Northern Pacific Railroad arrived in 1883 and promptly changed the name to Drummond, after either a Northern Pacific engineer or Hugh Drummond, a local trapper. In 1908, floodwaters washed out the track between Garrison and Drummond, stranding a train headed east. Among the passengers were several members of the Knights of Columbus from Butte and noted anarchist Emma Goldman. As the delay stretched on,

Goldman's manager attempted to organize an occasion for her to speak. On hearing this news, Butte attorney John A. Coleman promptly stated, "The American flag is good enough for me. My friends and I will tolerate no talk about anarchy." Discretion being the better part of valor, Ms. Goldman retired to her sleeping car without giving her speech. Elevation: 3,970 ft. Location: Granite County

Duck Creek Bay 1039 *map 7 D-1*

The original Duck Creek, for which the bay is named, is now buried under Fort Peck Reservoir; the Lewis and Clark Expedition had named it Werner's Creek for expedition member William Werner. Hundreds of ducks appear in a historic photo of the area, lending credence to the modern name. Elevation: 2,257 ft. Location: Valley County

Dunkirk 301 *map 3 C-4*

The Great Northern Railway named Dunkirk after Dunkirk, France, according to its practice of naming towns along the route for European cities. According to *Toole County Memories*: "We got our name when the railroad came in. They got a globe, blindfolded a guy, spun the globe, and where his finger lit became the town's name. The railroad purportedly followed this practice along the High Line." Established in 1892 as a station, the town acquired a post office in 1910, during the homestead boom. By 1916, Dunkirk had a population of 100 and a variety of businesses, including 2 hotels and 3 general stores. Elevation: 3,303 ft. Location: Toole County

Dunmore 1077 *map 22 A-3*

The origin of the name of this tiny community on the Crow Indian Reservation is not known. Elevation: 2,963 ft. Location: Big Horn County

Dupuyer 222 *map 3 D-2*

Dupuyer takes its name from Dupuyer Creek, which borders the town. The Blackfeet called the creek Osaks itukai, "Back fat." When French Canadian trappers came though the area, they translated it as Depouille, meaning "hide." Over the years, the name went through several spelling changes. The town of Dupuyer began in 1877 as a stage stop on the Fort Benton–Fort Browning road and later served as a supply center for ranches. In the 1890s, Dupuyer ran for the county seat for Teton County but lost to Choteau. County lines have since been redrawn. Elevation: 4,122 ft. Location: Pondera County

Durham 1255 *map 2 C-4*

Durham was a station on the Great Northern Railway from 1894 until at least 1918, between Browning and East Glacier. There were no businesses located there at that time. Elevation: 4,724 ft. Location: Glacier County

Dutton 330 *map 3 E-4*

Originally a station on the Great Northern Railway's Great Falls & Canada branch line between Great Falls and Conrad, Dutton was named for Charles E. Dutton, the railroad's general agent in Helena. In 1909, George and Sam Sollid purchased land from homesteader William "Stinking Bill" Frixel. The following year, they incorporated as the Dutton Townsite Company. The town grew rapidly and during the 1910s and '20s had a bank, a newspaper, grain elevators, and a variety of businesses. Unlike many small agricultural communities, Dutton has continued to prosper, in large part because of its operating grain elevators in the middle of wheat farms. Elevation: 3,724 ft. Location: Teton County

Northern Pacific Railroad trestle, Marent Gulch, near Evaro, 1883

F. Jay Haynes, photographer, MHS H-1071

Eagle Guard Station 559 *map 11 D-4*

About 1895, Dick Owen—known as "Dirty Dick" because he smeared himself with axle grease to ward off insects—and partner Jack Wilson built this 3-room log cabin nestled in the Elkhorn Mountains where eagles frequently nested. Wilson mysteriously disappeared on a hunting trip when the cabin was half-finished, and Owen's wife refused to live in it, settling instead at Radersburg. The USFS acquired the cabin in 1906 and restored it in 1992. The site serves administrative purposes and is available for public rental. Elevation: 5,830 ft. Location: Broadwater County

Eagle's Store 909 *map 20 D-1*

When the tracks of the Oregon Short Line reached West Yellowstone in November 1907, park employee Samuel P. Eagle applied for and received a permit to operate a business adjacent to the railroad right-of-way. Eagle, in partnership with Alex Stuart, built a tiny 12-by-12-foot general store on this site in 1908—the first commercial operation in West Yellowstone. Eagle enlarged the store in 1913, and in 1927 the Eagle family razed the old store and began construction on the present building, built in the Western Rustic style in 3 stages and completed in 1930. Prominent Bozeman architect Fred Willson, who designed other architecturally similar structures within Yellowstone, designed all 3 sections, donating his time out of a desire to promote the style. Massive red fir logs 18 to 36 feet long set in rhyolite and concrete support the building. Outstanding interior features include the back bar installed in the original store in 1910 and the original 1930 front bar and stools. National Register listed, and still operated as a gift shop and soda fountain owned and managed by the Eagle family, this impressive pioneer family business is one of West Yellowstone's most outstanding architectural landmarks. Elevation: 6,671 ft. Location: Gallatin County

Ear Mountain 225 *map 3 E-1*

Originally named Elephant's Ear Mountain by early trappers, this dramatic peak on the Rocky Mountain Front had long been used by Native Americans, including Blackfeet leader Heavy Runner, as a vision quest site. The mountain was designated an outstanding natural area by the BLM in 1986. Elevation: 8,527 ft. Location: Teton County

East Butte 362 *map 4 B-2*

East Butte is the name given collectively to 3 peaks—Mount Brown, Mount Royal, and East Butte—in the Sweet Grass Hills. The Isaac I. Stevens railroad survey mapped the area as the Trois Buttes (Three Buttes) in the early 1850s. East Butte was the site of a gold discovery by Alfred Bragg about 1884. The Great Northern Railway also acquired claims in the area around 1896, but very little gold was ever actually mined. The Blackfeet, Chippewa-Cree, and Gros Ventre tribes consider the area sacred and oppose any future mining in the Sweet Grass Hills. The tribes have lobbied to make the Sweet Grass Hills a world heritage site. Elevation: 5,499 ft. Location: Liberty County

East Fork Reservoir 396 *map 10 E-3*

This reservoir, created by a dam on the East Fork of Rock Creek built by the State Water Conservation Board in 1938, provided water for the Allendale Irrigation Company. Elevation: 6,064 ft. Location: Granite County

East Glacier Park 163 *map 2 C-4*

The Great Northern Railway platted the community of Midvale in the 1890s; residents changed the town's name to Glacier Park in 1913 to end the confusion with the town of Midvale in the southern part of the state. Home to Glacier Park Lodge and the Glacier Park Transportation Company's garages, the community thrived by providing services for tourists and area residents. The town's name officially became East Glacier Park in 1949. Elevation: 4,792 ft. Location: Glacier County

East Helena 488 *map 11 D-3*

In 1864, Jonathan and Elmira Manlove constructed a cabin at Prickly Pear Junction that served as a way station on the road to Diamond City. The settlement's name became East Helena in 1889, after the construction of the Helena & Livingston Smelting & Reduction Company's smelter there to process silver-lead ore from Wickes. In 1890, the United Smelting and Refining Company took over operation of the East Helena smelter until American Smelting and Refining Company (ASARCO) took charge in 1899. The Anaconda Company operated a zinc recovery plant at East Helena from 1927 to 1972 to supply material to its Great Falls zinc refinery. ASARCO purchased the Anaconda zinc operations in 1972 and shut them down 10 years later. ASARCO closed the smelter in 2001, and the largest of the smokestacks was dismantled in 2005. Cleanup of the site continues under supervision of the EPA. American Chemet, the world's largest producer of cuprous oxide, a toxin-free paint to protect oceangoing ships, set up shop in East Helena in 1946 because of access to zinc oxide, a by-product of lead-zinc smelting. Elevation: 3,888 ft. Location: Lewis and Clark County

East Pacific Mine 547 *map 11 D-4*

George Brooks located the East Pacific Mine in 1867. In 1886, P. O. and Philip Winston of Minneapolis, the brothers who built the Northern Pacific Railroad's line across eastern Montana, and John W. Kendrick, the railroad's chief engineer, purchased it. The mine produced about $500,000 worth of gold and galena ore between 1886 and 1895. Under the own-

ership of Robert A. Bell, who bought the property in 1896, the mine produced about $1.3 million of galena ore, which yielded equal parts of gold, silver, and lead. The mine operated sporadically from the 1910s to the 1940s, when it was put into full production to produce lead for the war effort. Elevation: 5,798 ft. Location: Broadwater County

East Rosebud Creek 943 *map 21 B-2*

East Rosebud Creek flows out of the craggy high country of the Beartooth Plateau north into the prairies and foothills, where it joins West Rosebud Creek near the town of Fishtail. The origin of the name is unknown, but wild roses are common along streams in Montana valleys. The largest ranch in Carbon County, owned by the Malcolm MacKay family, lay between West and East Rosebud creeks. The family donated their significant collection of Charlie Russell paintings to the Montana Historical Society in 1952, many of which are on permanent exhibit in the Society's museum in Helena. Location: Stillwater and Carbon counties

East Rosebud Lake 961 *map 21 C-1*

East Rosebud Lake, formed by creeks leaving the Beartooth high country, became the property of Crow Indian agent Maj. H. J. Armstrong in 1896. After a devastating fire in 1899, Armstrong sold his 108 acres to a group of Red Lodge bankers, who in turn sold it to Billings investor Christian Yegen and Red Lodge banker John Chapman in 1907. In 1912, Yegen and Chapman built a lodge on East Rosebud Lake, and in 1913 they established a nonprofit family association to grant leases for cabin sites along the lake. Elevation: 6,213 ft. Location: Carbon County

East St. Marys Peak 196 *map 10 A-2*

In 1841, the Jesuits established the St. Mary's Mission in the Bitterroot Valley to serve the Salish people, but by 1891 the Salish there had been forced to move to the Flathead Indian Reservation to the north. This peak to the east of St. Ignatius was named for the mission in the Bitterroot Valley. Elevation: 9,425 ft. Location: Lake County

Eddies Corner 745 *map 13 B-1*

W. E. "Ed" McConnell built the café, bar, and gas station known as Eddies Corner in 1949, using lumber supplied by the Edwards family—thus Eddies Corner was named for the several Eds involved. The Bauman family has owned the business since 1951. Elevation: 4,010 ft. Location: Fergus County

Eddy 98 *map 1 E-3*

The town of Eddy was built on the site of an 1824 trading post and named for Richard A. (Dick) Eddy. The Missoula firm of Eddy, Hammond & Company (later known as the Missoula Mercantile) held the contract to clear the right-of-way for the Northern Pacific Railroad. They built the wagon road from Missoula to Thompson Falls and then acted as the town's promoters beginning in 1883 with the arrival of the railroad. Elevation: 2,429 ft. Location: Sanders County

Eddy Mountain 99 *map 1 E-3*

The name Eddy was attached to this mountain to commemorate the work of Richard A. (Dick) Eddy, a partner in the Missoula Mercantile and builder of the wagon road connecting Missoula to Thompson Falls. Elevation: 6,957 ft. Location: Sanders County

Eden 478 *map 12 B-1*

Named for its idyllic location, Eden has never been more than a tiny settlement serving nearby farms and ranches. Robert Meisenbach was the first postmaster here, in 1899. According to local lore, Meisenbach and his neighbors received a list of potential names for the new post office and selected Eden as most appropriate. Eden Bridge State Park, a few miles to the west, is a takeout point for boaters on the popular Smith River. Elevation: 3,900 ft. Location: Cascade County

Edgar 1000 *map 21 B-3*

J. J. Thornton started the community of Edgar in 1907 when he purchased the Pendergast homestead and named it for his brother Edgar. Thornton insisted on a "dry" town and the establishment of a park near the railroad tracks, and he encouraged development of other businesses by donating land for the new town. The new community offered an alternative to area residents who did not wish to travel to Joliet, Gebo, or Rockvale to shop. Residents of Poverty Flats west of Pryor contributed to the town's stability and growth. Elevation: 3,466 ft. Location: Carbon County

Edith Lake 615 *map 12 D-1*

Nearby Mount Edith, the highest peak in the Big Belt Mountains, was named for 12 year-old Edith Wallace, who hiked up the mountain in 1881, in a party led by local ranchers C. W. Cook and J. O. Hussey. The assumption is that the lake was then given the same name as the peak. Elevation: 8,046 ft. Location: Meagher County

Egg Mountain 476 *map 3 E-2*

Egg Mountain, home of the *Maiasaura* dinosaur 80 million years ago, was discovered and named in 1979 by paleontologists Jack Horner and Bob Makela. The name

Ekalaka, c. 1890
MHS 946-777

came from the revolutionary discovery that the *Maiasaura*, or "good mother," dinosaur raised its young in nests, many of which are located in the vicinity of Egg Mountain. Fossilized bones, eggs, and babies were found in or near the nests. The site is believed to be relatively intact due to some cataclysmic event that very suddenly killed both adults and babies. Elevation: 4,413 ft. Location: Teton County

Ekalaka 1238   *map 16 E-3*

Ekalaka is named for Ijkalaka, the Ogal-lala Sioux niece of Chief Red Cloud and the bride of David Russell, who opened a store and saloon there in 1885. A trade center for cattle and sheep ranchers, the town became the county seat of Carter County in 1917 and reached its peak population of 400 a few years later. *Butte Standard* reporter Gary Langley wrote in 1975: "Ekalaka—This isn't the end of the world, but it's the end of the road." He clarified this comment by quoting a local resident who said, "We're supposed to be the only county in the U.S. where you can drive in but you have to back out." The heart of the economy remains cattle ranching. Medicine Rocks State Park is 11 miles north of Ekalaka and remains a sacred site to the Ogallala Sioux. Elevation: 3,427 ft. Location: Carter County

Electric Peak 887   *map 20 C-2*

The highest peak in the Gallatin Range, located just inside the northern boundary of Yellowstone National Park, Electric Peak was named by Henry Gannett, who encountered a severe lightning storm while climbing in July 1872. Gannett was a geographer and future president of the National Geographic Society. According to a USGS report by Ferdinand V. Hayden: "A thunder-shower was approaching as we neared the summit of the mountain. I was above the others of the party, and, when about fifty feet below the summit, the electric current began to pass through my body. At first I felt nothing, but heard a crackling noise, similar to a rapid discharge of sparks from a friction machine. Immediately after, I began to feel a tingling or prickling sensation in my head and the ends of my fingers, which, as well as the noise, increased rapidly, until, when I reached the top, the noise, which had not changed its character, was deafening, and my hair stood completely on end, while the tingling, pricking sensation was absolutely painful. . . . I started down again, and met the others twenty-five or thirty feet below the summit. They were affected similarly, but in a less degree." Elevation: 10,992 ft. Location: Park County

Montana Place Names

Elk Park Pass 529 *map 11 E-2*

At the turn of the nineteenth century, this high, narrow valley was home to several Italian-Swiss dairies that served Butte. It is named for the large ungulate that frequents the area. The town of Elk Park appeared in the 1880s to provide local mining operations with supplies, a school, and housing. Elevation: 6,968 ft. Location: Silver Bow and Jefferson counties

Elk Peak 669 *map 12 D-2*

Elk Peak, the highest peak in the Castle Mountains, and nearby Wapiti Peak are named for the same large ungulate common to the area. Elk Peak was officially known as Castle Peak for a time. Elevation: 8,566 ft. Location: Meagher County

Elkhorn 541 *map 11 E-3*

The community is named after the Elkhorn lode discovered by Swiss miner Peter Wyes in 1869. By 1883, Helena industrialist Anton M. Holter had constructed a 10-stamp mill and created a highly productive silver-lead operation. In 1886, the Northern Pacific Railroad constructed a spur line called the Helena, Boulder Valley & Butte Railroad, expanding opportunities for commerce and mining. The repeal of the Sherman Silver Purchase Act in 1893 led to a silver panic, shutting down numerous Montana silver mines, but Elkhorn survived until 1901. In 1889, most of Elkhorn's children died in a diphtheria epidemic and were buried in the local cemetery. In the 1980s, Montana designated the cemetery and 2 buildings in the Elkhorn ghost town a state park, one of Montana's smallest. In 1993, Montana Fish, Wildlife & Parks stabilized the Fraternity Hall and Gillian Hall; both are listed in the National Register. Elevation: 6,469 ft. Location: Jefferson County

Elkhorn Mountains 540 *map 11 D-3*

Silver miners who arrived in 1869 to develop the Elkhorn lode named the Elkhorn Mountains for the large number of elk found in the area. By the 1880s, the town of Elkhorn had grown up around the Anton M. Holter mine and mill. Significant gold and silver mining took place up and down the range, from Helena to Boulder. Elkhorn Peak rises above the town to 9,381 feet.

Elliston 409 *map 11 D-2*

Two stories explain the origin of Elliston's name. The more likely is that it honors Northern Pacific Railroad director John W. Ellis. In the more romantic story, the town was named Alicetown for the daughter of an early settler, Hubert Coty, operator of the MacDonald Pass tollgate until 1882. By the mid-1880s, Elliston was flourishing as a center for gold and quartz mining. The town burned twice, in 1894 and 1895. Many disheartened businessmen did not rebuild a second time. The Elliston Lime Company began processing lime in 1897 and by 1903 was producing 900 bushels per day. The lime kiln closed in 1965. Elevation: 5,051 ft. Location: Powell County

Elmo 112 *map 2 E-1*

Elmo's name is derived from that of a Blackfeet man, Elemie, who married a Kootenai woman and settled near the community. Eugene McCarthy purchased land from Elemie and platted the land that became the current townsite in 1917. Elmo had a dock and warehouse that served boat traffic on Flathead Lake, and the town acted as an overnight stop for people bound for Hot Springs. Elevation: 2,905 ft. Location: Lake County

Emigrant 845 *map 20 B-2*

In 1863, Thomas Curry found gold in Emigrant Gulch (on land that was then part of the Crow Indian Reservation); his

Emigrant Peak, Yellowstone River, and angler,
c. 1930
Brown, photographer, MHS 946-812

strike was followed the next year by a rich discovery made by David Weaver, David Shorthill, and Frank Garrett. The flood of prospectors and trappers from "the States" gave the nearby peak, creek, and gulch their name. In 1864, miners entering Emigrant Gulch discovered a single pine tree with some 20 elk antlers stuck in it, which they took as a mark of Jim Bridger's earlier arrival there. Emigrant first had a post office in 1872, which only lasted 4 years but was reestablished in 1911. Although the original settlement was on the east side of the Yellowstone River, today's Emigrant is on the west side, along US 89. Elevation: 4,894 ft. Location: Park County

Emigrant Peak 864 *map 20 C-2*

Emigrant Peak, creek, and gulch are named for Thomas Curry, David Shorthill, and other gold miners who appeared in the area in 1863–64. Over time, miners settled up Emigrant Gulch in White City and Chico. In the 1880s, a resort took shape at the mouth of Emigrant Gulch, taking advantage of the hot springs at Chico. In 1941, miners dredged Emigrant Gulch for gold with the world's second-largest dredge. Elevation: 10,921 ft. Location: Park County

Enid 1172 *map 8 E-2*

Named for Lossie and Lavinia Dawes's daughter Enid, the post office here opened in 1898 with the Daweses serving as the first postmasters. The town prospered with the arrival of homesteaders and the Northern Pacific Railway's line from Sidney to Circle in 1916. Elevation: 2,409 ft. Location: Richland County

Ennis 746 *map 19 B-3*

Scots-Irish immigrant William Ennis drove an ox-drawn freight wagon from Colorado to Bannack and then on to Alder Gulch, arriving in June 1863. Because of a lack of hay in Virginia City, he continued east about 14 miles to the Madison Valley, where he built a log cabin to live in while he hauled hay to sell in Virginia City. His wife, Katherine, and daughter, Jennie, joined him in 1865. In 1879, Ennis opened a general store. He established a post office in 1881, selecting the name Ennis. Although William Ennis was murdered in 1898, his family continued to run the many businesses he had founded. Agriculture and mines, including the Yellowstone Talc, Plago, and Washington mines, continued to be the economic mainstays of Ennis throughout the twentieth century. Today tourism focused on trout fishing has become a large part of the economy as well. Elevation: 4,940 ft. Location: Madison County

Essex 137 *map 2 C-3*

Named for a county in England, Essex (originally known as Walton) began as a small town on the Great Northern Railway's main line in 1890. Multiple work crews stayed here throughout the year, maintaining the line, clearing Marias Pass during winter, and operating the "pusher" engines used to assist trains over the pass. In 1939, in response to repeated requests, the Great Northern constructed the Izaak Walton Inn as a hostelry for the work crews, for $40,000. The use of diesel engines in the late 1940s eliminated the need for the Essex water towers and coal chute, but the "pusher" engines for Marias Pass remained into the 1990s. Today the inn serves winter and summer visitors to Glacier National Park and the surrounding area. Elevation: 3,859 ft. Location: Flathead County

Ethridge 251 *map 3 C-3*

Sometime in early 1900, the Great Northern Railway station named Galt was renamed Ethridge. Sir Alexander Galt, of Montreal, was a prominent Canadian statesman and entrepreneur. There is a rim to the north, which some note as a "ridge," but the source of the name Ethridge is unclear. In 1912, George Norman of Cut Bank laid out a townsite, and an agricultural center quickly grew adjacent to the tracks. By 1919, drought had taken a toll on area homesteaders, and by 1926 most of the buildings had been moved to the surrounding oil boomtowns. Elevation: 3,544 ft. Location: Toole County

Eureka 14 *map 1 A-3*

Elzeor Demers, Ovide Peltier, J. J. Sullivan, and Abram L. Jaqueth drew up the Deweyville Townsite Company articles of incorporation on April 28, 1903. The name Deweyville was proposed in honor of Elzeor Demers's wife, the former Amine Dewey. The directors changed the name of the proposed town to Eureka 3 months later when they discovered another Dewey in Montana. The town expanded along the new Great Northern Railway main line between Whitefish and Jennings, and the first train arrived from Kalispell on October 2, 1904. Hard on the heels of the first train was the construction of the Bader and Bottom Sawmill, which eventually became the Eureka Lumber Company. With the creation of Lincoln County in 1909, Eureka squared off against Libby in a special election for the coveted county seat and

won, 656 votes to 638. Libby challenged the results, claiming that the election was improper since the Montana legislature had declared Libby the county seat. In July 1911, the Montana Supreme Court reversed its April 1911 decision in favor of Eureka and eventually ruled in Libby's favor. A well-intentioned and slightly inebriated citizen of Eureka assumed that the county seat was literally a seat and, according to *The Story of Tobacco Plains* (p. 212), urged other stout hearts: "Come along you fellows, I'll hitch up my four-horse team to my wagon; I'll go down to that blankety-blank Libby and I'll load'er up, that county seat, and bring'er right up here in my wagon!" The Farmers and Merchants State Bank and the Eureka Community Hall are listed in the National Register. Elevation: 2,599 ft. Location: Lincoln County

Evaro 212 *map 10 B-1*

Adna Anderson, chief construction engineer for the Northern Pacific Railroad, chose the name Evaro for the railroad section house here in August 1883. There are 2 stories about this name. One is that it honors a French count, named Evreux or Evaraux, who frequented the area during the fur trade era. According to the other story, Anderson's fiancée, Eva Roe, a mail-order bride, was killed in an accident shortly before they could be married. Beginning in 1897, the town next to the railroad station was named Blanchard, but in 1905 the residents renamed it Evaro. O'Keefe Canyon, just south of Evaro, was named Coriaka's Defile by John Mullan in 1854 to commemorate one of 3 Hawaiians killed there by Blackfeet in the 1840s. The spectacular 226-foot-high Marent Trestle, constructed by the Northern Pacific Railroad in the 1880s, is located just south of Evaro. Elevation: 3,962 ft. Location: Missoula County

Threshing crew cooks, near Frazer, 1917
Detail, MHS PAc 82-65

Fairfield 318 *map 3 E-3*

The passage of the Newlands Reclamation Act in 1902 ultimately led to irrigation projects that made possible increased grain production in this area, particularly malting barley. In 1904, surveys began, followed by canal construction in 1915 and completion of Gibson Reservoir in 1929. Fairfield's origins are linked to the arrival of the Milwaukee Road in 1916 and the platting of the town by Elmer Genger. The completion of the Greenfields Irrigation District in 1936, which diverted water from the Sun River into the Pishkun and Willow Creek reservoirs, made increased barley production possible. Located just northwest of Fairfield, Freezeout Lake, a wildlife refuge manage by Montana Fish, Wildlife & Parks, attracts hundreds of thousands of snow geese, swans, and ducks during the spring and fall migration. Elevation: 3,983 ft. Location: Teton County

Fairmont Hot Springs 486 *map 11 E-1*

In 1869, brothers Eli and George Gregson, natives of Indiana, purchased 320 acres and built a hotel and bathhouse they called the Upper Deer Lodge Hot Springs; they also established a dairy farm. In 1891, they sold the health spa to Milo French, former proprietor of the Boulder Hot Springs Hotel, and he built 2 dance pavilions and a 2-story hotel on the site. The Butte, Anaconda & Pacific Railway offered train service from Butte beginning in the 1890s, allowing miners' families to use the springs as a place of recreation and relaxation. Fire destroyed the resort, and it changed ownership several times between 1914 and 1926, but in 1927 George Forsythe expanded the facilities to include a larger outdoor plunge with a "toboggan" run, a carousel, a playground for children, and a golf course. The facility finally closed in 1971 in disrepair, but in 1974 a Canadian purchased the property and renamed it Fairmont Hot Springs Resort. Today the resort includes an 18-hole golf course, waterslide, and convention center. Elevation: 5,131 ft. Location: Silver Bow County

Fairview 1219 *map 8 D-3*

Lewis E. Newlon arrived in Montana in 1903 and settled near the Montana–North Dakota state line intending to establish a town. He filed his homestead claim and set himself up in the mercantile business the same year. A year later, Newlon platted the townsite, selling his business in 1907 so he could devote himself full time to the town's growth. Fairview incorporated in 1913, but Newlon declined to have the town named after him; instead, residents drew names from a hat and Fairview was born, courtesy of "Grandma" Corbett. With the arrival of the Great Northern Railway a year earlier, the town's future looked bright. Newlon's dream of building a metropolis on the plains, however, suffered a crippling setback in the aftermath of World War I as Montana farmers saw prices plummet and a severe drought gripped the region. In 1909, irrigation water from the Lower Yellowstone Project, built by the U.S. Bureau of Reclamation, allowed Fairview farmers to cultivate sugar beets, which they sold to the Holly Sugar Company in nearby Sidney beginning in 1925. Today Fairview's economy depends largely on sugar beets. Because Fairview sits on the state line, the transition between the Mountain and Central time zones runs right through town. Elevation: 1,912 ft. Location: Richland County

Fallon 1178 *map 16 C-1*

The town and county of Fallon are named for O'Fallon Creek, which is in turn named for Benjamin O'Fallon, a nephew of Capt. William Clark and an Indian agent for the upper Missouri region from 1823 to 1827. The Northern Pacific Railroad established a station named Fallon in 1883, and a year later prominent rancher Cyrus Mendenhall became the first postmaster. In the late

1910s and early 1920s, Fallon had 2 grain elevators and a bank, grocery store, hardware store, garage, saloon, and newspaper to serve area cattle and horse ranches. Fallon became a railhead for shipping cattle east. Today Fallon depends on ranching and farming to support its economy. Elevation: 2,205 ft. Location: Prairie County

Fallon County 1231 *map 16 D-3*

Fallon County and the town of the same name (which is in Prairie County) are named for Benjamin O'Fallon, a nephew of Capt. William Clark and an Indian agent for the upper Missouri region from 1823 to 1827. This county in southeastern Montana was carved out of Custer County in 1913, and later contributed territory to Wibaux, Prairie, and Carter counties. The economy is largely wheat farming. Baker is the county seat.

Farmington 277 *map 3 E-3*

The area around Farmington was originally known as the Burton Bench, after early settler Z. T. Burton. In the late 1890s, a group of German and Norwegian Lutherans from Minnesota moved to the area and renamed it the Farmington Bench, after a farm community in Minnesota. The Minnesota settlers had a strong tradition of cooperation and established several cooperative enterprises, including a canal company, creamery, and telephone company. A post office named Farmington was established in 1899 but closed in 1951. Elevation: 3,884 ft. Location: Teton County

Fattig Creek 963 *map 14 D-1*

Fattig Creek is named for John Fattig, who worked as a miner in Meagher County in 1870. In 1880, he and partners William H. H. Healy and James Carpenter established a trading post at Junction City. The partners also owned a hunting and trapping business at the mouth of Fattig Creek,

which they sold to Balch & Bacon in 1882. Fattig and Healy later moved to Fort Belknap to be near the family of Healy's Gros Ventre wife. Location: Musselshell County

Ferdig 283 *map 3 B-4*

Established during the 1920s oil boom in the Kevin-Sunburst field of north-central Montana, Ferdig derives its name from its founder, Sylvester C. Fertig, who had been drawn to the area by the boom in 1926 and founded the Ferdig Oil Company. Ferdig soon supported a grade school, post office, and grocery, but by the 1940s the oil industry in the area had peaked and activities shifted to the Williston Basin farther east. Elevation: 3,524 ft. Location: Toole County

Fergus 807 *map 13 A-3*

Andrew Fergus had the distinction of living in the county named in his father James Fergus's honor and in the town

James Fergus, Fergus County's namesake,
c. 1900
W. H. Culver, photographer, MHS 942-160

named after himself. James Fergus was an early settler and territorial legislator. Andrew Fergus was his father's partner in a large ranch in the area. William Fergus, James's half-brother, established a post office named Fergus on his ranch in 1899, and when the Milwaukee Road built its branch line between Hilger and Roy, connecting the 2 Fergus ranches, it seemed only natural that the new town carry the same name. The post office moved into town in 1913. Eden Tait, postmaster and owner of the Fergus Mercantile, moved the store and post office to a location along US 191 in 1949. In 1972, the Milwaukee Road discontinued service. Elevation: 3,735 ft. Location: Fergus County

Fergus County 793 *map 13 A-3*
The Montana legislature created Fergus County, named for early settler and territorial legislator James Fergus, from a portion of Meagher County on March 12, 1885; the change went into effect in December 1886, allowing the 2 counties time to adjust their finances and elections. Lewistown, which became the seat of Fergus County, lies in the exact center of Montana. In the 1920s, the legislature created Petroleum and Judith Basin counties from the eastern and western parts of Fergus County.

Ferndale 1253 *map 2 D-2*
Ferndale traces its origins to homesteading and timbering in the 1890s. In 1911, the community built a 2-room log schoolhouse. The origin of the name remains unknown. Elevation: 3,071 ft. Location: Lake County

Fife 489 *map 12 A-2*
Fife began as a Great Northern Railway station 8 miles east of Belt, around 1914. Local lore suggests that the name derives from the Fife strain of wheat grown in the region. Elevation: 3,631 ft. Location: Cascade County

Finley Point 143 *map 2 E-2*
Finley Point is named for an old Flathead Valley ranching family, the Patrick Finleys, who originally settled near Polson. Abraham Finley, a French Canadian who came to the Flathead area in the 1840s with Father Pierre-Jean De Smet, operated the first ferry on the lower Flathead River near Polson. Elevation: 2,943 ft. Location: Lake County

First Peoples Buffalo Jump State Park 390 *map 11 A-4*
This site was formerly known as Ulm Pishkun. A pishkun is a cliff or cutbank over which buffalo were driven; in the Blackfeet language, *pishkun* refers to a "deep blood kettle" or "gathering place." Archaeological excavations have revealed arrowheads, stone tools, and pottery, verifying extensive use between 900 A.D. and 1500 A.D. In the early twentieth century, stonecutters quarried the cliffs here for buildings in Great Falls and Helena, and in the 1940s a local

First Peoples Buffalo Jump State Park, near Ulm, 1988
John Smart, photographer, MHS

family harvested thousands of pounds of bison bone for fertilizer. In 1972, the site was listed in the National Register. Montana Fish, Wildlife & Parks opened a visitor center in summer 1999 and it became a state park in 2001. Elevation: 3,746 ft. Location: Cascade County

Fish Creek 194   *map 9 B-4*
Trout populate most western Montana streams, and there are numerous Fish Creeks in the state. This one in Mineral County, in the Bitterroot Range, was home to Andrew Garcia from 1899 until his death in 1943. Garcia arrived in Montana with a herd of Texas cattle in 1868 and worked as a trapper, hunter, and U.S. Army agent during the Indian wars, all of which he recorded in his memoirs, published as *Tough Trip through Paradise*. On the banks of this Fish Creek stands Montana's largest ponderosa pine, measuring 75 inches in diameter and 194 feet tall. There is also a Fish Creek in Jefferson County.

Fisher River 22   *map 1 C-3*
The Fisher River is named for John S. "Jack" Fisher, a guide and gold prospector who worked out of Galbraith's Ferry (later Fort Steele, British Columbia), in the 1860s. Fisherville and Fisher Peak in British Columbia are also named for him. The Fisher River flows into the Kootenai River just below the Libby Dam. In 1868, Fisher moved to Libby and continued prospecting there for many years. He died in St. Ignatius after 1900.

Fishtail 940   *map 21 B-1*
Named for the nearby butte, the community of Fishtail was established in 1892 on John Maner's homestead, when the area was opened to homesteading following the ceding of this part of the Crow Indian Reservation in 1892. Joe and Addie Mason platted the town in 1913. Early businesses

included a mercantile, post office, hotel, and flour mill built in 1916 by S. B. Kennedy. Chrome and platinum mining in the nearby Stillwater Complex attracted residents from the 1940s to the present. Elevation: 4,465 ft. Location: Stillwater County

Fishtail Butte 926   *map 21 B-1*
In 1883, farmers John and James Fowler named the butte for its shape. Fishtail Creek and the town of Fishtail got their names from the butte. Elevation: 5,769 ft. Location: Stillwater County

Flaming Arrow Lodge 759   *map 20 A-2*
In 1934, Indianapolis businessman Arthur L. McKinney purchased this site with the intent to build a boys' camp, theater colony, and school for the arts. Under the capable direction of Walter Diteman, formerly of the 7-Up Dude Ranch near Lincoln, 75 workers built the lodge, 10 cabins, a theater that seated 1,000, and a private residence, but plans for the camp came to a halt when McKinney died in May 1935. The existing facilities opened the following Thanksgiving to winter sports enthusiasts. The theater included a spectacular indoor ski jump, an unplanned use that later expanded. During the 1940s and '50s, Eva and Erwin Lachenmaier ran a year-round dude ranch here. Eventually, the home sold separately from the lodge, and from 1956 to the mid-1970s it served part of its original purpose as a Boy Scout camp. Today the Flaming Arrow Lodge, named after the ceremony of truce that supposedly ended a major Sioux–Nez Perce battle at this site, remains a masterpiece of Western Rustic architecture. The lodge is listed in the National Register. Elevation: 5,927 ft. Location: Gallatin County

Flathead County 84   *map 2 D-4*
The 1893 Montana legislature created Flathead County from the northern portion

of Missoula County, with Kalispell as the county seat; a small piece of Deer Lodge County was added in 1903. The county was presumably named for Flathead Lake, since the entire lake was originally included within its boundaries. Later, in 1923, most of the portion containing the lake became Lake County. Traditionally, wood products dominated the economy, but today the area attracts out-of-state retirees and tourists.

Flathead Indian Reservation 152
map 10 B-2

The Flathead Indian Reservation, established by the Hellgate Treaty of 1855, is governed by the Confederated Salish and Kootenai Tribes and is home to members of the Salish, Pend d'Oreille, Kalispel, and Kootenai tribes. The reservation derives its name from a name erroneously given to the Salish by the Pend d'Oreille and later Euro-Americans, since the tribe never bound their children's heads on cradleboards. In 1855, Isaac I. Stevens negotiated the Hellgate Treaty at Council Grove near Missoula with 4 tribes, creating a reservation in the Jocko Valley south of Flathead Lake. Salish Chief Charlo, however, refused to move his people from their traditional home in the Bitterroot Valley until 1891, when his band resettled in the Mission Valley alongside the St. Ignatius Mission. The Flathead Allotment Act in 1904 required tribal members to claim individual 160-acre parcels, and it opened unclaimed lands to non-Indian homesteaders in 1910. In all, more than half a million acres of the most productive tribal lands were transferred to non-Indian agriculture. By the 1920s, the Salish-Kootenai people owned only a small portion of their own reservation. After the passage of the Indian Reorganization Act of 1934, a tribal council known as the Confederated Salish and Kootenai Tribes emerged to manage reservation affairs. In the 1930s, the tribal government began purchasing land, and the tribes currently own about 70 percent of the reservation. At the time of the Hellgate Treaty, the Flathead Reservation covered 20 million acres; today only 1.3 million acres remain. In the 1970s, the tribe created the Salish-Kootenai Tribal College.

Flathead Lake 123   *map 2 D-2*

Glaciers scoured out the Flathead Valley during the last ice age about 12,000 years ago. As the glaciers retreated, the Polson terminal moraine dammed up melting ice, creating Flathead Lake. In more recent history, between 1885 and 1910, steamboats traversed the length of the lake from Demersville on the north to Polson on the south, transporting passengers and freight. The lake is named for the Salish tribe, who were erroneously labeled "flathead" by the Pend d'Oreille tribe, who mistakenly thought the Salish bound their babies on cradleboards, artificially flattening the backs of their heads. Elevation: 2,896 ft.

Flathead Range 128   *map 2 C-3*

Named for the Salish tribe who occupied the reservation in the lower Flathead Valley, the Flathead Range covers an area 60 miles long, from near West Glacier through the Great Bear and Bob Marshall wilderness areas.

Flathead camp, Flathead Lake, Polson, c. 1910
MHS 957-712

Flathead River 150 *map 9 A-4*

The river is named for the Salish tribe, who were erroneously labeled "flathead" by the Pend d'Oreille tribe. The Flathead River's North Fork flows south from Canada along the western boundary of Glacier National Park; the Middle Fork forms the southern boundary of Glacier National Park; and the South Fork flows out of the Bob Marshall Wilderness. The three forks join east of Columbia Falls as the Flathead River and flow into Flathead Lake. Water leaving the lake is still the Flathead River, locally called the Lower Flathead, which joins the Clark Fork River at Paradise.

Flatwillow 920 *map 13 C-4*

Flatwillow is named for the willows that line Flatwillow Creek. According to Granville Stuart's journal, in about 1880, Pike Landusky and Jo Hamilton opened a general store at Flatwillow Crossing that drew business from Fort Maginnis and the gold miners in the Judith Mountains. When a post office was established in 1883, the name officially became Flatwillow. It later became a market town for neighboring homesteaders and ranchers. Elevation: 3,225 ft. Location: Petroleum County

Flatwillow Creek 964 *map 14 C-1*

Flatwillow Creek flows out of the Big Snowy Mountains and into the Musselshell River. John Mullan, a member of the Raynolds Expedition, which conducted a topographical survey for the U.S. Army, named this stream Yellowwater Creek in July 1860. An 1875 map included in a report by William Ludlow lists the creek as both Yellowwater Creek and Flatwillow Creek, after the willow trees that line the creek banks. In 1879, 25 families of Métis, led by Ben Kline and Francis Janeaux, settled along Flatwillow Creek. In 1885, Thomas Cruse, of Drumlummon Mine fame, purchased the land along the creek that became the famous N Bar Ranch, just north of the

Little Snowy Mountains. Location: Fergus and Petroleum counties

Flaxville 1123 *map 7 B-4*

Named for the flax grown in the region, Flaxville began in 1913 with the arrival of the Great Northern Railway's branch line from Culbertson to Scobey. The area attracted homesteaders, and agriculture sustained the community through the drought and recession of the 1920s and '30s. The 1940s were prosperous; improved roads allowed better auto transportation coupled with an increased demand for wheat. The town incorporated in 1955. Elevation: 2,780 ft. Location: Daniels County

Flesher Pass 348 *map 11 B-2*

The town of Flesher took its name from its first postmaster, Gideon Flesher, in 1902, as did the pass. The route over the pass allowed wagon traffic between Helena and the mining camps around Lincoln. Elevation: 6,131 ft. Location: Lewis and Clark County

Flint Creek 323 *map 10 D-4*

Flint Creek takes its name from the deposits of flint that the Salish used for making arrowheads. Early settlers found large deposits of flint-knapping debris at a popular campsite between what is now Maxville and Stone Station in Granite County.

Flint Creek Range 370 *map 10 D-4*

The Flint Creek Range takes its name from Flint Creek. The highest peak is Mount Powell, at 10,168 feet. The range runs north-south between the Deer Lodge Valley and the Flint Creek Valley. It is rich in silver and manganese deposits, which were developed extensively in the late 1800s and early 1900s. Manganese, critical to both World War efforts for hardening steel and for batteries, was mined near Philipsburg as late as the 1970s.

Florence 262 *map 10 C-1*

During the first decade of the twentieth century, construction of the Bitterroot Valley Irrigation Canal precipitated the emergence of an apple industry around Florence. Florence was named for Florence Abbott Hammond, the wife of Missoula businessman A. B. Hammond, who helped secure the coming of the Bitterroot Valley branch of the Northern Pacific Railway, which was instrumental in developing the area lumber industry and apple production in the 1910s. Florence was the center of a rich wheat-growing area, shipping up to 100 carloads of wheat per day during the harvest. Today Florence boasts several large ranches, farms, and fruit orchards that support the local economy. Elevation: 3,258 ft. Location: Ravalli County

Floweree 449 *map 4 E-2*

Floweree is named for Texas cattleman Daniel Floweree, who came to Montana in the 1860s gold rush. In 1873, he brought 1,500 head of cattle over the Chisholm Trail to what is now Chouteau County, where he established a large cattle and horse ranch using the F Triangle brand. The post office was established in 1910, and the town grew into a lasting community with a mercantile, a school, grain elevators, and other businesses serving the surrounding farm families. The post office closed in 2004 after 94 years of operation. Elevation: 3,223 ft. Location: Chouteau County

Forest Green 610 *map 12 C-2*

In about 1900, Homer Ward homesteaded in the area that became Forest Green. During the 1950s, the Thale Post Office was established at this location. It is unclear when and why Thale was renamed Forest Green. The community is currently a Christian resort and retreat center. Elevation: 6,088 ft. Location: Meagher County

Forestgrove 830 *map 13 B-3*

Named for the dense stands of trees in this fertile valley at the junction of Tyler, Sure Enuf, and McDonald creeks, Forestgrove, also spelled Forest Grove, began in 1885 when sheep and cattle ranchers arrived in the area. Homesteaders followed the ranchers, and by 1913 the town was home to a new public school that also served as the local community center. Elevation: 4,072 ft. Location: Fergus County

Forsyth 1098 *map 15 E-1*

Forsyth was created in 1882 when the Northern Pacific Railroad purchased part of the Thomas Alexander homestead along the Yellowstone River for a townsite and division point. The railroad named the community for Col. James Forsyth, a member of the 1875 Yellowstone Expedition, which traveled through the area. When Rosebud County was created in 1901, Forsyth became the county seat; it gained its city charter 3 years later. Although Forsyth remained a Northern Pacific town—the railroad employed 200 men there in 1907—the arrival of the Milwaukee Road that year brought thousands of homesteaders to Rosebud County, which expanded Forsyth's mercantile opportunities. In 1923, Forsyth lost the roundhouse and railroad shops, but it has remained a crew change point for the Burlington Northern Santa Fe Railway and is an important transfer point for coal from the mines at Colstrip. As such, it is one of only a handful of Montana towns whose railroad heritage remains a vibrant part of its economy. Forsyth has 2 historic districts listed in the National Register. Elevation: 2,522 ft. Location: Rosebud County

Fort Assinniboine 617 *map 5 C-1*

According to the U.S. War Dept., Fort Assinniboine was named after the Assiniboine tribe. The army added an extra "n" presumably to distinguish the fort from

Students and teacher, Fort Belknap Agency school, c. 1890
Detail, MHS 946-972

the tribe. According to a U.S War Dept. report, it was established in 1879 "for the purpose of protecting the citizens of Montana from the hostile incursions of Indian tribes dwelling in that region; and especially the Sioux who had withdrawn across the international boundary line after its victory over the U.S. troops in the Yellowstone country in 1876." Garrisoned troops were to monitor the Blackfeet, Gros Ventre, Assiniboine, Sioux, Cree, and Métis; deter raiding parties; and guard wagon trains. In addition, soldiers drilled on the parade ground, patrolled the prairies, made bricks, and put up fort buildings; during the 1880s and '90s, more than 100 buildings were built at a cost in excess of $1 million on this 220,000-acre military reserve. Fort Assinniboine troops never saw significant action, and the post, which could accommodate 746 enlisted men and officers, seldom hosted more than 500 families. Later, the fort housed some of the famous African American "buffalo soldiers" of the 10th U.S. Cavalry, whose famous Lt. John "Black Jack" Pershing earned his name while stationed here in the mid-1890s. Abandonment of the post by 1911 influenced the subsequent history of northern Montana. Demolished buildings provided the brick for construction of Pershing Hall at Montana State University–Northern; 58,000 acres of fort land became part of Rocky Boy's Indian Reservation; and another portion became an experimental station for Montana Agricultural College (now Montana State University). The fort is listed in the National Register. Elevation: 2,661 ft. Location: Hill County

Fort Belknap 783 *map 5 C-3*

In 1871, Abe Farwell, agent for Leavenworth, Kansas, trading company Durfee and Peck (Elias H. Durfee and Campbell K. Peck), constructed a fort/trading post on the south bank of the Milk River. In 1873, the U.S. government moved the administrative headquarters for the Gros Ventre and Assiniboine tribes from the old Fort Browning to this site. The new agency was named Fort Belknap, after President Grant's secretary of war, William Belknap. In 1889, with the establishment of the Fort Belknap Indian Reservation, the agency moved from the town of Fort Belknap to its current location near Harlem. Elevation: 2,376 ft. Location: Blaine County

Fort Belknap Indian Reservation 784
map 5 D-4

As a result of treaties between the U.S. government and the Assiniboine and Gros Ventre tribes, in March 1889, Congress established the Fort Belknap Indian Reservation, encompassing 1,200 square miles along the Milk River in northern Montana. The Assiniboine, or Nakoda, people had split off from the Yanktoni Sioux in the seventeenth century and traveled west into Montana, Alberta, and Saskatchewan. Gros Ventre, meaning "large belly," was the result of French-speaking fur trappers misinterpreting a sign language word. The Gros Ventres' own name for themselves is I Ah-Ah-Ne-Nin, or "White clay people." The Fort Belknap Community Council governs the reservation from tribal headquarters at Fort Belknap Agency. The tribe administers Fort Belknap College and also has an active native language immersion program. There are more than 5,000 tribal members; approximately one third of the reservation land is tribally owned. An abandoned cyanide heap-leach gold mine near the towns of Zortman and Landusky in the Little Rocky Mountains has caused significant water pollution on the reservation.

Fort Benton NHL 511 *map 4 F-2*

Maj. Alexander Culbertson of the American Fur Company established a trading post on the banks of the upper Missouri River in 1846 and named it for U.S. Senator Thomas Hart Benton, the company's congressional ally. As the demand for buffalo hides replaced beaver pelts and the gold rush began, a settlement outside the post walls catered to a new kind of traffic. Throughout the 1860s, Fort Benton's mile-long levee docked 50 steamboats a season. These boats brought prospectors, traders, and merchandise to this gateway to the Northwest and carried buffalo hides, bullion, and passengers back to "the States." Fort Benton's merchants

Grand Union Hotel, Fort Benton
MHS 947-095

sent traders laden with rifles and whiskey into Canada to siphon off the Hudson's Bay Company trade. The lawlessness that resulted brought the newly created North West Mounted Police into present-day Alberta and Saskatchewan. As the Mounties worked to curtail the whiskey and gun trade, they bought their supplies from the same Fort Benton companies. Convoys of freight wagons carried tons of food, supplies, mail, and treaty rations to Canada and returned with buffalo bones and hides, furs, wolf pelts, and coal. Fort Benton's glory, however, was short-lived. The Great Northern Railway's line from Havre to Great Falls replaced the steamboats in the 1880s, trade trails became a thing of the past, and the ambitions of the town once called the "Chicago of the Plains" faded. Fort Benton, a NHL, is the southernmost point of the Old Forts Trail. National Register listings at this county seat include the Fort Benton Historic District, the Fort Benton Bridge, the I. G. Baker House, the Chouteau County Courthouse, St. Paul's Episcopal Church, and the fully restored Grand Union Hotel. Elevation: 2,620 ft. Location: Chouteau County

Fort C. F. Smith Historic District 1071
map 22 B-2

Fort C. F. Smith, along with forts Phil Kearny and Reno in Wyoming, functioned

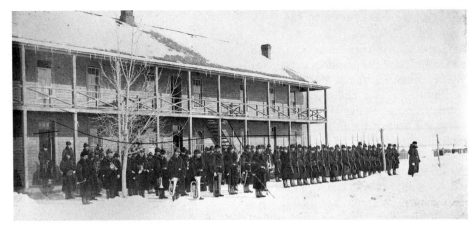

Guard mount in buffalo coats, Fort Keogh, June 1882
Detail, L.A. Huffman, photographer, MHS 981-363

as military posts to guard the Bozeman Trail wagon route that brought hundreds of emigrants to Montana Territory. Constructed by Col. Henry B. Carrington in summer 1866, the short-lived fort named for Maj. Gen. Charles Ferguson Smith was destroyed by Sioux warriors in 1868. Traces of the limestone quarry used during the fort's construction along with remnant foundations remain, and wagon ruts are still visible in the vicinity. In 1892, the soldiers' remains buried in the post cemetery were removed to the national cemetery at what was then known as the Custer Battlefield (now the Little Bighorn Battlefield National Monument). The district is listed in the National Register. Elevation: 3,265 ft. Location: Big Horn County

Fort Connah 177   *map 10 A-2*

The Hudson's Bay Company established a trading post, Fort Connah, on this site in 1847. It was the powerful company's last post built within the boundaries of the United States and represented the British effort to stave off competition from American traders west of the Continental Divide. Angus McDonald took charge of the post, naming it Fort Connen, after a river valley in his native Scotland. The Hudson's Bay Company continued to operate the post

until 1871. McDonald's son Duncan, who was born at the fort, served as its last factor. Duncan and his wife, Red Sleep (Louisa Quill), and their descendants were prominent in developing this region. They are buried in the nearby cemetery. The sole surviving fort structure, built of channeled log, is Montana's oldest standing building. The site, listed in the National Register, is under the care of the Fort Connah Restoration Society. Elevation: 2,796 ft. Location: Lake County

Fort Fizzle 237   *map 10 C-1*

Volunteers and troops from Fort Missoula under Capt. C. C. Rawn built a log barricade on this site in July 1877 in an effort to intercept Chief Joseph and the Nez Perces as they left Idaho. The Nez Perces, however, simply flanked the barricade, and from that time forward the site has been dubbed "Fort Fizzle." The USFS maintains the site, listed in the National Register, where there is a replica of the breastworks and interpretive signage. Elevation: 3,383 ft. Location: Missoula County

Fort Keogh 1138   *map 15 D-3*

Fort Keogh, the successor to the Tongue River Cantonment, was officially established in August 1876 in the few weeks following the Battle of the Little Bighorn, although materials to construct the fort did not arrive until the next year. This U.S. Army cavalry post takes its name from Capt. Myles Keogh, an adjutant general to Lt. Col. George Armstrong Custer, who died in the battle. The fort's commander was Gen. Nelson Miles, for whom Miles City was named a few years later. In 1879, Miles City became the first seat of Custer County, and the fort grew to be the largest in the territory. Sixty buildings once sprawled across the diamond-shaped grounds. In 1907, the army withdrew its infantry troops, and in 1909 the fort became a remount station where the army trained and shipped horses worldwide; more horses came from Fort Keogh during World War I than any other post. The military withdrew in 1924 and transferred the land to the U.S. Dept. of Agriculture for experimental stock raising and forage crops; this work continues today. The remains of the historic fort, listed in the National Register, include the parade ground, an 1883 wagon shed, an 1887 flagpole, and 7 other pre-1924 structures. Elevation: 2,361 ft. Location: Custer County

Fort Kipp 1167 *map 8 D-2*

Employees of the American Fur Company constructed the fur trading post in 1860, naming it for employee James Kipp. W. D. Debb, a member of the 1862 Fisk Expedition to Montana, wrote on August 14 that the wagon master described Fort Kipp as "a very bad campground—stinks like a slaughter house!" A Sioux raiding party destroyed the fort later that year. Sporadic settlement occurred in the early twentieth century as homesteaders moved into the region, prompting the opening of a post office in March 1920, but postal officials rescinded its charter in July of that year. Elevation: 1,943 ft. Location: Roosevelt County

Fort Logan 574 *map 12 C-1*

Originally built as Camp Baker in 1869 at a location nearby, the fort, named after Maj. Eugene M. Baker, moved to this site in 1870. Its purpose was to protect local miners and travelers along the Fort Benton–Helena road. The U.S. Army occupied the fort from 1870 to 1880. Its name was changed to Fort Logan in 1879, for Capt. William A. Logan, who died at the Battle of the Big Hole in 1877. The original blockhouse, officers' quarters, and other log buildings, listed in the National Register, remain visible from the road; the site is part of a working ranch and not open to the public. Elevation: 4,639 ft. Location: Meagher County

Fort Missoula 228 *map 10 C-2*

Fort Missoula, established in 1877, was the only permanent military post in Montana west of the Continental Divide. Its purpose was to control western Montana's Indian tribes and to protect settlers. Since there was little conflict in the region, however, the fort amassed a long and diverse record of noncombative service. From 1888 to 1898, it housed the African American 25th Infantry Regiment. Twenty men of the 25th explored military applications of the bicycle, riding 1,900 miles from Missoula to St. Louis in 40 days. During the Spanish-American War in 1898, volunteers known as Grigsby's Cowboys were garrisoned at the fort. Shortly thereafter, soldiers engaged in an ambitious building program, erecting 18 Mission-style buildings between 1904 and 1912; today these buildings form the core of the present complex. The fort served as a technical training center during World War I, and in the 1930s it became the nation's largest regional CCC headquarters. During World War II, it was the nation's largest civilian detention camp, interning German and Italian nationals. After the war, the fort served as a medium-security military prison until its closure in 1948. Listed in the National Register, Fort Missoula's historical museum currently occupies some of the old fort buildings; others are occupied by the Northern Rockies Heritage Center. Elevation: 3,155 ft. Location: Missoula County

Fort Owen State Park 275   *map 10   D-1*

Trader John Owen purchased Fort Owen after the Jesuit fathers who had established St. Mary's Mission in 1841 closed their doors in 1850. Owen operated and expanded St. Mary's mills, cultivated the fields, enlarged the fort, and kept a well-stocked trade room, thereby transforming the mission compound into a vibrant trading post complex. A man of many talents, Owen also served as Flathead Indian agent from 1856 to 1862. For a time, the fort served as agency headquarters, and Owen and his Shoshone wife, Nancy, created a refined and comfortable haven, extending hospitality to Indians, traders, trappers, missionaries, settlers, and travelers. With the 1860s came gold seekers and a fresh clientele, but the newly completed Mullan Road bypassed Fort Owen and trading dwindled. After Nancy's death in 1868, Owen's mental health deteriorated. In 1872, Fort Owen was sold at a sheriff's sale to Washington J. McCormick, who operated the fort's mills until 1889. In 1937, the Fort Owen site was donated to the State of Montana, and the donors sponsored stabilization and partial reconstruction of its sole remaining building, the East Barracks. Archaeological investigations initiated in 1957 by the University of Montana continued through 1980, exposing the fort's walls and foundations. Since 1971, the Stevensville Historical Society has been instrumental in interpretive reconstruction, continued stabilization, and maintenance of this noteworthy site, listed in the National Register. Elevation: 3,293 ft. Location: Ravalli County

Fort Peck 1042   *map 7   D-1*

The name Fort Peck is associated with Col. Campbell K. Peck, the partner of Elias H. Durfee in the Leavenworth, Kansas, trading firm of Durfee and Peck. In 1867, company employee Abe Farwell constructed the Fort Peck trading post along the Missouri River, which enjoyed a virtual monopoly in trade with the Sioux and Assiniboine people. After its short life as a trading post, Fort Peck served as an Indian agency from 1873 until 1878. At that time, the agency was moved to its current location at Poplar. Fort Peck had a post office from 1879 to 1881. A new town of Fort Peck, located about 2 miles north of the original, was built in 1934 to house employees involved in the construction of the Fort Peck Dam. Designed to be temporary, the government-owned town nevertheless included many features of a permanent town, including an administrative headquarters, a hospital, stores, a theater, a recreation hall, and other facilities. Totally inadequate to house the 10,000-plus employees, Fort Peck was soon joined by numerous shanty towns, including Wheeler, New Deal, Delano Heights, and Park Grove. The Fort Peck Original Houses Historic District, the Fort Peck Theatre, and the hospital, administration building, and other associated public works properties are listed in the National Register. Elevation: 2,125 ft. Location: Valley County

Fort Peck Dam and Reservoir 1047
map 7   D-2

The Fort Peck Dam represents one of the largest public works projects in U.S. history, employing more than 10,000 workers during its 6 years of construction, which began in 1934. The name Fort Peck is derived from the Fort Peck trading post built by the Leavenworth, Kansas, trading firm of Durfee and Peck in 1867. When completed in 1940, the Fort Peck Dam was recognized as the largest hydraulically filled earthen dam in the world, containing more than 125 million cubic yards of earth, 4 million cubic yards of gravel, and 1 million cubic yards of rock. In 1936, a Margaret Bourke White photograph of the spillway, designed to discharge 250,000 cubic feet of water per second, graced the very first cover of *Life* magazine. Originally built for improvement of downstream navigation, irrigation, and flood control, the dam became a major hydroelectric facility in 1943 with the completion of the first powerhouse. Listed in the National Register, the Fort Peck Reservoir, 135 miles in length, with a shoreline of 1,520 miles, has a longer coastline than California. The reservoir flooded out many of the homesteaders who had survived the drought years of the 1920s. It is currently a popular boating and fishing destination. The Fort Peck Dam Interpretive Center and Museum opened in 2005, featuring a reproduction of a *Tyrannosaurus rex* found near the dam. Elevation: 2,230 ft. Location: Valley County

Fort Peck Dam, spillway gate structure, 1939
MHS

Fort Peck Indian Reservation 1106
map 8 C-2

The Milk River Agency was established in 1870 about 15 miles from the mouth of the Milk River. In 1873, the agency moved to the abandoned Fort Peck trading post that the U.S. Office of Indian Affairs had bought from the Leavenworth, Kansas, trading firm of Durfee and Peck. The agency stayed there until 1878, when it moved to its current location at Poplar. During the late 1870s and early 1880s, many of the Sioux settled near the agency at Camp Poplar. The next few years were devastating to the tribes, due to starvation, disease, the slaughter of bison, and the severe winter of 1886–87. The modern reservation, the second-largest in the state, encompassing 3,200 square miles, was officially established in 1888. The year 1913 marked the opening of the reservation to homesteaders, under the Fort Peck Allot-

ment Act of 1908, with more than 1.3 million acres of reservation lands (roughly half the total) ultimately sold to non-Indians. Today the reservation is home to about 6,000 members: Assiniboines of the Wadapana "Canoe Paddler" and Red Bottom clans, and the Hunkpapa, Yanktonai, Sisseton, and Wahpeton Sioux. An additional 5,000-plus enrolled tribal members live off the reservation. The reservation is governed by the 15-member Tribal Executive Board under a constitution adopted about 1960. Fort Peck Community College offers 25 associate degree programs oriented toward economic opportunities in the area. The reservation, located in northeastern Montana, hosts several celebrations and pow-wows each summer.

Fort Shaw 352 *map 11 A-4*

First called Camp Reynolds, Fort Shaw is named for Col. Robert G. Shaw of Boston. The U.S. government established this fort on the Mullan Road in 1867, in the wake of Indian hostilities. The fort was home to the 13th, 7th, and 25th U.S. Infantries until it was decommissioned in 1891. The site was then used as an Indian boarding school. Between 1902 and 1906, the Fort Shaw Indian girls' basketball team won every

Fort Shaw, 25th U.S. Infantry company, 1890
Detail, C. Eugene LeMunyon, photographer, MHS 947-375

Fort Union Trading Post NHS 1216 *map 8 D-4*

In 1828, John Jacob Astor's American Fur Company established the Fort Union trading post near the confluence of the Missouri and Yellowstone rivers. In 1837, a disastrous outbreak of smallpox spread to the tribes trading there. At the end of the Civil War, the privately owned post hosted military troops engaged in combat against Red Cloud's armed resistance to the Bozeman Trail during 1866–67. In 1867, the U.S. Army bought the post and dismantled it to build nearby Fort Buford. The Fort Union Trading Post NHS has an extensive rebuilt fort and a museum. Although it is in North Dakota, the original post may have been in Montana. Elevation: 1,912 ft. Location: Montana–North Dakota state line

game but one and played in exhibition matches at the 1904 Louisiana Purchase Exposition in St. Louis, Missouri, taking home the title of "world champions." The U.S. Reclamation Service, in charge of the Fort Shaw Irrigation Project, laid out the townsite 1 mile south of the old fort in 1906. The influx of farmers brought many merchants to the area, and by the mid-1920s the new town was flourishing. The fort is listed in the National Register. Elevation: 3,504 ft. Location: Cascade County

Fort Smith 1070 *map 22 C-2*

The Crow name for this town is Annu'ucheepe, "Mouth of the canyon." The English name derives from Fort C. F. Smith, which was established in 1866 along the Bozeman Trail, 4 miles south of the present-day town. The establishment of forts C.F. Smith, Reno, Phil Kearny, and Fetterman in 1866–67 to protect the Bozeman Trail enraged the Sioux, Northern Cheyenne, and Arapaho people. Sioux warriors destroyed the fort in 1868. Elevation: 3,257 ft. Location: Big Horn County

Fort William Henry Harrison 440 *map 11 C-3*

The U.S. Army built a new military post near Helena in 1892 to take advantage of the nearby Great Northern and Northern Pacific rail lines and named the post Fort Benjamin Harrison, after the twenty-third president of the United States. (President Harrison's son, Russell, had served as head of Helena's federal assay office in the 1880s.) The post was renamed Fort William Henry Harrison in honor of Benjamin's grandfather, the ninth president of United States. By 1897, the expanded facilities included bachelor officers' quarters, a double set of noncommissioned officers' quarters, and barracks for a band. The fort remained an active army post until 1913. With the U.S. involvement in World War I, the Montana Regiment of the National Guard assembled at Fort Harrison in 1917. In 1919, the U.S. Public Health Service took over management. The 1st Special

Service Force, an elite group of Canadian and American military personnel, trained here at the start of World War II. Today the Veterans Affairs Medical and Regional Office Center based at the fort provides medical care to veterans. Elevation: 3,974 ft. Location: Lewis and Clark County

Fortine 21 *map 1 B-4*

Fortine takes its name from Octave and Phillipe Fortin (or Forten), who filed a homestead claim near this branch of the Tobacco River in the 1890s. A construction camp called Harrisburg developed on the east side of Fortine Creek when the Great Northern Railway began constructing a new main line between Whitefish and Rexford in 1903, but the railroad selected a location on the west side of the creek for its station, forcing businesses to pack up and move. Like many other towns in northwestern Montana, Fortine prospered with the development of the timber industry between 1908 and 1928. Elevation: 2,951 ft. Location: Lincoln County

Four Buttes 1097 *map 7 B-3*

Originally known as Whiskey Buttes, these 4 distinctive buttes rise "like small mountains above the surrounding rolling prairies." When the Great Northern Railway's branch line came west from Scobey in 1926, land speculator J. V. Bennett, president of the North Country Townsite and Land Company, bought the land and subdivided the original townsite. The Farmers Elevator, already in operation in August 1926, has always been a focal point of the community. Elevation: 2,483 ft. Location: Daniels County

Four Horns Lake 208 *map 3 C-1*

Built in 1911 as part of the Blackfeet Irrigation Project, Four Horns Lake receives water from Badger Creek via the Four Horns Feeder Canal. The Four Horns

Outlet Canal conveys the water some 5 miles east to irrigate about 6 square miles of farmland. The lake is stocked with rainbow trout. Elevation: 4,115 ft. Location: Glacier County

Fourchette Creek 938 *map 6 E-2*

Lewis and Clark named this creek Weiser's (or Wiser's) Creek for expedition member Peter Weiser. It was renamed Fourchette Creek about 1832, probably for the French word meaning "fork." (The creek forms a major fork with the Missouri River.) In 1870, Thomas Curry established Fort Fourchette, a trading post at Hermon Point, at the confluence, now the western end of Fort Peck Reservoir. Location: Phillips County

Fox Lake WMA 1185 *map 8 E-2*

Homesteaders settled near Fox Lake, named for the small mammal common to the area, in the early 1900s and built a post office and general store at the east end of the lake. In 1913, the town was renamed Lambert. Montana Fish, Wildlife & Parks administers the WMA, which is more a cattail-and-bulrush marsh than a true lake. Elevation: 2,346 ft. Location: Richland County

Frazer 1079 *map 7 D-2*

The St. Paul, Minneapolis & Manitoba Railway established Frazer as a station in 1888, naming it for a railroad contractor or foreman. A post office opened in 1907. By 1914, the town had a general store, meat market, lumberyard, café, grain elevator, and other businesses. The local school board and the BIA built a high school here in 1931. The town is now a grain-shipping center with several grain elevators. Elevation: 2,061 ft. Location: Valley County

Fred Robinson Bridge, Missouri River, north of Roy, 1959
MHS PAc 86-15.100-A

Frazier Creek 1052 *map 15 A-1*

Frazier Creek takes its name from Steele and John Frazer (or Frazier), early-day buffalo hunters in this central Montana region. Location: Garfield County

Fred Burr Creek (Ravalli) 293 *map 10 D-1*

Like the Fred Burr Creek in Granite County, this creek is named for Fred H. Burr, a member of the Isaac I. Stevens 1853 railroad survey and an early trader of horses and cattle in the Bitterroot Valley in 1856. Burr worked the Gold Creek placer diggings in the early 1860s and later served as Deer Lodge County sheriff. He was a member of the Constitutional Convention in 1866. Burr left Montana for Canada in 1868 and died in Washington, D.C., in the 1890s. In 1948, the State Water Conservation Board dammed Fred Burr Creek, west of Victor, creating Fred Burr Reservoir.

Fred Burr Lake 371 *map 10 D-4*

In 1889, the Fred Burr and Granite Ditch Company dammed the Fred Burr Creek (named by Granville Stuart for Fred H. Burr, an engineer with the Isaac I. Stevens 1853 railroad survey, and Stuart's brother-in-law) that runs south and east of Philipsburg, creating Fred Burr Lake to provide water to Philipsburg and Granite and their surrounding mines. Elevation: 7,641 ft. Location: Granite County

Fred Robinson Bridge 833 *map 5 E-4*

Fred Robinson homesteaded north of Wagner starting in 1912, joined the military during World War I, and returned to Malta to open an auto dealership. Robinson served as county assessor and as a state legislator from 1937 to 1959. Throughout his career he promoted the idea of a highway and bridge connecting Malta and

Lewistown. This bridge, one of the few Missouri River crossings in central Montana, was completed in 1959. Elevation: 2,248 ft. Location: Phillips County

Freezeout Lake WMA 309 *map 3 E-3*
A stage station named Camp Freezeout was established in the area in the winter of 1885–86. Several stories attribute the origin of the name: the area was so cold that nobody would stay the entire winter; freighters were stranded here during a blizzard; a stage driver froze to death here; and a type of poker game known as "freezeout" was popular at the stage stop. The surrounding area became known as Freezeout Flats and Freezeout Bench. Freezeout Lake is a Montana Fish, Wildlife & Parks WMA, created in 1953. A spectacular array of snow geese and other migrating waterfowl stop here each spring and fall. Elevation: 3,768 ft. Location: Teton County

French Gulch 485 *map 10 E-4*
French Gulch was named for a group of Canadians who staked placer-mining claims here in 1864. The gulch's trees attracted the Anaconda Company for mine timbers and for constructing the Anaconda smelters in the early 1900s. USFS director Gifford Pinchot authorized extensive logging here, and the McClure log flume was built to bring down the timber. William R. Allen, future lieutenant governor (1909–13), spent his summers here working a claim with his father. Location: Deer Lodge County

Frenchman Reservoir 962 *map 6 B-3*
In 1953, the State Water Conservation Board built a dam on Frenchman Creek, creating this irrigation reservoir. Elevation: 2,262 ft. Location: Phillips County

Frenchtown 209 *map 10 B-1*
The Salish called the valley in which Frenchtown sits Qua elth, "State of tranquility." In the late 1850s and '60s, French Canadians from Quebec and Ontario, beginning with the Louis Brun family, settled in the area. Fathers Joseph Menetrey and Urban Grassi built a log cabin church here in 1868. In 1884, the beautiful St. John the Baptist Church, with its gleaming steeple, replaced the earlier church. Today Frenchtown Pond State Park offers picnic tables and water-based recreation. Elevation: 3,044 ft. Location: Missoula County

Fresno 579 *map 4 C-4*
The Great Northern Railway in 1913 established a station stop here named for the California gold mining city. By 1916, Fresno was a thriving community of 75 people, with a post office, general store, hardware store, livery, newspaper, and other businesses. Elevation: 2,692 ft. Location: Hill County

Fresno Dam and Reservoir 586 *map 4 B-4*
The U.S. Bureau of Reclamation built this reservoir and earthen dam in 1939 as part of the Milk River Irrigation Project, to provide irrigation for area farms. Elevation: 2,572 ft. Location: Hill County

Froid 1182 *map 8 C-3*
Homesteaders began arriving along the banks of Sheep Creek and Lost Creek in 1906 and soon discovered the near-surface lignite coal. They burned it to survive the long, cold winters and established the town of Froid in 1908. Ambrose Olson named the town for an engineer he admired, and residents later discovered that the word, appropriately, meant "frigid" in French. The Great Northern Railway's branch line between Bainville and Scobey arrived at Froid in 1910, the year the town was officially platted; residents observe this date

as the official birthday of the town. Froid businesses watched with delight when the LaLonde Construction Company paved Main Street in 1959. Elevation: 2,029 ft. Location: Roosevelt County

Fromberg 1006 *map 21 B-3*

The Northern Pacific Railway constructed a spur line to the Gebo coal mines in the Clarks Fork Valley in 1898 and named the depot Fromberg, after Northern Pacific stockholder Conrad Fromberg. William Swallow, recognizing that his land near the new depot offered potential, platted a 6-block townsite in "T-town" form, with the main street perpendicular to the tracks. Referred to as the "fruit basket" of Carbon County, Fromberg grew rapidly. In 1911, residents placed a petition before the legislature to change Fromberg's name to Fordberg, as there were 6 Ford automobiles in town, more per capita, the petitioners believed, than in any of the surrounding communities. Despite the perceived abundance of cars, the depot continued to be the town's main transportation hub. Constructed by the railroad from standardized plans for "fourth class combination stations," the depot originally included a ticket office and waiting room on one end, a freight room on the other, and central living quarters for the agent. The depot served passengers and freight until 1970. It was later moved 75 feet to its present location, and the building today serves as the Clarks Fork Valley Museum. Elevation: 3,533 ft. Location: Carbon County

Froze to Death Creek 1056 *map 14 D-4*

The standard explanation for this name is that a party of Crow warriors froze to death along its banks. The more unusual story is that bachelor ranchers made a tacit agreement to "freeze to death" with unfriendliness any women who arrived, so as to maintain the harmony of this community of ranchers near Hysham. Location: Treasure County

Blackfeet in Glacier National Park, 1915
Herford T. Cowling, photographer, MHS 956-504

Galata 336 *map 4 C-1*

The Great Northern Railway made Galata, named for nearby Galata Ravine, a station on its line in 1894. In 1901, David R. McGinnis, retired immigration agent for the railroad and area homesteader, hired Kalispell civil engineer A. L. Jaqueth to plat a townsite. By 1916, the town had a population of 200 and a wide variety of businesses, including a bank and newspaper. Elevation: 3,110 ft. Location: Toole County

Galen 436 *map 11 E-1*

This site began in 1912 as the Montana State Tuberculosis Sanitarium and was named for Montana's attorney general, Albert J. Galen. The sanitarium traced its origins to Jim McNally, a Butte carpenter and progressive state legislator, who introduced the bill to establish the facility one year after his brother died of "miner's lung." Soon after the site was selected, the Anaconda Company donated $35,000 toward the sanitarium's construction, and the first miner arrived for treatment in 1913. As the incidence of tuberculosis declined, the hospital began treating respiratory diseases and drug and alcohol abuse and handled transfer patients from Warm Springs State Hospital. Galen closed its doors as a state hospital in 1993, and the State Land Board sold the 80-acre, 28-building campus to Anaconda–Deer Lodge County in 1998. Nine of the original hospital buildings still stand, forming part of the Montana State Tuberculosis Sanitarium Historic District. Elevation: 4,756 ft. Location: Deer Lodge County

Gallatin County 773 *map 20 B-2*

Gallatin County, along with the river and mountain range of the same name, is named after Albert Gallatin, Thomas Jefferson's secretary of the treasury. One of the original counties approved by the territorial legislature in February 1865,

Gallatin County over the years transferred land to all its neighbors. Bozeman is the county seat, and agriculture and Montana State University–Bozeman dominate the county's economy.

Gallatin Gateway 761 *map 20 B-1*

Zachariah Sales, a lumberman from Wisconsin, came over the Bozeman Trail by wagon train in 1865 and settled with his family near the entrance of Gallatin Canyon. Sales soon established a sawmill here, and as more families arrived in the Gallatin Valley, a small community grew up around Sales's sawmill. Locals called the settlement Slabtown, for the sawmill, but in 1883 changed the name to Salesville, for its owner. In 1928, locals permanently changed the name to Gallatin Gateway, a year after the Milwaukee Road built the elegant Gallatin Gateway Inn to accommodate visitors traveling to and from Yellowstone National Park. Elevation: 4,961 ft. Location: Gallatin County

Gallatin Gateway Inn 760 *map 20 B-1*

In 1927, the Milwaukee Road built a spur line from Three Forks to this site, with the idea of building a hotel that could serve as an interim stop or a home base for Yellowstone National Park visitors. Designed by Seattle architects Schack, Young and Myers, the fabulous inn opened on June 27, 1927, creating the county's first traffic jam and even overshadowing Lindbergh's flight across the Atlantic. On opening day, 10,000 people enjoyed lunch and 2,000 attended a gala ball that evening. The Spanish Colonial Revival–style hotel featured skillfully landscaped grounds, Philippine mahogany finish work and beamed ceilings, and a grand ballroom and dining room with narrow oak flooring and stone fireplaces. The kitchen, hailed a "marvel of modern machinery," included the latest technology as well as a device that cut blocks of ice into cubes that perfectly

Gallatin Gateway Inn, 1930s
MHS 947-480

fit the water glasses on the dining room tables. Within the next decade, however, as buses and automobiles replaced trains, many tourists went directly to the park without an interim stop, and the inn fell into disrepair and changed hands several times. Now extensively refurbished and listed in the National Register, the Gallatin Gateway Inn is again a gracious, full-service hotel. Elevation: 4,941 ft. Location: Gallatin County

Gallatin Range 812 *map 20 B-1*

This mountain range forms the divide between the Gallatin and Yellowstone river drainages and takes its name from the Gallatin River. Several peaks exceed 10,000 feet, including Electric, Ramshorn, and Hyalite. The north end of the range near Bozeman is popular for hiking because of its numerous waterfalls. Capt. William Clark designated the range the Snow Mountains on July 15, 1806.

Gallatin River 657 *map 20 B-1*

The Gallatin River combines with the Madison and Jefferson rivers to form the Missouri River at Three Forks. On July 28, 1805, Lewis and Clark named it for Secretary of the Treasury Albert Gallatin. The range, valley, and canyon, and the town of Gallatin City, all later took their names from the river, which originates in the extreme northwest corner of Yellowstone National Park and flows generally northward to Three Forks. The canyon portion of the river is popular for white-water rafting.

Gardiner 892 *map 20 C-2*

In 1870, the Washburn-Langford-Doane party, exploring the area that became Yellowstone National Park, named this area Gardiner. It had been known by early trappers as Gardner's Hole, after Johnson Gardner, who trapped in the Yellowstone region in 1831–32. The town was established in 1880 and began thriving as the park's northern entrance. In addition, in 1883 gold was discovered northeast of town, up Bear Gulch. Prosperity increased when the Northern Pacific Railway extended its branch line from Cinnabar to Gardiner in 1903. That same year, on April 24, Theodore Roosevelt attended the ceremony to mark the placement of the cornerstone of the Roosevelt Arch, which was designed to act as the gate to the park's northern entrance. Constructed of basalt, it stands 50 feet tall and 20 feet wide and is inscribed "For the Benefit and Enjoyment of All People," a line from the congressional act that created the park. The Northern Pacific line operated until 1976, when it was discontinued and the tracks dismantled. Today Gardiner bustles with tourist activity as a year-round entrance to Yellowstone National Park. Elevation: 5,226 ft. Location: Park County

Garfield County 1032 *map 14 A-3*

Named for the twentieth U.S. president, James A. Garfield, the county was created in 1919, with Jordan its seat of government. In the heart of "Big Dry Country" south of Fort Peck Reservoir, it's one of the least populated places in the nation, with approximately 0.4 resident per square mile.

Garneill 772 *map 13 C-1*

The history of Garneill is actually the history of Ubet and Garneill. Ubet sat on the Carroll Trail and at the crossroads of the Helena–Fort Benton and Billings–Great Falls roads. It received its name from A. R. Barrows, who, when asked if his place was the stage station and could accommodate travelers for the night, briefly replied, "You bet." When he applied for a post office in 1881, Barrows shortened his standard response to Ubet. In 1891, Frank Hassett platted and sold town lots near the Ubet school. He named this community Garneill in honor of the first couple to marry in the town—Garnette Currier and W. T. Neill. Being temperance-minded, Hassett sold lots with the proviso that if a business ever sold alcohol, the land would revert back to him. In response, civic-minded Ed Beach gave a piece of his land south of the townsite for the construction of a saloon. This resulted in the establishment of South Garneill. When the Montana Railway Company built its line, locally called the "Jawbone Railroad," through the area in 1903, it put a station a quarter mile west of Garneill and named it Ubet in honor of the old stage station. Businesses and the school relocated next to the rail line, and residents successfully petitioned the railroad to name the station Garneill. Elevation: 4,426 ft. Location: Fergus County

Garnet 285 *map 10 C-3*

The area's first placer-gold discovery took place near Garnet in 1865, but the rush that created the town did not start until 1895. Originally named Mitchell, for stamp mill manager A. H. Mitchell, the boomtown's name changed in 1897 to Garnet, for the semiprecious red stone found in the surrounding mountains. The highest gold-producing mine at Garnet took its name from Abraham Lincoln's mother, Nancy Hanks. The rush ended by 1905, and though there was a brief resurgence in the 1930s, by 1942 Garnet had withered into a ghost town. The site is co-managed by the BLM and the Garnet Preservation Association. Elevation: 5,916 ft. Location: Granite County

Mail stage at post office, Main Street, Garnet, 1899
MHS 947-521

Garnet Range 299 *map 10 C-4*

This mountain range in west-central Montana is named for the garnet, a semiprecious red stone that formed when magma penetrated Madison limestone. The range is better known for significant gold deposits found at Garnet, Coloma, and Beartown.

Garrison 367 *map 11 D-1*

Garrison is definitely a town at the crossroads—it developed at the junction of the Northern Pacific Railroad and the Montana Union Railroad and today is at the junction of highways leading to Helena, Butte, and Missoula. Some sources suggest that Northern Pacific president Henry Villard named Garrison in 1883 after his father-in-law, William Lloyd Garrison, the abolitionist editor of the *Liberator* newspaper. With the railroad's decline and the bypassing of the town by I-90, Garrison experienced its own decline in population

and importance. Elevation: 4,369 ft. Location: Powell County

Garryowen 1090 *map 22 B-3*

Settled shortly after the famous battle at the Little Bighorn, Garryowen is named for the Irish marching tune adopted by Custer's 7th Cavalry. Today it is a mostly Crow community on the Crow Indian Reservation. Elevation: 3,119 ft. Location: Big Horn County

Gates of the Mountains Wilderness 377 *map 11 C-3*

Congress designated this 29,000-acre wilderness in the Big Belt Mountains bordering the Missouri River in the Wilderness Act of 1964. Capt. Meriwether Lewis named the towering limestone cliffs along the upper Missouri River "the gate of the rocky mountains" on July 19, 1805.

Gebo 998   *map 21 B-3*

Named after Sam Gebo, who opened the first coal mines here, Gebo enjoyed prosperity between 1899 and 1912, its population peaking at 1,000. The town in its heyday included a drugstore, café, boardinghouse, confectionery, laundry, barbershop, post office, newspaper, and 5 bars. The mines closed in 1912 after the discovery of better grades of coal at Bearcreek and Red Lodge and as the result of long-term disputes over ownership of the Gebo operation. Gebo was nearly abandoned; most of its residents moved to Fromberg and took many of Gebo's buildings with them. Only a few residents remained in Gebo into the Great Depression. In 1987, the remaining buildings, foundations, mine adits, and cisterns were razed for public safety. However, the Gebo cemetery overlooking the mines is still intact and is listed in the National Register. Some 200 graves are marked with wooden or iron crosses, or granite tombstones. Elevation: 3,754 ft. Location: Carbon County

Geiger Lake 36   *map 1 D-2*

Geiger Lake is named for John H. Geiger, a Libby-area rancher and state legislator who arrived in Montana Territory in 1879 and hauled freight from Fort Benton to Missoula in those early years. Elevation: 4,745 ft. Location: Lincoln County

Georgetown 393   *map 10 E-4*

Named for prospector George Cameron, Georgetown began as a placer-mining camp in Georgetown Flats in 1867. The placers played out in less than 10 years. Some miners attempted quartz mining, but the low-grade ore made these ventures unprofitable. Most residents abandoned the town by 1886. With the completion of the Montana Water, Electric Power & Mining Company's dam on Flint Creek in 1901, Georgetown disappeared under the waters of Georgetown Lake. The current

town is just east of the lake. The old Butte, Anaconda & Pacific Railway grade passes just south of the town. Elevation: 6,537 ft. Location: Deer Lodge County

Georgetown Lake 384   *map 10 E-3*

The dam that flooded Georgetown Flats and created Georgetown Lake was begun in the early 1890s by the Flint Creek Electric Power Company and completed in 1901 by the Montana Water, Electric Power & Mining Company, a subsidiary of the Granite-BiMetallic Consolidated Mining Company of Philipsburg. Wooden flumes carried the water down the canyon to the powerhouse, which generated electricity with Pelton water wheels. In 1907, the owners sold the plant to Amalgamated Copper Company, the parent corporation of the Anaconda Company. Georgetown Lake is a popular recreational destination for residents of Butte, Anaconda, and Philipsburg. Elevation: 6,403 ft. Location: Granite and Deer Lodge counties

Geraldine 598   *map 12 A-4*

Originating as a depot on the Milwaukee Road, this town is named for Geraldine Rockefeller, wife of one of the railroad's owners. Among the town's founders were William and Abbie Welch, the first merchants, and Jack Phelan and Ed Fuller, all of whom had journeyed to the area by Model T Ford from Lewistown to lay out the townsite in 1913. Workers put the finishing touches on the depot, the only custom-built one on the central branch, and townsfolk christened the building in 1914 with a gala New Year's Eve dance. Its hardwood maple floors were pronounced "splendid." The "rustic bungalow of the California pattern" featured 2 waiting rooms, a ticket room, a freight room with scales embedded in the floor, nickel-trimmed hot-blast stoves, and a ventilating system that changed the air every 5 minutes. Geraldine was a busy stopover, serving 2 daily passenger trains and freight crews. Passenger service ended in 1955 and, after the Milwaukee Road's demise in 1980, salvage companies removed the rails from the Great Falls–Geraldine section. The nonprofit Geraldine Historical Committee acquired the depot in 1995; it is listed in the National Register. Elevation: 3,133 ft. Location: Chouteau County

Geyser 599 *map 12 B-3*

Searching for stray horses in 1881, George Hay happened on some strangers mapping a stage route between Great Falls and Lewistown. They were looking for a place to build a stage station, and Hay showed them some mud springs nearby. The men pushed a 20-foot pole into one of the springs, and when they pulled it out, a spout of water and mud followed. One of the men called this a "geyser," and that became the name of the new stage station. P. J. O'Hara, considered the father of Geyser, started a hotel here in 1887, and other businesses soon followed. The Great Northern Railway's branch line between Belt and Lewistown, built in 1908, missed the town, and residents abandoned the site to move closer to the railroad, marking the birth of the "new" Geyser. Offers of free land enticed homesteaders, mostly Finns, to the area during Montana's homestead era. During the dry 1930s, the "mud geysers" became active, then inexplicably dried up when the rains returned. Elevation: 4,187 ft. Location: Judith Basin County

Giant Springs State Park 433 *map 12 A-1*

On June 18, 1805, Capt. William Clark encountered "the largest fountain or Spring I ever Saw, and doubt if it is not the largest in America Known." Later, E. V. Smalley, a publicity man for the Great Northern Railway, named the spring Giant Springs during a visit sponsored by Paris Gibson. Aptly named, the spring sends forth more than 380 million gallons daily. In 1888, the

Montana Smelting and Refining Company capitalized on the water source for its smelting operations, building a large complex to process silver and lead. The smelter closed in 1901 and lay in ruins until 1928, when the city of Great Falls razed the buildings. The Springs were known for pure, cool waters and were tapped for a trout hatchery created by the Montana Fish and Game Commission in 1922. The 117-acre Giant Springs State Park was created in 1977. The Roe River connects the springs to the Missouri River. Elevation: 3,251 ft. Location: Cascade County

Gibson Reservoir 241 *map 3 E-1*

In 1926, the U.S. Bureau of Reclamation began constructing Gibson Reservoir's 200-foot-high concrete dam. Completed in 1929, the 6-mile-long reservoir can irrigate as much as 100,000 acres of the Greenfields Irrigation District. The dam and reservoir took the name of Great Falls's founder, Paris Gibson, a Minneapolis entrepreneur and agricultural promoter. Elevation: 4,725 ft. Location: Lewis and Clark County

Gildford 523 *map 4 C-3*

In 1910, homesteaders established the town of Gildford (named for Guildford, England) a mile east of Dayton, which had begun as a general mercantile at the Sage Creek crossing. Joe Casey wrote in the *Gildford Times*: "Gildford is a town that can do nothing but grow and prosper for it lies in the middle of over 800,000 acres of highly productive chocolate loam soil which has no known productive limitations." G. F. Mundy built a flour mill at Gildford in 1915 and milled Golden Grain Flour, marketed along the High Line until the mill closed in 1951. Elevation: 2,832 ft. Location: Hill County

Gilman 290 *map 11 A-2*

In 1912, Great Northern Railway officials decided to build a branch line up the Sun River Valley to tap that rich agricultural region. They chartered the Gilman Townsite Company, named after company officer L. C. Gilman. After intense rivalry between the new town of Gilman and the nearby community of Augusta, Gilman was selected as the western terminus of the line. Many businesses, including a bank, moved from Augusta to Gilman. However, with the failure of the Gilman State Bank in 1923, the town withered and died. Now the only thing left of Gilman is Abraham Lincoln Bradley's abandoned brick bank building. Elevation: 4,018 ft. Location: Lewis and Clark County

Giltedge 806 *map 13 B-2*

W. E. "Limestone" Wilson discovered gold in the vicinity of Giltedge about 1883. He named his mine the Gilt Edge because the ore was contained in a rim encircling a ridge. The Gilt Edge produced little ore until the Giltedge Mining Company built a cyanide mill in 1893. The mill, the first of its type in the nation, produced profitably for about a year, but by January 1894 the company was in deep debt. To avoid the confiscation of processed ore to pay on this debt, company manager Robert A. Ammon directed an employee to escape with $25,000 in bullion, ahead of the sheriff. The mine and mill later reopened, and Giltedge reached its zenith about 1906; it had a large miners' boardinghouse, a 2-story school, and numerous business establishments. The mines shut down about 1912, and the town declined. Elevation: 4,496 ft. Location: Fergus County

Glacier County 172 *map 3 B-2*

Created in 1919 from Teton County, Glacier County received its name because of its location on the eastern side of Glacier National Park. The bulk of the Blackfeet Indian Reservation lies within this county, which reaches to the Canadian border; the seat of government is Cut Bank.

Glacier National Park 90 *map 2 B-3*

Congress established Glacier National Park in 1910, after years of effort by George Bird Grinnell and others to preserve this unique northern Montana area from development by miners, homesteaders, and tourist entrepreneurs. The Great Northern Railway, led by Louis Hill, son of James J. Hill, lobbied for creation of the park with an eye to developing a series of luxury hotels there along its main line to the West Coast. The portion of the park east of the Continental Divide, in Glacier County, had been removed from the Blackfeet Indian Reservation in the 1890s in the interest of opening exploration for copper ore. In 1900, most of the area that became the park was designated a forest reserve, closed to settlement but open to mining and logging.

Great Northern Railway train and Mount Nyack, Glacier National Park, 1966
MHS

Glacier National Park Great Northern Railway Buildings NHL 92 *map 2 B-3*

Glacier National Park contains more than 350 structures listed in the National Register and several NHLs. These include ranger stations, hotels, lookouts, cabins, camps, roads, and homesteads. Great Northern Railway chairman Louis Hill dubbed the rugged mountains of Glacier National Park "America's Alps." Between 1909 and 1915, the railroad constructed 5 building complexes in the Swiss Chalet style. Belton Chalet was the first of the hotels, built in 1910–11. The other 4 are the Granite Park Chalet, Many Glacier Hotel, Sperry Chalet, and Two Medicine Chalet. These latter 4 buildings as a group have been designated a NHL. Location: Glacier National Park

Glasgow 1031 *map 7 D-1*

This town grew up near a railroad siding named by the Great Northern Railway around 1887 for the city in Scotland. The opening of the Fort Peck Indian Reservation to homesteaders in 1910 and the Milk River Irrigation Project lured a large number of homesteaders to the area, ensuring Glasgow's growth as a supply center. Construction of Fort Peck Dam in the late 1930s brought a flood of 10,000 workers and their families, invigorating Glasgow's economy during the otherwise bleak days of the Great Depression. The U.S. Army established an airbase north of Glasgow during World War II, which grew dramatically in the mid-1950s. In 1955, the U.S. Air Defense Command reactivated the base as part of the nation's defenses against Soviet bombers. It became a Strategic Air Command unit in 1960 and was staffed by 3,500 military personnel by the early 1960s. Glasgow's post office and courthouse are listed in the National Register. Elevation: 2,096 ft. Location: Valley County

Glasgow Air Force Base 1035 *map 7 C-1*

The origins of the Glasgow Air Force Base date from 1942, when satellite airdromes were established at Glasgow, Lewistown, and Cut Bank. B-17 Flying Fortresses were based at the Glasgow facility. With the end of the war, the base was deactivated. In 1955, the U.S. Air Defense Command established the Glasgow Air Force Base as a defense against Soviet bombers potentially carrying atomic bombs. The base was taken over by the Strategic Air Command in 1960, and enlarged to accommodate B-52 bombers. Three years later, the base was expanded to Wing strength and hosted the 91st Bombardment Wing and the 13th Fighter Interceptor Squadron. Beginning in 1964, the Dept. of Defense attempted to phase out the base but was met by vigorous opposition from the city of Glasgow and the Montana congressional delegation. The base eventually closed in 1968; numerous attempts have been made to find a viable commercial use for the property, including as a Boeing test flight facility. Elevation: 2,749 ft. Location: Valley County

Glaston Lakes 854 *map 13 E-1*

Upper and Lower Glaston lakes are named for William, James, John, and Alex Glass, who in 1904 formed the Glass Brothers Land Company. In 1908, the company reorganized, with partner Frank Lindsay, as the Glass-Lindsay Land Company and contracted with the state Carey Land Act Board to build several reservoirs and irrigation canals as part of the Big Timber Project. In addition to 2 reservoirs, the company built about 35 miles of canals to transport water to irrigate sugar beets and fruit. The project was completed about 1915. Elevation: 4,659 ft. Location: Sweet Grass County

Glen 629 *map 19 B-1*

Glen started out in 1878 as Willis Station, named for Ozias Willis, the first postmaster. When the Utah & Northern Railway came through in 1880, the name was shortened to Willis. Willis became Reichle in 1913, when Margaret Reichle took over the post office, and, finally, Glen, in about 1950, reflecting its position nestled in the Big Hole River Valley. Elevation: 4,990 ft. Location: Beaverhead County

Glen Lake 18   map 1 A-4

The name Glen comes from a USGS engineer who surveyed in the area. In 1915, the Glen Lake Irrigation Ditch tapped the lake to supply water to farmers and ranchers throughout the Tobacco Valley. Elevation: 2,960 ft. Location: Lincoln County

Glendale Smelter 577   map 19 A-1

The Hecla Consolidated Mining Company of Indianapolis, Indiana, built a smelter at Glendale in 1877 to process the gold ore mined at the company's Hecla Mine and others. The site included a 10-stamp mill, leaching works, furnaces, copper refinery, concentrator, and tramway. Burned in 1880, it was rebuilt that same year but closed in 1886. According to one source, the name was chosen by tossing a piece of paper in the air with the name Glendale on one side and Clinton on the other. Elevation: 5,727 ft. Location: Beaverhead County

Glendive 1198   map 16 B-2

In 1856, Sir George Gore, a British nobleman, hunted along a creek in the vicinity of present-day Glendive and named it for a stream in his native Ireland. As the Northern Pacific Railroad approached in 1880, the Yellowstone Land & Colonization Company platted the community;

Glendale Smelter, 1880
MHS 947-691

the first train arrived in the new town of Glendive (named after the creek) on July 5, 1881. The Montana territorial legislature had created Dawson County in 1869 but had not named a county seat, instead placing it administratively under Meagher County. In September 1881, citizens of Glendive petitioned to have the new county more formally organized and to designate Glendive the county seat. As it grew, Glendive became the marketing center for eastern Montana's cattle industry, and later for its sugar beet and grain farms. Glendive is home to Dawson Community College and is adjacent to Makoshika State Park. The Merrill Avenue Historic District, Glendive's commercial area, is listed in the National Register. Elevation: 2,061 ft. Location: Dawson County

Glendive Creek 1200   map 16 B-2

According to local lore, Sir George Gore, a wealthy British nobleman, camped beside this stream during an 1856 hunting expedition. Gore's retinue included 40 men, 112 horses, 12 yokes of oxen, 6 wagons, and 21 carts. The setting inspired the name Glendale, after a stream in Ireland. Over time, the name became Glendive Creek. Location: Dawson County

Glengarry 770   *map 13 B-1*
Glengarry received its name as a gesture of thanks from surveyors for the Montana Central Railway. In 1902, homesteader Angus McMillan opened his home to a 2-man survey crew, rescuing them from the wintry winds. They stayed at the McMillan place for 14 months, using it as a base while they surveyed the rail line. When the surveyors' superintendent decided to build the depot and townsite a mile east of McMillan's homestead, he asked Angus where he was born. McMillan told him Glengarry, Ontario, Canada. The new Montana town became Glengarry; the first train arrived in 1902. Elevation: 4,131 ft. Location: Fergus County

Glentana 1043   *map 7 B-2*
A community meeting in about 1910 brought forth this name, combining a nearby glen with the last 4 letters of "Montana." The Glentana post office opened in 1913 with William J. O'Connor as postmaster. In the late 1910s, the town boasted a variety of businesses, including 2 banks, a newspaper, a hardware store, and a saloon. During summer 1926, the whole town was moved nearer the Great Northern Railway's branch line between Scobey and Opheim. Elevation: 3,085 ft. Location: Valley County

Going-to-the-Sun Road NHL 100   *map 2 B-2*
A 48-mile road crossing the Continental Divide, the Going-to-the-Sun Road opened the alpine interior of Glacier National Park to automobile traffic and brought increasing numbers of tourists into the park. Survey of the mountainous route began in 1917, and by 1925 a total of 28.5 miles had been completed, including tunnels through solid rock. During the early 1930s, the CCC did much of the work. On July 15, 1933, with much fanfare, the NPS opened the road. Park officials named the road for Going-to-the-Sun Mountain, which in turn had been named in the mid-1880s by George Bird Grinnell and Tail Feathers Coming Over the Hill, a member of the Blackfeet tribe. Location: Glacier National Park

Gold Butte 325   *map 4 B-1*
Gold was first discovered in the Sweet Grass Hills by the Blackfeet in the 1860s. It was not until 1884, however, that a number of placer miners, in violation of the law, entered the Blackfeet Indian Reservation to prospect for gold on Middle Butte, the most central of the 3 buttes that form the Sweet Grass Hills. The butte and nearby town were known interchangeably as Middle Butte and Gold Butte, until the town acquired a post office in 1895 under the name Gold Butte, for the Gold Butte Mining Company. During World War I, the Anaconda Company explored the area for oil and gas, and during the 1930s, the town was the center of dredge-mining activities. Years of controversy have marked proposed new exploration in this area, which has long been sacred to the Blackfeet and other Montana tribes. In response to the mining threat, the Blackfeet tribe has initiated efforts to have the Sweet Grass Hills declared a world heritage site. Elevation: 6,412 ft. Location: Toole County

Gold Creek 351   *map 10 D-4*
French/Iroquois fur trader François Finlay, "Benetsee," is credited with first finding gold in 1852 along what was then called Benetsee Creek. Six years later, Granville and James Stuart arrived in the area and began prospecting for gold. They renamed the stream American Fork. In 1862, residents named the settlement Gold Creek. It briefly prospered but in 1863 was abandoned when richer gold discoveries were made at Grasshopper Creek and Alder

Gulch. In September 1883, the Northern Pacific Railroad marked the completion of the transcontinental line with the Last Spike ceremony at Gold Creek. The railroad established a station named Gold Creek, ten miles west of Garrison Junction, in 1888. Gold continued to play an important role in the area. Five miles up Gold Creek, the town of Pioneer, established by placer miners in the 1860s, became the site of massive dredge mining during the early twentieth century. Elevation: 4,190 ft. Location: Powell County

Golden Valley County 881 *map 13 D-3*
Established in October 1920 from the northern part of Sweet Grass County and the western part of Musselshell County, Golden Valley County was so named because boosters thought the name would draw more homesteaders to this county in central Montana. Ryegate is the county seat.

Granite 365 *map 10 D-4*
The discovery of silver on Granite Mountain in 1872 prompted development around the mines and stamp mill. By 1890, the population of Granite had swelled to 3,000, making it the state's eleventh-largest city. The stone-and-brick Miners' Union Hall functioned as the social center. When the silver market crashed in 1893, so did Granite. The mines experienced a brief recovery between 1898 and 1905, before the low price of silver forced closure of the mines once again, and another revival in 1910 when they started producing manganese. Today Granite is one of Montana's most popular ghost towns and a state park, Granite Ghost Town State Park. Elevation: 7,072 ft. Location: Granite County

Granite County 334 *map 10 C-4*
The Montana legislature named Granite County, formed in 1893 from a portion of Deer Lodge County, for the predominant rock in the surrounding mountains, rich in gold and silver ore. Granite Mountain, the town of Granite, and the Granite Mountain Mining Company share the name. The county seat is Philipsburg.

Granite County mines 363 *map 10 D-4*
The Philipsburg-Granite area was one of the richest mining areas in the state. Philip Deidesheimer, for whom Philipsburg is named, arrived in the area in 1864 as a representative of the St. Louis & Montana Mining Company. Among the early mines were the Hope, BiMetallic, Granite Mountain, and Algonquin mines. Although the Philipsburg-Granite area produced some gold, it was best known for its silver. The mines fell victim to the silver crash of 1893, which was linked to the repeal of the Sherman Silver Purchase Act, but in the 1910s they again became productive, supplying manganese for military use during World War I. Location: Granite County

Granite Mountain Mine 366 *map 11 E-1*
The Granite Mountain Mine was opened in Butte in 1887 by the Boston & Montana Consolidated Copper and Silver Mining Company, owned by the Lewisohn brothers of Boston. They sold the mine to the North Butte Mining Company in 1909. On June 9, 1917, it was the site of a deadly fire that killed 168 men, known as the Granite Mountain–Speculator Mine fire, since the smoke vented out the nearby Speculator Mine shaft. To this day, it remains the nation's deadliest hard rock mining disaster. The mine reopened and operated sporadically until 1944. Elevation: 7,408 ft. Location: Silver Bow County

Granite Peak 951 *map 21 C-1*
There are 2 Granite Peaks in Park County. The better known, named by the USFS for the gigantic granite formations that shape it, is in the heart of the Absaroka-Beartooth

Wilderness northeast of Cooke City. The highest peak in the state, at 12,799 feet, it was rated by *Backpacker Magazine* as one of the toughest peaks to climb in the lower 48 states. In August 1923, Elers Koch became the first white man to climb the peak. The other Granite Peak is between Crazy Peak and Conical Peak in the Crazy Mountains. Elevation: 12,799 ft. Location: Park County

Grannis 809 *map 20 A-3*

Also called Grannis Crossing, Grannis takes its name from Thirza Grannis, who granted the right-of-way for the Shields River Valley Railway, the Northern Pacific Railway's Shields River branch line to Wilsall. Grannis operated as a station from 1909 until the abandonment of passenger service in the early 1970s. Elevation: 4,479 ft. Location: Park County

Grant 700 *map 18 C-4*

The tiny community of Grant, in Horse Prairie Valley, acquired a post office in 1899. It is named in honor of Ulysses S. Grant, eighteenth president of the United States. Elevation: 5,812 ft. Location: Beaverhead County

Grant-Kohrs Ranch NHS and NHL 404 *map 11 D-1*

Johnny Grant, son of Richard Grant, the Hudson's Bay Company factor at Fort Hall, acquired horses and cattle in trade with immigrants along the Oregon Trail and brought them to the Deer Lodge Valley in 1859. He settled on this site in 1861. Grant sold the property to Conrad Kohrs in 1867, and Kohrs's operation shipped between 8,000 and 10,000 head of cattle to market every year. Ownership of the working ranch remained in the Kohrs family, through grandson Conrad Warren, until the 1970s. The NPS began restoration in 1974, and today the site preserves all aspects of a working cattle ranch on the frontier. Elevation: 4,520 ft. Location: Powell County

Grantsdale 324 *map 10 E-1*

Grantsdale started out with an unusual name in 1872. The first residents named the post office after nearby Skalkaho Creek, which empties into the Bitterroot River near Hamilton. According to the "English-Flathead Dictionary" compiled by Father Urban Grassi, that name is a combination of *skalkalen* ("beaver") and *kalalko* ("green wood"), with the literal translation "place of beaver." H. H. Grant, a miller, moved to the Bitterroot Valley in 1884 and settled near Skalkaho, where he purchased land and a gristmill. As the mill prospered and the settlement grew, Grant referred to it as "the Dale." Henry Chambers, who lived nearby, moved the Skalkaho post office to his residence in 1886. In 1888, Carl T. Jones platted the townsite for Grant, and residents began calling it Grantsdale after the town's benefactor and founder. Elevation: 3,678 ft. Location: Ravalli County

Grass Range 871 *map 13 B-3*

A stage station on the Fort Maginnis–Junction City road named by Frank Chamberlain in the 1870s, Grass Range sat in the middle of the Judith Basin open-range cattle country, the stomping grounds of cowboy artist Charlie Russell and prominent cattleman Granville Stuart. The post office opened in 1883, and in 1889 James Charters began operating a general store here. Elevation: 3,483 ft. Location: Fergus County

Grasshopper Creek 704 *map 19 C-1*

Lewis and Clark named this stream Willard's Creek for expedition member Alexander Hamilton Willard. It became Montana Territory's most famous creek when John White discovered gold along its

Grasshopper Glacier, 1898
Anders B. Wilse, photographer, MHS 957-474

banks on July 9, 1862, setting off Montana's first major gold rush. Miners renamed the creek for the hordes of insects on its banks. A sign near the mouth of the creek at Bannack read: "Tu grass Hop Per diggins 30 myle Kepe the Trale nex the bluffe." Location: Beaverhead County

Grasshopper Glacier 946 *map 20 C-4*
USGS mining engineer J. P. Kimball first scientifically described Grasshopper Glacier in the early 1900s, naming it for the thousands of frozen grasshoppers embedded in the ice. In 1914, a government entomologist determined them to be migrating Rocky Mountain locusts (*Melanoplus spretus*) that had been caught in a blizzard hundreds of years ago. With climate warming melting the glacier, the grasshoppers have been disintegrating as they thaw. A second Grasshopper Glacier lies several miles to the east. Elevation: 10,678 ft. Location: Park County

Gravelly Range 827 *map 19 D-3*
The Gravelly Range, on the west side of the Madison Valley, is named for the deposits of coarse gravels found here. The basement rock in the western part of the range contains marble and one of North America's largest deposits of talc, an industrial mineral used by the ceramics, paper, paint, and cosmetics industries. The highest point is 10,545-foot Black Butte. Location: Madison and Beaverhead counties

Gray Wolf Lake 205 *map 10 A-2*
Gray Wolf Lake (also spelled Grey Wolf) is named for the plentiful wolves and wolverines that roamed the area in the early days. The name may also be a translation of an unknown Salish word. A 1923 sketch map by Theodore Shoemaker labels it Dumbbell Lake. Nestled high in the Mission Mountains, the lake is the source of the Swan River. Elevation: 6,654 ft. Location: Missoula County

Great Bear Wilderness 162 *map 2 D-4*
Following decades of effort by local conservationists and sportsmen to protect this area, Congress formally designated it the Great Bear Wilderness in 1978. Among the key advocates were grizzly bear researchers Frank and John Craighead and *Missoulian* reporter Dale Burk. The name was chosen to honor the native grizzly bear. The 285,771-acre wilderness is part of the Bob Marshall Wilderness Complex, consisting of the Great Bear Wilderness, the Bob Marshall Wilderness, and the Scapegoat Wilderness. Together, the wilderness complex protects most of the Continental Divide from Lincoln to Glacier National Park.

Great Falls 423 *map 12 A-1*
Recognizing the potential for hydroelectric power from the Great Falls of the Missouri, Paris Gibson, with the assistance of railroad magnate James J. Hill, acquired title to the land east and south of the river for a townsite, which he platted and named

Black Eagle Falls of the Missouri River, Great Falls, 1892
Detail, C. E. LeMunyon, photographer, MHS 949-532

Great Falls in 1884. Gibson demonstrated great vision when he created broad avenues and set aside large parcels of land for future city parks. Hill's St. Paul, Minneapolis & Manitoba Railway arrived in 1887. Gibson became the first mayor when Great Falls incorporated in 1888. The Great Falls Water Power & Townsite Company began building the first dam at Black Eagle Falls in 1890. In 1892, the Boston & Montana Consolidated Copper and Silver Mining Company built a smelter on the north side of the river, powered by Black Eagle Dam; a 506-foot-tall smokestack built in 1908 vented the smelter. All 4 of the large waterfalls (Black Eagle, Rainbow, Ryan, and Morony) had hydroelectric dams by the 1950s, leading to Great Falls's nickname, "The Electric City." The Northside Residential and the Railroad historic districts are listed in the National Register. The Charles M. Russell House and Studio and the Great Falls Portage are NHLs. Elevation: 3,330 ft. Location: Cascade County

Great Falls Portage NHL 435 *map 12 A-1*
On June 13, 1805, traveling overland with a small advance party, Capt. Meriwether Lewis saw "the spray arise above the plain like a collumn of smoke" and soon heard "a

roaring too tremendious to be mistaken." When the magnificent Great Falls of the Missouri came into view, the sight was so spectacular that Lewis felt his "imperfect description" was wholly inadequate. The expedition's grueling 18-mile portage around the 5 falls of the Missouri River proved a monthlong ordeal of heat, grizzly bears, rattlesnakes, mosquitoes, and prickly pear cactus. The sun beat relentlessly as they dragged supplies across gullies and around ravines in a race to cross the Continental Divide before winter. Different segments of the Great Falls Portage route are under varied ownership, in areas that range from highly developed to near pristine. The Lewis and Clark National Historic Trail Interpretive Center in Great Falls, operated by the USFS, provides an overview of the expedition. Elevation: 3,503 ft. Location: Cascade County

Greenfields Bench 320 *map 3 F-3*
The name Greenfields refers to a large bench of land east of Fairfield, made green by the Sun River Irrigation Project. By the end of the 1920s, the U.S. Bureau of Reclamation had completed Gibson Reservoir, Pishkun Reservoir, and Willow Creek Reservoir, along with 174 miles of main

canals and 442 miles of laterals, providing the Greenfields Irrigation District enough water to irrigate more than 60,000 acres of cropland by 1961. Elevation: 3,930 ft. Location: Teton County

Greenhorn Range 769 *map 19 C-3*
Located a few miles south of Virginia City, the Greenhorn Range extends from Browns Gulch south to the Ruby River. Its geology is entirely different from the famous gold-mining town's. Talc is the only mineral mined here commercially, though garnets can be found in the Barton Gulch area. The origin of this name remains unknown; however, in western slang, a greenhorn is a person without experience.

Greenough 263 *map 10 B-3*
Thomas L. Greenough supplied railroad ties to the Northern Pacific Railroad as it was being built through the Missoula area in 1883. His sawmill at Greenough became part of the Anaconda Copper Mining Company Lumber Dept. during the late 1920s. Today the 2-room Sunset School constitutes the core of the community. Elevation: 3,766 ft. Location: Missoula County

Greycliff 884 *map 21 A-1*
Named for the gray cliffs along the Yellowstone River, this community was established in 1883 by the Northern Pacific Railroad to serve the nearby sheep ranches and, after 1900, dryland farmers. Known for its dance hall, Greycliff drew farmers and ranchers from great distances to shake a leg or just listen to fiddle music. Elevation: 3,937 ft. Location: Sweet Grass County

Greycliff Prairie Dog Town State Park 883 *map 21 A-1*
Named for the nearby community, this state park, established in 1974, protects 98 acres of black-tailed prairie dog habitat.

Since the early 1900s, populations of these animals have dropped by 90 percent overall, due to the destruction of habitat and ranchers' extermination efforts. Prairie dog towns provide habitat for more than 100 vertebrates, including endangered black-footed ferrets as well as rare burrowing owls and swift foxes. Elevation: 3,968 ft. Location: Sweet Grass County

Grinnell Glacier 93 *map 2 B-3*
Named for naturalist George Bird Grinnell by Lt. J. H. Beacom in 1887, Grinnell Glacier is one of the 2 largest glaciers in Glacier National Park. Located in the Swiftcurrent Valley below the scenic Garden Wall, Grinnell Glacier covered more than 500 acres in 1901 but had shrunk to less than 200 acres by 2006. At the rate they are currently melting, all of the park's glaciers will be gone by 2030. Elevation: 6,684 ft. Location: Glacier National Park

Grizzly Gulch 471 *map 11 D-3*
Grizzly Gulch commemorates an encounter between gold seeker David Wright and a grizzly bear that had come down into Helena's Last Chance Gulch to feed on chokecherries. A second Grizzly Gulch in Lewis and Clark County runs through the Bob Marshall Wilderness and Sun River Game Preserve. Elevation: 4,359 ft. Location: Lewis and Clark County

Gunsight Pass 102 *map 2 B-3*
George Bird Grinnell, Henry L. Simpson, and William H. Seward named Gunsight Pass in 1891 for its resemblance to the V-shaped gun sight of a rifle. In 1902, University of Minnesota students under the direction of Lyman B. Sperry built the trail over the pass. Elevation: 6,946 ft. Location: Glacier National Park

Hungry Horse Dam, South Fork of the Flathead River, 1953
MHS

Hagan Site NHL 1195 *map 16 B-2*
Hagan is the only archaeological site in Montana with evidence of early horticulture and permanent settlement. After the Crow tribe split from the Hidatsas on the Missouri River, they established a village here between 1550 and 1675. Archaeological studies support the theory that native peoples grew corn and tobacco at the site. It is named for Thomas F. Hagan, a rancher and early mayor of Glendive. Elevation: 2,050 ft. Location: Dawson County

Hail Columbia Gulch 502 *map 19 A-1*
It is likely that the gulch was named in 1876 in honor of the nation's centennial. Reuben Geary and Charles F. Collins owned claims in the gulch in the 1890s. In 1949, Jim Edwards, a local farmer, bought a Hungarian horse that had been captured in Nazi Germany by Gen. George Patton at the end of World War II. Eventually, Edwards partnered with Margit Sigray-Bessenyey, Marcus Daly's granddaughter, to breed these horses at the Bitterroot Stock Farm in Hamilton. Elevation: 5,553 ft. Location: Silver Bow County

Hailstone NWR 912 *map 13 E-2*
The refuge is named for Hailstone Basin, which presumably takes its name from the aftermath of a hailstorm, a common occurrence on the Montana prairie. Hailstone NWR, created in 1934, occupies more than 1,900 acres, dominated by an alkaline lakebed. The refuge is home to thousands of nesting waterfowl. It was the site of a gun battle over stolen horses between Piegans and Crows (aided by Park City ranchers) in February 1885. Elevation: 4,003 ft. Location: Stillwater County

Halfbreed Lake NWR 922 *map 21 A-3*
The USFWS established Halfbreed Lake NWR to protect wetlands for migratory birds and waterfowl. The refuge land was purchased in 1987 and originally managed as a wildlife protection easement. It is now administered by the Charles M. Russell NWR. Elevation: 3,944 ft. Location: Stillwater County

Hall 326 *map 10 C-4*
Henry Hall granted the right-of-way to the Northern Pacific Railroad to construct a branch line across his land in 1877. Originally known as Hall's Crossing, by 1910 this town boasted 2 stores, a telephone exchange, 2 hotels, a butcher shop, a creamery, and a candy store, all serving the Philipsburg-area miners and railroad men. Elevation: 4,204 ft. Location: Granite County

Hamilton 315 *map 10 D-1*
At the behest of Copper King Marcus Daly, in 1890 James W. Hamilton platted the town that bears his name and shortly thereafter sold the rights to Daly. The Bitter Root Development Company, a private enterprise affiliated with the Anaconda Company, owned the townsite, mill, store, hotel, and company houses. Hamilton's lumber mill processed timber from Anaconda Company–owned timberlands. A year after the town's founding, the Bitter Root Development Company's mill produced 35 million board-feet of lumber. Daly played a significant role in Hamilton's winning the Ravalli County seat from Stevensville in 1898. From the 1890s through the 1910s, agriculture was an economic mainstay, especially apple orchards. Oddly, Rocky Mountain spotted fever, or "black measles," which is fatal in 80 percent of adult cases, became another boon to Hamilton's economy. The prevalence of this disease among settlers in the Bitterroot Valley led Dr. Howard T. Ricketts of the U.S. Public Health Service to investigate. He concluded in 1906 that ticks transmitted the disease from infected animals to humans; in 1921, the U.S. Public Health

Service agreed to fund a vaccine development program. This program produced a vaccine, but its manufacture required large-scale tick rearing, a dangerous proposition. The Rocky Mountain Laboratory, funded by the Montana legislature in 1927, began producing the vaccine in 1928; the federal government purchased the lab in 1931. In 1938, an improved method for producing vaccines eliminated the need for live ticks. By 1940, research expanded to include the study of other insect-borne diseases. Today the Rocky Mountain Laboratory continues to research immunologic, allergic, and infectious diseases. Hamilton's National Register properties include the Southside Residential and Commercial historic districts. Elevation: 3,577 ft. Location: Ravalli County

Hammond 1242 *map 24 C-2*
In response to the construction of US 212 in the 1930s, Ernest Bushan opened a small store and gas station here. In November 1933, Bates Eccles applied for a post office named for homesteader Billy Hammond; a year later, it opened and officially put the town on the map. Today the post office is about all that remains. Elevation: 3,713 ft. Location: Carter County

Hanging Woman Creek 1155 *map 23 B-1*
A Northern Cheyenne story relates the name of this creek to a young woman who took her own life after being rebuked by her family for her liaison with a cavalryman stationed at Lame Deer. According to the story, the woman was the sister of Bobtail Horse and Hollow Wood. Elevation: 3,124 ft. Location: Rosebud County

Happys Inn 35 *map 1 D-3*
Located approximately halfway between Libby and Kalispell, Happys Inn serves a diverse group of travelers as well as area residents recreating along the nearby Thomp-

son Chain of Lakes. The inn includes a bar and restaurant. The origin of the name is unknown at this time. Elevation: 3,389 ft. Location: Lincoln County

Hardin 1059 *map 22 A-2*
In 1907, the Lincoln Land Company laid out the town of Hardin, named for Wyoming cattleman Samuel B. Hardin. The town, situated on the fringes of the Crow Indian Reservation, incorporated in 1911. Thomas Campbell operated the nation's largest wheat farm on 95,000 acres near here and pioneered the use of industrial machinery in farming. The Holly Sugar Company established a sugar beet–processing plant in Hardin in 1937. Community growth has ebbed and flowed, in large part with the development and progress of the Campbell Farms and the Holly Sugar Company. The factory closed in the 1970s, along with 5 of the 6 implement dealers who served the farming community. Hardin includes National Register–listed commercial and residential districts. Elevation: 2,906 ft. Location: Big Horn County

Hardy 389 *map 11 B-4*
The town was named by Montana Central Railway officials for Rufus Hardy, who in 1866 became one of the first settlers to live on the scenic west side of the Missouri River in this area. Hardy had a post office from 1888 to 1915. The area has 2 Hollywood connections: actor Gary Cooper's father owned a ranch nearby, and the 1987 movie *The Untouchables* featured a gun battle filmed at the Hardy Bridge. Elevation: 3,387 ft. Location: Cascade County

Harlem 776 *map 5 C-3*
Like other towns along the High Line, Great Northern Railway officials chose the name of a European city, in this case Haarlem, in the Netherlands. A. A. Cecil

platted the townsite in 1889. Harlem is just outside the boundaries of the Fort Belknap Indian Reservation. Elevation: 2,365 ft. Location: Blaine County

Harlowton 798 *map 13 D-1*
Harlowton was established in 1881 with the name Merino, for the breed of sheep raised in the area. Merino was renamed and platted as Harlowton in 1900 when Richard A. Harlow's Montana Railway Company, or "Jawbone Railroad," reached the town. In 1916, Harlowton became the eastern end of the Milwaukee Road's 438-mile electrified line between Harlowton and Avery, Idaho. During the homesteading boom, Harlowton became the state's second-largest grain-shipping terminal. The drought beginning in 1919 led to a rash of foreclosures during the next few decades, and the town's fortunes declined. Always a railroad town, Harlowton was especially hard hit by abandonment of the Milwaukee Road in 1979. The Graves Hotel is listed in the National Register. Elevation: 4,208 ft. Location: Wheatland County

Harrison 672 *map 19 A-3*
Henry C. Harrison settled in the Willow Creek Valley in 1865 near Ferguson, a stage stop on the road to Virginia City. The arrival of a Northern Pacific Railroad branch line in 1889 precipitated an identity crisis for the community, and over the next 16 years residents could not decide if they lived in Ferguson or Harrison. Harrison won the battle. Harrison today remains true to its ranching heritage. Elevation: 4,917 ft. Location: Madison County

Harwood Lake 560 *map 4 E-3*
This lake southeast of Fort Benton, originally named Gravel Lake by USGS geologists Louis N. Pirrson and Walter H. Weed, was renamed for Thomas B. Harwood, a rancher and stage stop operator along the Fort Benton–Judith Basin road, around 1882. Harwood promoted the lake's waterfowl hunting as far away as Minneapolis, and he built a hotel to lodge hunters. Elevation: 3,204 ft. Location: Chouteau County

Hathaway 1124 *map 15 E-2*
The Northern Pacific Railroad established a section stop named Martin here in 1882 and built a section house, telegraph office, and depot. In 1883, the railroad changed the name to Hathaway in honor of Gen. Forrest Henry Hathaway, commander of a regiment guarding the Northern Pacific construction crews against hostile Indians. The town that grew up around the depot became the center of social life for neighboring farm and ranch families. Elevation: 2,440 ft. Location: Rosebud County

Haugan 121 *map 9 A-2*
Haugan takes its name from H. G. Haugan, a comptroller and land commissioner for the Milwaukee Road. The rail-

Montana Flour Mills Company, Harlowton, c. 1920
MHS 948-190

Boxing match at Shorty Young's Honkey Tonk, Havre, 1907
MHS 948-268

road founded Haugan as a pusher station, for adding extra engines to assist trains making the climb up to the tunnel at St. Paul Pass. In 1933, a flood washed out the Northern Pacific Railway's tracks between Haugan and St. Regis. The Milwaukee Road allowed the Northern Pacific to use its tracks, which it did until the Northern Pacific closed its Coeur d'Alene branch line. Elevation: 3,128 ft. Location: Mineral County

Hauser Dam 452 *map 11 C-3*

Hauser Dam was named for Samuel T. Hauser, entrepreneur and territorial governor from 1885 to 1887. His company, the Helena Power Transmission Company, contracted the Wisconsin Bridge and Iron Company to build a steel dam and hydroelectric power station on the Missouri River below Canyon Ferry. It was completed in early 1907. In April of the following year, the dam, due to a flawed design, collapsed during an exceptionally high spring runoff. The dam was rebuilt of concrete in 1911, and through a series of corporate reorganizations, the property became part of the Montana Power Company. In 2000, with utility deregula-

tion, PPL Montana, a Pennsylvania energy company, purchased Hauser Dam along with all of Montana Power's electrical generating facilities in Montana. There is a popular hiking and fishing access trail below the dam. Black Sandy State Park provides boat access and a campground. Elevation: 3,649 ft. Location: Lewis and Clark County

Havre 635 *map 5 C-1*

Havre (pronounced "HAV-er") was known as Bull Hook Bottoms or Bull Hook Siding when the St. Paul, Minneapolis & Manitoba Railway (later the Great Northern Railway) first used the site in September 1887. Bull Hook Siding was incorporated as a town in 1892, but citizens renamed the community in 1894 for Le Havre, France, the ancestral home of local teamster Gus Descelles. Havre was selected as the county seat of Hill County in 1912. Havre's Residential Historic District is listed in the National Register and features homes whose owners' fortunes were made providing supplies and services to homesteaders, soldiers at nearby Fort Assinniboine, and Great Northern employees. Havre is the home of Montana State University–Northern. Elevation: 2,517 ft. Location: Hill County

Hawk Creek 978 *map 14 D-1*

It is not known how, why, or when Hawk Creek was named. Old Custer Road followed the lower part of Hawk Creek in the 1880s. A large forest fire raged through the drainage in August 1984, burning some 175,000 acres and destroying 44 homes. Location: Musselshell County

Hays 810 *map 5 D-3*

When the Assiniboines and Gros Ventres settled the southern end of the Fort

Belknap Indian Reservation, among the communities they founded was Hays, in 1890. The town was named after a Major Hays, who helped the Gros Ventres establish themselves in this area, which had more plentiful resources than along the Milk River at the northern end of the reservation. One of the area employers was the Circle C Ranch. The Bureau of Catholic Missions built St. Paul's Mission Church at Hays in 1887. A few years later, the town moved 4 miles south of "old Hays" to its present site. Elevation: 3,533 ft. Location: Blaine County

Buttrey's department store and delivery wagon, Havre, 1912
MHS 948-291

Haystack Butte 350 *map 4 B-1*
Haystack Butte, one of 19 peaks in Montana named for a resemblance to a haystack, is about 4 miles south of East Butte in the Sweet Grass Hills. It stands alone, an igneous intrusion in the surrounding sedimentary rock. Elevation: 4,737 ft. Location: Liberty County

Headquarters Creek Pass 216 *map 3 E-1*
The pass, an eastern entry point into the Bob Marshall Wilderness, has the same name as a creek just to its west that runs into the North Fork of the Sun River at Gates Park. The creek had been named in the 1910s for a tie-cutting camp. Elevation: 7,743 ft. Location: Teton County

Heart Butte 199 *map 3 C-1*
Heart Butte, on the Blackfeet Indian Reservation, takes its name from the small heart-shaped peak southwest of town. In 1910, under the leadership of Father Aloysius Soer, members of the community built St. Peter Claver Church, which was replaced by a modern structure in the late 1990s. The town also has a school, general store, volunteer fire department, and senior center. Elevation: 4,466 ft. Location: Pondera County

Heart Lake 191 *map 9 B-3*
There are 3 Heart Lakes in Mineral County, all near the Montana-Idaho state line. The largest, identified on the map in this book, is a popular hiking destination. Another Heart Lake is about 10 miles northwest, near the head of Lost Creek; the third is about 10 miles south of Haugan. Elevation: 5,772 ft. Location: Mineral County

Hebgen Dam and Hebgen Lake 872 *map 20 D-1*
Hebgen Dam, completed in 1915 by the Madison Reservoir & Irrigation Company, is named for Max Hebgen, a hydroelectric engineer who in 1890 moved from Wisconsin to Butte to work for the Butte Electric Light Company. Hebgen was the general manager of Montana Power Company at the time of his death in 1915. The earth-filled dam with concrete core, 718 feet in length, captures the waters of the Madison River, creating a reservoir approximately 15 miles long. The dam survived the 1959 earthquake that caused a massive landslide and created Earthquake Lake, below Hebgen. Elevation: 6,537 ft. Location: Gallatin County

Hecla Mine 571 *map 18 B-4*

The Hecla Consolidated Mining Company of Indianapolis, Indiana, purchased the Hecla Mine, on Lion Mountain, in January 1877. Among the early managers were Noah Armstrong, E. C. Atkins, and Henry Knippenberg. In the 1880s, some 500 miners and merchants clustered around the Hecla Mine in a community they called Lion City. Ore wagons hauled silver-lead concentrate from the mill at Lion City down the primitive road to the smelter at Glendale. The mine produced profitably until 1893 and ceased operation in 1904. Elevation: 8,858 ft. Location: Beaverhead County

Hedstrom Lake 1096 *map 15 B-2*

Hedstrom Lake, created by damming Hay Creek, is named for Ole Hedstrom, a Swedish widower, and his 2 sons, Albert C. and Kingman W. Hedstrom, who settled in the area about 1901. The family eventually acquired 5 sections of land (3,200 acres) in McCone and Prairie counties, on which they raised sheep, cattle, and crops. Elevation: 2,561 ft. Location: McCone County

Helena 469 *map 11 D-3*

Four prospectors, down on their luck, took a "last chance" along a narrow gulch and found significant "color." The name of Helena's main street, Last Chance Gulch, memorializes the town's chaotic beginnings in the summer of 1864. Miners named the gold camp Helena, after a town of the same name in Scott County, Minnesota. Within a year of the discovery of placer gold, a boomtown flourished. Helena survived after the placer gold played out because pioneer entrepreneurs had invested in homes and businesses here. The

Main Street, Helena, c. 1902
MHS 954-213

territorial capital moved to Helena from Virginia City in 1875, and Helena received one of the nation's 5 U.S. Assay Offices—acknowledgment of the area's extensive wealth in gold. Arrival of the Northern Pacific Railroad in 1883 and Helena's election as state capital in 1894 confirmed the community's survival, though the Panic of 1893 and the end of guaranteed federal silver purchases slowed its momentum. The Lewis and Clark County Courthouse survives as Montana's only standing territorial-period capitol and as the first state capitol (1889–1902). National Register listings in Helena include the Downtown, South-Central, Rodney Street, House of the Good Shepherd, West Main Street, and Railroad Depot historic districts as well as many individual homes and buildings and several cemeteries. Elevation: 4,060 ft. Location: Lewis and Clark County

Hell Creek State Park 1030 *map 6 E-4*

Millions of years ago, a tropical inland sea covered this area, creating a home for dinosaurs, sequoia trees, and other species. Paleontologist Barnum Brown discovered the first *Tyrannosaurus rex* fossils here in 1905. Situated on a peninsula of shale and sandstone jutting into Fort Peck Reservoir, 172-acre Hell Creek State Park, established in 1966, is typical of the badlands landscape found along the Missouri River. Extreme temperature fluctuations characterize the area. Elevation: 2,328 ft. Location: Garfield County

Hellgate Canyon 231 *map 10 C-2*

This place, known to the Salish as Im-i-sul-e'-tiku, "Place of dread by the water," eventually took on an even more ominous name. Since it was the site of many Blackfeet ambushes of Salish and fur traders, the French named it Porte de l'Enfer, "Door of hell." Elevation: 3,198 ft. Location: Missoula County

Helmville 307 *map 10 C-4*

Helmville, near the confluence of Nevada Creek and the Blackfoot River, is named after early homesteader J. H. Helms, who applied for a post office in the area. It was granted in 1872, when more settlers began ranching and farming in the valley. Elevation: 4,311 ft. Location: Powell County

Henderson 129 *map 9 A-3*

Henderson takes its name from Ben W. Henderson, who, along with partner Edward Donlan, opened a sawmill in De Borgia in 1904. That same year, the town of Henderson acquired a post office, which operated until 1930. Eventually, the sawmill moved from De Borgia to Henderson, where it operated until 1928 as the Mann Lumber Company. Henderson's primary industry was logging, though it also served for a time as a station for the Northern Pacific Railway. Elevation: 2,985 ft. Location: Mineral County

Heron 30 *map 1 D-1*

Built in 1883 by the Northern Pacific Railroad as a division point, Heron in its earliest days boasted a roundhouse, an engine repair shop, and a sawmill. The town is named after nearby rapids. On October 12, 1809, explorer David Thompson reported seeing Salish fishing for herring on the Clark Fork River, and several weeks later he mentioned fishing on "Herring Rapid." In his journal entry of January 5, 1826, Hudson's Bay Company trapper John Work referred to a "Heron Rapid." Elevation: 2,248 ft. Location: Sanders County

Highland Mountains 580 *map 19 A-2*

On July 25, 1866, E. B. and J. B. S. Coleman and William Crawford discovered placer gold in Fish Creek, on the north side of Red Mountain. The miners named the area Highland Gulch and established the Highland Mining District, which boasted

2 towns: Highland City and Red Mountain City. In 1895, Ron Leggat, owner of most of the claims, sold his property on Fish Creek and Basin Creek to the Butte Water Company. There was a revival of placer-gold mining during the Great Depression, when many Butte miners supplemented their wages by panning gold. The highest point is 10,223-foot Table Mountain. Location: Silver Bow County

Highwood 513 *map 12 A-2*

Homesteaders began arriving in the Big Sag Valley as early as the 1860s, and the area quickly developed into prime ranching and farming country. Starting about 1910, larger numbers of homesteaders began moving in. The Milwaukee Road surveyed a branch line to connect Great Falls and Lewistown in 1912. On December 10, 1913, when the railroad reached Highwood, named for the nearby Highwood Mountains, longtime resident Evan J. "Dad" Price drove the golden last spike. Highwood has both an "old" town and a "new" town. Because the railroad and landowner Frank H. McGowan could not agree on a price for the planned townsite along Highwood Creek, the railroad purchased a site from H. O. Lyng. Construction had already started on McGowan's site—old town—when the railroad platted the different site—new town. The valley was popularized in the 1962 movie *Shoot Out at Big Sag*, starring Walter Brennan. Elevation: 3,395 ft. Location: Chouteau County

Highwood Mountains 565 *map 12 A-3*

Named Shonkin by the Blackfeet and later identified by USGS geologists Louis N. Pirrson and Walter H. Weed as the Highwoods, this isolated range north of the Little Belt Mountains is a remnant of volcanic intrusions called laccoliths and dikes.

Hilgard Peak 851 *map 19 D-4*

Hilgard Peak is named for Eugene Woldemar Hilgard (1833–1916), a German-born chemist, geologist, and soil scientist. From 1881 to 1883, Hilgard participated in the Northern Transcontinental Survey, studying the agricultural potential of Montana, Oregon, and Washington. E. W. Hilgard's cousin was Henry Villard, president of the Northern Pacific Railroad. Villard was born Ferdinand Heinrich Gustav Hilgard and changed his name to Villard when he arrived in the United States. This second connection with the Hilgard name may also have been a factor in naming the peak, in addition to Hilgard Creek, Hilgard Lake, and Hilgard Basin. At 11,297 feet, Hilgard Peak is the highest in Montana outside of the Beartooth Range. The first recorded ascent of the peak was by Dave Wessel in 1948. Location: Madison County

Hilger 774 *map 13 B-2*

The community of Hilger is named for David J. Hilger, who came to the territory with his parents from Minnesota in 1867 when he was 9 years old. Hilger established a sheep ranch on Dog Creek in Fergus County in 1881 and married Christina Fergus (for whom the town of Christina is named) in 1884. Later in life, Hilger became a prominent resident of Lewistown and a state legislator. He served as the librarian at the Montana Historical Society from 1923 to 1937. The town he established benefited from the arrival of the Milwaukee Road in November 1911. Miners from the Judith and North Moccasin mountains would catch the 4:30 train in Hilger and ride into Lewistown on Saturday nights. Elevation: 4,080 ft. Location: Fergus County

Hill County 555 *map 4 B-3*

Formed from part of Chouteau County in 1912, Hill County is named for Great Northern Railway founder James J. Hill in recognition of the role the railroad played in the development of north-central Montana. Havre is the seat of this county, which abuts the international border.

Hillsboro 1062 *map 22 C-1*

The Bighorn Canyon placer mines lured Grosvenor W. Barry to the area, but failure to find the mother lode led Barry to pursue other ventures. In 1915, a post office designated Hillsboro opened in Barry's log house. Barry raised hackney horses for a time, then redesigned his ranch, called Cedarvale, as a dude ranch. After Barry's death in 1920, his wife continued to operate the dude ranch. The post office closed in 1945. The ruins of the ranch are near Barry's Landing. Elevation: 3,897 ft. Location: Carbon County

Hingham 503 *map 4 C-3*

Established in 1910, Hingham grew quickly, as the *Hingham Review*'s editor noted on April 21, 1911, when he wrote: "This time last year there was no semblance of a town here while the adjacent country was all wild prairies, very little of it having been filed on. Now, we have a thriving town in which over twenty firms are each doing business." Hingham dubbed itself "the progressive city—a city built on the square." Elevation: 3,028 ft. Location: Hill County

Hinsdale 985 *map 6 C-4*

According to local lore, Hinsdale, a station on the Great Northern Railway as early as 1889, is named for a Reverend Hinsdale, friend of James J. Hill, the builder of the Great Northern Railway. The town got a post office in 1891. Residents moved the town about one and a half miles west in 1898, after flooding on the Milk River inundated the settlement. At the turn of the twentieth century, sheep ranching dominated the local economy, but after the Milk River Irrigation Project brought water to the area, sugar beets became a major crop. Elevation: 2,167 ft. Location: Valley County

Hobson 721 *map 13 B-1*

Located at the freight-wagon crossing of the Judith River between Fort Benton and the Musselshell River country, this community was once known as the "Gateway to the Judith Basin." In 1881, E. J. Morrison bought a house and saloon from the Clegg family, established a post office, and named the new community Philbrook, his wife's maiden name. Philbrook experienced a burst of growth, adding 2 hotels, 2 stores, a saloon, and 2 blacksmith shops. In 1908, however, the Great Northern Railway's Billings and Northern branch line established another town 4 miles west. Local rancher and legislator S. S. Hobson and 3 partners purchased this townsite from the railroad and formed the Philbrook Townsite Company. Residents, however, could not agree on the name. As the opponents squared off, the signboard read Hobson one morning and Philbrook the next. The railroad solved the problem when it decided on Hobson. Elevation: 4,098 ft. Location: Judith Basin County

Hodges 1221 *map 16 B-3*

Hodges was established as a station stop on the Northern Pacific Railroad in 1879, named for Leonard B. Hodges, a surveyor and superintendent of tree planting for the railroad. Hodges, long a Scandinavian agricultural community, operated its first school and post office out of Charles Anderson's ranch house. Community members built the first "real" school in 1912 and the first grain elevator in 1914. Elevation: 2,505 ft. Location: Dawson County

Hogeland 790 *map 5 B-4*

Named for A. H. Hogeland, the Great Northern Railway's chief engineer, Hogeland began as a station stop on the railway about 1928. Before the Great Depression, Hogeland supported 2 general stores, 3 restaurants, 2 pool halls, and a hotel, hardware store, butcher shop, lumberyard, and weekly newspaper. Hogeland lost its high school in 1970, and by the late 1970s the population had dwindled to 35 residents. Elevation: 3,137 ft. Location: Blaine County

Holland Lake 200 *map 10 A-3*

In the 1890s, Ben Holland, George Grant, and Ed Thompson hunted and prospected in the Swan Valley, and in 1897 Holland filed a water right on Holland Creek, which flows into Holland Lake. In 1924, Babe Wilhelm and Art White built the Holland Lake Lodge to accommodate tourists interested in hunting and fishing. Elevation: 4,035 ft. Location: Missoula County

Hollowtop Mountain 664 *map 19 B-3*

According to local forester Merlin Stock, Hollowtop is named for the unusual shape of the mountain when viewed from the northeast. Located at the northern end of the Tobacco Root Mountains, Hollowtop is near several historic gold mines in the Pony area. Elevation: 10,604 ft. Location: Madison County

Holter Lake and Holter Dam 399
map 11 B-3

Construction of a dam named for investor Anton Holter began in 1908, downriver from the Gates of the Mountains and Hauser Dam. Begun under the auspices of Holter and business partner Samuel Hauser's United Missouri River Power Company, the dam was one of dozens of municipal power stations and hydroelectric facilities across western Montana that were consolidated by the creation of the Montana Power Company in 1912. Upon

the concrete dam's completion in 1918, it measured 104 feet high and 1,364 feet long, and became Montana Power's highest hydroelectric dam along the Missouri River. The dam created a reservoir 24 miles long, reaching into the canyon through the Gates of the Mountains. PPL Montana purchased the property after utility deregulation and the dissolution of Montana Power. Elevation: 3,510 ft. Location: Lewis and Clark County

Homer Youngs Peak 578 *map 18 B-2*

Named for a miner whose claims lay above Rock Island Lakes, southwest of Jackson, Homer Youngs Peak is the highest in the Beaverhead Range. Elevation: 10,610 ft. Location: Beaverhead County

Homestake Pass 556 *map 19 A-2*

Homestake Pass crosses the Continental Divide between Silver Bow and Jefferson counties, just east of Butte. It is named for the mining camp of Homestake, established in 1885 by a group of miners who made their "stake" there when they found gold. The Northern Pacific Railroad laid tracks over the pass in 1889–90. Homestake Precinct No. 34 became notorious during Montana's first general election, in 1889, when widespread voting by railroad construction workers led to a challenged election. This, in turn, led to a stalemated legislature, with Democrats and Republicans meeting in separate chambers. At the height of its success, Homestake had a stone schoolhouse, a large log boardinghouse, 2 stamp mills, and several mines. In the 1960s, the H. K. Mining Corporation mined gold, silver, and platinum ore here and shipped it to California for processing. Elevation: 6,375 ft. Location: Silver Bow County

Homestead 1175 *map 8 C-2*

The original name of this town was Barford, after the nearby ford across Big Muddy Creek used by the N Bar N Cattle Ranch in 1893. Peder Pederson began calling the town Pederson after he opened the first business and became the first postmaster in 1908. Mail began arriving at the depot for Barford and for Pederson, causing some confusion. In a spirit of compromise, residents chose the name Fort Peck for the new community. The town of Poplar objected to this name, since it was the headquarters of the Fort Peck Indian Agency. In a stroke of inspiration, residents resolved the issue with the name Homestead, in honor of the homesteaders who had settled the town and surrounding area. No one objected this time. With the 1910 arrival of the Great Northern Railway's Bainville to Scobey branch line, the townsite company purchased 80 acres from Anna Olson and officially platted the community. Elevation: 1,982 ft. Location: Sheridan County

Homestead Lake 1174 *map 8 C-2*

Homestead Lake, named for the nearby town, spans the county line between Roosevelt and Sheridan counties. The lake is part of the Medicine Lake NWR, established in 1935 by President Franklin D. Roosevelt. The CCC created nesting islands, planted trees and shrubs, and constructed a 100-foot lookout tower. Elevation: 1,933 ft.

Hopley Creek 789 *map 12 D-4*

Hopley Creek was originally named Hopley's Hole Creek sometime before 1876. According to the story told by Two Dot farmer James A. Freeser, whose father settled on the Musselshell River in 1872, the creek is named for an early hunter, trapper, and Pony Express rider who hid in a hole in the rocks near the creek when attacked by Indians in the 1860s. Location: Wheatland County

Hornaday Buffalo Camp NHL 1015 *map 14 B-3*

A Smithsonian Institution expedition whose purpose was to acquire bison specimens from the last free-roaming herd of wild bison used this site as its base in November and December of 1886. Expedition leader and Smithsonian chief taxidermist William T. Hornaday described the site in his journals as the "camp on the Big Porcupine." A depression marks the location of the cook shack, the only man-made feature now visible. Hornaday's experiences in Montana led him to write scathingly of the bison's extermination and to publicize its plight. One of the animals Hornaday collected near the camp served as the model for the bison on the $10 bill of 1901 and is also part of the famous American Buffalo Group exhibit on display at the River and Plains Museum in Fort Benton. In 1908, Hornaday helped establish the National Bison Range near Moiese. Elevation: 3,157 ft. Location: Garfield County

Horseshoe Hills 674 *map 12 E-1*

The arid, sagebrush-covered Horseshoe Hills are named for a horseshoe bend in the Missouri River to the north and for the outline formed by the hills. More than 550 million years ago, a shallow inland sea covered the Gallatin Valley, fostering tropical vegetation that sustained dinosaurs and trilobites (the first animal with a well-defined backbone), whose fossils can be found today in the Horseshoe Hills. Elevation: 6,713 ft. Location: Gallatin County

Hot Springs 120 *map 1 E-4*

Previously known as both Camas and Camas Hot Springs, Hot Springs was founded in 1905 by Frank Lamoureaux, who named it for the camas plant that grows abundantly in the region. The medicinal properties of the site's numerous hot springs were well known to Native Americans, who came from what are now Montana, Idaho, and Washington each spring to camp on Camas Prairie and bathe in the springs. Today's town continues to host visitors who come to soak in the pools. Elevation: 2,832 ft. Location: Sanders County

Hudson Bay Divide 140   *map 2   B-4*

Water that flows north of the Hudson Bay Divide (from waterways such as the Waterton, Belly, and St. Mary rivers) eventually makes it way into Hudson Bay, hence the name. Water south of the divide eventually flows into the Gulf of Mexico. Elevation: 7,982 ft. Location: Glacier County

Hughesville 600   *map 12   B-3*

The town of Hughesville takes its name from Patrick H. Hughes, who found silver ore here in 1879. The town prospered while miners extracted silver from the surrounding countryside, but after the demonetization of silver brought about the Panic of 1893, the town began to wilt. Its economy picked up a little when the St. Joseph Lead Company opened a mine here in 1941, but that closed 2 years later, bringing hopes of Hughesville's resurgence to an end. Today the area is part of a large EPA Superfund site encompassing more than 140 abandoned mines and waste dumps. Elevation: 5,968 ft. Location: Judith Basin County

Hungry Horse 73   *map 2   C-2*

The creek, dam, and mountain draw their name from a local legend about 2 horses, Tex and Jerry, that were lost for more than a month in deep snow in the South Fork of the Flathead River country. The town owes its existence to construction of the Hungry Horse Dam, a U.S. Bureau of Reclamation dam on the South Fork, authorized by Congress in 1944. By 1948, a collection of more than 100 prefabricated buildings housed construction workers at the site. The town is now primarily a tourist center

on the road to Glacier National Park. Elevation: 3,103 ft. Location: Flathead County

Hungry Horse Dam 83   *map 2   C-2*

The dam is named for a creek and a mountain near the South Fork of the Flathead River called Hungry Horse after a story about 2 horses that were lost for more than a month in deep snow. Beginning in 1948, the U.S. Bureau of Reclamation oversaw construction of the hydroelectric dam. Twenty-five hundred workers poured more than 3 million cubic yards of concrete, creating the fourth-largest dam in the world. When the dam was completed in 1953, it measured 564 feet tall and 2,115 feet long and created a reservoir 34 miles long. Federally subsidized, low-cost electricity available to industries within 15 miles of the dam encouraged the Anaconda Company to construct an aluminum plant at nearby Columbia Falls in 1955. Elevation: 3,278 ft. Location: Flathead County

Hunters Hot Springs 831   *map 20   A-4*

Hunters Hot Springs was a noted landmark for both Crows and pioneers. At times, as many as 1,000 tipis surrounded the hot springs, and the Crows continued to use the springs at least until the mid-1870s, when the western portion of their reservation, which included the springs, was ceded to the federal government. Dr. A. J. Hunter, a surgeon in the Confederate Army, first noticed the hot springs in the spring of 1864. In 1883, he built a small hotel at the site and later sold it to Butte attorney James A. Murray, who built the elegant Hotel Dakota in 1909. That resort featured a golf course, tennis courts, and a spring-water bottling plant. The hotel burned in November 1932. After years of abandonment, the plunge reopened in 1948 and continued to operate until its final closure in 1974. The building was razed in the mid-1990s. For a few years thereafter, a Japanese company used the greenhouse

Hunters Hot Springs Hotel, c. 1920
MHS 948-675

to grow hydroponic tomatoes. Elevation: 4,422 ft. Location: Park County

Huntley 1014 *map 22 A-1*

Huntley was first established in 1877 as a Gilmer and Salisbury Company stage station, store, ferry, and post office run by Omar Hoskins and Thomas McGirl. Since both Gilmer and Salisbury had previously worked for Silas S. Huntley's stage line, it was logical to name the station for him. In 1881, Huntley became a Northern Pacific Railroad station. In 1907, the Huntley Irrigation Project began diverting water from the Yellowstone River just upriver of Huntley, making possible sugar beet crops and, ultimately, a sugar beet refinery in Billings. Elevation: 3,019 ft. Location: Yellowstone County

Huson 206 *map 10 B-1*

Established as a railroad station about 1894, Huson is named for H. S. Huson, a Northern Pacific Railroad construction engineer. In 1897–98, the post office opened as Glaude, named for Napoleon Glaude, who owned the Glaude Hotel and store and also ran a livery stable and lime kiln.

In 1898, the post office's name was changed to Huson. A reduction in area mining and sawmills, and a disastrous fire, led to the town's decline in the early 1900s. Elevation: 3,012 ft. Location: Missoula County

Hutchins Bridge 842 *map 19 D-4*

Madison County commissioners began discussing the feasibility of a road along the Madison River in 1869. When Congress established Yellowstone National Park in 1872, the area was accessible only by horse. Not until a year later was the first good wagon road to the park constructed, along the Madison River route. Mathew Dunham built a toll bridge across the river here in 1885 but soon sold it to rancher Ammon Hutchins, who continued to collect tolls. In 1900, Madison County purchased the bridge with a right-of-way through Hutchins's ranch for $300. Portions of the bridge collapsed when a herd of cattle crossed, and it was not rebuilt; ruins of the original stone piers are still visible in the river. In 1902, John Towle of Omaha, whose builder's plaque is mounted on the bridge's southeast hip, constructed a new bridge for Madison County at a cost of $5,999. By 1917, the Hutchins Bridge was part of the Banff–Grand Canyon Road, known as the Red and White Trail. The West Yellowstone–Butte portion was known as the Vigilante Trail. A new route to the park in 1922 bypassed the Hutchins Bridge, and it has since served only local traffic. The bridge, listed in the National Register, is significant as an example of a pin-connected Pratt through-truss, a pre-fabricated design that was the most common form of metal truss bridge until about 1915. Elevation: 5,879 ft. Location: Madison County

Hutterite Colonies (Milford) 321
map 11 A-2

The Hutterite Brethren is an Anabaptist sect started by John Hutter during the sixteenth century in Europe's Tirol and Moravia. Persecuted for their religious belief in pacificism and communal life, the Hutterites moved frequently and by 1771 had settled in the Ukraine. In the 1870s, the Russian government required all men to join the army, so the Hutterites moved again, this time to the United States. During World War I, faced with military conscription and the banning of the German language, most Hutterites moved to Canada. Many returned to the United States following the war, settling in Montana. Milford is one of more than 40 colonies scattered around the state. Among the larger of these are Milford (Augusta), Hilldale (Havre), Gildford (Gildford), and Spring Creek (Lewistown). The Hutterites live communally, have their own schools, and maintain traditional religious beliefs and German language.

Hyalite Creek 740 *map 20 A-1*
Hyalite Creek takes its name from the glasslike hyalite crystal deposits at the head of the creek, located at the base of Hyalite Peak. The creek was known as Middle Creek until local residents, led by P. C. Waite, petitioned for the name change. It

is dammed to form Hyalite Reservoir and then flows through Hyalite Canyon, eventually joining the Gallatin River. Location: Gallatin County

Hyalite Peak 815 *map 20 B-2*
Hyalite Peak is the tallest peak in the north end of the Gallatin Range, towering over Hyalite Lake nestled below, from which it is accessible by trail. The name refers to the glasslike hyalite crystals found in a crevice near the top of the peak. Elevation: 10,299 ft. Location: Gallatin County

Hysham 1053 *map 14 D-3*
Rancher Charlie J. Hysham, owner of the Flying E Ranch, ran thousands of cattle south of the Yellowstone River and north of the Wyoming border during the latter part of the nineteenth century. In 1906, the area around Hysham was ceded from the Crow Indian Reservation and opened to settlement, expanding the demand for goods and services around the Northern Pacific Railway station. Hysham grew into a merchandising center and the county seat of Treasure County by 1919. It was home to the longest-serving state legislator in U.S. history, Dave Manning, who served under 11 different governors over 53 years. The impressive Mission-style Yucca Theatre is listed in the National Register. Elevation: 2,660 ft. Location: Treasure County

Ingomar School, c. 1915
Mabel Van Duzen, photographer, MHS PAc 93-67 Box 2

Indian Creek 584 *map 11 D-4*

Indian Creek was named by the first prospector on the creek, who had an Indian wife. Placer mining occurred here during the 1860s and '70s, producing about $500,000 in gold, and in later years the Park Mines operated a cyanide mill along the creek. The Iron Mask was a prominent gold mine near the creek. Near the Townsend turnoff for Indian Creek Road were the mining camps of Hog 'Em, Cheat 'Em, and Rob 'Em. Elevation: 3,843 ft. Location: Broadwater County

Ingomar 1033 *map 14 D-3*

Ingomar began in 1908 as a Milwaukee Road depot town. Unfortunately, the railroad chose a townsite without a water supply, forcing it to haul in water each week with a 22,000-gallon tender. The town did not have a municipal water system until 1985. Ingomar for many years boasted about being the largest sheep-shearing and wool-shipping point in Montana, but a devastating fire in 1923, followed by years of drought and abandonment of the railroad in the 1970s, forced the town into decline. The Jersey Lilly Bar and Café, housed in the former Wiley, Clark and Greening Bank, is listed in the National Register. The bar was established in 1948 by Robert Francis Seward, who began a tradition of serving a free Christmas dinner to residents. The tradition later became a Christmas potluck. Also in the Register are the J. A. Bookman General Store and the Ingomar School. Elevation: 3,014 ft. Location: Rosebud County

Intake 1205 *map 16 A-2*

Dubbed the "Dam Town," Intake began in 1907 with the construction of the Lower Yellowstone Diversion Dam and the Glendive to Sidney branch line of the Northern Pacific Railway. The intake of water into the irrigation ditch inspired the town's name. The town prospered briefly—many people who arrived in the area to work on the railroad or the irrigation project stayed on as homesteaders—but it suffered severe setbacks during the 1920s drought that forced many to leave the area. Elevation: 2,003 ft. Location: Dawson County

Inverness 445 *map 4 C-3*

James "Scotty" Watson, a Great Northern Railway employee, named Inverness for the Scottish town of the same name. Inverness began as a section house in 1909 and was soon a thriving community that included a school, church, grain elevator, hardware store, and grocery. Elevation: 3,297 ft. Location: Hill County

Ismay 1213 *map 16 D-2*

The Milwaukee Road established Ismay in 1907 at the point where the old stage road from Fort Lincoln to Fort Keogh crossed O'Fallon Creek. The town's name derives from either Isabelle and Mary Peck, daughters of railroad official George Peck, or from Isabel and May Earling, daughters of another railroad official. In 1993, a Kansas City radio station contacted the town of Ismay to request that it change its name to Joe, in honor of Joe Montana, the San Francisco 49ers quarterback, for the duration of the football season. Ismay, population 22, agreed. The town organized a parade, rodeo, and show and drew more than 2,000 guests, but the football player did not embrace the idea and the town's name reverted to Ismay. The Ismay Jail is listed in the National Register. Elevation: 2,529 ft. Location: Custer County

Italian Peaks 824 *map 18 E-4*

This subrange of the Bitterroot and Beaverhead mountains, in the southwest corner of the state, separates Idaho from Montana. It contains the highest mountain in the Bitterroot Range, Scott Peak, whose 11,378-foot summit is actually a mile inside Idaho.

Artesian well, Ismay
T. O. Boven, photographer, MHS 948-687

Izaak Walton Inn 138 *map 2 C-3*

The Izaak Walton Inn, named for the author of *The Compleat Angler* (1653), illustrates the difficulty of keeping the nation's northernmost transcontinental railroad open during Rocky Mountain winters. Originally, the days of fighting snow and frequent avalanches ended with the 60 workers returning to minimal shelter in abandoned railcars and wall tents, for Essex had only 150 permanent residents and nowhere for workers to board. After numerous petitions, the Great Northern Railway built this 29-bedroom structure in 1939, following its standard pattern for a division hotel, despite the railroad policy that called for only a section house anywhere except a division point. The railroad also realized that the hostelry could serve summertime tourists. Naming it for the renowned English fisherman underlined the intended double use. Though the Great Northern Railway sold the hotel to private interests in the 1950s, this Craftsman-style inn, listed in the National Register, has been in continuous use since its construction and to this day serves railroad workers and tourists. Elevation: 3,867 ft. Location: Flathead County

Jardine, c. 1905
Detail, MHS 948 691

Jackson 585 *map 18 B-3*

East of present-day Jackson, Capt. William Clark on July 7, 1806, noted finding a "boiling Hot Spring, which cooked meat in 25 minutes." Benoil O. Fournier later located the hot springs in 1884. The Jackson post office, named after Anton H. Jackson, the first postmaster and proprietor of Jackson's hotel, opened on August 1, 1896. A hotel and spa have operated at the hot springs for several decades. Elevation: 6,483 ft. Location: Beaverhead County

Jardine 893 *map 20 C-2*

In 1866, Joe Brown discovered a gold-quartz vein in Bear Gulch, but no large-scale mining occurred until 1884, when several mills were constructed. The Bear Gulch Mining Company, founded by Harry Bush, began mining in 1898, and Jardine takes its name from company superintendent A. C . Jardine, who operated a 20-stamp gold mill in Bear Gulch. Jardine is the site of the first commercial tungsten deposits found in the United States, in about 1906. Over the next 50 years, Jardine's mines changed ownership many times. In 1964, San Francisco developer Richard Blankenship purchased Jardine hoping to create a ski area, but gave up on building it. During the 1960s and 1970s, many of the town's buildings were lost to fire and demolition. TVX Mineral Hill Inc. restarted gold-mining operations in 1989 but closed down their Mineral Hill Gold Mine in 1996, putting more than 130 people out of work. Elevation: 6,463 ft. Location: Park County

Jeffers 748 *map 19 B-4*

Myron D. Jeffers came to Alder Gulch in 1864 as a freighter. Recognizing the miners' need for a steady supply of beef, between 1869 and 1871, Jeffers would head to Texas, buy cattle, and herd them back to Montana Territory. With his last herd, Jeffers started his own ranch across the Madison River from Ennis. Jeffers died in May 1900. In 1903, his widow, Florence Switzer Jeffers, became the first postmaster of the new town of Jeffers. The Jeffers and Switzer families continued to be prominent in the area, including operating a general store. Elevation: 4,929 ft. Location: Madison County

Jefferson City 510 *map 11 D-3*

This stop along the Fort Benton and Virginia City stage line quickly grew into a settlement. It took its name when Jefferson County was named one of Montana Territory's original counties on February 2, 1865. Area mines produced millions of dollars worth of silver and gold during the late 1800s. A large open-pit mine has produced gold for the Montana Tunnels Project since the late 1990s. One of Jefferson City's summertime attractions is Tizer Gardens' thousands of blooming flowers, including 100 varieties of roses and 150 varieties of clematis. Elevation: 4,560 ft. Location: Jefferson County

Jefferson County 549 *map 11 E-3*

Created on February 2, 1865, Jefferson County is one of Montana's original counties. It is named for the river that Lewis and Clark called the Jefferson River, in honor of President Thomas Jefferson. Although the new county took Jefferson City as its first county seat, that distinction moved to Radersburg in 1869 and to Boulder, the current county seat, in 1883.

Jefferson Island 744 *map 19 A-3*

Named for an island in the Jefferson River, the town changed its name to Cardwell in 1909, when the post office moved to the south side of the Jefferson River to be next to the railroad station. Elevation: 4,285 ft. Location: Jefferson County

Parson's Bridge, Jefferson River, 1866
MHS 957-841

Jefferson River 659 *map 19 A-4*

Named by Capt. Meriwether Lewis on July 28, 1805, for the third president of the United States, this river, one of the 3 forks of the Missouri, finds its source in what we now call the Beaverhead, Big Hole, and Ruby rivers. In 1810, Andrew Henry and Pierre Menard constructed a post for the St. Louis Missouri Fur Company on the east bank of the Jefferson River, near the headwaters of the Missouri River.

Jimtown 1261 *map 23 A-1*

Located south of Colstrip and just north of the Northern Cheyenne Indian Reservation, Jimtown today maintains few services. There is nothing known about the origin of the town's name or any of its history. Elevation: 3,228 ft. Location: Rosebud County

Jocko River 175 *map 10 A-1*

The Jocko River flows into the Flathead River at Dixon. It is named for Jacques Raphael Finlay, the son of a North West Company trader who served as assistant to explorer David Thompson from 1800 to 1806. In 1810, Finlay built Spokane House, a trading post near present-day Spokane, Washington. Jacques, also known as Jocco, married a Chippewa woman, and today their descendants still reside in the area.

Joliet 984 *map 21 B-3*

The construction of the Rocky Fork & Cooke City Railway in 1892 made the spot that would become Joliet a shipping point for agricultural products. Although locals began developing the site as early as 1893, it was not until 1899 that the Joliet Townsite and Improvement Company purchased the 32 acres that became the town. Named for Joliet, Illinois, in 1895 the town unsuccessfully vied with Red Lodge to become the county seat of newly created Carbon County. Properties listed in the National Register include the Joliet Bridge over Rock Creek, Joliet High School, the Southern Hotel, and the Joliet Fire Hall. Elevation: 3,736 ft. Location: Carbon County

Joplin 427 *map 4 C-2*

As early as 1902, Joplin was a station house on the Great Northern Railway. When homesteaders began arriving in the spring of 1910, E. C. Tolley, a North Dakota land developer, assisted many settlers with their claims and laid out a townsite. Joplin residents, however, recognize Syrian immigrant Joseph E. Rehal as Joplin's founder; he built the town's first 4 buildings. As more homesteaders arrived in the area, the town's population exploded, and in 1915 the Joplin Commercial Club coined the phrase the "Biggest Little Town on Earth." Elevation: 3,323 ft. Location: Liberty County

Jordan 1036 *map 14 A-4*

Arthur J. Jordan began homesteading along Big Dry Creek in 1896. A few years later, the entrepreneurial spirit struck Jordan, who realized that he could make money by purchasing extra supplies and selling them to area ranchers and homesteaders. He opened the Jordan post office in 1899. According to local legend, Arthur named the town not for himself but after his good friend W. B. Jordan of Miles City. With the creation of Garfield County in 1919, the town squared off against Cohagen, Sand Springs, and West Edwards to be designated the county seat, with the *Jordan Times, Edwards Journal,* and *Sand Springs Star* waging an acrimonious campaign in the service of their communities. Ultimately, Jordan edged out the contenders. As of 1986, the Garfield County High School in Jordan still had a dormitory for students who lived too far away to return

home every night. Elevation: 2,602 ft. Location: Garfield County

Judith Basin County 655 *map 12 C-4*

Named for the Judith River, which flows through it, central Montana's Judith Basin County was formed in 1920 from portions of Cascade and Fergus counties, with Stanford as the county seat. The county, best known for Yogo sapphires, also is a rich agricultural area.

Judith Gap 756 *map 13 C-1*

Judith Gap is a low pass that forms the divide between the Musselshell and Judith rivers. It provided a convenient route for travelers moving between the Yellowstone River and Fort Benton on the Missouri. In 1877, Chief Joseph and the Nez Perces came through Judith Gap, fleeing the U.S. Army. The Carroll Trail and early stagecoach routes also passed through the gap en route to the Missouri River. In 1904, the "Jawbone Railroad" (Montana Railway Company) built a section house north of present-day Judith Gap and called it Ubet, but when the Great Northern Railway embarked on completing the line, they moved the townsite to the Olof Sandberg homestead. The first issue of the *Judith Gap Journal*, November 20, 1908, proclaimed Judith Gap "the fastest growing town in Montana," praising the climate and soils for growing wheat, oats, and barley. The Great Northern Railway established a locomotive shop and roundhouse in Judith Gap that employed 250 men. The town lost population during the drought of the 1920s and the depression that followed. Judith Gap's economic prospects soared in 2005 with the construction of a major wind farm, featuring 90 turbines generating 135 mW (enough to power 30,000 households), which has been touted as the most productive wind farm in the United States. The 260-foot towers dot the agricultural landscape. Judith Gap, like the river and mountains, derives its name from Capt. William Clark's fiancée, Julia (Judith) Hancock. Elevation: 4,639 ft. Location: Wheatland County

Judith Landing 1262 *map 5 E-1*

Francis A. Chardon established a fur trading post near the confluence of the Missouri and Judith rivers in 1844 for the American Fur Company. Although it was established to serve the Blackfeet, the Indians did not like the location of the post since it was not near their prime hunting grounds. A year later, when Alexander Culbertson took over, he relocated the post upriver. At the rivers' confluence, on September 13–14, 1846, Father Pierre-Jean De Smet arranged a council between the Salish and Blackfeet, which resulted in an agreement between the two to cease hostilities in the face of Crow encroachment. Less than a decade later, Isaac I. Stevens held a treaty negotiation with the Blackfeet near Judith Landing that resulted in the establishment of the first Blackfeet Agency in Fort Benton and defined the limits of Blackfeet territory. Judith Landing became a favorite stop for steamboats to take on more wood during the upper Missouri River steamboat era. The federal government established Camp Cooke (1866–70) to protect the steamboats operating on the river, but in fact the military post had little purpose, and the army abandoned it in 1870. At the same spot, in 1869, T. C. Power established Fort Clagett, named for William H. Clagett, who owned the land. The post office opened in 1872. Power diversified his cattle interests and eventually went into partnership with G. R. "Bill" Norris to establish the PN Ranch, running approximately 20,000 sheep by 1884. The community, on the line between Fergus and Chouteau counties, thrived as a service center for area ranchers and homesteaders before slowly dying out. Judith Landing became a national historic district in 1975 and is listed in the National Register. Elevation: 2,421 ft.

Judith Mountains 802 *map 13 B-2*

In May 1805, Capt. William Clark named the Judith River for his future wife, Julia (Judith) Hancock of Fincastle, Virginia. The mountains take their name from the river. Composed primarily of igneous intrusions, the Judiths extend about 18 miles north and east of Lewistown, and are a source of water for irrigating the many surrounding farms and ranches.

Judith River 695 *map 5 E-1*

The Crow tribe called this waterway Buluhpa'ashe, "Plum river." Capt. Meriwether Lewis named this central Montana river the Bighorn. On May 20, 1805, Capt. William Clark renamed it in honor of his future wife, Julia (Judith) Hancock. Beginning in the 1880s, the area surrounding the Judith River at Judith Landing was home to 2 large ranching operations: the DHS Ranch of A. J. and Erwin Davis, Samuel T. Hauser, and Granville Stuart; and the PN Ranch of Thomas C. Power and G. R. Norris.

Wedge Saloon, Kendall, c. 1903
Detail, George Carolus, photographer, MHS 948-871

Kalispell 67   *map 2 C-1*

As the tracks of the Great Northern Railway inched westward toward Seattle, Flathead Valley towns vied for designation as a railway division point. In spring 1891, railroad officials purchased land from Rev. George Fisher and other early residents to found a new settlement. The new town of Kalispell was platted in "T-town" form, with Main Street perpendicular to the proposed tracks. Some who doubted that the railroad would ever touch the new settlement dubbed it "Collapsetown" and "Wait a Spell," but even so, lots sold for as much as $1,250. Construction boomed on Main Street, and many businesses were moved on log rollers 4 miles across the prairie from once-thriving Demersville. On New Year's Day 1892, the tracks reached Kalispell. Banners mounted on an arch over the tracks proclaimed "Kalispell and St. Paul United by Steel," and "beer and whiskey were as free as the fresh air."

Although the railroad moved its division point to Whitefish in 1904, Kalispell prospered. Designated the county seat in 1893 and later bolstered by homesteading, the lumber industry, and tourism, Kalispell became an important trade, financial, and service center. It is named for the Pend d'Oreille tribe, the Kalispels. Kalispell has numerous properties listed in the National Register as well as 3 historic districts: Main Street Commercial, Courthouse, and East Side. Lone Pine State Park lies just south of town. Elevation: 2,960 ft. Location: Flathead County

Kendall 758   *map 13 B-2*

Harry Kendall bought several claims in the Kendall area, north of Lewistown, and in 1898 began developing them. Kendall owned a small smelter nearby, and in 1900 he built a cyanide mill at his Kendall mine. Over the next 10 years, the mill

Kalispell Fire Department, c. 1900
Detail, William M. Inglis, photographer, MHS 948-767

produced $6 million in gold. In 1915, the Barnes-King Development Company bought the mines and mill, which operated through lease until about 1923. The North Moccasin Mines Syndicate operated the mines during the 1930s. Canyon Resources Corporation bought the property in 1990 and operated it through 1997. Since shutting down the Kendall mines, Canyon Resources has been embroiled in a controversy with the State of Montana about the cleanup of mining pollution, including cyanide and arsenic. Elevation: 4,614 ft. Location: Fergus County

Kent Dairy Round Barn 986 *map 21 C-2*

Finnish immigrant Ephraim Kent settled in Red Lodge in the early 1900s to work in the coal mines. His wife, Fiina, began a small dairy business that was a family venture from the start, with all the children pitching in to deliver raw milk in buckets and, later, bottles to local customers. The business grew, and by 1938 the Kent sons and their wives were all involved in the dairy. When a city ordinance prohibited cows in town, the family purchased land north of town and an abandoned commercial building in the town of Bear Creek. They meticulously salvaged the building's bricks, wood joists, and decorative tin ceiling, which they used to build their barn. Steam pipes recovered from a nearby mine served as stall dividers; hand-hewn beams were finished with a plane whose cutting bit was a piece of leaf spring from a car; and 37 log support posts were shaped with a draw knife. Many locals remember summertime dances held in the spacious second floor before it was filled with winter feed. When Armas and Sylvia Kent retired in 1969, the barn was converted for use as a restaurant; it's listed in the National Register. Elevation: 5,280 ft. Location: Carbon County

Kerr Dam 141 *map 2 E-1*

Kerr Dam, constructed in 1938, was the largest dam and power plant among Montana Power Company's 13 hydroelectric projects. The dam, named for Frank Kerr, president of the company from 1933 to 1940, is taller than Niagara Falls and has more than 200,000 kW of power generating capacity. The Confederated Salish and Kootenai Tribes, which own the land on which the dam sits, receive an annual rental fee from PPL Montana (who purchased Montana Power Company's facilities in 2000). The tribes will have the option to purchase the dam in 2015. Elevation: 2,789 ft. Location: Lake County

Kershaw 653 *map 4 E-3*

Originally built in 1887 as a stockyard station on the St. Paul, Minneapolis & Manitoba Railway, Kershaw today consists of a grain elevator and a grain loading station. It is now on the Burlington Northern Santa Fe line. Elevation: 2,897 ft. Location: Chouteau County

Kevin 258 *map 3 B-3*

Founded during the homestead boom in 1910, Kevin (pronounced "Kee-vin") takes its name from Canadian Thomas Kevin, an Alberta Railway and Irrigation Company official. Kevin is most noted for its proximity to the Kevin-Sunburst Oil Field, which produced oil and gas in the 1920s. The Kevin Depot is listed in the National Register. Elevation: 3,327 ft. Location: Toole County

Keystone 156 *map 9 A-3*

Initially called O'Rourke, by miner Phillip O'Rourke, this town emerged with the discovery of silver in the area in 1887 and a year later claimed 500 residents. In 1890, townsfolk decided to rename it Carter, after Thomas H. Carter, a U.S. senator who helped the town obtain its first post office. The post office did not remain open for long, however, because the price of silver plummeted, and many residents left after the repeal of the Sherman Silver Purchase Act of 1890. The fortunes of the town reversed a few years later when the price of silver rebounded; this time townspeople renamed the town Keystone, after a local mine. Keystone prospered for a time, and the post office operated between 1913 and 1925, but when silver production diminished again, the residents departed, leaving behind only remnants of the past. Elevation: 3,375 ft. Location: Mineral County

Keystone Peak 154 *map 9 A-3*

Keystone Peak, Keystone Creek, and the town of Keystone are all named for the Keystone Mine, discovered and developed by Phillip O'Rourke and others in 1887, and operated on a larger scale beginning in June 1891 by the Keystone & King Mining Company. The silver mine operated sporadically until the 1930s. There was a fire lookout on the peak from 1934 until 1980. Elevation: 5,843 ft. Location: Mineral County

Kicking Horse Reservoir 171 *map 10 A-2*

This reservoir on the Flathead Indian Reservation, built by the Flathead Irrigation Project, was named for Antoine and Angelica Kicking Horse. The irrigation project, initiated by the U.S. Reclamation Service in 1909, now includes 15 storage reservoirs and more than 1,300 miles of canals and ditches. Elevation: 3,066 ft. Location: Lake County

Kila 64 *map 2 D-1*

Called Sedan by the Great Northern Railway when homesteaders settled the area in 1892, Kila derives its name from William Kiley. When Kiley filed for a post office in 1901, the spelling was somehow changed to Kila. The town was platted in 1914. The

Enterprise Lumber Company, which built the mill on Smith Lake, was the town's main employer for many years. Logging operations closed down in the 1930s. Elevation: 3,184 ft. Location: Flathead County

Kilbrennan Lake 6 *map 1 B-1*

This small mountain lake in northwestern Montana derives its name from a lake in Scotland. The date of its naming is not known. Elevation: 2,826 ft. Location: Lincoln County

Kings Hill Pass 627 *map 12 C-2*

Kings Hill Pass is named for the King family, early settlers in Meagher and Judith Basin counties. Cris King, his wife, Krazenta, and his sons, Joseph and Anton, came from Switzerland and settled in Diamond City sometime before 1880. They later established a large ranch in Judith Basin County. The Kings Hill road was built as part of the Yellowstone-Glacier-Banff highway in 1921. At elevation 7,393 feet, Kings Hill Pass is Montana's highest pass that is maintained year-round, and is the location of Showdown Ski Area. Location: Meagher and Cascade counties

Kingsbury Lake 587 *map 12 A-3*

This lake, named Mallard Lake by USGS geologists Louis N. Pirrson and Walter H. Weedin, was renamed for A. W. "Ike" Kingsbury, who arrived in Jefferson City in 1864 and later moved into the Boulder Valley. In the late 1870s, Kingsbury moved the first sheep into the Sun River country, and in 1880 he established the Big Sag Land & Livestock Company. Elevation: 3,185 ft. Location: Chouteau County

Kinsey 1147 *map 15 D-4*

Kinsey, named after pioneer rancher Jack Kinsey, acquired a post office in 1898. The area was originally settled by dryland farmers and ranchers. By 1918, it had a population of 50 and boasted a hotel, general store, and lumberyard. In 1938, the U.S. Resettlement Administration established the Kinsey Farms Resettlement Project, an irrigation project featuring 28 miles of canals in its initial phase. Families from 13 neighboring counties moved to the area, leasing land from the Farm Security Administration and establishing multicrop farms. Elevation: 2,305 ft. Location: Custer County

Kinsey Bridge 1145 *map 15 D-3*
The American Bridge Company of New York built the Kinsey Bridge for the Milwaukee Road in 1907, spanning the Yellowstone River near the town of Kinsey. This four-span pin-connected Parker through-truss structure is 1,080 feet long. There are 2 other identical railroad bridges in Montana: the Calypso Bridge southwest of Terry and the Paragon Bridge near Miles City. Elevation: 2,282 ft. Location: Custer County

Kintla Lakes 42 *map 2 A-1*
An 1846 Jesuit map refers to Lac et Riviere de Joset, named for Joseph Joset, a Jesuit missionary who worked in the area. Kintla is derived from a Kootenai word for a sack. According to legend, a man had drowned in one of the lakes, and the Kootenai said the lake was like a sack—once you got in, you couldn't get out. Upper Kintla Lake is the site of an early Montana oil well. Kintla Glacier lies just to the south of the lakes. Elevation: 4,012 ft. Location: Glacier National Park

Kintla Peak 51 *map 2 A-2*
Kintla Peak, part of the mudstone Kintla Formation, is distinguished by its red color. The name is derived from the Kintla Lakes. Elevation: 10,101 ft. Location: Glacier National Park

Kiowa 157 *map 2 C-4*
Kiowa is a town on the Blackfeet Indian Reservation, named for the Southern Plains tribe. A small campground and motel cater to Glacier National Park visitors. Elevation: 5,092 ft. Location: Glacier County

Kipps Lake 186 *map 3 C-1*
Kipps Lake is named for Joseph Kipp and his Mandan wife, Martha. Joseph was a merchant, whiskey trader, and son of James Kipp, an American Fur Company employee at Fort Benton. Joseph owned more than a section of land in the vicinity and was the first postmaster at Kipp, now called Blackfoot. Elevation: 4,111 ft. Location: Glacier County

Klein 937 *map 13 D-4*
Mike Klein was a native of Bohemia who came to Montana in 1879 to work for the Montana Cattle Company. In 1902, Klein established his own ranch in the Bull Mountains, south of the town of Roundup. Employees of the Milwaukee Road discovered coal on Klein's property in 1909. By 1918, the town had 2 general stores and 3 saloons that served the coal miners living there. Mike Klein sold the mine to the railroad's subsidiary, the Monarch Coal Company, which developed Republic Mine No. 2 to provide fuel for locomotives. When the railroad converted to diesel, the demand for coal declined, and the town of Klein was essentially abandoned. Elevation: 3,300 ft. Location: Musselshell County

Kleinschmidt Lake 288 *map 10 B-4*
Albert and Theodore Kleinschmidt were prominent early Helena businessmen engaged in banking, utilities, and ranching. Several members of the Kleinschmidt family homesteaded around the lake in the 1880s. Elevation: 4,182 ft. Location: Powell County

Koch Peak 822 *map 19 C-4*

Peter Koch, with his sons Stanley and Elers, made an early ascent of this summit in the Taylor Peaks of the Madison Range. Peter was a Gallatin Valley pioneer, bank cashier, county attorney, and amateur archaeologist. He helped found Bozeman's library and Montana State College. Elers Koch was one of Montana's first forest rangers. Elevation: 11,181 ft. Location: Madison County

Kolin 725 *map 13 B-1*

Kolin was born when the Great Northern Railway established a line between Great Falls and Lewistown around 1910. The settlement quickly boomed as homesteaders flocked to the area. Bohemian settlers named the small Montana town after one of their home towns in what is now the Czech Republic. Elevation: 3,945 ft. Location: Judith Basin County

Kootenai Creek 274 *map 10 D-1*

Kootenai Creek has gone through several name changes over the years. The 1863 John Owen Donation Claim Survey by Walter W. DeLacy showed it as Lyons Creek. It was called Mill Creek in 1864, Kootenoy Creek in 1872, and Lion Creek in 1879. The name was later normalized as Kootenai, which comes from the name of the northwestern Montana tribe. Location: Ravalli County

Kootenai Falls 9 *map 1 C-2*

Kootenai Falls, on the Kootenai River, has long been sacred to the Kootenai people. In 1808–09, Finan McDonald built a fur trading fort several miles upstream from the falls. Explorer David Thompson made a difficult portage around the falls in 1809, following Indian cairns. Thirty-five years later, Father Pierre-Jean De Smet described the portage in harrowing terms. Frank R. Miles filed water rights on the falls in 1891,

hoping to build a hydroelectric dam. He sold that right to lumberman James A. Coram about 1906. Coram's Kootenai Falls Power Construction Company completed the initial planning for a dam but gave it up. As recently as 1978, plans to build the Northern Lights Dam were proposed, but again, because of opposition by the Kootenai tribe and conservationists, the idea was abandoned. There is a foot trail and swinging bridge for viewing the falls. Elevation: 1,943 ft. Location: Lincoln County

Kootenai Lodge 126 *map 2 D-2*

Cornelius "Con" Kelley and Orvis Evans, aspiring young attorneys for the Anaconda Company, purchased this former homestead site in 1908 as a seasonal retreat. Both men rose to positions of great power and wealth. Kelley became the Anaconda Company's president and Standard Oil's vice president. Evans became chief counsel for both the Anaconda Company and the Montana Power Company. Together they expanded their rustic family retreat between 1914 and 1928, transforming it into a sprawling $2 million, 2,700-acre vacation spot for business associates and company executives. The finely crafted, elegantly appointed collection of log buildings and exquisite landscaping represents a most unusual juxtaposition of urban opulence and Arts and Crafts–inspired Western Rustic–style architecture against a backdrop of remote mountain timberland. Upturned rooflines on lakeshore arbors, "yin and yang" placement of outdoor flagstones, and peaceful gardens radiate Japanese charm. Etchings in concrete around the main lodge's courtyard are attributed to cowboy artist Charlie Russell, once a regular visitor. During the hard times of the 1920s, the lodge bolstered the local economy, employing many area craftsmen and 70 domestic servants. In 2005, the property, listed in the National Register, was sold to a Florida developer. Elevation: 3,085 ft. Location: Lake County

*Kootenai River and
Dome Mountain, 5
miles above Libby*
K. D. Swan, photographer,
MHS 948-901

Kootenai River 5 *map 1 B-1*

The Kootenai River, a tributary of the Columbia River, is named for the Kootenais who migrated from eastern Washington into northwestern Montana. The Kootenais fished the river for white sturgeon, paddling reed canoes that had long, sturgeon-like projections on the bow and stern. The Kootenai name for the river meant "bow," but early maps refer to it as McGillivray's River, honoring Duncan McGillivray, a North West Company compatriot of David Thompson. Thompson explored the Kootenai River drainage for the company in spring 1808. The lowest elevation in Montana is where the Kootenai River exits Montana at the Idaho state line at 1,820 feet.

Kremlin 564 *map 4 C-4*

Kremlin, "in the center of the Chocolate loam," received its first large group of homesteaders in 1910, many of them Russian. One explanation for the town's name, which is Russian for "fortress" or "citadel," is that Russian farmers claimed to see the citadel of Moscow in prairie mirages. On the main line of the Great Northern Railway, the town grew with the homestead boom of the 1910s. It underwent changes as the drought and recession of the 1920s forced many homesteaders to leave the area. Elevation: 2,857 ft. Location: Hill County

Kuester Lake 1163 *map 8 E-1*

William C. Kuester was a German immigrant who homesteaded here in 1913 with his wife, Augusta, and their 6 children. The family eventually grew to 13 children. Kuester and his wife died within 10 days of each other in August 1942. There is a fishing access site near the north end of the reservoir. Elevation: 2,397 ft. Location: Richland County

Organ Room, Morrison Cave, Lewis and Clark Caverns, c. 1910
N. A. Forsyth, photographer, MHS 957-791

La Hood Park 632 *map 19 A-3*

La Hood Park takes its name from Shadan "Dan" LaHood, a Lebanese immigrant who came to the United States in 1899 and moved to Butte shortly after. He married a Butte woman, Fannie Zinnie. In 1909, they opened a general store at Jefferson Island, which lay on the Yellowstone Trail auto route that was developed in the 1910s. LaHood proved an active booster for the road, and provided services for tourists traveling the route. In 1928, the Montana Highway Dept. built a road (now MT 2) between Three Forks and Whitehall, bypassing Jefferson Island. LaHood then purchased land along the new route and constructed a hotel, café, and service station. The area became known as La Hood Park. LaHood promoted the Lewis and Clark Caverns beginning in 1937. Elevation: 4,266 ft. Location: Madison County

Lake Bowdoin and Bowdoin NWR 919 *map 6 C-2*

President Roosevelt established the 15,551-acre Bowdoin NWR in 1936 by executive order to enhance waterfowl habitat in the region, particularly on Lake Bowdoin, a 4,000-acre horseshoe bend that is a former channel of the Milk River. During periods of drought, the lake dried up, hurting bird populations. A series of dikes constructed after the refuge's establishment captures spring runoff from the Milk River, creating nesting habitat for white pelicans, Caspian terns, various wading birds, and numerous other bird species. More than 200 bird species have been counted on the refuge over the years. Elevation: 2,211 ft. Location: Phillips County

Lake Como 345 *map 10 E-1*

Jesuit missionary Father Anthony Ravalli named Lake Como sometime in the 1840s for the lake in Italy. Pioneer orchardist Wilson B. Harlan arrived in the Bitterroot Valley in 1868, and in the 1880s he established one of the valley's first commercial apple orchards. A few sources credit him, not Father Ravalli, with naming the lake. Harlan served as the first postmaster of Como in 1882. The Bitter Root Valley Irrigation Company built a dam to raise the level of Lake Como and dug associated irrigation ditches about 1909, as part of the Bitter Root Valley Project that supplied water to apple orchards in the valley, but by 1918 the irrigation company had declared bankruptcy. Elevation: 4,249 ft. Location: Ravalli County

Lake County 155 *map 2 E-2*

Lake County, one of Montana's youngest counties, was formed in 1923 from portions of Missoula and Flathead counties. Its county seat is Polson. It is named after Flathead Lake, which lies mostly within the county's borders, as does half of the Flathead Indian Reservation. The county is famous for its cherry orchards.

Lake Frances 244 *map 3 C-2*

Lake Frances was created by a dam begun about 1909 by several private companies in cooperation with Montana's Carey Land Act Board, as part of the Conrad-Valier Project. The project selected the name Frances for W. G. Conrad's wife, Frances (Fannie). When construction was completed in 1927, the lake covered 6 miles by 3 miles (5,600 acres) to a depth of 36 feet, with storage for irrigating 70,000 acres. The town of Conrad draws its water from Lake Frances. Elevation: 3,816 ft. Location: Pondera County

Lake Helena 467 *map 11 C-3*

Completion of Hauser Dam on the Missouri River in 1907 created Hauser Lake. In addition, it created an arm of the lake, flooding 8 miles of Prickly Pear Creek and surrounding wetlands to form Lake Helena. In 1945, a causeway was built to separate the lake from the flooded canyon portion of the old Prickly Pear Creek. Water from Tenmile Creek, Prickly Pear Creek, Silver Creek, and the Helena Valley Irrigation Canal flows into the west end of the lake. Lake Helena supported a commercial carp fishery for decades. The marshy west end of the lake is now a popular birding location. Elevation: 3,655 ft. Location: Lewis and Clark County

Lake Koocanusa 11 *map 1 B-3*

Lake Koocanusa, a 90-mile-long reservoir created by Libby Dam, derives its name from an amalgamation of Kootenai, Canada, and USA. The U.S. Army Corps of Engineers began work on the 370-foot-long hydroelectric and flood-control dam in 1967, following an agreement with Canada for use of Kootenai River water. The powerhouse has the potential to produce 840,000 kW of electricity. Completed in 1975, the project cost $466 million. The town of Warland disappeared under the reservoir, but Rexford was relocated to a bench above the original townsite. Elevation: 2,465 ft. Location: Lincoln County

Lake Mary Ronan State Park 91 *map 2 D-1*

According to Mary Ronan, the wife of Flathead Indian agent Peter Ronan, "The Indians who guided [my husband] to this remote, beautiful lake northwest of Flathead Lake could tell him no name for it, so he named it in honor of his wife and eldest daughter." The lake, shaded by Douglas-fir and western larch, is a popular place for picking wild huckleberries and mushrooms, bird watching, hiking, and camping. Elevation: 3,727 ft. Location: Lake County

Lake Mason NWR 900 *map 13 D-3*

Administered by the Charles M. Russell NWR, Lake Mason NWR is one of several small refuges established by executive order in 1941 primarily to protect wetlands for migratory birds and waterfowl. Elevation: 3,750 ft. Location: Musselshell County

Lake McDonald 78 *map 2 B-2*

Lake McDonald and nearby McDonald Creek have had many names. Prior to 1878, the lake was known as Terry Lake, after Gen. Alfred Terry. Today, according to the predominant theory, the lake is named for Duncan McDonald, son of Hudson's Bay Company factor Angus McDonald, and his Salish wife, who visited the area in 1878. Duncan carved his name in a birch tree by the lake, and gradually, people began referring to it as McDonald's Lake. With the coming of the Great Northern Railway in 1892, settlers, including Milo Apgar, began arriving at the lake. Apgar built cabins on his land to accommodate visitors. The NPS formalized the name as Lake McDonald. The Kootenais referred to the cascades above the lake as a "good place to dance." A translation of the

Lake McDonald, Glacier National Park, 1909
Fred H. Kiser, photographer, MHS 956-733

Blackfeet name for McDonald Creek is "the bear wags its tail." Elevation: 3,157 ft. Location: Glacier National Park

Lake McDonald Lodge NHL 81 *map 2 B-2*
One of the finest examples of the Swiss Chalet style in the United States, Lake McDonald Lodge was the second hotel constructed on this site. George Snyder built the first in 1895. John E. Lewis, a land speculator from Columbia Falls, acquired the property in 1906 and set out to build a hotel "worthy of the park." The Spokane firm of Kirtland, Cutter, and Malmgren designed the hotel, called the Lewis Glacier Hotel, carrying the Swiss Chalet detailing throughout. The Great Northern Railway's Glacier Park Hotel Company obtained the concession rights to the property in 1930 and changed its name to Lake McDonald Lodge, completing the company's monopoly of the major park hotels. Its Western Rustic style and craftsmanship of the highest quality blend well with the park's other hotels. Elevation: 3,172 ft. Location: Glacier National Park

Lake Sherburne 115 *map 2 B-3*
Created by a dam in 1920 at the head of Swiftcurrent Creek, the lake is named for Joseph H. Sherburne, owner of Sherburne Mercantile in Browning and Swiftcurrent Oil, Land & Power Company (which made the first oil discovery in Montana). The lake was a main source of water for the Milk River Irrigation Project. This project began in 1902 to bring water to the lower Milk River from more reliable sources in the upper Milk River. Since the Lake Sherburne Dam had been planned prior to the establishment of Glacier National Park, and the dam was just outside the park boundaries, it was grandfathered in. The water level in the lake fluctuates greatly; during dry times, the shoreline is stark and bare. In recent years, the Blackfeet tribe has been working with the U.S. Bureau

of Reclamation to resolve environmental problems. Elevation: 4,792 ft. Location: Glacier County

Lake Sutherlin 647 *map 12 C-2*
Lake Sutherlin is named for the R. N. Sutherlin family, who homesteaded in the area in the 1880s and '90s. Sutherlin was a journalist and agricultural promoter who began his career at Diamond City publishing the *Rocky Mountain Husbandman*, which he later moved to White Sulphur Springs. The North Fork Smith River Dam, built in the 1930s by the State Water Conservation Board, created the lake. It provides irrigation water to 29 registered users on 11,000 acres. Elevation: 5,486 ft. Location: Meagher County

Lake Thibadeau NWR 639 *map 5 B-1*
Lake Thibadeau NWR, named for local farmers Solomon and John Thibadeau, was established on September 23, 1937, by executive order, to provide a breeding ground for migratory birds and other wildlife. The refuge consists of 3 small lakes: Lake Thibadeau, Grassy Lake, and Dry Lake. Elevation: 2,661 ft. Location: Hill County

Lakeside 95 *map 2 D-1*
The community of Stoner, named for John J. Stoner, proprietor of a hotel near the shores of Flathead Lake, grew up around Stoner's business establishment in 1892. Residents wished to call the town Lakeside, but such a place already existed, in Roosevelt County. They settled briefly on Lacon. After the demise of the Roosevelt County community in 1920, this Flathead County town changed its name to Lakeside. West Side State Park is south of town. Elevation: 2,907 ft. Location: Flathead County

Lakeview 875 *map 19 E-3*

Originally named Shambow, for George H. Shambow, one of the area's earliest residents and its first postmaster, this Centennial Valley town was renamed Magdalen and finally, in the late 1890s, Lakeview, for its scenic location. Lakeview served as a supply center for Centennial Valley ranchers. Newspaper correspondent Lillian Hackett Hanson Culver wrote of life in the valley in the *Dillon Tribune* in 1897: "It looks like some of the women in this valley will soon be entitled to divorces if their husbands don't spend a little more time at home with them. It is rather a lonesome place to expect their wives to be content, living alone so much." Elevation: 6,709 ft. Location: Beaverhead County

Lambert 1189 *map 8 E-2*

The Great Northern Railway surveyed the Lambert townsite in 1914 as a station on the branch line it was building from Sidney to Circle. Though the population never exceeded 1,000 people, Lambert, with 4 grain elevators and a railroad siding, was the largest wheat-shipping point in the world between 1914 and the 1920s. Donald Nutter, Montana's governor from 1961 to 1962, was born in Lambert. Elevation: 2,372 ft. Location: Richland County

Lame Deer 1127 *map 23 B-1*

Named for Sioux leader Lame Deer, this town on the Northern Cheyenne Indian Reservation is home to the tribal headquarters. It was the site of a trading post from the late 1870s on, and in 1884 the settlement became home to the Tongue River Agency when the Northern Cheyenne returned from exile in Oklahoma. Elevation: 3,352 ft. Location: Rosebud County

Lame Deer Agency, Northern Cheyenne Indian Reservation, 1904
L. A. Huffman, photographer, MHS 981-038

Lamesteer NWR 1232   *map 16 C-4*

President Franklin D. Roosevelt established Lamesteer NWR on May 19, 1942, by executive order. The refuge is named for nearby Lame Steer Creek, which, according to local sources, recalls a 3-legged steer raised by a local rancher. It is administered by the Medicine Lake NWR. Elevation: 2,890 ft. Location: Wibaux County

Landusky 825   *map 5 E-4*

Landusky takes its name from Powell "Pike" Landusky, a Missourian from Pike County who came to Montana in 1864 and settled in Alder Gulch. Landusky worked as a cattleman for a time, then discovered gold in the Little Rocky Mountains in 1887, which led to a boom there. The town that bears his name was founded in 1894 to supply the influx of miners. Pike Landusky died on December 27, 1894, after being shot by outlaw Kid Curry (Harvey Logan) in an altercation in Pike's saloon. Elevation: 4,011 ft. Location: Phillips County

Larb Hills 956   *map 6 C-3*

The names Larb Hills and Larb Creek are a corruption of the French word *l'herbe,* meaning an herb or a plant; it was used to describe the kinnikinnick plant commonly smoked locally. Scandinavians settled in the Larb Hills in the early 1910s. The town of Harb, which no longer exists, was a further corruption of *l'herbe,* made when postal officials misread the name of the requested post office. Elevation: 2,548 ft. Location: Phillips County

Laredo 606   *map 5 C-1*

Great Northern Railway officials in 1912 named Laredo for the town in Spain. By 1915, the little town boasted 12 businesses, laid out in a single row along the tracks. Elevation: 2,642 ft. Location: Hill County

Larslan 1050   *map 7 B-2*

The Larslan post office opened in 1918 in Otho B. Moore's sod house. Moore had requested the name Hyatt, after a local family, but was overruled by postal officials who replaced the name with Larslan for an unknown reason. Beginning in the late 1920s, the town had a sizeable Mennonite population; the Mennonite Brethren Church held services from 1928 to 1990. Elevation: 2,906 ft. Location: Valley County

Laurel 983   *map 21 A-3*

The history of Laurel, once known as Carlton, is tied to the Northern Pacific Railroad. Laurel first appeared as a post office in 1886. One story links the town's name to a railroad official from North Carolina, where the laurel is a dominant shrub. The town of Laurel eventually served 3 railroads: the Northern Pacific, the Great Northern, and the Chicago, Burlington & Quincy. In 1906, the Great Western Sugar Company erected a sugar beet–processing plant here. Agriculture has always been important to the local economy, but oil refining is the town's main industry. The Laurel Leaf Refinery opened in 1930 and expanded into the Farmers Union Refinery in the 1940s; today it is known as the CENEX Refinery. Elevation: 3,300 ft. Location: Yellowstone County

Laurin 708   *map 19 B-2*

Jean Batiste Laurin (pronounced "Lahray") settled on the Ruby River in 1863 and operated a general store at a location he named Cicero. The post office that opened here in 1874 was named Laurin for this early settler. One resident described Mr. Laurin as looking like "a little 8 gallon keg of beer." The town served as a supply center for the Alder Gulch mines and surrounding agricultural areas, but after the 1930s it experienced a steady decline. Laurin's Saint Mary of the Assumption Church is listed in the National Register. The infamous Hangman's Tree, where on January 4, 1864, members of the Vigilance Committee hanged Erastus "Red" Yager and G. W. Brown—members of Sheriff Henry Plummer's outlaw gang, the Innocents—stands half a mile from town. Elevation: 5,065 ft. Location: Madison County

Lavina 910 *map 13 E-3*
Working for T. C. Power & Bro., Walter Burke selected Lavina as a stage stop in 1882. It lies at the crossing of the Musselshell River, between Fort Benton and Billings; audaciously, Burke named the station after a former girlfriend rather than his wife. Lavina was an important stop on the stage line since, in 1903, it took 12 hours to travel by stage from Billings. The town did not experience significant growth until the arrival of the Milwaukee Road in 1907. The railroad purchased land for a depot east of the town. The town that grew up around the depot adopted the name Lavina as well, resulting in the abandonment of Old Lavina in 1908. The new town incorporated in 1920. The Adams Hotel and Slayton Mercantile are listed in the National Register. Elevation: 3,451 ft. Location: Golden Valley County

Lebo Lake 788 *map 12 D-4*
Lebo Lake is a reservoir created in the early 1900s by the Lake Lebo Irrigation Company, headed by W. J. Beecher. Over the years, the irrigation system has been upgraded by a series of owners. The reservoir is unusual in that it stores and releases water from 2 creeks, Lebo Creek and American Fork Creek. The origin of the name Lebo is uncertain. Elevation: 4,925 ft. Location: Wheatland County

Ledger 296 *map 3 D-4*
This tiny settlement has had at least 5 names in its short lifetime. The townsite

of Esper was originally laid out in 1914 and named for N. Esper Norman. The post office, opened in 1916 under the name Esper, changed its name in 1917 to Ledgerwood in honor of local resident Dan Ledgerwood. Since North Dakota already had a Ledgerwood, some residents shortened the name to Ledger. In 1922, 3 different names represented the small town: Ledger (the townsite), Storrenberg (the post office, named for the postmaster), and Price (the railroad station, named for a local merchant). Finally, in 1926, postmaster Frank Stuart led a petition to declare one name for all the sites, and the residents chose Ledger. Elevation: 3,256 ft. Location: Pondera County

Lee Metcalf NWR 269 *map 10 C-2*
Ravalli NWR was established in 1963 to provide habitat for migratory birds. The refuge lands had been part of the Peter Whaley farm, which in the early 1900s was managed as an apple orchard by the Bitter Root Valley Irrigation Company. In 1978, the refuge changed its name to honor U.S. Senator Lee Metcalf for his strong advocacy in preserving Montana's natural places and wilderness. Elevation: 3,261 ft. Location: Ravalli County

Lee Metcalf Wilderness 853 *map 20 D-1*
Congress designated the Lee Metcalf Wilderness in 1983, in honor of longtime U.S. Senator Lee Metcalf, who was a strong proponent of wilderness preservation. This southwest Montana wilderness is in 4 separate units in the Madison Range, administered by the BLM and the USFS.

Lemhi Pass NHL 675 *map 18 C-3*
On August 12, 1805, Capt. Meriwether Lewis and 3 of his men followed a winding Indian trail west. As they stood on the Continental Divide, the snowcapped mountains that lay before them shattered

their hopes of an easy crossing. In the decades that followed, traders, fur brigades, and Blackfeet used the pass along the route known then as the Blackfoot Road. In 1855, Mormon settlers founded a colony on the west side of the Continental Divide and named it Fort Limhi, after fair-skinned King Limhi in the *Book of Mormon*. Settlers later corrupted the spelling to Lemhi. Lemhi Pass was on the stage route from Salmon, Idaho Territory, to Red Rock, Montana Territory. The pass was abandoned after construction of the Gilmore & Pittsburgh Railroad, and then Route 324 over Bannock Pass. Elevation: 7,373 ft. Location: Beaverhead County

Lennep 707   *map 12   D-3*

Norwegian immigrant M. T. Grande started a sheep ranch on Comb Creek in 1877, and a small settlement began to develop nearby as other Norwegian immigrants arrived. Many of them worked for Grande until they established themselves. This trend caused one Ringling resident to quip that the only English the Norwegian shepherds could speak was "M. T. Grande." The settlement shifted and coalesced after the arrival of the Milwaukee Road, which purchased the Montana Railway Company's "Jawbone Railroad" in 1907 and established a station here. It is thought that a railroad auditor named the town after his home town of Lennep, Germany. The Trinity Lutheran Church was built in Lennep in 1914 to serve the Norwegian residents. Elevation: 5,240 ft. Location: Meagher County

Lewis and Clark Caverns State Park

637   *map 19   A-3*

Named for the explorers Meriwether Lewis and William Clark, these caverns first became known to Euro-Americans in 1892, when Bert Pannell and Tom Williams found the limestone caves while deer hunting along the Jefferson River. In 1903, Dan

Morrison, manager of a lime quarry owned by the Northern Pacific Railway, began exploring the caves with the idea of creating a tourist attraction called Morrison Cave. In 1908, the Northern Pacific deeded the property to the federal government, and on May 11 President Theodore Roosevelt named the caverns a national monument. In 1935, the federal government committed a contingent of 200 CCC workers to building roads, trails, and a visitor center. Six years later, on May 4, 1941, Lewis and Clark Caverns State Park opened to the public, a 2,735-acre park featuring tours of brilliantly colored calcite stalactites and stalagmites and a large population of little brown bats. The caverns were the first state park in Montana. Elevation: 4,921 ft. Location: Jefferson County

Lewis and Clark County 328   *map 11   B-2*

Edgerton was one of the original counties established by the territorial legislature in 1865, with Silver City as its county seat. The leaders of the growing town of Helena, however, wanted Helena as the county seat. To achieve this end, attorney Wilbur Fisk Sanders rode to Silver City in 1865, stole the county records, and rode back to Helena with the documents in his saddlebags. In December 1867, the legislature renamed the county for explorers Meriwether Lewis and William Clark and designated Helena the county seat. It is suggested that the change came about because southern members of the legislature were unhappy with the affiliation of former territorial governor Edgerton with the national Radical Republican faction.

Lewistown 782   *map 13   B-2*

In 1874, Maj. William H. Lewis established a store in what is now Lewistown, and a community grew up around it and the nearby Reedsfort post office, which was in operation between 1881 and 1885. Starting in 1879, a group of Métis—people of French and

Making up a logging train, Libby
MHS PAc 97-14.9

Chippewa-Cree descent—homesteaded in this area, and many Lewistown street names memorialize these settlers, including Francis A. Janeaux and Paul Morase. But open-range cattle ranching, nearby gold discoveries, and growth of the sheep industry quickly made Lewistown, at the geographic center of Montana, a regional supply center. Fergus County was created in 1885, with Lewistown as its county seat. C. E. Bell, one of the Montana State Capitol architects, designed the jail in 1904. The elegant stone Carnegie library was built in 1907. The Lewistown Art Center is housed in what was once the Charles Lehman Bunkhouse. Several Croatian builders and stonemasons settled in Lewistown and left a tangible legacy in the stone buildings that grace the town's streets. Some of these are listed in the National Register. Also listed are the Central Business, Courthouse, Judith Place, and Silk Stocking historic districts. Elevation: 3,942 ft. Location: Fergus County

Lewistown Satellite Airfield Historic District
775 *map 13 B-2*
The U.S. Army selected Great Falls as the site of a large air base after the Decem-

ber 7, 1941, Japanese attack on Pearl Harbor and the massive congressional defense appropriations that followed. Concurrent with the Great Falls construction were satellite airfields at Cut Bank, Glasgow, and Lewistown. On October 28, 1942, the first Boeing B-17 Flying Fortresses roared over Lewistown's Main Street with their bomb bays open, buzzed the treetops, and landed at the Lewistown airfield. Crews trained day and night, combining navigation, bombing, and gunnery practice. The men familiarized themselves with all aspects of the B-17 and trained with the top-secret Norden bombsight, a computerized aiming device that reportedly could "put bombs in a pickle barrel." After one to three months of instruction, aircrews flew directly to Europe to join the war. Nearly 1,000 GIs trained at the Lewistown Satellite Airfield until it was deactivated in 1943 after 11 months of service. Because the U.S. Dept. of Defense systematically removed "temporary" World War II–era buildings, this intact airfield is a rarity, and its Norden bombsight storage shelter is the only known identifiable example remaining in the United States. Elevation: 4,143 ft. Location: Fergus County

Libby 15 *map 1 C-2*
John S. Fisher led a group of miners through Kootenai River country in the early 1860s. As they panned for "color" in the streams of northwestern Montana, they named many of the Kootenai's tributaries. One small stream was named Libby Creek by Stephen Allen, after his daughter Elizabeth "Libby" Allen. Miners flocked to Libby Creek in 1867 as word of a promising placer strike spread, and the mining camp of Libbysville was established. Miners deserted Libbysville by the 1870s, and the camp did not experience a revival until 1885. Six years later, B. F. Howard and several other miners received

word that the Great Northern Railway was going to construct its transcontinental rail line along the Kootenai River. As a result, they moved downstream from Libbysville and established a townsite near the confluence of Libby Creek and the Kootenai River. The new town shortened its name to Libby and replaced Libbysville in 1892. Throughout most of its history, Libby, the Lincoln County seat, has relied on the mining and timber industries. Elevation: 2,087 ft. Location: Lincoln County

Libby Creek 16 map 1 C-2

Libby Creek flows out of the Cabinet Mountains. The discovery of gold here in 1867 led to the establishment of a mining camp named Libbysville. Stephen Allen named the nearby creek for his daughter Elizabeth "Libby" Allen. Location: Lincoln County

Liberty County 382 map 4 B-2

Liberty County was formed in 1920 from portions of Chouteau and Hill counties, in part due to public dissatisfaction with Chester losing out to Havre as county seat for Hill County. Chester is now the seat of Liberty County. There is no official explanation of the name, but it can be assumed to be an expression of patriotism after World War I. The county's economy is dominated by agriculture.

Lima 808 map 19 E-1

This community (pronounced "Lie-ma") appeared when the Utah & Northern Railway established a maintenance facility in 1880. L. Eugene Simmons became the first postmaster a year later. The town, originally named Allerdice, became Spring Hill and finally Lima in 1889, after pioneer Henry Thompson's home town in Wisconsin. Montana's first railroad community boomed and then declined as advances in railroad technology eliminated the need

for the services the town provided. For several decades, the railroad maintained a roundhouse and machine shop in Lima, until they were consolidated into the facility in Pocatello, Idaho. Elevation: 6,257 ft. Location: Beaverhead County

Lima Reservoir 828 map 19 E-2

A dam on the Red Rock River forms this irrigation reservoir created by the State Water Conservation Board in 1934. The reservoir takes its name from the town. Elevation: 6,577 ft. Location: Beaverhead County

Limestone 902 map 20 B-4

Limestone is named for nearby Limestone Butte and Limestone Creek. This town, in the mountains northwest of Nye, was settled by the Lowe, Holt, and Hawkes families. For many years, Milton C. Lowe farmed and ran a general mercantile here, and his wife, Frances, was postmaster. Elevation: 5,523 ft. Location: Stillwater County

Lincoln 319 map 11 B-1

The area where Lincoln now stands was well known to travelers. The fabled Coka-lihishkit, "River of the road to the buffalo," was followed by the Nez Perce, Salish, and other tribes to the buffalo grounds of the Montana plains. Capt. Meriwether Lewis led a small contingent along this same route on his return trip to the Great Falls of the Missouri River in July 1806 and noted that "the road was a well beaten track we could not miss our way." In 1865, prospectors David Culp and Thomas Patterson struck gold near here. They decided to name the site Lincoln Gulch in memory of the recently assassinated president, Abraham Lincoln. By 1880, most of the placer mines had played out, and the local economy converted to farming and logging. The present town of Lincoln developed 4 miles east of Lincoln Gulch, on the road between Missoula and Great Falls. Numerous small sawmills operated in the valley, primarily supplying local needs. A notable event in Lincoln's history occurred in 1996, when federal authorities tracked down the Unabomber, Ted Kaczynski, living in a cabin southeast of Lincoln. The 1918 Lincoln Community Hall is listed in the National Register. Elevation: 4,542 ft. Location: Lewis and Clark County

Lincoln County 13 *map 1 B-2*
The Montana legislature created Lincoln County from Flathead County in 1909 in response to petitions from Libby and Eureka residents. The new county in far northwestern Montana takes its name from President Abraham Lincoln. After a spirited campaign, Libby defeated Eureka in the election for county seat. Wood products have historically dominated the county economy.

Lindbergh Lake 197 *map 10 A-3*
Lindbergh Lake is named for aviator Charles A. Lindbergh, who spent several days at the lake in summer 1927 seeking solitude from his adoring crowds. The lake had previously been named Elbow Lake for its shape. Nearby Lindy Peak was also named for the aviator, by "Cap" Eli Laird. Elevation: 4,324 ft. Location: Missoula County

Lindsay 1164 *map 16 B-1*
This town is named for Willam Lindsay, an Ohio-born businessman and the first rancher and freighter in the region. Present-day Dawson County was opened up to homesteading about 1905, and by 1908 there were more than 30 families in the vicinity of Lindsay. The town moved when the Northern Pacific Railway built its branch line to Circle in the 1920s. Elevation: 2,696 ft. Location: Dawson County

Little Beaver Creek (Fallon) 1243 *map 16 E-4*
There are 9 Little Beaver Creeks, and even more Beaver Creeks, around the state—testament to the importance of this small fur-bearing mammal. Little Beaver Creek in Fallon County rises in the Chalk Buttes in Carter County and flows into the Little Missouri River in North Dakota. Several exploratory oil wells were drilled near the creek in the 1920s, with no success. In 1936, Montana-Dakota Utilities discovered oil in several wells and built a compressor plant southeast of Baker near Little Beaver Creek. There is also a Beaver Creek in the northeast corner of Fallon County.

Little Belt Mountains 609 *map 12 C-2*
Originating before 800 million B.C., the Little Belts stretch in an arc of Precambrian sedimentary rocks overlaid by younger formations, with igneous intrusions called laccoliths. The name is derived from a geological designation, the Belt Formation. The map created by the Isaac I. Stevens 1853 railroad survey showed the mountains as the Girdle Mountains, referring to their distinctive banding he called a "girdle," or belt. The Little Belts were a prodigious source of timber, gold, silver, sapphires, and coal during the late nineteenth and early twentieth centuries, and they remain a primary source of Missouri River water, which emanates from the Smith, Musselshell, and Judith rivers and Belt Creek.

Little Bighorn Battlefield National Monument 1085 *map 22 B-3*
Sioux, Northern Cheyenne, and Arapaho warriors defeated 12 companies of the 7th U.S. Cavalry under Lt. Col. George Armstrong Custer here on June 25–26, 1876. In 1879, the battlefield received designation as a national cemetery, and in 1940 jurisdiction transferred to the NPS. The battle was long known as "Custer's Last Stand" and the place called Custer Battlefield. In

1991, Congress changed it to Little Bighorn Battlefield National Monument. A memorial to honor the Indian participants who fought and died in the Battle of the Little Bighorn was dedicated on June 25, 2003. The Crow name for the battlefield is Ihkale'axdaaku, "Where Child of the Morning Star was wiped out," referring to Custer by his Crow name. Elevation: 3,167 ft. Location: Big Horn County

Little Bighorn River 1064   map 22   A-3

Named for bighorn sheep, the Little Bighorn River gained notoriety as the site of the battle between Lt. Col. George Armstrong Custer of the 7th U.S. Cavalry and a large gathering of Sioux, Northern Cheyenne, and Arapaho warriors on June 25–26, 1876. The seat of Crow tribal government is along the river's banks at Crow Agency. The Little Bighorn flows north out of the Bighorn Mountains in Wyoming and joins the Bighorn River at Hardin.

Little Bitterroot Lake 55   map 1   D-4

Little Bitterroot Lake, previously known simply as Bitterroot Lake, is named for the wildflower of the same name—Montana's state flower. The route of the Great Northern Railway over Haskill Pass ran along the east shore of the lake, and the railroad built an ice plant at the lake to cut and store ice for use by passengers on the trains. When the main line was moved, a spur line continued to serve the lake for several years. On the northeast edge of the lake, a man named Pomeroy built what became known as the Crazy Man's Castle. He started building it for his fiancée, and when she jilted him he reportedly became insane and continued to build his castle in an eclectic style. The castle burned in 1929. A dam, completed in 1918, raised the level of the lake. Elevation: 3,907 ft. Location: Flathead County

Little Blackfoot River 369   map 11   D-1

John Work, chief trader for the Hudson's Bay Company, mentioned both the Little Blackfoot River and the Blackfoot River by name in his journal entries for October 22 and November 4, 1831. He did not mention the origin of the names, but they most likely refer to the Blackfeet. He did mention that Americans had been heavily trapping the river ahead of him. John Mullan later traveled down this river, heading west from Little Blackfoot Pass, which later became Mullan Pass.

Little Dry Creek 1076   map 15   A-2

Like its brother Big Dry Creek, Little Dry Creek was named by Lewis and Clark for its lack of water. Together, the 2 intermittent creeks drain the southern half of Garfield County. The last 40 miles of the combined creeks are now flooded by Fort Peck Reservoir. The area around the 2 creeks is known colloquially as the "Big Dry." Location: Garfield County

Little Missouri River 1252   map 24   B-4

Lewis and Clark named the Little Missouri River on April 12, 1805. It rises near Oshoto, Wyoming, flows across southern Carter County in Montana and through a corner of South Dakota, and empties into the Missouri River on the Fort Berthold Indian Reservation in North Dakota.

Little Powder River 1224   map 24   B-1

The Powder River, after which the Little Powder River is named, derives from the Lakota word *yela*, which means "powdery," a reference to the fine silt found in the river. The Little Powder River Valley in southeastern Montana attracted Clinton Graham and, later, S. F. Biddle to the area in the late 1880s. These ranchers eventually established the Cross Ranch, and the area has continued to have a ranching economy.

Natural Bridge, Little Rockies, Blaine County
MHS 949-090

Little Rocky Mountains 832 *map 5 E-3*

The origin of the name Little Rocky Mountains is not known, but this range in north-central Montana is on the Northern Plains, isolated from the main stem of the Rocky Mountains. Euro-American habitation of these mountains followed the discovery of gold by Frank Aldridge in 1885 and subsequent construction of a mill in Alder Gulch by Pete Zortman. During this period, Powell "Pike" Landusky discovered gold in Montana Gulch near Landusky. In 1904, Ben Phillips and Charles Whitcomb organized the Ruby Gulch Mining Company, which operated the mines until about 1951. In the 1970s, Pegasus Gold Corporation began a large cyanide heap-leach mine near the Zortman mines, which leaked thousands of gallons of cyanide solution into adjacent creeks in the 1980s. Pegasus declared bankruptcy in 1998, leaving the State of Montana to clean up the toxic waste. The northern part of the mountain range is on the Fort Belknap Indian Reservation. The tribe has played an active role in trying to enforce cleanup of the mines.

Livingston 813 *map 20 A-2*

Johnston Livingston was a stockholder and director (1875–81 and 1884–87) of the Northern Pacific Railroad. The town of Livingston grew out of a trading post called Benson's Landing, sited 3 miles downstream. When Northern Pacific Railroad construction contractors arrived in July 1882, the trading post became known as Clark City, named for railroad contractor Herman Clark. The railroad officially reached the area on November 22, 1882, and moved the entire town to its present location a month later, renaming it Livingston. Livingston became county seat of the newly created Park County in 1887, and in the 1890s Livingston welcomed several manufacturing businesses into the area, including sawmills and cigar factories. The Northern Pacific remained its largest employer; it operated the largest Northern Pacific shops west of the Mississippi here. Livingston has 4 historic districts in the National Register: Commercial, East Side Residential, West Side Residential, and B Street. Elevation: 4,501 ft. Location: Park County

Livingston Range 61 *map 2 A-2*

The Livingston Range in northwestern Glacier National Park was named in 1873 for the famous British explorer David Livingstone, who had been tracked down in Africa by Henry M. Stanley the previous year. Earlier, in 1858, Lt. Thomas Blakiston had named a Canadian range on the east side of the Rocky Mountains for Livingstone, who had recently crossed the entire African continent. Elevation: 10,142 ft. Location: Glacier National Park

Lloyd 703 *map 5 D-2*

Situated in the shadow of the Bears Paw Mountains, Lloyd is named for an early prospector, "Old Man Lloyd." The town achieved permanency when William Wilson established a post office and store in 1890. Its proximity to the Tiger Ridge Oil Field and the Bowes Oil Field resulted in prosperity in the 1920s. Elevation: 3,908 ft. Location: Blaine County

Lodge Grass 1104 *map 22 B-3*

The community of Lodge Grass is at the confluence of Lodge Grass Creek and the Little Bighorn River, on the Crow Indian Reservation. This is the site of the traditional Crow summer hunting camp. They called the creek "Greasy Grass" because of the rich grass that was said to make the animals fat. The words *grease* and *lodge* are very similar in the Crow language, and the name of the creek was accidentally interpreted as Lodge Grass instead of Greasy Grass. The community now serves as a supply center for the surrounding ranches. Several homes and businesses and the Lodge Grass Jail are listed in the National Register. Elevation: 3,366 ft. Location: Big Horn County

Lodge Grass Creek 1105 *map 22 C-3*

The Crows named this creek Bikkaatashee ashe, "Greasy grass," for the rich grass, which "makes the horses fat." It empties into the Little Bighorn River at the town of Lodge Grass. This confluence was the site of a large battle between the Crow and Gros Ventre tribes in the 1860s. The creek's headwaters are in the Bighorn Mountains in northern Wyoming. Location: Big Horn County

Lodge Pole 829 *map 5 D-4*

Lodge Pole, a community on the Fort Belknap Indian Reservation, had a post office as early as 1899. The name comes from the distinctively tall, straight pines used for poles of Assiniboine and Gros Ventre tipis. The Lodge Pole Community Hall is listed in the National Register. Elevation: 3,417 ft. Location: Blaine County

Lodge Grass, Crow Indian Reservation, c. 1910
MHS PAc 88-84

Logan 684 *map 19 A-4*

Logan began in 1866 as a cluster of buildings around a stage stop called Canyon House. Eventually, the town was renamed Logan, in honor of early resident Edelia Logan, whose husband, John, was killed at the Battle of the Little Bighorn. In 1883, the Northern Pacific Railroad centered its siding operations at Logan, building a roundhouse, water tank, section house, coal dock, sand house, and company housing, bringing new life and long-term prosperity to Logan. Madison Buffalo Jump State Park, 7 miles south of Logan, is one of the largest such archaeological sites in Montana. Elevation: 4,113 ft. Location: Gallatin County

Logan Pass 101 *map 2 B-3*

Logan Pass is named after the first superintendent of Glacier National Park, William Richard Logan, who began his career as an army scout during the Great Sioux War of 1876–77. According to James Willard Schultz, author and adopted member of the Blackfeet tribe, early mountain men knew this pass as Trapper Pass; the Blackfeet called it Misam-ohsokoi, "Ancient road." Elevation: 6,646 ft. Location: Glacier National Park

Logging Lake 60 *map 2 B-2*

The Kootenai name for Logging Lake and Logging Creek is translated "Big beaver," for a legendary 20-foot beaver. During the 1890s, there was extensive logging in the area, and the first settlers coined the name to commemorate the felling of large ponderosa pines in the area. Elevation: 3,814 ft. Location: Glacier National Park

Lohman 679 *map 5 C-2*

Established first as a division point on the Great Northern Railway, Yantic became Lohman when its post office opened on November 2, 1916. A. S. Lohman, a local rancher and later a banker, was a good friend of James J. Hill's son, Louis. Lohman's wife, Lillie, was the first postmaster. Elevation: 2,442 ft. Location: Blaine County

Lolo 242 *map 10 C-1*

When the Lewis and Clark Expedition spent the night in the vicinity of present-day Lolo, members of the Corps of Discovery named the campsite Travelers' Rest. There are many explanations about the origin of the name Lolo. According to historian Olin Wheeler, the Salish referred to the creek as Tum-sum-lech, meaning "No salmon." Another version attributes a corruption of the French name for Meriwether Lewis, "Le Louis." A third points to the Chinook word for "pack" or "carry," or it may be based on the Nez Perce word for "muddy water." Elevation: 3,195 ft. Location: Missoula County

Lolo Pass 233 *map 9 C-4*

Sources point to several different origins for the name Lolo (see the previous entry). On September 13, 1805, the Lewis and Clark Expedition ascended Lolo Pass and continued west on their arduous trek to the Pacific Ocean. Elevation: 5,235 ft. Location: Missoula County

Lolo Peak 248 *map 10 C-1*

Lolo may be derived from the Chinook word for "pack" or "carry," the Nez Perce word for "muddy water," or a corruption of the French name for Meriwether Lewis, "Le Louis." Elevation: 9,139 ft. Location: Missoula County

Lolo Trail NHL 232 *map 9 C-4*

The 140-mile Lolo Trail winds through thick mountain timberland, following ridgetops along an ancient Nez Perce route. The Lewis and Clark Expedition found the trail strewn with fallen timber that made it treacherous and difficult to follow. Sick with dysentery, hungry, and wet, the explorers still managed to cover about 18 miles a day. On the return in June 1806, Patrick Gass dreaded recrossing "the most terrible mountains I ever beheld." Despite 7 feet of snow, they safely reached Travelers' Rest on the eastern side of the Continental Divide. The Lolo Trail was the corridor the Nez Perces traveled to seasonal buffalo hunts. It was also the route they used to flee their homeland during the Nez Perce War of 1877. The Nez Perce NHP encompasses the Lolo Trail NHL; US 12 follows parts of it from Travelers' Rest State Park to Lolo Pass in the Lolo National Forest and west to Weippe Prairie in Idaho's Clearwater National Forest.

Loma 531 *map 4 E-3*
Local lore suggests that Loma received its name in 1911 from a Mexican railroad worker who translated James J. Hill's last name into Spanish, *loma*, meaning "knoll" or "hill." Another story has it that Loma is shorthand for Lower Marias—from "Lo Ma," telegraph operators' shorthand for the Great Northern Railway station. Just upstream of the confluence of the Marias and Missouri rivers, the area received high praise from Capt. William Clark, who thought it offered "a proper and handsome situation for a trading establishment." James Kipp of the American Fur Company founded the first community here in 1831 with the establishment of Fort Piegan. The Blackfeet laid siege to the fort, and inhabitants quickly abandoned the site. The next year, the American Fur Company established another trading post, Fort McKenzie, a few miles upstream of the old site. During the 1860s, as Fort Benton prospered from the steamboat trade on the Missouri River, Virginia City businessmen decided to cash in on the trade and established a townsite near the confluence of the Marias and the Missouri, called Ophir. This new location offered a longer

shipping season for the steamboats because of its deeper channel. On May 25, 1865, the Blackfeet killed 10 men in the developing town. This signaled the end of Ophir. The few buildings that remained became fuel for the steamboats. Elevation: 2,575 ft. Location: Chouteau County

Lombard 642 *map 11 E-4*
Named for A. G. Lombard, a Northern Pacific engineer, the town of Lombard was founded about 1895. It was a thriving community early in the twentieth century, situated at the junction of the Northern Pacific Railway and the Milwaukee Road. Lombard's first mayor was Billy Kee, a Chinese man who also owned the first hotel and restaurant in town. Elevation: 3,991 ft. Location: Broadwater County

Lone Mountain 787 *map 19 C-4*
Lone Mountain takes its name from its prominent position among lower peaks in the Madison Range. The mountain attracted Chet Huntley, Montana native and cohost of the Huntley-Brinkley NBC news program, when he visited the Lone Mountain Guest Ranch in 1968. In 1974, Huntley's Big Sky Ski Resort opened. Today the complex runs a tram to the summit of Lone Mountain. Elevation: 11,166 ft. Location: Madison County

Lonepine 107 *map 1 E-4*
Prior to establishment of a post office in 1911, ranching dominated the Little Bitterroot River Valley, situated southwest of Flathead Lake. The McDonald family, related to Angus McDonald of the Hudson's Bay Company, had become the largest ranching family in the area, but that all changed with the arrival of homesteaders in 1910 and the creation of an elaborate irrigation system in 1916. The name Lonepine is attributed to William Whiteside, a Canadian immigrant and the first postmaster, who thought

Lombard and railroad bridge over the Missouri River, c. 1910
MHS 949-105

it appropriate to name the settlement after the solitary tree located next to his log store and house. From the 1910s forward, Lonepine supported a local school and community hall. In 1921, the U.S. Reclamation Service built the Lower Dry Fork Reservoir to provide irrigation for the region. The 2,800-foot-long dam impounds 4,200 acrefeet of water. The BIA currently maintains the reservoir as part of the Flathead Agency Irrigation Division. Elevation: 2,861 ft. Location: Sanders County

Lonetree 602 *map 12 A-3*

Christopher and Edward Wilson chose this narrow canyon as headquarters for their ranching operation in 1887. The brothers lived in a dugout while they built a more serviceable 2-room cabin, using granite and sandstone from the nearby hillside. By 1895, when Edward brought his bride to the ranch, the brothers had finished a 2-story home of hand-cut sandstone, complete with running water piped in from the nearby spring. In 1900, Lonetree was designated a post office and served as both mail and stage stop between the railroads at Fort Benton and Lewistown. When the "sodbusters" began arriving between 1908 and 1912, Lonetree, named for the single cottonwood tree that marked the Wilson ranch headquarters, became the mailing address for hundreds. New homesteaders filled their wooden barrels at the Lonetree spring until their own wells could be dug. In 1912, the Lonetree School was established in the original 2-room cabin. On colder days, students gathered in an upstairs room of the "big house." Lonetree had become the focal point of a community scattered over 400 square miles, but when the Milwaukee Road bypassed it in favor of developing the new towns of Geraldine and Square Butte, Lonetree's importance dwindled. In 1915, the stage line disbanded and the school closed. In 1928, Lonetree had a new beginning when newlyweds John and Mary Tanner added the Wilson ranch to their holdings. The Tanner family has preserved the ranch. Elevation: 3,113 ft. Location: Chouteau County

Lookout Pass 97 *map 9 A-1*

From the vantage point of this mountain pass, a person can "look out" west into the Coeur d'Alene Mountains in Idaho. The pass was originally known as Coeur d'Alene Pass. Lookout Pass Ski and Recreation Area now spans the pass, located half in Montana and half in Idaho. Elevation: 4,725 ft. Location: Mineral County

Loring 894 *map 6 B-2*

Loring began as a stop on the Great Northern Railway's branch line between Saco and Hogelund. The name possibly came from Charles M. and Albert C. Loring, flour mill owners in Minneapolis. The post office opened in 1929. For a time, Loring bustled with activity. Eventually, it became a stopover for tourists on their way to Canada. Elevation: 2,705 ft. Location: Phillips County

Lost Creek State Park 411 *map 10 E-4*

According to miner W. J. Garrity, Lost Creek is so named because it disappears near its head. Founded in 1957, Lost Creek State Park is named for the 50-foot-high Lost Creek Falls. The park features spectacular gray limestone cliffs and unusual folded, pink-and-white granite formations rising 1,200 feet above the canyon floor. Elevation: 6,391 ft. Location: Deer Lodge County

Lost Trail Pass 461 *map 18 A-1*

The Lewis and Clark Expedition was searching this pass on September 4, 1805, when their guide, failing to recognize it, led them over a tortuous route to the west. The pass became known as Lost Trail Pass in the 1930s, when the State Highway Commission replaced an earlier route over Gibbon Pass with a route over Lost Trail Pass. This pass in extreme southwestern Montana sits astride the Montana-Idaho state line. Elevation: 7,014 ft. Location: Ravalli County

Lothair 355 *map 4 C-1*

Originally a station on the Great Northern Railway, Lothair became a town in 1910 when Peter A. Greiner opened a lumberyard and built shacks for newly arrived homesteaders. At the peak of its prosperity in the 1910s, it had 4 grain elevators, 2 churches, a bank, a hotel, and assorted other businesses. Elevation: 3,321 ft. Location: Liberty County

Lower Yellowstone Diversion Dam 1204 *map 16 A-3*

Passage of the Newlands Reclamation Act in 1902 prompted a survey of the lower Yellowstone River Valley in 1903 to determine the viability of an irrigation system. When complete in 1912, the Lower Yellowstone Irrigation Project included a main canal 72 miles long as well as 225 miles of lateral canals. Construction of a sugar beet–processing plant in Sidney by the Holly Sugar Company in 1925 promoted widespread planting of sugar beets. Today sugar beets are still processed each autumn in Sidney. Elevation: 1,985 ft. Location: Dawson County

Lozeau 178 *map 9 B-4*

This town is named for Adolph Lozeau and his wife, Louise, who built a trading post on the Mullan Road in the mid-1860s; Louisville, an early Cedar Creek mining town, was named for Mrs. Lozeau. The post office in Lozeau opened in 1921 and closed in 1925; it reopened in 1927 and operated until 1963. Elevation: 2,826 ft. Location: Mineral County

Lump Gulch 494 *map 11 D-3*

Prospectors Fred Jones and William M. Sprague named Lump Gulch in 1864 for a lump of gold they found there. The gold did not live up to its original promise and the site was abandoned, but miners started mining lode silver there in the 1890s. A town known as Lump began about a mile up the gulch, with a post office that operated from 1895 to 1898. The largest mine in the gulch was the Liverpool, which produced rich silver ore from the 1890s until it closed in 1940. The creek flowing down the gulch originates above Park Lake. Elevation: 4,191 ft. Location: Jefferson County

Lustre 1082 *map 7 C-3*
The Lustre area began attracting homesteaders about 7 years after the Fort Peck Indian Reservation was opened to non-Indian settlers in 1908. Most of these early residents were German-Russian Mennonites. When store owner Henry C. Dick applied for a post office, he held a contest to name the community. Claus K. Dick looked through a dictionary and chose the name Luster. Postal officials changed the spelling to Lustre when the post office opened in 1917. Elevation: 2,843 ft. Location: Valley County

Luther 967 *map 21 C-2*
Grace Luther became the first Luther postmaster in 1907; the community takes its name from this pioneer family. Residents laughingly referred to tiny Luther and the nearby town of Linley as the "Twin Cities." Although Linley no longer exists, the small community of Luther still serves surrounding farmers. Elevation: 5,187 ft. Location: Carbon County

M

McDonald Peak and Crow Creek, Glacier National Park, 1921

Herman Schnitzmeyer, photographer, MHS PAc 96-42.3

CROW CREEK AND McDONALD

MacDonald Pass 1263 *map 11 D-2*

In 1869, the territorial legislature authorized Constant Guyot to construct a toll road from Helena west to the Little Blackfoot River. A year later, E. M. Dunphy bought the contract and completed construction of the 10-mile road over this pass south of Mullan Pass. Dunphy hired Canadian prospector Alexander MacDonald to manage the toll road, and MacDonald bought it from him in 1876. As many as 3 stages a day crossed the pass, en route to Deer Lodge. Valentine Priest assumed management of MacDonald's toll road in 1876, but in 1879 he established a competitive route to the north, which was eventually named for him (Priest Pass). At first, Priest lured away the stagecoach traffic because Priest Pass was hundreds of feet lower, but by 1912 improvements to MacDonald Pass had established it as the primary auto route between Helena and Deer Lodge. Elevation: 6,320 ft. Location: Lewis and Clark County

Macon 1257 *map 7 D-4*

Macon began as a stop on the Fort Peck Indian Reservation along the Great Northern Railway's route through northern Montana. Nothing is known about the origin of the name. Elevation: 1,982 ft. Location: Roosevelt County

Madison Buffalo Jump State Park 696
map 19 A-4

Native tribes stampeded huge numbers of buffalo off this massive semicircular cliff. Runners used drivelines (piles of rock) above the cliff to funnel the stampeding herd over the edge. Men waiting at the bottom dispatched wounded animals. The women butchered the carcasses, prepared the meat, and made jerky and pemmican, a dietary staple made from buffalo fat and berries. The layers of bones that still line the cliff's base are evidence of generations of use, from 2,000 years ago to as recently as 200 years ago. Archaeologists have found tipi rings near this site, indicating that groups used the area as an extensive seasonal village. Acquisition of the horse in the 1700s changed hunting practices, making buffalo jumps obsolete, but some were used periodically for ceremonial purposes, until the demise of the buffalo herds in the late nineteenth century. Madison Buffalo Jump State Park is listed in the National Register. Elevation: 4,713 ft. Location: Gallatin County

Madison County 735 *map 19 C-3*

Madison County takes its name from the Madison River, named in 1805 by Lewis and Clark after secretary of state and future president James Madison. The territorial legislature created Madison County on February 2, 1865, with Virginia City as the county seat. This southwest Montana county's boundaries remained unchanged until 1911, when the state legislature gave part of it to Beaverhead County. Madison County covers 3,541 square miles, encompassing the Madison Valley, Ruby Valley, Tobacco Root Mountains, and Gravelly Range.

Madison County Fairgrounds 645
map 19 B-2

Twin Bridges in 1887 had few public gathering places, so these 50 acres, once part of the Lott and Seidensticker homesteads, were developed as "the Park." A "harvest home barbecue" was held that year, and 2 years later the event blossomed into the county's first annual fair. Early fairs were privately run and, later, partially supported by the county. The fair gave ranchers and farmers a chance to show their best produce and livestock while promoting local pride and friendly rivalry. In 1928, the depressed economy ended the event, and in 1930 Madison County purchased the fairgrounds property. The economy worsened through 1934, leaving more than half of

Madison County's workforce unemployed. In 1935, the WPA approved funding assistance to rebuild the unused fairgrounds. Engineer C. D. Paxton drew the plans, and Tosten Stenberg, well known for his log structures in Yellowstone National Park, directed construction. Foreman Fred Sommers came out of retirement to supervise the project. Construction began in 1936, putting a great number of unemployed residents back to work. Workers gathered and prepared local lodgepole pine, fir, and other building materials on site. When the project was completed in 1937, 7 masterfully crafted new buildings and 1 remodeled 1890s structure greatly expanded the traditional fair. Today the buildings, listed in the National Register, are architecturally significant for their fine design, as well as historically important for the WPA construction that used entirely local materials and labor. Elevation: 4,635 ft. Location: Madison County

Madison Dam 729 *map 19 B-4*

In 1906, the Butte Electric & Power Company built this dam in Bear Trap Canyon, on the Madison River, north of Ennis. It replaced an earlier power plant built by Lucius Lucien Nunn. Rebuilt and enlarged in 1913, Madison Dam backs up 3 miles of the river into the canyon and up into a portion of the valley to form Ennis Lake. Elevation: 5,531 ft. Location: Madison County

Madison Range 818 *map 19 C-4*

The range takes its name from the Madison River, named by Capt. Meriwether Lewis and Capt. William Clark for secretary of state and future president James Madison. The Madison is one of the largest mountain ranges in the state, extending from Yellowstone National Park to south of Bozeman. It contains several peaks over 10,000 feet, including Blaze Mountain, Lone Mountain, the Sphinx, and the highest, 11,297-foot Hilgard Peak. Portions of the range are in the Lee Metcalf Wilderness.

Madison River 1126 *map 19 B-4*

On July 28, 1805, Capt. Meriwether Lewis and Capt. William Clark agreed to name the middle fork of the Missouri River at Three Forks for secretary of state and future president James Madison. The river is one of several major river systems that originate in Yellowstone National Park, including the Snake River and the Yellowstone River. The name of the river was later given to the county and the mountain range.

Madoc 1118 *map 7 B-4*

Homesteaders began arriving on the Big Bench in 1909. In 1910, the community acquired a post office under the name Orville. Dissatisfied with that name, residents finally selected Madoc as a compromise among several competing suggestions. The Great Northern Railway's branch line from Bainville to Scobey arrived in 1913. In its early years, residents referred to Madoc as the "Hub City of the Big Bench" because of its size, prime farmland, and proximity to the northern entrance of the Fort Peck Indian Reservation. Elevation: 2,778 ft. Location: Daniels County

Mahan and Hoyt Reservoir 1026 *map 7 D-1*

The Mahan and Hoyt Reservoir is named for Archibald Mahon (though the spelling was corrupted) and his brother-in-law, Dr. Mark D. Hoyt, partners in a pharmacy business from about 1898 to 1902. Mahon also served as county surveyor, superintendent of irrigation on the Fort Belknap Indian Reservation, and state engineer. Hoyt had an active medical practice, helped establish Glasgow's hospital, served as mayor of the town, and was involved in numerous charitable endeavors. Elevation: 2,120 ft. Location: Valley County

Maiden 800 *map 13 B-2*

"Skookum Joe" Anderson, David Jones, and others first discovered gold in Virgin and Alpine gulches in the vicinity of Maiden in 1880. C. C. Snow and J. R. Kemper established the townsite of Maiden in April 1881. Mrs. James H. (Jennie) Connely named the town for her daughter, whom the miners had nicknamed the "Little Maiden." Maiden's gold mines were originally on the Fort Maginnis military reservation; reservation boundaries were redrawn to exclude the developing mines. The district included the productive Maginnis, Spotted Horse, and Collar gold mines. The town was almost totally destroyed by fire in August 1905. Elevation: 4,819 ft. Location: Fergus County

Makoshika State Park 1202 *map 16 B-2*

As early as 1893, Andrew Larson proposed a park for the extraordinary Makoshika (pronounced "Ma-KO-shi-ka") badlands, in eastern Montana which consist of sandstone rock formations with stripes of scoria that were formed when lightning ignited seams of lignite coal. The idea of a park was espoused by other proponents over the years, including A. A. Baker in 1923 and a group called the Badlands Park Boosters in 1939, the year the WPA built roads into the area. The Montana State Park Commission officially established Makoshika State Park in 1953. *Makoshika* (or *Maco Sica*) is a Sioux word for "badlands." Fossilized remains of wooly mammoths and dinosaurs have been discovered in the park. Elevation: 2,575 ft. Location: Dawson County

Malmstrom Air Force Base 443 *map 12 A-1*

The U.S. Army established East Base in 1942 as a fueling stop for airplanes bound for the Soviet Union, part of the Lend-Lease program during World War II. It also served as a training facility for 4 bombardment groups. After the war, it became a training base for the Berlin Airlift. On June 15, 1956, the name Malmstrom Air Force Base was adopted to honor Col. Einar Axel Malmstrom, who died in 1954 when his T-33 crashed a few miles south of the base. In 1954, the U.S. Strategic Air Command stationed the 407th Strategic Fighter Wing at Malmstrom. In response to Cold War fears, in 1960 Boeing Corporation began building the Minuteman missile field in a wide oval stretching from Heart Butte to Shawmut. Between 1960 and 1967, crews built 200 missile launch control facilities, better known as missile silos, connected by cable to 20 launch control centers staffed by officers on alert 24 hours a day. In 2007, about 6,600 military personnel worked at Malmstrom, contributing more than $287 million to the local economy annually. In 2007, approximately 200 Minuteman III missiles, each capable of carrying three 20-megaton nuclear warheads, remained on alert beneath the Montana prairie. Elevation: 3,470 ft. Location: Cascade County

Malta 898 *map 6 C-2*

Like many High Line towns, Malta, a railroad siding established in 1887, was named by Great Northern Railway officials for a European locale (in this case a Mediterranean island). The open area around Malta attracted many cattlemen and some of

Men playing poker, probably in Malta
MHS 949-176

the largest cattle companies in Montana, including the Bloom Cattle Company, the Coburn Circle C, and the N Bar N. One of Malta's most exciting moments occurred on July 3, 1901, when the Kid Curry gang robbed a Great Northern train near here, escaping with nearly $40,000. When the surrounding area was opened for homesteading in the 1910s, Malta boomed; it became the county seat when the Montana legislature created Phillips County in 1915. During the Great Depression, Malta was the base for the Milk River Resettlement Project, the federal government's effort to relocate poor dryland farmers to farms in the irrigated Milk River Valley. The CCC also established a camp at Malta. Today Malta remains a cattle town that offers many tourist attractions, including the nearby Bowdoin Wildlife Refuge. Elevation: 2,253 ft. Location: Phillips County

Mammoth 650 *map 19 A-3*

A ghost town, Mammoth is named for the Mammoth Mine it served. John Hughes and James Howe started the gold mine about 1876, and in the early 1900s as many as 7 mining companies operated in Mammoth. The Mammoth Mine operated sporadically from 1914 until its closure in the 1930s. Elevation: 6,027 ft. Location: Madison County

Manchester 397 *map 11 A-4*

Manchester developed as a station stop on the Great Northern Railway, named for the Vermont-based Manchester Woolen Mills established here about 1906. About 1908, J. T. Rundell opened the Manchester Distillery (later renamed the Montana Distilling Company and then the Sun River Distilling Company), possibly the first commercial distillery in Montana. The distillery closed about 1915. Today Manchester has all but disappeared, although a handful of ranches and residences still form a community. Elevation: 3,351 ft. Location: Cascade County

Manhattan 702 *map 20 A-1*

Known as Hamilton when established in 1865, this town became a Northern Pacific Railroad station stop in 1883. In 1884, English investors incorporated the Moreland Ranch Stock Company and started Moreland, a new community on the railroad near the older town of Hamilton. When the Manhattan Malting Company of New York arrived in 1891, the town changed its name to Manhattan. The malting operation employed fewer than a dozen men, but several barley-producing agricultural communities, including Churchill and Amsterdam, grew up around the plant. Manhattan malt supplied breweries in Montana and around the world. The business came to an end in 1916 as Prohibition loomed nationwide, but by this time Manhattan was firmly established as an agricultural center. Elevation: 4,245 ft. Location: Gallatin County

Manicke 41 *map 1 D-3*

Fred and Augusta Manicke homesteaded in the Pleasant Valley–Fisher River area of southern Lincoln County in 1912. Augusta was postmaster of the Manicke post office from 1915 until 1924. The Manickes were instrumental in establishing the Manicke School in 1919, and they supervised a rural library that operated out of the post office. The Manicke schoolhouse is still visible today along US 2. Elevation: 3,066 ft. Location: Lincoln County

Manternach Coulee 1110 *map 7 B-4*

This coulee is named for John Manternach, who homesteaded nearby about 1902. The first year, Manternach sowed 20 acres of oats, and during the hard winter of 1906–07 the family lost more than 300 of their 335 cattle. During the next 2 decades, other members of the Manternach family homesteaded in this vicinity on the Poplar River. Elevation: 2,333 ft. Location: Daniels County

Marias Pass 160 *map 2 C-4*

Named for the Marias River, which Capt. Meriwether Lewis called Maria's River in honor of his cousin Maria Wood, Marias Pass has long been an important crossing over the Continental Divide for the Salish and other tribes. When John Frank Stevens, principal engineer for the Great Northern Railway, was searching with his Blackfeet guide Coonstah for a rail route over the mountains, he was attracted by the gentle grade of the approaches to this pass. The Great Northern constructed its line over the pass in 1890–91 and heavily promoted Glacier as a tourist destination after it became a national park in 1910. A statue of Stevens stands atop the pass, along with an obelisk honoring Theodore Roosevelt. The pass straddles the line between Glacier and Flathead counties. Elevation: 5,280 ft.

Marias River 532 *map 4 D-3*

On June 8, 1805, Capt. Meriwether Lewis named this Maria's River, after his cousin Maria Wood. Initially, Lewis and his party thought this northern tributary of the Missouri might be the mighty river's main stem. Lewis described it as a "noble river; one destined to become . . . an object of contention between the 2 great powers of America and Great Britin." For an unknown reason, the spelling and pronunciation changed from Maria's to Marias (pronounced "Ma-RI-as"). The river is formed by the confluence of the Medicine River, Birch Creek, and Cut Bank Creek.

Marion 57 *map 1 D-4*

The Great Northern Railway created Marion in 1891 as the terminus of a short spur line that ran west from Kalispell. The town acquired a post office in 1892. Established by Charles Haverlandt in about 1906, the Marion Store, with its eatery, hotel, saloon, dance hall, and livery stable, was the town's social center for many years. Today's Lang Creek Brewery, located in Marion, bills itself as "America's Most Remote Brewery." Elevation: 3,944 ft. Location: Flathead County

Martin City 79 *map 2 C-2*

Martin City, established on the homestead of Gaspard Martin near Abbott Creek, owes its existence to the early 1950s construction of the Hungry Horse Dam on the South Fork of the Flathead River. While the U.S. Bureau of Reclamation worked the appropriations bill for the dam through Congress in 1947, Martin City's population swelled in anticipation of the coming boom. Montana author Joseph Kinsey Howard remarked: "On and around the dam site a group of 'boom-towns' living solely on beer and hope have sprung up." He marveled at the cocksure attitude of Martin City, which, when less than a year old, planned a Pioneer Days to honor its old-timers. Martin City lives on as a tourist town, on the road from Columbia Falls to Glacier National Park. Elevation: 3,208 ft. Location: Flathead County

Martinsdale 730 *map 12 D-3*

The settlement was first known as Gauglersville to honor Franklin J. Gaugler, who built a general store and hotel at the site in 1876. The name changed to Martinsdale, after Martin Maginnis, Montana Territory's delegate to Congress, who assisted the town in getting a post office in 1878. When the Montana Railway Company ("Jawbone Railroad") laid track through the Musselshell Valley in 1899, Martinsdale moved 2 miles south to be closer to the rail line. Martinsdale's 2 most famous early-day residents are Charles M. Bair, one of Montana's most successful sheepmen, and Grace Stone Coates, a nationally recognized fiction writer. Elevation: 4,823 ft. Location: Meagher County

Thomas Cruse, founder of Marysville, c. 1900
MHS 941-810

Martinsdale Reservoir 739 *map 12 D-4*

Named after the town of Martinsdale in neighboring Meagher County, the WPA constructed the reservoir in 1938–39, under the auspices of the State Water Conservation Board as part of the Upper Musselshell Irrigation Project. Elevation: 4,784 ft. Location: Wheatland County

Marysville 392 *map 11 C-2*

In 1876, Thomas Cruse discovered and developed the famous Drumlummon Mine, named for his home parish in Ireland. It made the penniless Irish immigrant a wealthy man. Cruse supposedly named the town after Mary Ralston, an early settler. Cruse sold his mine to English capitalists in 1882. Marysville prospered during the next decade, especially with the coming of a Northern Pacific Railroad branch line in 1886. The Marysville Mining District eventually yielded $30 million in gold. In the early twentieth century, fire destroyed much of the original commercial district. The Methodist Episcopal Church, listed in the National Register,

and the Marysville school are reminders that several thousand people once lived in the vicinity. A handful of residents still live in the town. Elevation: 5,420 ft. Location: Lewis and Clark County

Maudlin 1084 *map 15 C-1*

Now one of eastern Montana's many abandoned communities, Maudlin was named for Lloyd Maudlin, proprietor of the first post office in 1916. The settlement never amounted to more than a school, the post office, and a few other buildings. Elevation: 3,075 ft. Location: Rosebud County

Maudlow 670 *map 12 E-1*

Named as a combination of Richard A. Harlow's wife, Maud, and their last name, Maudlow began as a railroad town on the Montana Railway, on a line that began north of Three Forks at Lombard and headed northeast through Maudlow toward Lewistown. The town got a post office in 1898. The Montana Railway Company, owned and financed by Harlow, was almost always called the "Jawbone Railroad." According to the story, Harlow encountered so many difficulties building the road (weather, right-of-way disputes, finances) that he had to repeatedly talk his way out of bankruptcy—hence the moniker. Elevation: 4,412 ft. Location: Gallatin County

Maxville 341 *map 10 D-4*

Named for nearby Flint Creek, Flint was a station on the Northern Pacific Railroad's spur line from Drummond to Philipsburg as early as 1888. Residents changed the name to Macville, in honor of Robert R. MacLeod, a Philipsburg livery stable owner, when they submitted their application for a post office in 1912. When the paperwork was returned, the name on the official form was Maxville. Elevation: 4,844 ft. Location: Granite County

McAllister 724 *map 19 B-3*

Originally called Meadow Creek and boasting a post office beginning in 1869, McAllister was renamed in 1896 for James Alexander McAllister Jr., son of one of the earliest settlers in the area. When the local school burned in the 1890s, James Jr. had rallied local support to construct a new one. In 1896, James Jr. purchased land from the Northern Pacific Railway's Norris branch line for an expanded townsite, named McAllister. Elevation: 4,906 ft. Location: Madison County

McCabe 1193 *map 8 C-3*

Originally named Leland, this community began in 1909 as a café owned and operated by Andrew and Anna Jern, located near the John Hofman farm. A year later, H. B. Johnson opened a general store. With the arrival of the Great Northern Railway's Bainville to Scobey branch line in 1912, the railroad built a commercial scale here to weigh grain prior to shipment, and more businesses moved to the community. About the same time, Bainville resident John Lundquist purchased 40 acres of land for the townsite. The town's name is most likely related to Oscar McCabe, who became the first postmaster of Homestead, north of Froid, and allowed the railroad to establish a work camp on his property during construction of the branch line. Elevation: 2,202 ft. Location: Roosevelt County

McClellan Creek 491 *map 11 D-3*

A tributary of Prickly Pear Creek, which drains the northwest corner of the Elkhorn Mountains, McClellan Creek was explored by prospectors in the 1860s. The area, including Mitchell Gulch to the east, became known as the McClellan Mining District. The most likely source for the name was John L. McClellan, who led several 1860s prospecting expeditions in Montana. Location: Jefferson and Lewis and Clark counties

McClellan Gulch 332 *map 11 C-1*

A rich placer discovery, McClellan Gulch yielded $7 million in gold between 1864 and 1875. The diggings were reworked numerous times, and in 1927 a miner uncovered a nugget weighing 57 ounces and valued at more than $1,000. The name is likely related to either Civil War general George McClellan or early prospector John L. McClellan. Elevation: 4,851 ft. Location: Lewis and Clark County

McClure Reservoir 1146 *map 15 C-4*

McClure Reservoir is named for Lewis G. McClure, who homesteaded this area about 1910. Nothing is known about when, or by whom, the reservoir was built. McClure's land reverted to the General Land Office in 1937 and was sold to private parties as part of a land exchange in 1984. Elevation: 2,552 ft. Location: Prairie County

McCone County 1102 *map 7 E-3*

Although the Montana legislature officially created McCone County on April 1, 1919, it had tentatively approved the new county 2 months earlier but spent the interim debating what to call it. Some legislators advocated for Redwater, after the Redwater River, but another noted that "it would help a lot in the Senate if the name remained McCone. Several senators told me they would vote for it just to honor the old man." The legislature agreed to it, honoring Montana pioneer Senator George McCone of Dawson County. McCone County voters awarded the county seat to Circle by a narrow margin.

McCormick's Livery and Feed Stable Sign 581 *map 11 D-4*

Painted in black and orange directly on a vertical, gray limestone rock wall, this 8-by-15-foot sign reads, "The Best in Town, McCormick's Livery and Feed Stable, Near Depot—Townsend." Ficklin T. McCormick

Circle, McCone County seat, 1907
Detail, L. A. Huffman, photographer, MHS 981-075

established his business in 1883, and was the largest livery in Townsend; he sold the business in 1915. The sign, listed in the National Register, is a rare example of early advertising and a vivid reminder of the time when horses were the primary mode of transportation. Elevation: 3,964 ft. Location: Broadwater County

McDonald Peak 185 *map 10 A-2*
The highest point in the Mission Mountains, McDonald Peak is named for Angus McDonald, a Hudson's Bay Company employee who in 1847 established a trading post at Fort Connah in the Flathead Valley. Angus's son Duncan McDonald made a name for himself as a railroad surveyor and historian of the Flathead Indian Reservation and early fur trading posts. Elevation: 9,820 ft. Location: Lake County

McGregor Lake 54 *map 1 D-4*
McGregor Lake is named for Forester McGregor, who homesteaded at the head of this lake in late 1887. McGregor emigrated from Scotland in 1852 to work in coal mines in Pennsylvania and metal mines in California and Nevada. He settled briefly at Tobacco Plains before moving to McGregor Lake, where he established a large cattle and hay ranch. He died in 1910. Elevation: 3,895 ft. Location: Flathead County

McGuire Creek 1080 *map 7 E-2*
McGuire Creek flows into McGuire Creek Bay on the southern end of Fort Peck Reservoir's Dry Arm. The McGuire Creek area contains important geological sites, including the Tullock Formation (Early Paleocene). The state operates a recreation area and campground nearby. The origin of the name is uncertain. Location: McCone County

McLeod 868 *map 20 A-4*
This settlement was named for W. F. McLeod, who brought 125 head of cattle and 200 horses from Oregon and established a general store on this site in 1882. The community sits at the confluence of the West Boulder and Boulder rivers and originally served the miners coming and going along the river. McLeod's most famous resident, writer Tom McGuane, is known for his novels, including *The Sporting Club* and *92 in the Shade*. Elevation: 4,804 ft. Location: Sweet Grass County

McLeod Peak 213 *map 10 B-2*

After rejecting several other names for the summit, in 1921 the U.S. Board of Geographic Names selected the name McLeod Peak for this, the highest summit in the Rattlesnake Mountains, to honor Charles H. McLeod, a manager of the Missoula Mercantile. Elevation: 8,620 ft. Location: Missoula County

Meagher County 634 *map 12 C-2*

The territorial legislature created Meagher County in 1867. Thomas Francis Meagher made the announcment in Diamond City, which became the first county seat, followed by White Sulphur Springs in 1880. During his tenure as territorial secretary, Meagher served as acting governor in the absence of Sidney Edgerton and Green Clay Smith. In 1867, Meagher disappeared off a docked steamboat at the Fort Benton levy. Rumors abound regarding his disappearance, ranging from foul play to accidental drowning. Over the next several decades, the legislature donated portions of Meagher County to Gallatin, Fergus, Cascade, Sweet Grass, Yellowstone, Broadwater, Lewis and Clark, and Wheatland counties. A statue of Meagher on horseback anchors the Montana State Capitol lawn in Helena.

Medicine Rocks State Park, Carter County, c. 1927
Himsl, photographer, MHS 949-225

Medicine Lake 1177 *map 8 C-2*

Edward Stubban named this place Flandrem for his home town in Norway and established a post office and store in 1906. The community flourished until 1910, when the Great Northern Railway constructed the Bainville to Scobey branch line about 2 miles from town. The town moved to its present location and changed its name to Medicine Lake, after the nearby lake the Assiniboine referred to as Bda wauka, "Medicine water." Elevation: 1,962 ft. Location: Sheridan County

Medicine Lake NWR 1187 *map 8 C-3*

The Medicine Lake NWR, established in 1935, protects more than 31,000 acres and shelters thousands of nesting white pelicans and nearly a million migrating waterfowl. In 1937, the CCC constructed dams, dikes, and shelterbelts to create habitat for the refuge. Indians who used the area called the lake Bda wauka, "Medicine water." The Medicine Lake Wilderness, established in 1976, encompasses 11,366 acres of the refuge. Elevation: 1,953 ft. Location: Sheridan County

Medicine Rocks State Park 1234
map 16 E-3

As the name Medicine Rock indicates, these wind-weathered sandstone formations held spiritual and cultural significance to Native American tribes; the Siouan name for the rocks was Inyan-oka-la-ka, "Rock with a hole in it." In 1883, Theodore Roosevelt described the Medicine Rocks, which he visited during a hunting trip, as "fantastically beautiful a place as I have ever seen." In 1957, the Carter County commissioners donated 320 acres for a state park, which was officially created in 1965. Elevation: 3,428 ft. Location: Carter County

Melrose 593   map 19 B-1

Melrose was established in 1881 at the junction of the road from Corinne, Utah, and the road to the rich Hecla Mine and the smelter at Glendale. Situated on a scenic stretch of the Big Hole River, Melrose today is famous for the nearby trout fishery. The origin of the name is not known. Elevation: 5,185 ft. Location: Silver Bow County

Melstone 990   map 14 D-2

Melstone is named for Associated Press reporter Melvin Stone, who rode a Milwaukee Road train with the railroad's president and his daughter as they named stations along the rail line about 1909. Melstone started as a station and freight division point on this line. Later, homesteading brought settlers to the area, but many eventually left due to the drought of the 1920s and '30s. The Melstone Oil Field west of town developed in the 1950s and saw renewed production in the 1990s. Elevation: 2,931 ft. Location: Musselshell County

Melville 819   map 12 E-4

Originally known as "the Settlement," this community was established in 1881

by Norwegians John Hoff, Eric Solberg, and Ben Hoyseth. In 1883, postmaster and shopkeeper Herbert Hickox renamed it in honor of a friend, arctic explorer George Wallace Melville. By 1888, the community had added a store, school, sawmill, blacksmith shop, harness shop, and hotel. Elevation: 5,020 ft. Location: Sweet Grass County

Mid Canon 385   map 11 B-3

Named for its scenic location about halfway between the entrance and exit of the Missouri River from a spectacular canyon south of Great Falls, Mid Canon started as a railroad siding and station on the Montana Central Railway about 1890. Elevation: 3,406 ft. Location: Cascade County

Mildred 1194   map 16 C-2

Mildred was platted in 1908 along the Milwaukee Road and the banks of O'Fallon Creek. Local lore suggests that the town is named for the daughter of a railroad official or an early settler. Since it was on the Yellowstone Trail, which passed along O'Fallon Creek through Ismay to Miles City, Mildred saw its share of early automobile tourists—until US 10 and US 12 were routed around the community. Mildred's population dwindled after construction of the highways and discontinuation of railroad activity. Elevation: 2,372 ft. Location: Prairie County

Miles City 1142   map 15 D-3

Miles City, the county seat of Custer County, was originally called Miles Town, for Gen. Nelson Miles, commander of nearby Fort Keogh. In the weeks following the defeat of Lt. Col. George Armstrong Custer, Congress appropriated $400,000 to establish 2 forts in Montana. One, Fort Custer, was at the mouth of the Little Bighorn River. General Miles was commanding officer over the second post, first established as the Tongue River Cantonment in August 1876. Construction of the permanent post, Fort Keogh, began in spring 1877. Miles Town grew to serve the fort. In 1877, the town boasted 200 residents; that number doubled by 1879 when Miles Town became the county seat. It became a city with the arrival of the Northern Pacific Railroad in 1881, and was rechristened Miles City. The population reached 2,600 by 1882. Arrival of the railroad solidified Miles City's future as a leading cattle-shipping point; the Miles City Montana Stockgrowers Association formed in 1884. Since then, Miles City has been a trade, service, and social center for eastern Montana, and the region's governmental hub. The first Ursuline convent in Montana opened in Miles City on January 18, 1884. The nuns came at the invitation of Fort Keogh chaplain Father Eli Lindesmith. The convent is listed in the National Register, as are 3 historic districts: Miles City Carriage House, East Main Street, and Main Street. Elevation: 2,367 ft. Location: Custer County

Bull train on Main Street, Miles City, 1881
Detail, L. A. Huffman, photographer, MHS 981-523

Milk River 1054   *map 7 D-2*

On May 8, 1805, Capt. Meriwether Lewis wrote in his journal: "The water of this river possesses a peculiar whiteness, being the colour of a cup of tea with the admixture of a tablespoonfull of milk." The Hidatsas had told Lewis and Clark about the river, referring to it as the "River which scolds all others." In 1902, the U.S. Reclamation Service proposed the Milk River Irrigation Project. The U.S. secretary of the interior authorized the project in 1903, pending an agreement with Canada for diversion of water from the St. Mary River. The project was an elaborate engineering scheme to divert water from the St. Mary River into the North Fork of the Milk River, trapping it in a reservoir near Havre, then releasing the water via diversion dams at Dodson and Vandalia into canals that could irrigate up to 200,000 acres. With the signing of the Boundary Waters Treaty in 1909, the project moved forward. Construction continued for 4 decades on a variety of irrigation canals and diversions.

Mill Creek 847   *map 20 B-2*

This Mill Creek, one of 3 in Park County, is named for a sawmill run by John J. Tomlinson from 1864 until 1867. The mill boasted a waterpowered circular saw. Tomlinson, born in 1812 in Maryland, also built boats to ferry passengers down the Yellowstone River. He later settled in Salesville (later known as Gallatin Gateway), where he operated a shingle mill and flour mill. Location: Park County

Mill Iron 1246   *map 24 A-4*

The Mill Iron post office was established in 1916 on the Harris-Franklin cattle ranch near the Montana–South Dakota state line. The name came from the Mill Iron Ranch in Texas, owned by the Continental Land and Cattle Company, which brought herds of cattle to Montana for summer grazing during the 1880s to 1890s. Nearby, on land inaccessible to the public, is the Mill Iron Site NHL, a prehistoric buffalo kill site dating to at least 11,000 B.C., making it one of the oldest Paleoindian sites in Montana. Elevation: 3,099 ft. Location: Carter County

Millegan 493   map 12 B-1

This settlement takes its name from Reuben Millegan, an early pioneer who came to the area in 1885. Millegan was soon joined by other families, and by 1890 the community boasted a school and post office. Although the community lost its post office in 1928, it has continued as a service center for local farm and ranch families. Elevation: 4,496 ft. Location: Cascade County

Milltown 239   map 10 C-2

The settlement that would become Milltown began in 1886 as a place for mill workers to live while they worked in the Bonner mill, owned by the Big Blackfoot Milling Company. The town grew and in 1903 received the unofficial name Riverside, for the Clark Fork and Blackfoot rivers that flow together nearby. Many Finns lived there, and for a time the community was called Finntown to prevent confusion with a Riverside near Butte. Townspeople were dissatisfied with the name Finntown and changed it to Milltown. Milltown's post office was established in 1912. W. A. Clark's Missoula Light & Power Company built the Clark Dam (later known as the Milltown Dam) near Milltown in 1904–06. For over a century, the dam trapped millions of tons of copper tailings that washed downriver from Butte and Anaconda. In 1994, the EPA announced the Milltown Dam as a Superfund site. Faced with continued pollution and structural weakness in the dam, the EPA decided in 2003 to remove

it. Elevation: 3,284 ft. Location: Missoula County

Miner 857   map 20 C-2

The town of Miner had a post office from 1898 until 1967. Thomas J. Miner, for whom the Paradise Valley town and basin is named, was a native of Indiana who arrived in the area in the 1860s. He ranched in the area during the 1880s and maintained a road for Yellowstone visitors. Elevation: 5,044 ft. Location: Park County

Mineral County 166   map 9 A-3

As the forest fires of 1910 cooled, residents of western Missoula County fumed over the sense of abandonment they had felt during the disaster. Four years later, concerned citizens established the New County Club of Superior and Iron Mountain and petitioned to create Mineral County. The Montana legislature agreed, establishing Mineral County in 1914, with Superior as the county seat. Orville G. Willett suggested the name Mineral County since most of those involved in the petition owned mining claims. Willett became the first state senator for the new county, serving in the 14th and 15th legislative sessions (1915 and 1917).

Mission Mountains Wilderness 211
map 2 E-2

In 1975, Congress designated 84,000 acres in the Mission Range overlooking the Mission Valley as wilderness, and in 1982 the Salish-Kootenai Confederated Tribes added an additional 89,000 acres of tribal land, creating a wilderness area totaling over 174,000 acres. The tribal wilderness is the only Native American–managed wilderness in the lower 48 states.

Mission Peak 823 *map 5 E-4*

Mission Peak is named for the St. Paul's Mission Church established by the Bureau of Catholic Missions in 1887 at Hays, on the Fort Belknap Indian Reservation. The 5,512-foot peak is the second highest in the Little Rocky Mountains. Elevation: 5,503 ft. Location: Phillips County

Mission Range 174 *map 2 E-2*

The Mission Range is named for the Jesuit mission built near the base of the range at St. Ignatius in 1854. According to Missoula attorney and Flathead reservation agent Washington J. McCormick, the Salish name for these mountains was Sin-yale-a-min, "Surrounded." The range is noted for jagged peaks (9,820-foot McDonald Peak its tallest) and high mountain lakes. Its western slope includes the Mission Mountains Tribal Wilderness.

Mission Reservoir 187 *-map 10 A-2*

Mission Reservoir is a natural lake formed by moraine from the glaciers that sculpted the Mission Mountains. The lake level is augmented by the Mission Dam, built as part of the Flathead Irrigation Project around 1912. Elevation: 3,412 ft. Location: Lake County

Missoula 227 *map 10 C-1*

In 1860, C. P. Higgins and Frank Worden established a trading post they named Hellgate on the newly finished Mullan Road about 4 miles west of present-day Missoula. The name Hellgate came from the canyon French trappers called Porte de l'Enfer. In 1864–65, Worden and Higgins began constructing a flour mill and saw-mill where Rattlesnake Creek enters the Clark Fork River, and the settlement of Missoula Mills grew up around the mills. Higgins and Worden quickly moved their trading post to the new location, which took its name from the original county when the area was still part of Washington Territory. In 1866, the county commissioners moved the county seat from Hellgate to Missoula. Over the next decade, the town evolved into a regional commercial

Missoula's Clark Fork Bridge, after a 1908 flood
MHS 949-408

and transportation center, and in 1877 the U.S. Army constructed Fort Missoula to control western Montana's Indian tribes and to protect settlers. In 1893, the state located the new university in Missoula. Missoula includes many properties listed independently in the National Register, and 6 historic districts: University of Montana, University Area, Southside, Northside Railroad, Lower Rattlesnake, and East Pine Street. Elevation: 3,211 ft. Location: Missoula County

Missoula County 215 *map 10 B-3*

Created in 1860 as part of Washington Territory, Missoula County in 1863 became part of Idaho Territory for one year. Montana's territorial legislature approved Missoula County as one of the original counties in 1864. Missoula County shares its name with the city of Missoula, which is also the county seat. Although the origins of the name Missoula are disputed, most sources say the name goes back to at least 1812, when explorer David Thompson sketched an extraordinary map of the valley and named it Ne-missoola-takoo. Later shortened to Missoula, it incorporates the Salish word for "chilly waters." Other explanations range from "Horrible" (Issoul) to "By or near the place of fear or ambush" (Im-i-sul-e-etikee), and "River of awe." During the 1970s and 1980s, some

environmentalists even claimed the Salish word meant "bad air."

Missouri River 1217 *map 8 D-3*

The Missouri headwaters are found in Gallatin County at the Three Forks, the confluence of the Gallatin, Madison, and Jefferson rivers. The name Missouri seems to be derived from the name of a small Sioux band described by an Illinois tribe as the people who dwelled on the "Big muddy." A variety of names appear on early French maps, including references to Emossouritsu and Le Missouri de R. de Pekatenoui. The Missouri River initially flows north, then makes a wide turn and runs east across the plains into North Dakota and on to St. Louis.

Mizpah Creek 1191 *map 16 E-1*

Capt. William F. Raynolds led the Raynolds Expedition that in 1859–60 conducted a topographical survey for the U.S. Army. He lost his Masonic medallion with the name Mizpah (a region in ancient Palestine) engraved on it in this creek. Mizpah Creek and adjacent Pumpkin Creek gained notoriety in 1928 when Congress created the first grazing district on the public domain, the Mizpah–Pumpkin Creek Grazing District. The success of this new policy during a period of intense drought led to passage of the Taylor Grazing Act in 1934. Location: Custer County

Moccasin 712 *map 12 B-4*

Moccasin, "the pride of the prairies," started in the 1880s as a post office at the Fort Benton Road's crossing of Warm Spring Creek. D. O. Holt established a hotel and store here in 1905. The townsite moved the following year, antici-

Hunters in camp on the Missouri River, c. 1885
Dan Dutro, photographer, MHS 948-578

pating the arrival of the Montana Railway Company ("Jawbone Railroad"). It seemed logical to name the town after the nearby Moccasin Mountains, which were named for their shape. The residents of Moccasin and the surrounding area took their farming seriously. The local newspaper once reported the arrest of a farmer who had allowed Russian thistles to go to seed on his place. The legislature made this a crime in 1895, with a fine of no less than $5 but no more than $50 for persons "guilty of supporting and maintaining a common nuisance." Elevation: 4,180 ft. Location: Judith Basin County

Moiese 169   *map 10 A-1*

When President Theodore Roosevelt created the National Bison Range on May 23, 1908, Moiese became its entrance. The name is derived from a Salish leader who lived from 1851 to 1918. His 2 Salish names were Crane With a Ring Around His Neck and Door of the Grizzly Bear. Homesteading began around Moiese in 1910, when the Flathead Indian Reservation was opened to non-Indians. Elevation: 2,625 ft. Location: Lake County

Molt 953   *map 21 A-3*

Originally a post office established in 1909 as Stickley, this town was renamed when a Northern Pacific Railway branch line was built to it in 1918. The new name honored Rudolph Molt, who sold the railroad the right-of-way. Elevation: 3,960 ft. Location: Stillwater County

Monarch 567   *map 12 B-2*

After staking the King, Czar, Emperor, Rex, and Sultan mining claims in July 1889, area residents created the Monarch Townsite Company, naming it for the common theme of the mining claims. The Montana Central Railway connected Monarch to Great Falls in autumn 1889, and Monarch

acted as a hub for materials coming to the mines, as well as a shipping point for ore from the mining camps of Hughesville and Barker. The line continued operation until November 3, 1945. Elevation: 4,564 ft. Location: Cascade County

Monida 844   *map 19 E-2*

The name Monida, credited to a Utah & Northern Railway dispatcher, is derived from the first 3 letters of Montana and Idaho. The Monida post office opened in 1891. From here, tourists wishing to visit Yellowstone National Park caught the Monida and Yellowstone stagecoach which took them through the Centennial Valley to the park. Monida also became the shipping point for Centennial Valley livestock. Elevation: 6,789 ft. Location: Beaverhead County

Monida Pass 846   *map 19 E-2*

The 1860s stage line between Corrine, Utah, and the gold fields at Bannack and Virginia City established a route over Monida Pass. The Utah & Northern Railway followed this route to Dillon and on to Butte, becoming the first railroad into Montana. A train dispatcher is credited with the name, derived from the first 3 letters of Montana and Idaho. Elevation: 6,820 ft. Location: Beaverhead County

Montague 561   *map 4 E-3*

Named by railroad officials for Montague, Massachusetts, this tiny town began as a station stop on the Great Northern Railway in 1914. After 1928, Montague saw an exodus of farmers and town residents; the hotel, garage, depot, bank, store, and even some homes were moved to other locations, leaving only 1 store, the school, a dance hall, and 2 houses. Elevation: 3,156 ft. Location: Chouteau County

Montana State Capitol, Helena, 1918
Edward Reinig, photographer, MHS 952-697

Montana City 492 *map 11 D-3*

For thousands of years, Native Americans quarried chert for arrowheads and spear points in the Prickly Pear Valley region that surrounds what now is Montana City. The first gold prospectors arrived here in the summer of 1862, and 2 years later the Lower Prickly Pear Mining District was established to govern the area. The Montana Town Company laid out Montana City in October 1864, naming it in honor of the newly designated territory. By 1868, the placer mines were proving less profitable, and Chinese miners began moving in to rework the claims. In 1887, there was a brief revival with the arrival of the Helena and Wickes Railroad and a Great Northern Railway branch line, and the establishment of a post office. In the late 1940s, Henry Kaiser built a cement plant for Permanente Cement Company just east of what remained of the town, because of its proximity to an Anaconda Company lime quarry. A new Montana City began to grow in the 1960s, and is now a prospering bedroom suburb for Helena. Elevation: 4,053 ft. Location: Jefferson County

Montana State Capitol 474 *map 11 D-3*

In 1902, the original Montana State Capitol was completed on a prominent rise in a largely unsettled Helena neighborhood east of Last Chance Gulch. Iowa architects Charles Bell and John Kent drew upon classical models but relied on local materials, including granite quarried from Columbus in Stillwater County. Montana copper caps the central dome, topped by Philadelphia sculptor Edward Van Lendeghem's *Montana*. This was the first capitol in the nation wired for the new electric lighting. As soon as lawmakers moved in, however, it was obvious that the space was inadequate. Montana architects John Link and Charles Haire, in association with New York architect Frank Andrews, designed 2 wings, completed in 1912. Matching granite for the wings came from Jefferson County. Historical paintings and murals portraying Montana's heritage decorate the interior spaces. The mural art of Charles Pedretti and Amedee Joullin combine with the art of Montana painters Charles M. Russell, Edgar S. Paxson, and Ralph DeCamp. Though less elegant than many capitol buildings of its era, the Montana State Capitol, listed in the National Register, reflects Montana's turn-of-the-twentieth-century optimism, financial reality, and closely linked political and business arenas. Elevation: 4,130 ft. Location: Lewis and Clark County

Montana State University 763 *map 20 A-1*

The 1893 Montana legislature established the Agricultural College of the State of Montana at Bozeman. The evolution of this land-grant school's name has been tortuous. Starting in 1893, the college referred to itself as the Montana College of Agriculture and Mechanic Arts in its course catalogs, but it was popularly known as Montana Agricultural College. In 1913, the official name became the Montana State College of Agriculture and Mechanic Arts, and in the 1920s the name Montana State College came into use. In 1965, in recognition of the school's commitment to scientific and humanistic research, the state legislature bestowed a new name: Montana State University. Architect Cass Gilbert designed the campus plan in the early twentieth century. The school has experienced steady growth, with enrollment at more than 12,500 in 2005 and degrees in 50 fields of study. MSU's physical boundaries today include campuses at Billings, Havre, and Great Falls. Elevation: 4,871 ft. Location: Gallatin County

Montana Tech of the University of Montana 520 *map 11 E-1*

The foundation of the Montana School of Mines, the historical name of this institution, was laid in 1889 when a federal enabling act provided the first federal land grants for the establishment of mining schools, thereby declaring the significance of mining industries to the new western states of Montana, North Dakota, South Dakota, and Washington. A commission appointed by Governor John E. Rickards decided that the heart of Montana's mining industry—Butte—would be the ideal location. Completed in 1897, Main Hall

stood empty until 1900 because the state pushed its educational building programs so fast that immediate funding gave out. Thanks to the generosity of local benefactors, the school opened to 39 students in 1900, and the first class graduated in 1903. Butte offered unsurpassed facilities in practical observation and firsthand experience in the mines, a facet of training other mining schools did not emphasize. The original 4 professorships have expanded to include a teaching faculty of 150; as of 2006, the campus accommodates almost 2,000 students. The campus is a contributing element in the Butte-Anaconda NHL. Elevation: 5,777 ft. Location: Silver Bow County

Montana Territorial and State Prison 405 *map 11 D-1*

The federal government established its first prison in Montana with the opening of a territorial penitentiary at Deer Lodge in 1871. The early prison was primitive and overcrowded. Upon statehood in 1889, federal authority passed to the state. Under controversial longtime warden Frank Conley, who served from 1889 until Governor Joseph Dixon removed him from office in 1921, prisoners built the fortress-like walls and crenellated towers, in 1908 the women's prison, and in 1912 the cell block. In 1919, Copper King W. A. Clark donated funds for a state-of-the-art theatre, the first such facility built within prison walls in the nation. During the economically depressed 1930s, the prison deteriorated. A nationally publicized riot occurred in 1959, and fire left the theatre a burned-out shell in the 1970s, but the prison continued to house inmates until the state completed a more modern facility in 1979. The prison, listed in the National Register, is now a museum. Elevation: 4,532 ft. Location: Powell County

Moss Mansion,
Billings

Hunt, Witham & Lass,
photographers,
MHS PAc 2004-17

Monture Creek 267 *map 10 B-4*

On July 5, 1806, Capt. Meriwether Lewis named Seaman Creek for his Newfoundland dog. It was later named Monture Creek for George Monture, a mixed-blood trader who lived in the upper Blackfoot River area. Sam Pierre, a Coeur d'Alene man, stabbed and killed Monture on the Blackfoot's North Fork on October 10, 1877, during an argument over trading a horse for a keg of whiskey. In the 1920s, Ovando banker John Blair erected a marker on Monture's grave. Location: Powell County

Moore 750 *map 13 C-1*

Moore was established in 1903 on the Montana Railway Company's "Jawbone Railroad" line west of Lewistown. Company president Richard A. Harlow named the community after Henry D. Moore, who had helped finance the railroad. In 1908, Moore produced more wheat than any other community in the Judith Basin and boasted a modern creamery and ice cream plant. Elevation: 4,161 ft. Location: Fergus County

Morony Dam 468 *map 12 A-1*

The Phoenix Utility Company built Morony Dam between 1928 and 1930 for the Montana Power Company, to provide power for the Anaconda Company's new electrolytic zinc plant at Great Falls. It was the fourth of the 5 hydroelectric dams to be built in the vicinity. The dam was named for John G. Morony, one of Montana Power's first directors. Elevation: 2,803 ft. Location: Cascade County

Mosby 966 *map 14 B-2*

Originally known as Baldwin, this town takes its name from the area's first settler, who arrived in 1891. Most homesteaders in the area stayed only a short time. In 1904, a post office was established in William Henry Mosby's home. The area is dotted with the oil wells of the Mosby Dome–Cat Creek Oil Field. Elevation: 2,526 ft. Location: Garfield County

Moss Mansion 1001 *map 21 A-4*

The bustling activity of Billings so impressed Preston B. Moss that he relocated here from Missouri in 1892 and became one of Montana's most diversified investors and a leading Billings entrepreneur and banker. Moss built this red sandstone mansion in 1901–03. The 28-room residence, designed by New York architect R. J. Hardenbergh (whose works include the Waldorf Astoria), features mahogany, birch, oak, ash, and white pine woodwork, an onyx fireplace, rose silk and gold leaf wall coverings, and stained-glass windows. The nonprofit Billings Preservation Society operates tours of the mansion. Elevation: 3,134 ft. Location: Yellowstone County

Mouat Mine 911   *map 20   B-4*
Jack V. Nye and the Hedges brothers first discovered copper-nickel deposits in the Nye region in 1883. World War I created a demand for chromite, an iron-chromium oxide that was also abundant in the area. William M. Mouat and several other men developed their claims, including the Mouat Mine, and work continued through the 1930s. At the outbreak of World War II, when Germany cut off supplies of chromite from Africa and Russia, there was again a strong demand for the mineral from the Mouat Mine. To facilitate wartime production, the U.S. government built a town here, with a school, a recreation center, and structures to house about 900 workers and their families. At the end of the war, foreign sources for chromite again became available and the mine was shut down. The American Chrome Company reopened the mine for the duration of the Korean War. Elevation: 7,054 ft. Location: Stillwater County

Mount Aeneas 117   *map 2   D-2*
There is considerable confusion about the origin of this name. The most common explanation is that it was a corruption of the name Ignace. An Iroquois fur trader, Ignace, was part of the 1835 delegation to St. Louis that brought Father Pierre-

Jean De Smet to the Salish and Kootenai people in what would become Montana. However, there were several Aeneases and Ignaces in the area at that time. Both Ignace Lamouse and a Young Ignace are described as Iroquois. Young Ignace's son Aeneas Paul became a leader of the Kootenai during the time of increasing white settlement. Additionally, a Chief Aeneas led the Kootenais over Marias Pass on snowshoes in the 1860s. Elevation: 7,528 ft. Location: Flathead County

Mount Baldy 608   *map 12   D-1*
Montana has 6 peaks called Mount Baldy. This Mount Baldy, the second-highest peak in the Big Belt Mountains, is named for its treeless summit, dramatically visible from afar when snow-covered. Elevation: 9,472 ft. Location: Broadwater County

Mount Brown 358   *map 4   B-1*
Mount Brown on East Butte bears the name of an early homesteader, John Brown. This second-highest point in the Sweet Grass Hills has been sacred to the Blackfeet, Chippewa, and Cree peoples for centuries. Elevation: 6,958 ft. Location: Liberty County

Mount Cleveland 72   *map 2   A-2*
Named by conservationist and author George Bird Grinnell in 1898 for President Grover Cleveland, Mount Cleveland is the highest summit in Glacier National Park. During the 1872 Northern Boundary Survey, the peak was called Kaiser Peak. According to ethnologist James Willard Schultz, the Blackfeet name for the mountain was Napi, named for the trickster of Northern Plains legends. Elevation: 10,466 ft. Location: Glacier National Park

Mount Cowen 869 *map 20 B-3*

Mount Cowen is named for George Cowan. Fleeing pursuit by the U.S. Army, the Nez Perces led by Chief Joseph passed through Yellowstone National Park in August 1877. There, a smaller party of Nez Perces encountered a group of tourists, including George and Emma Cowan, in the lower Geyser Basin. A fracas ensued. George Cowan survived several gunshot wounds, and his story became legendary over his long legal career. Elevation: 11,206 ft. Location: Park County

Mount Douglas 901 *map 20 C-4*

Mount Douglas towers just north of Lake Plateau in the Absaroka-Beartooth Wilderness. It was named for Edward M. Douglas, USGS "geographer in charge" in Montana, in 1886. In the course of mapping in the region, Douglas climbed many of the area's high peaks, including the first recorded attempt to scale Granite Peak in 1889. Elevation: 11,298 ft. Location: Sweet Grass County

Mount Fleecer 535 *map 19 A-1*

Mount Fleecer, the highest point on Fleecer Ridge, is named for the Fleecer family who settled on Moose Creek, in the Melrose area, in the 1870s. In 1962, the Montana Fish and Game Commission established the Fleecer Mountain WMA on the southeast flanks of the peak. Elevation: 9,436 ft. Location: Silver Bow County

Mount Haggin 432 *map 10 E-4*

Mount Haggin, which towers over the town of Anaconda, is named for James Ben Ali Haggin, one of the founders of the Anaconda Company. It had formerly been one of several peaks around the state named Mount Baldy. The Mount Haggin WMA, popular with cross-country skiers and snowmobilers, does not actually include the mountain but is named for Mount Haggin Ranch, which the Anaconda Company donated to the state in 1976. Elevation: 10,607 ft. Location: Deer Lodge County

Mount Hague 931 *map 21 C-1*

In July 1898, young Norwegian photographer Anders Wilse and geologist James P. Kimball left Cooke City to map the high country of the Beartooth Mountains. They named Mount Hague for USGS geologist Arnold Hague. Hague had accompanied a mineral survey of Nevada during the 1860s and a geological survey of Yellowstone National Park in the 1890s. Elevation: 12,303 ft. Location: Stillwater County

Mount Headley 62 *map 1 E-3*

Mount Headley is named for Roy Headley, the second forest supervisor of the Cabinet National Forest. From 1913 to 1917, Headley directed USFS District 5. In the 1930s, he led the agency's Division of Fire Control and wrote widely on the topic of fire suppression. A fire lookout stood on this peak for decades. Elevation: 7,429 ft. Location: Sanders County

Mount Helena Historic District 465
map 11 D-3

Mount Helena stands out as a grand, dramatic backdrop for the city from which it takes its name. Since picnickers first enjoyed its quiet refuge during mining camp days, Mount Helena has served the community in various ways. First, miners searched in vain for its minerals. Settlers next stripped its slopes of timber and quarried its limestone. In 1883, residents by the hundreds trekked up the mountainside to watch the first trains smoking slowly westward across the valley to Helena. Then, on November 12, 1894, a huge bonfire at the summit lit the night sky, confirming Helena's victory as state capital. Near the twentieth century's turn, forest fires further denuded

Mount Powell, Deer Lodge, and Montana State Prison, c. 1909
MHS 946-694

the near-barren mountain. A city park was proposed in 1898, and on Arbor Day 1899, Helena schoolchildren armed with baskets of evergreen seedlings hiked the lightning-scorched slopes and planted trees. On July 4, 1904, residents dedicated the 700-acre park, and in 1906 the USFS donated 30,000 pine and fir seedlings for planting the hillsides laid bare by logging and fire. Today the city's century-old invitation still stands: "Do not deny yourself the health and pleasure of the delightful walk. Go all and go often." Mount Helena Historic District is listed in the Historic Register. Elevation: 5,433 ft. Location: Lewis and Clark County

Mount Henry 4 *map 1 A-2*
Mount Henry takes its name from Henry Wegner, who homesteaded on the East Fork of the Yaak River about 1906. In 1925, the Kootenai National Forest constructed a stone-and-frame cupola lookout atop Mount Henry, replacing it with a new structure in 1942. Mount Henry Lookout was partially restored in the 1990s and now is used only in emergencies. Elevation: 7,257 ft. Location: Lincoln County

Mount Jackson 106 *map 2 B-3*
George Bird Grinnell named this peak in 1891 for William Jackson, the part Piegan grandson of Hugh Monroe, a fur trader and guide in Blackfeet country. Jackson served as a scout under Maj. Marcus Reno at the time of the Battle of the Little Bighorn. Elevation: 10,052 ft. Location: Glacier National Park

Mount Powell 387 *map 10 D-4*
Mount Powell was named for John W. Powell, a Virginian who arrived in Montana in 1856 and settled at the foot of the Flint Creek Range in 1864. Powell made the first documented ascent of this peak, which is the highest in the Flint Creek Range. He died as a result of a quarrel with a butcher at Dewey's Flat in 1880. Elevation: 10,168 ft. Location: Powell County

Mount Silcox 75 *map 1 E-3*
One of the earliest USFS lookouts in the Cabinet National Forest was built on this mountain named for Ferdinand Silcox, the first supervisor of the Cabinet National

Chinese workers at Mullan Tunnel, Mullan Pass, 1884

F. Sumida, photographer, MHS 950-124

Forest and later head of the USFS. Elevation: 6,900 ft. Location: Sanders County

Mount St. Nicholas 136 *map 2 C-3*

This dramatic peak, clearly visible from US 2, takes its name from the legendary fourth-century bishop now associated with Christmas, but why this peak was so named is not known. The Kootenai called the mountain Kasinquwa, "Two feathers." Elevation: 9,376 ft. Location: Glacier National Park.

Mount Stimson 125 *map 2 C-3*

George Bird Grinnell named this mountain for Henry L. Stimson, a member of Grinnell's 1891 expedition into the region. Stimson later served as secretary of war under President William Taft, as governor-general of the Philippines and secretary of state under President Herbert

Hoover, and as secretary of war under President Franklin D. Roosevelt. Stimson is the highest peak in the Livingstone Range. Elevation: 10,142 ft. Location: Glacier National Park

Mount Villard 949 *map 21 C-1*

Named for Henry Villard, president of the Northern Pacific Railroad, Mount Villard is in the Beartooth Range just south of 12,799-foot Granite Peak, Montana's tallest summit. In 1883, Villard sponsored an excursion into Yellowstone National Park to generate interest among journalists and investors in a branch line through the park from Gardiner to Cooke City. It never came to be. Elevation: 12,254 ft. Location: Park County

Mount Wilse 947 *map 21 C-1*

Anders Wilse moved to Seattle in 1890 to work as a surveyor and engineer. After photographing the building of the Great Northern Railway through the Cascades and working as a cartographer in 1897, he turned to commercial photography. In 1898, James P. Kimball hired the young Norwegian immigrant to photograph his mapping and mineral survey expedition to the Beartooth Range, funded by the Rockefeller family and the Rocky Fork Coal Company. During the course of his work, Wilse climbed a high peak from which he photographed Grasshopper Glacier. He named the peak for himself. In 1900, Wilse left for a visit to Norway and never returned. Elevation: 11,788 ft. Location: Park County

Mulherin Creek 874 *map 20 C-2*

Mulherin Creek (also spelled Mol Herron and Mol Heron), a tributary of the Yellowstone River that originates in Yellowstone National Park, is named for John Mulherin, who filed a mining claim in Emigrant Gulch in 1876. Location: Park County

Mullan Pass 408 *map 11 C-2*

John Mullan crossed over this pass in 1853 with the Isaac I. Stevens railroad survey. The pass was later named for him. Mullan conceived of the idea of building a road between Walla Walla, in present-day Washington, and Fort Benton that would go over this pass. Stevens pushed through a congressional bill in 1857 that authorized this road. The Northern Pacific Railroad tunneled under the pass in building its main line across the Continental Divide in 1883. Elevation: 5,932 ft. Location: Powell County

Mullan Road 402 *map 4 E-1*

In 1859, John Mullan began constructing a military road to connect Walla Walla with Fort Benton. At the time, both towns were in the vast expanse of Washington Territory. Mullan began building his road east from Walla Walla, following the Coeur d'Alene River, and then the St. Regis River in what would later become Montana. In 1860, Mullan's crews worked along the Clark Fork and Little Blackfoot rivers, headed over Mullan Pass, and turned north to Fort Benton. Completed in 1860, the 624-mile-long Mullan Road was the first engineered road in the Pacific Northwest. It was initially designed for military traffic but served this purpose only once before the Civil War intervened. After the Montana gold rush began in 1862 with the discovery of gold at Grasshopper Creek, the Mullan Road between Fort Benton, Helena, and Missoula was heavily traveled by miners and freighters. In places, mostly west of Missoula, it was too narrow for wagons. Camel trains carrying supplies to the mining camps trekked over the road, but it never evolved into a major thoroughfare because the mountainous country was too treacherous and there were no funds to maintain it. Portions of the road still exist in several locations in western Montana, and wagon ruts of some segments between Fort Benton and Helena—used primarily for mining traffic—are visible from the air. One well-preserved portion in Cascade County is listed in the National Register. The Montana Dept. of Transportation owns a 2-mile segment in Mineral County that is open to the public.

Murphy Lake 25 *map 1 B-4*

Murphy Lake is named for Tom Murphy, who filed on a homestead here in the early 1890s. Murphy was a partner of Charles Loring, who later served as the Minnesota Supreme Court's chief justice from 1944 to 1953. Elevation: 2,999 ft. Location: Lincoln County

Musselshell 979 *map 14 D-1*

Musselshell takes its name from the Musselshell River, named by Lewis and Clark for the freshwater mussels lining the riverbank. In 1866, the Rocky Mountain Wagon Road Company built a trading post near the mouth of the river and named it Kerchival City, after a steamboat captain. In 1868, the Musselshell River flooded the post. The Montana Hide and Fur Company later built a post and warehouse on the site and renamed it Musselshell. During the early 1900s, the town was the center of a prosperous homestead boom. The Handel brothers owned a general mercantile company, bank, and hotel. Elevation: 2,984 ft. Location: Musselshell County

Musselshell County 950 *map 13 C-4*

In 1911, the Montana legislature created Musselshell County from Fergus and Yellowstone counties, with Roundup as the county seat. Residents named the county after the Musselshell River, which runs through the area.

Musselshell River 965 *map 14 C-2*

The name Muscle Shell is attributed to Lewis and Clark, bestowed as they passed

Musselshell River, Harlowton, c. 1915
Detail, MHS PAc 95-30.9

this central Montana river's mouth on May 19, 1805. Hidatsas had told the Lewis and Clark Expedition that they would encounter a river called Mahtush-ahzhah, "Muscle shell," for the freshwater mussels. The usage changed to Musselshell in 1875.

Mussigbrod Lake 464 *map 18 A-2*
The usual story is that Mussigbrod Lake is named for Dr. Charles F. Mussigbrod, founder of the Warm Springs State Hospital. It is, however, more likely named for his son Herman S. Mussigbrod, who established a homestead in the vicinity with his uncle, Peter S. Mussigbrod. Herman's wife, Mary, also filed on her own homestead nearby. Elevation: 6,488 ft. Location: Beaverhead County

Myers 1049 *map 14 E-3*
The Northern Pacific Railroad established Myers about 1888 as a station, named for a civil engineer on the railroad construction crew. The Myers post office opened in 1911; by 1914, the town had a general store and a lumber and grain business. The post office closed in 1975. Elevation: 2,684 ft. Location: Treasure County

Mystic Lake 944 *map 21 C-1*
Originally a natural lake in the Beartooth Mountains known as Long Lake, Mystic Lake was dammed by the Montana Power Company in 1926, raising the water level and increasing the surface acres. The lake's name is credited to a surveyor for the Montana Power Company named Mystic who, in 1918, helped the company launch its effort to dam the lake to generate hydroelectricty. During construction, Montana Power built a 1.5-mile-long, 48-inch wood stave pipe along the face of the mountain that led to a penstock at the power station. The power station generated 22,000 kW of electricity beginning in 1926; the station remains in operation today. It is currently (2003–09) undergoing the relicensing process, which takes into account wildlife, aesthetics, water quality, and other factors. Elevation: 7,673 ft. Location: Stillwater County

Road crew, Noxon, c. 1910
Detail, MHS PAc 2003-31.1

Nashua 1048 *map 7 D-1*

The St. Paul, Minneapolis & Manitoba Railway established Nashua in 1888 as a station. The name is said to be a Native American word meaning "The land between" or "Meeting of two streams." According to the Nashua town clerk, the town was named by early settler Charles Sargent. A Texan, Sargent was a woodcutter in the area in the early 1880s and later established a mercantile business. By the 1910s, the town had a wide variety of businesses, including a hotel, a bank, a livery stable, 2 general stores, a barbershop, and a hardware store. Nashua had a brief economic boom during the building of Fort Peck Dam in the 1930s. Elevation: 2,063 ft. Location: Valley County

National Bison Range 751 *map 10 A-1*

President Theodore Roosevelt created the National Bison Range on May 23, 1908, to preserve the animal from extinction. The bison range started with 34 bison (historically called buffalo) purchased from the Charles Conrad estate by the American Bison Society. The National Bison Range's most famous resident was Big Medicine. Born on May 3, 1933, this white buffalo—originally named Whitey—quickly became the premier attraction. When Big Medicine died on August 25, 1959, Browning sculptor and taxidermist Bob Scriver mounted Big Medicine's tanned hide on a molded standing mannequin for the Montana Historical Society. Governor Donald Nutter dedicated the exhibit on July 13, 1961, at the Montana Historical Society, where it still resides. Every October, the range rounds up bison for branding, inoculation, and sale. Between 2004 and 2006, the USFWS and the Confederated Salish and Kootenai Tribes shared management of the range. However, in 2006, the USFWS rescinded its management agreement with the Tribes. Location: Lake and Sanders counties

Big Medicine (white buffalo), National Bison Range, Moiese

MHS 945-868

Natural Bridge State Park 816   *map 5   D-4*

The natural stone bridge for which the state park is named is a popular attraction in the scenic Mission Canyon on the Fort Belknap Indian Reservation. Outlaw Kid Curry (Harvey Logan) hid out in this area during his career as a train robber about 1894–1900. Fort Belknap Tourism Office staff provide tours of the canyon. The park has picnic and camping areas. Elevation: 3,850 ft. Location: Blaine County

Navajo 1130   *map 8   B-1*

The Northern Town and Land Company developed Navajo in 1913 when the Bainville to Scobey branch line of the Great Northern Railway arrived. Local residents do not know why railroad officials called this town Navajo; there is no known connection with the southwestern U.S. tribe of the same name. Elevation: 2,430 ft. Location: Daniels County

Neihart 607   *map 12   C-2*

Prospectors James LeRoy Neihart, John O'Brien, and Richard Harley discovered rich silver deposits soon after they arrived in the area in 1881; among the early mines were Queen of the Hills, Galt, Mountain Chief, and Ball. These mines and others produced about $16 million in silver between 1882 and 1929. Ore was initially shipped to the smelter at nearby Barker and Hughesville, but those facilities closed in 1883 and ore had to be shipped by wagon to Fort Benton for eventual processing in Swansea, Wales. Two years later, the Mountain Chief

Mine built a concentrator/smelter that again allowed local processing of silver ores. Arrival of a Montana Central Railway branch line in 1891 allowed ore to be shipped to Great Falls for processing. The Panic of 1893 shut down most of the silver mines, but production continued sporadically during periods of higher silver prices. During World War II, Neihart was a major zinc producer for the war effort. Elevation: 5,661 ft. Location: Cascade County

Nelson Reservoir 930   *map 6   C-2*

Nelson Reservoir is named for Henry H. Nelson, a Vandalia rancher instrumental in promoting the Milk River Irrigation Project. Nelson Reservoir lies in a natural basin, enhanced by 5 long dikes. The dikes were raised in 1921–22 to enlarge the reservoir. The project diverted water from the Milk River by way of the Dodson South Canal, stored it in Nelson Reservoir, and then dispersed it for irrigation. There is a campground and fishing access at the reservoir. A much smaller Nelson Reservoir lies about 30 miles south-southwest. Elevation: 2,224 ft. Location: Phillips County

Nevada City 728   *map 19   B-3*

Nevada City likely takes its name from veteran prospectors who came up from the gold camps in Nevada, a territory created in 1861. Nevada City and Virginia City

Nevada City,
Alder Gulch, 1899
Detail, MHS 950-142

were the largest of the 9 booming gold camps that sprawled along Alder Gulch in the months following the May 1863 gold strike. In December 1863, Nevada City's main street was the scene of the miners' court trial and hanging of George Ives. This event catalyzed people into forming Montana's first vigilance committee, on December 23, 1863, 2 days after Ives's hanging. Between 1863 and 1866, Nevada City vied with Virginia City as the largest of the Alder Gulch camps. Dozens of stores and cabins were spread out in a 6-block radius. Nevada City was the first Montana town to incorporate, on February 9, 1865, but its fame quickly faded. By 1876, only a few residents remained. MT 287, then called the Vigilante Trail, had cut the town in half by 1920. By the 1950s, Cora and Alfred Finney were the only residents. In the meantime, Great Falls legislator Charles Bovey and his wife, Sue, had begun collecting endangered historic buildings, placing them at their "Old Town" at the Great Falls fairgrounds. When the fairgrounds asked Bovey to remove his collection in 1959, he acquired the Nevada City property and moved the buildings there. Nevada City became the Boveys' haven for endangered structures, and today more than 90 buildings from across Montana line the streets. The State of Montana purchased the Bovey properties in 1997 and today maintains the historical resources at Nevada City. Buildings original to Nevada City include the Byam House and the Finney Homestead, both listed in the National Register. Elevation: 5,604 ft. Location: Madison County

Nevada Creek 308 map 11 C-1

Washington J. Stapleton made the first placer-gold strike near Nevada Creek in 1866, with additional strikes over the next few years. In 1871, 2 companies—the Wilson Brothers and Pierson, Ogden and Brown—built a ditch to supply water to the claims. The Nevada Creek Placer Mining Company was incorporated in 1887 to

work the claims. The State Water Conservation Board dammed the creek in 1938 to form Nevada Creek Reservoir. The source of the name is not known. Location: Powell County

Niarada 89 map 1 E-4

Named for the waterfall and creek of the same name in Washington, this community (pronounced to rhyme with Nevada) was established as a store and post office about 1910 by brothers Edward and Valjean Riley. Elevation: 2,921 ft. Location: Sanders County

Nilan Reservoir 276 map 11 A-2

Nilan Reservoir is named for John and Margaret Nilan, who homesteaded just west of Augusta in the 1890s. John had come west working for the Canadian Pacific Railroad and then settled in Montana, where in 1888 he married Margaret Owen. She had come to Montana in 1863, a young child of a family who established a ranch in the area in 1882. Elevation: 4,420 ft. Location: Lewis and Clark County

Ninemile Creek 203 map 10 B-1

Ninemile Creek was so named because it was 9 miles west of the town of Frenchtown on the Mullan Road. It had previously been known as Skiotah Creek, for the mountain of the same name. There is a historic USFS remount station about 3 miles up Remount Road, just east of Ninemile Road. Just north of the remount station was a large CCC camp in the 1930s. Location: Missoula County

Ninepipe NWR 168 map 10 A-1

Established by Executive Order 3503 on June 23, 1921, this 2,062-acre wildlife refuge is named for a Salish man, Joseph Ninepipes, and managed jointly by the BIA, the Confederated Salish and Kootenai

Norris Mercantile, Norris, 1911
Detail, MHS 950-167

Tribes, and the USFWS to provide water-fowl and upland game bird habitat. More than 185 bird species have been counted on the refuge, and as many as 200,000 birds migrate through the refuge during the fall, with a variety of waterfowl nesting during the spring. The refuge encompasses Ninepipe Reservoir. Elevation: 3,012 ft. Location: Lake County

Ninepipe Reservoir 170   *map 10   A-1*
This reservoir is named for Joseph Ninepipes, a member of the Salish nation who sold his allotment to the federal government for its Flathead Irrigation Project. Between April and September 1910, a crew employing Fresno scrapers and graders excavated more than 11,000 yards of soil and constructed 29 miles of canals and ditches. The reservoir contains approximately 1,672 acres of water as part of the BIA Flathead Irrigation Project, which provides flood control and irrigation. Elevation: 3,010 ft. Location: Lake County

Norris 709   *map 19   B-4*
Alexander Norris built the first house in what became the town of Norris in September 1865. Norris proved an indiffer-

ent booster for the new town, selling a few lots but mainly working diligently to establish his own ranch. He discovered and sold the Revenue Mine and, with the proceeds, started cattle ranching. Local mines produced approximately $3.9 million in gold between 1864 and 1930. Five mining districts surrounded the community: Washington, Lower Hot Springs, Meadow Creek, Upper Hot Springs, and Norwegian Gulch. The Northern Pacific Railroad built a branch line with the terminus at Norris in 1890, and the community continues to be a significant shipping point for cattle ranchers. A popular attraction is Norris Hot Springs, on the banks of Hot Springs Creek. Elevation: 4,859 ft. Location: Madison County

North Fork of the Blackfoot River 282
map 10   B-4
The Salish referred to the main stem of the Blackfoot River as Cokahlarishkit, "River of the road to buffalo," since the river marked their route to fall buffalo hunts. From the North Fork, the trail climbed over what came to be known as Lewis and Clark Pass and dropped down to the Sun River country. On July 6, 1806, Capt. Meriwether Lewis and a contingent of

the Corps of Discovery crossed the North Fork of the Blackfoot River, which Lewis referred to in his journals as the North Fork of the Cokahlarishkit. Over time, both forks gained the name Blackfoot, referring to the Blackfeet tribe's propensity to follow the rivers when raiding Salish camps on the west side of the Continental Divide. This river flows into the Blackfoot River southeast of Ovando.

Northern Cheyenne Indian Reservation 1133 *map 23 B-1*

As a result of their participation in the Great Sioux War of 1876–77, the federal government exiled the Northern Cheyennes to Oklahoma. Under the leadership of Dull Knife and Little Wolf, in 1878 over 300 Northern Cheyennes fled Oklahoma in an attempt to return to the Tongue River country of Montana and Wyoming. Little Wolf managed to make it to southeastern Montana with his followers, settling near Miles City and the adjacent Fort Keogh. They began spreading south along the Tongue River and Rosebud Creek. The federal government created the Northern Cheyenne Indian Reservation in November 1884, sparking controversy. Ranchers attempted to have the executive order reversed. Instead, the federal government expanded the reservation in 1890, and again in 1900, making the Tongue River the eastern boundary and swelling the reservation from its previous 256,000 acres to approximately 400,000 acres. The Northern Cheyenne retain over 90 percent ownership of reservation lands. During the 1960s and 1970s, the tribe resisted efforts by coal companies to develop extensive coal resources on the reservation, pressures it again faces as coalbed methane develops. Tribal headquarters are in Lame Deer, which is also the location of Dull Knife Memorial College. Location: Big Horn and Rosebud counties

Northern Montana Fairground Historic District 416 *map 12 A-1*

Daniel Burnham, superintending architect for the World's Columbian Exposition held in Chicago in 1893, instructed those developing the fair to "make no small plans. They have no magic to stir men's blood." This sentiment influenced fairgrounds planning for the next 40 years. Reflecting the concept of "Exposition" planning, the Great Falls fairgrounds buildings were begun in 1919 with construction of the Montana Livestock Pavilion, designed by Great Falls architect George Shanley. Subsequent buildings were constructed between 1928 and 1938 and represent a variety of planners, architects, landscapers, styles, and ideas. Many were constructed during the Great Depression with Public Works Administration assistance, and thus the fairgrounds illustrate community spirit during the hardest times. By 1939, the 102-acre fairgrounds, listed in the Historic Register, had become the venue for the Montana State Fair, which had been held in Helena prior to this time. Elevation: 3,326 ft. Location: Cascade County

Northwest Peak 1 *map 1 A-1*

C. A. Fenn, a district ranger in the Kootenai National Forest, named Northwest Peak for its location near Montana's boundary with Idaho and British Columbia. It is the highest summit in the Purcell Mountains. Elevation: 7,705 ft. Location: Lincoln County

Noxon 34 *map 1 D-1*

Established as a Northern Pacific Railroad station in 1883, Noxon is named for an early prospector in the area. It thrived for many years as a railroad and logging town. In 1960, Washington Water Power completed construction of the Noxon Rapids Dam, which is capable of generating 400,000 kW of electrical power with its 4 generators. Elevation: 2,179 ft. Location: Sanders County

Noxon Rapids Dam 37 *map 1 D-2*
In the late 1950s, Washington Water Power began constructing a large concrete dam at Noxon, employing several thousand men and women. It was completed in July 1960, creating 38-mile-long Noxon Reservoir. The powerhouse contains 4 generators, each capable of generating 100,000 kW of electricity. Elevation: 2,281 ft. Location: Sanders County

Nyack 103 *map 2 C-3*
Located on the Great Northern Railway's main transcontinental line as a depot, this place was first referred to as Red Eagle. A community began to develop around the depot in the 1890s as prospectors filtered into the area. Homesteaders began arriving in the 1910s, and a post office opened in 1912 under the name Nyack, after a town in New York. When 2 lumber companies located in Nyack about 1920, the population rose to about 60, and the community built a school in 1923. Elevation: 3,355 ft. Location: Flathead County

Nye 914 *map 21 B-1*
Jack V. Nye, H. A. Thompson, E. R. Nichols, and E. S. Case, discoverers of gold and copper in the area, founded Nye in 1887. The Minnesota Mining and Smelting Company built a copper smelter here in 1889 to process the ore, but the secretary of the interior shut down the operation when it was discovered that they were illegally on the Crow Indian Reservation. Mining resumed after the reservation boundary moved in 1890 and the Crow ceded the land. The region around Nye is known as the Stillwater Complex (a geological province with a uniform mineralogical history), a rich chromium-mining area. The Stillwater Mining Company currently mines an abundant deposit of platinum and palladium, the only known deposit in North America. Elevation: 4,854 ft. Location: Stillwater County

Jack Nicklaus playing inaugural round on Old Works Golf Course, Anaconda, 1997
Detail, © John Reddy

O'Fallon Creek 1176 *map 16 C-1*

Capt. William Clark led a contingent of the Corps of Discovery down the Yellowstone River in 1806. They passed a stream on July 31 that Clark named Oak Tar pon er River, or Coal River, due to the numerous deposits of coal visible in the bluffs above the creek. It later became known as O'Fallon Creek, after Benjamin O'Fallon, William Clark's nephew, who served as an Indian agent from 1819 until poor health forced his retirement in 1826. He was a staunch supporter of the fur trade industry; it is assumed that one of his acquaintances named the creek after him. O'Fallon died in Missouri in 1842.

Oilmont 273 *map 3 B-4*

The community of Oilmont developed around Clarence Davis's business, the Oilfield Supply Company, which he constructed south of the Absure Refinery, which processed petroleum from the Kevin-Sunburst Oil Field. Early residents wanted to call the town Koby, after an oil town in Oklahoma, but by combining "oil" and "Montana" the community became Oilmont. During the oil boom that peaked in 1930, the town sustained a Chinese restaurant, several bars, a bakery, a movie theater, and a hotel. Elevation: 3,498 ft. Location: Toole County

Old Works Golf Course 438 *map 10 E-4*

The Old Works Golf Course, developed on the ruins of the first copper smelter in Anaconda, is the creation of golf legend Jack Nicklaus. Grappling with the closure of the Washoe Reduction Works and Washoe Stack in the early 1980s, citizens decided to turn a Superfund site into a world-class golf course. Nicklaus's design incorporated innovative techniques for capping the mining waste and incorporating ruins into the course, such as filling sand traps with the black slag that had been generated during the smelting process. Today the 18-hole championship course lures golfers from across the nation. Elevation: 5,263 ft. Location: Deer Lodge County

Olive 1209 *map 23 B-4*

In 1909, the residents around Mizpah Creek founded the Olive post office. According to local lore, each person wrote a suggestion for a name on a scrap of paper and placed it in a hat. The name selected was Olive, for local resident Olive Coon. In 1920, when the county seat election was held, Olive ran against Broadus but lost 1,624 to 198. Elevation: 3,228 ft. Location: Powder River County

Ollie 1241 *map 16 C-4*

Homesteader Leander Greiner started the town of Ollie in 1910 with the construction of a general store and trading post. He named the community after his daughter, Ollie Greiner Larson. The Northern Pacific Railway opened a branch line between Beach, North Dakota, and Ollie in 1915. In 1928, the Independent Order of Odd Fellows Lodge in Ollie sponsored the first rabbit roundup. Members chose sides, and whichever side brought in the fewest rabbits had to feed the winners and their families an oyster supper. The community lost a significant part of its population when the railroad discontinued the branch line, and by 1955 it had become a ghost town. Elevation: 3,103 ft. Location: Fallon County

Olney 39 *map 2 B-1*

The Olney post office takes its name from a local rancher. It opened in 1907 to serve homesteaders between Whitefish and Eureka. Elevation: 3,178 ft. Location: Flathead County

One-room schoolhouses of Gallatin County 765 *map 20 B-1*

Gallatin County, one of the original 9 counties established in 1865, was Montana's first extensively settled agricultural area. Homesteaders arriving in the late 1860s first established schools in private homes or one-room cabins. Tiny one-room schoolhouses soon dotted the countryside, often no more than 5 miles apart. Weather constraints dictated a short school year of 4 months. When the population grew, a more permanent frame schoolhouse usually replaced the original log cabin. These structures had a central door on an open front porch, a standard feature employed to make younger students feel at home. By 1915, one-room schools reflected stylistic changes, and many schools of this period employed the Bungalow style. A bulletin published in 1919 by W. R. Plew of Bozeman's Montana State College recommended that classroom windows be on one side only, to prevent eye discomfort thought to be caused by cross lighting. Some schools reflect this recommendation, as well as another suggestion to provide a vestibule for added protection against harsh weather. Such adaptations became the norm in the 1920s in small schools throughout the West. There are 16 one-room schools listed in the National Register. Location: Gallatin County

Opheim 1037 *map 7 B-1*

The town of Opheim, named for homesteader Alfred S. Opheim, began in 1910 with construction of the family's sod house. The place grew during the homestead boom on the High Line, in part because of the Great Northern Railway's construction of the Bainville to Scobey branch line. Opheim went from a single dwelling to a community that supported a bank, several mercantile stores, a bakery, a lumberyard, and a saloon. Elevation: 3,262 ft. Location: Valley County

Opportunity 472 *map 11 E-1*

Dr. Henry Gardiner, director of the Anaconda Company's ranch properties, founded and named Opportunity as a community where Anaconda families would have an "opportunity" to raise their children in a rural atmosphere. Mining families received 10-acre lots where they grew vegetable gardens and raised horses, cows, pigs, and chickens. The company provided these early residents with streetcar service and, later, bus service into Anaconda and the smelter. Elevation: 4,972 ft. Location: Deer Lodge County

Opportunity Ponds 460 *map 11 E-1*

In 1910, the Anaconda Company began constructing a series of ponds 1 mile north of Opportunity, between Warm Springs and Mill creeks, designed to contain copper and zinc tailings from the Washoe Reduction Works and Washoe Smelter at Anaconda. The Opportunity Ponds accommodated expanded production until the 1940s, when copper and zinc production for the war effort taxed their capacity. The ponds, which occupied more than 3,000 acres in the Deer Lodge Valley, to an average depth of 40 feet, were closed in 1972. Currently the EPA plans to transport millions of tons of tailings from the base of the Milltown Dam near Missoula to the Opportunity Ponds for disposal and reclamation. Many residents of Opportunity have expressed opposition to the plan, citing their own struggles as part of the Anaconda Smelter Superfund cleanup. Elevation: 4,955 ft. Location: Deer Lodge County

Oswego 1088 *map 7 D-3*

The Great Northern Railway established Oswego in 1888 as a station, named for a town in New York. It is derived from a Mohawk word meaning "Where the river widens." The federal government opened the Fort Peck Indian Reservation to home-

Circle Bar O Ranch, Otter Creek
L. A. Huffman, photographer, MHS 981-292

steaders under the Fort Peck Allotment Act of 1908, resulting in a growth spurt for Oswego. It served as an important cattle-shipping center for the N Bar N Ranch, owned by the Niedringhaus brothers. A prairie fire destroyed most of Oswego in 1971. Elevation: 2,029 ft. Location: Valley County

Otter 1188   *map 23   C-2*

Established in 1895, Otter began as a post office on Charles Bull's ranch, where local ranchers could pick up their mail without having to travel to Miles City. Levi Howes recalled the effort he put forth to obtain enough signatures on the post office application, to the extreme of traveling to an outlaw hangout to request their signatures as well. While explaining his purpose for calling on them, he reached into his pocket for the petition and looked up—into the business end of a Colt .45. Howes quickly explained that he did not have a warrant and was only soliciting signatures to establish a post office. The pistol disappeared, and the boys all trooped into the cabin to sign the petition. Elevation: 3,461 ft. Location: Powder River County

Otter Creek 1156   *map 23   B-2*

Otter Creek flows north into Montana out of the highlands in Wyoming and empties into the Tongue River at Ashland. Capt. Calvin Howes developed one of the earliest ranches on Otter Creek. He arrived in Montana in the early 1880s and established the Circle Bar O Ranch on the lower Powder River. In 1884, Captain Howes drove 2,000 head of cattle from Texas to Otter Creek and maintained a successful cattle operation that survived the disastrous winter of 1886–87. The creek's naming is attributed to Howes.

Outlook 1151   *map 8   A-1*

Established on the Minneapolis, St. Paul & Sault Ste. Marie Railway in 1909 to provide supplies and services to the homesteaders rushing to the area, Outlook incorporated in 1913. There appears to be only one story about the origin of the name: A gentleman was entering the saloon one day when someone shouted, "Look out!" He ducked, and a glass sailed over his head. Amused by the episode and inspired by the phrase, the locals named their town after the incident but reversed the order of the words. The town's first building was C. E. Styers's store and post office in 1910, soon followed by more than a dozen other buildings and businesses. Like most of the other small towns in the area, this one declined after its initial boom. Unlike many of its neighbors, however, Outlook experienced a decided upswing when, on December 22, 1956, the first oil well was completed west of town near Big Muddy Creek. It produced a stunning 915 barrels of oil in its first 24 hours. Residents soon referred to their town as the "Oil City." When a wildfire hit the town in 1999, 20-some buildings were completely destroyed. The Outlook Depot is listed in the National Register. Elevation: 2,351 ft. Location: Sheridan County

Ovando 271 *map 10 B-4*

Ovando takes its name from Ovando Hoyt, a rancher and businessman who came to the Big Hole Basin in 1865, served as miller on the Flathead Indian Reservation, and appeared in the Blackfoot Valley in 1882. Hoyt served as Ovando postmaster from 1883 to 1898. Settlers were attracted by the rich agricultural land in the vicinity, swelling the town's population to 100 residents by 1919. Unfortunately, that same year a fire destroyed 7 buildings. Today the area offers access to the Bob Marshall and Scapegoat wilderness areas, as well as to numerous fly fishing streams. The town is probably best known for Trixie's Bar, located along MT 200, named for Trixie McCormick, a former owner and Montana rodeo queen. Elevation: 4,092 ft. Location: Powell County

Pipestone Pass Tunnel II, south of Butte, c. 1910
Butte Photo View Co., photographer, MHS PAc 94-53.6

Pablo 158 *map 2 E-2*

Pablo got its start in 1917, when the Northern Pacific Railway completed a branch line between Dixon and Polson. The town takes its name from Salish pioneer cattleman Michel Pablo, who is perhaps best known for his efforts to save the American bison from extinction. The timber industry was an early economic boon. Boosters predicted that Pablo would surpass Spokane, Washington, in size and importance, but by 1923 several disastrous fires had taken their toll and the dream of expansion diminished. Today Pablo is the headquarters of the Confederated Salish and Kootenai Tribes and home to Salish-Kootenai College and the Sqelix'u/Aqtsmaknik, "The People's" Cultural Center. Elevation: 3,091 ft. Location: Lake County

Pablo NWR 153 *map 2 E-2*

Built in 1912 as part of the Flathead Irrigation Project, Pablo Reservoir became part of the Pablo NWR in 1921; both are named for Michel Pablo, the Salish man known for his efforts to save the American bison from extinction. The refuge, administered by the USFWS, primarily protects the marshland surrounding the reservoir; the Confederated Salish and Kootenai Tribes own and administer the reservoir. Popular with birders, the refuge supports abundant wildlife. Elevation: 3,215 ft. Location: Lake County

Painted Rocks Lake 419 *map 18 A-1*

Painted Rocks Lake is named for the colored rock cliffs surrounding it. It was built by the State Water Conservation Board, in cooperation with the West Fork Water Users Association in 1938. The reservoir displaced the original West Fork Ranger Station and several homesteads. Painted Rocks State Park, established in 1963, encompasses 293 acres and is managed by Montana Fish, Wildlife & Parks. Elevation: 4,717 ft. Location: Ravalli County

Paradise 145 *map 9 A-4*

According to locals, Paradise is a corruption of the name of a local roadhouse: "Pair o' Dice." Other explanations have circulated over the years, but what is certain is that the name was formally recorded as Paradise in 1883, when the Northern Pacific Railroad chose the site as a division point and the place where railroaders would change their watches from Mountain to Pacific time. Elevation: 2,503 ft. Location: Sanders County

Paradise Valley 841 *map 20 B-2*

Early settlers awed by the natural beauty and fertile soil of this area along the Yellowstone River named it the Paradise Valley. The valley remained part of the Crow Indian Reservation until the arrival of the Northern Pacific Railroad in 1883. Hollywood transplants Peter Fonda and Jeff Bridges are longtime residents, and San Francisco hippie poet Richard Brautigan lived up Pine Creek in the north end of the valley. Paradise Valley provides a dramatic backdrop for tourists traveling to and from Yellowstone National Park. Elevation: 4,861 ft. Location: Park County

Park City 976 *map 21 B-3*

Alonzo Young established a boat landing on the Yellowstone River near this site and opened a post office named Young's Point in 1878. A colony of settlers from Ripon, Wisconsin, arrived in 1882, planted a grove of elms and maples, and established their own post office called Park City here. The Northern Pacific Railroad's main line passed through the community shortly thereafter, and the railroad constructed a station, calling it Rimrock for the sandstone cliffs north of town. The name Park City persisted, however, which prompted railroad officials to establish the railyards and shops at Laurel in retaliation. Today many people who work for the oil refinery and railroad in nearby Laurel make their homes in Park City. Elevation: 3,399 ft. Location: Stillwater County

Park County 850 *map 20 C-3*
The Crows had inhabited this area as part of their original reservation. Beginning in 1882, the Northern Pacific Railroad built tracks through here and established a division point at Livingston. The Montana legislature created Park County in 1887 from parts of Gallatin, Carbon, and Sweet Grass counties; the name reflects its proximity to Yellowstone National Park. Livingston became the county seat.

Park Grove 1256 *map 7 D-1*
This town, named for a nearby grove of trees, emerged during construction of Fort Peck Dam in 1934, one of a handful of boomtowns. In 1934, the makeshift town housed approximately 350 families and boasted Tom's Black Cat Lunch, which offered 35¢ plate lunches, and the Riverview Park Tavern, which was made out of train cars. Today the town still supports a bar and grocery. Elevation: 2,067 ft. Location: Valley County

Pattengail Creek 542 *map 18 A-4*
This creek is named for George Pattengill, "Wild Man of Montana," a Civil War veteran who returned home to Wisconsin from the war to find his wife with another man. Pattengill dispatched his wife's lover, his wife then shot herself, and Pattengill headed to Montana with his son, who contracted diphtheria and died. Pattengill set up camp in a wickiup along the West Fork of the Wise River, now called Pattengail Creek, a misspelling of his name. He lived off the land and regularly frightened Butte fishermen until his demise in 1895. Location: Beaverhead County

Peerless 1081 *map 7 B-3*
Established in 1914 as Tande (for postmaster and store owner Andrew Tande), this town prospered until 1925 when the Great Northern Railway extended its branch line west from Scobey. Recognizing the benefits of being situated right on the railroad, residents moved homes and businesses to the present location and took the name Peerless for the town. The idea for the new name came from Schlitz-Peerless beer, the budding community's brew of choice. Elevation: 2,852 ft. Location: Daniels County

Pendroy 254 *map 3 D-2*
Great Northern Railway founder James J. Hill planned to extend a branch line from Great Falls northwest to Essex, on the railroad's main line. Levi "Boots" Pendroy, who lived near the proposed route, asked his old friend Hill to establish a station on his homestead. However, as the railroad tracks approached the site, they encountered Farmer's Coulee. Railroad officials decided that the cost of filling the coulee or building a trestle to span it was not cost efficient, so they established the townsite south of the coulee, missing Pendroy's homestead. They planned to name the

T. R. Larson general store, Pendroy, c. 1925
MHS PAc 85-45

Home of W. Q. Amison and Episcopal rectory, Philipsburg
Detail, MHS 950-223

new community either Mountain View or Long View, but Hill settled the issue by naming it Pendroy after his old friend. The railroad constructed a depot, roundhouse, and section house there by 1916. The town's population peaked during the 1920s. Elevation: 4,272 ft. Location: Teton County

Pennel Creek 1208 *map 16 C-2*

Pennel Creek in eastern Montana is named for Joe Pennel, a station agent on the Fort Abraham Lincoln–Fort Keogh wagon road in the 1870s. Pennel's station was burned by Indians about 1880. Just north of the creek, on Dead Man's Butte, is a monument to a stage driver named Fritz or Fries, killed near there in 1880. Location: Fallon and Custer counties

Peoples Creek 835 *map 5 C-4*

Known to the Assiniboine as Many Peoples Creek, the name Peoples Creek was shortened in translation. This tributary of the Milk River has its headwaters in the Bears Paw Mountains and flows into the Milk between Coburg and Dodson. Location: Blaine and Phillips counties

Perma 159 *map 9 A-4*

The Northern Pacific Railroad established Perma as a station stop in 1883, near the Weeksville Road ferry crossing on the Flathead River. The town's name, derived from the Greek word for ferry, is immortalized in the title of Debra Magpie Earling's novel *Perma Red*, which describes life on the Flathead Indian Reservation during the 1940s. Elevation: 2,509 ft. Location: Sanders County

Petroleum County 916 *map 14 B-1*

The Montana legislature created Petroleum County in 1925 from Fergus County, with Winnett as the county seat. The county owes its name to the petroleum produced from the Cat Creek Oil Field discovered in 1920. It also has the distinction of being the last county formed in the state. With only 493 residents, according to the 2000 census, it remains Montana's least-populated county.

Petrolia Lake 928 *map 14 C-1*

Petrolia Lake, presumably named for the oil for which Petroleum County is named, was formed in 1951 by impounding Flatwillow Creek behind Petrolia Dam. The dam is 900 feet long and 55 feet high; 3 irrigation canals take water to local farms. Montana Fish, Wildlife & Parks stocks the lake with walleye. Elevation: 2,898 ft. Location: Petroleum County

Philipsburg 361 *map 10 D-3*
Philipsburg, the county seat of Granite County, is named for mining engineer Philip Deidesheimer, who platted the townsite near rich gold and silver mines in 1867. Subject to the boom-and-bust cycles of a mining economy, the town was considered dead in 1869 but revived a little with the arrival of the Northern Pacific Railroad's branch line, the Drummond and Philipsburg Railroad, in 1887. Philipsburg boomed again in the 1890s, and the newly merged Granite-BiMetallic Consolidated Mining Company produced silver in large quantities until the repeal of the Sherman Silver Purchase Act and the Panic of 1893. During World War I, manganese deposits proved the source of yet another boom. The Philipsburg Historic District, listed in the National Register in 1986, includes the commercial area and other structures. Elevation: 5,266 ft. Location: Granite County

Phillips County 897 *map 6 B-2*
The Montana legislature created Phillips County in 1915 from Blaine and Valley counties, with Malta as the county seat. The county takes its name from former Chouteau County senator Benjamin D. Phillips, who operated a sheep ranch and several area mines; Phillips used his political influence to ensure that the new county fell within the boundaries of his mining properties. Phillips County encompasses 6,565 square miles, making it one of Montana's largest counties.

Pictograph Cave State Park and NHL
1018 *map 21 A-4*
Pictograph, Middle, and Ghost caves sheltered generations of prehistoric hunters as long ago as 4,500 years. Archaeologists in the 1930s recorded more than 100 fragile paintings in red, black, yellow, and white on the cave walls that dated to between 500 A.D. and 1900 A.D. By the 1990s, because of exposure, fading, and vandalism, only 44 images remained. In 1937, amateur archaeologists discovered prehistoric cultural deposits in Pictograph Cave. The find attracted national attention, and within months the WPA funded excavations in the caves. The substantial collection of Native American artifacts presented a rare complete picture of multiple occupations. Archaeologist William Mulloy suggested that the longest occupation at the site was by ancestors of the Crows who were in transition from an agricultural economy to a nomadic lifestyle. World War II halted the excavations in 1941. Middle Cave is the only cave of the 3 with no evidence of habitation. Ghost Cave has yielded cultural material and human remains dating to the Late Prehistoric period (500 A.D. to 1800 A.D.). The

Pictograph Cave, south of Billings, 1979
MHS PAc 84-91 A7910-7

caves received NHL status in 1964, and the site became a state park in 1991. Improvements include trails, outhouses, and picnic facilities, but protection of the fragile site is critical and remains problematic. The park is open April through October. Elevation: 3,433 ft. Location: Yellowstone County

Pilgrim Creek 1222 *map 24 B-1*
John R. and Harriet Edwards and their son Byrd established a sheep ranch at the mouth of Pilgrim Creek in the late 1800s. They proved up on their homesteads in 1912. Byrd Edwards diversified to cattle ranching and raised his family in the area. The origin of the name is not known. Location: Powder River County

Pine Butte Swamp Preserve 245 *map 3 E-2*
The Nature Conservancy owns and manages the 28-square-mile Pine Butte Swamp Preserve, established in 1979. The preserve is named for the butte that rises dramatically 500 feet above the marshland. It is the largest wetland complex on the Rocky Mountain Front. The preserve was established on what was Alice and Kenneth Gleason's Circle 8 dude ranch from 1930 until 1978. The Nature Conservancy operates the Pine Butte Guest Ranch based on the traditions established by the Gleasons, as an international nonprofit organization dedicated to natural diversity. Elevation: 5,004 ft. Location: Teton County

Pine Creek 837 *map 20 B-3*
Pine Creek, named for the trees along its banks, is popular with fly fishers and hikers. It flows out of the Absaroka Mountains into the Paradise Valley and empties into the Yellowstone River. Location: Park County

Pinesdale 300 *map 10 D-1*
Pinesdale is a relatively new community, incorporated in 1980. It was settled in the early 1960s by fundamentalist Mormons, who selected its secluded location for the privacy. Dee Jessop, one of the town founders, said they chose the name "to make it as insignificant as we could." The community has a cooperative philosophy, sharing many of the tasks and facilities among the members. Most of the children attend the private Pines Academy. Elevation: 3,986 ft. Location: Ravalli County

Pinnacle 132 *map 2 C-3*
Originally known as Paola, the town of Pinnacle served as a station stop on the Great Northern Railway and was home to railroad employees, lumbermen, and USFS employees. Nothing is known about the origin of the name. Elevation: 3,711 ft. Location: Flathead County

Pioneer Mountains 572 *map 18 B-4*
Named to commemorate the first gold miners and settlers along Grasshopper Creek at Bannack, this range is bounded on the west and north by the Big Hole River and split east and west by the Wise River. The range has 48 peaks higher than 10,000 feet. Significant silver mines operated at Lion City (Hecla Mine) and Coolidge (Elkhorn Mine).

Pipestone 582 *map 19 A-2*
The name Pipestone recalls the clay along the creek bank that various Indian tribes harvested to make pipes. The Pipestone post office opened in 1880. The *Butte Miner* reported on March 24, 1893, that the Pipestone Mineral Springs and Townsite Company had incorporated to develop the nearby hot springs into a summer resort. Although a small resort opened around the springs and a townsite was laid out, a community never devel-

oped. Elevation: 4,567 ft. Location: Jefferson County

Pipestone Hot Springs 583 *map 19 A-2*
In 1870, John Paul bought a ranch property that included thermal springs, about 16 miles east of Butte. Eight years later, he opened the property to the public as a health resort, served by a triweekly stage from Butte. Paul and investors created the Pipestone Mineral Springs and Townsite Company in 1893, with plans for an enlarged bathhouse, hotel, and hospital. Pipestone Hot Springs was a stop along the Northern Pacific's main line. Elevation: 4,538 ft. Location: Jefferson County

Pipestone Pass 569 *map 19 A-2*
The name Pipestone refers to a soft, red stone preferred by Native Americans for making pipes. In the late 1870s, a rough wagon road over the pass connected Butte and Whitehall. During the late 1880s, a stage "Halfway House" 19 miles from Butte sat here; it eventually became known as the Grace post office, named for the wife of W. W. McCall, who operated the stage station. In 1909, the Milwaukee Road built its main line over the Continental Divide at Pipestone Pass, constructing a spectacular tunnel with classic Milwaukee Road portals. The pass marks the line between Jefferson and Silver Bow counties. Elevation: 6,453 ft.

Piquett Mountain 421 *map 18 A-1*
This mountain in the southern end of the Sapphire Range is named for early homesteader Edward Piquett, who settled on the West Fork of the Bitterroot River at the mouth of the canyon in 1889. Elevation: 8,831 ft. Location: Ravalli County

Pirogue Island State Park 1143 *map 15 D-4*
Capt. William Clark and his party camped on this island, once known as Doeden Island, on July 29, 1806, on their return trip down the Yellowstone River. The State of Montana acquired Doeden Island in 1982; it was renamed Pirogue Island State Park, after the boats used by the expedition. During most of the year, the park is accessible only by boat. Elevation: 2,350 ft. Location: Custer County

Pishkun Reservoir 261 *map 3 E-2*
The U.S. Bureau of Reclamation built Pishkun Reservoir in 1925 as part of the Sun River Irrigation Project. The reservoir stores water diverted from the North Fork of the Sun River. Eight earth-filled dams create the reservoir, which has a total of 550 acres of surface water and 13 miles of shoreline. A "pishkun" is a cliff or cutbank over which buffalo were driven; butchering was done at the cliff base. Pishkun Reservoir is designated a wildlife management area. Elevation: 4,374 ft. Location: Teton County

Placid Lake 226 *map 10 B-3*
New Yorker Hiram Blanchard, who arrived in the area in 1892 and formed the Clearwater Land and Livestock Company, named this lake after Lake Placid, New York. The lake is the site of Placid Lake State Park. Elevation: 4,125 ft. Location: Missoula County

Plains 130 *map 9 A-4*
Shortened from Wild Horse Plains to Horse Plains to simply Plains, this community was established in 1883 as a Northern Pacific Railroad station. British and American trappers used the area as a wintering site for horses as early as 1800. Elevation: 2,478 ft. Location: Sanders County

Plentywood 1168 *map 8 B-2*

According to local legend, Plentywood Creek and the town of Plentywood derive their name from a search for firewood. One day, cowboys from the Diamond Ranch watched in exasperation as the chuck wagon cook attempted to start a fire with damp buffalo chips. Finally, in frustration, the notorious Dutch Henry said, "If you'll go 2 miles up this creek, you'll find plenty wood." George Bolster arrived in the area in 1900 and opened the first business. The post office opened in 1902. The Great Northern Railway surveyed a route through the area for the Bainville to Scobey branch line in 1911. Two years later, the Dakota and Great Northern Townsite Company platted the town and Plentywood incorporated; Plentywood residents mark 1912 as the town's birth. Sheridan County was a hotbed of Socialist and, later, Communist sentiment from about 1918 to 1937. The WPA undertook a tree-planting campaign in Plentywood in the 1940s, inspiring this clever Associated Press line: "At last there's going to be plenty of wood in Plentywood, a town that's had more sun than shade." Elevation: 2,047 ft. Location: Sheridan County

Riba's Bank of Plentywood, c. 1913
MHS 950-242

Plevna 1226 *map 16 D-3*

Bulgarian railroad workers employed by the Milwaukee Railroad named the town of Plevna. *Plevna* in Russian translates into "city of churches." The town opened its post office in 1909, and homesteaders trickled into the area. Many of these immigrants were descendents of the German farmers invited by Catherine the Great, Empress of all the Russias, to settle the Russian steppes. Plevna grew up as a cluster of churches, bars, and mercantile operations serving the growing dryland farming community. Elevation: 2,809 ft. Location: Fallon County

Polaris 611 *map 18 B-4*

This community takes its name from the Polaris Mine, which operated as a silver mine from 1885 until 1922. The town declined after the mine closed, and by 1955 the Polar Bar was the sole business. The post office operated from May 1898 to July 1985. Elevation: 6,355 ft. Location: Beaverhead County

Polebridge 46 *map 2 B-1*

Ben Henson named the post office Polebridge in 1920, after the bridge made of poles that spanned the North Fork of the Flathead River. The first community sat on the east side of the North Fork in 1904, where Bill Adair constructed a store and boardinghouse. He moved both businesses to the other side of the river when the North Fork was established as the western boundary of Glacier National Park in 1910. Adair's 2 businesses formed the heart of the community of Polebridge and served residents of the remote region and tourists who braved the road up the North Fork. Homesteads were filed for under the Forest Homestead Act of 1906—commonly referred to as June 11 claims, the day the bill was enacted. Elevation: 3,524 ft. Location: Flathead County

Polson 144 *map 2 E-2*
The Salish named the place where Polson now sits Pied e' lai, "Foot of the lake." In 1864, Baptiste Eneas built and operated a ferry across the Flathead River where it exited the lake. When Henry Lambert opened a trading post and general store nearby in 1881, the spot became known as Lambert's Landing. In 1898, the community took the name of pioneer rancher David Polson, but it did not incorporate until 1910, when the area boomed with the sudden influx of homesteaders attracted by the opening of the Flathead Indian Reservation to non-Indians. When the Montana legislature created Lake County in 1923, Polson won the coveted county seat from Ronan. Elevation: 2,927 ft. Location: Lake County

Pompeys Pillar National Monument
1025 *map 14 E-1*
Pompeys Pillar, a large sandstone butte, was named in July 1806 by Capt. William Clark in honor of Sacagawea's son, Jean Baptiste Charbonneau, whom he had nicknamed "Pomp." Clark carved his name on the rock on July 25, 1806. Nicholas Biddle, the first editor of the Lewis and Clark journals, changed the name from Pompy's Tower to Pompeys Pillar. Native Americans called the pillar Lisbi'iaassaao, "Place where the mountain lion lies." Pompeys Pillar, named a NHL in 1965, received further recognition as a national historic monument in 2001. Elevation: 2,985 ft. Location: Yellowstone County

Pompey's Pillar, c. 1925
Herman Schnitzmeyer, photographer, MHS 950-257

Pondera County 253 *map 3 D-4*
The Montana legislature created Pondera County in 1919 from Chouteau and Teton counties, with Conrad as the county seat. Local lore suggests that Pondera is either the phonetic spelling of the French *pend d'oreille* ("hanging earring") or *pain d'or* ("golden bread," for the color of the native grasses). Wheat production remains the main industry in the county.

Pony 667 *map 19 A-3*
About 1866, a prospector of very small stature, Tecumseh "Pony" Smith, gave his nickname to the creek where he found gold. In 1875, a settlement called Pony grew to serve local miners. By the 1880s, mines like the Boss Tweed and Clipper were yielding fortunes in gold ore. In 1890, the Northern Pacific Railroad's Red Bluff and Pony Railroad branch line came through the town, and by 1895 Pony had a school, a public hall, 2 hotels, and numerous businesses. As the mines began to play out at the turn of the twentieth century, cyanide processing of gold tailings sparked a new interest in the area. Pony prospered, acquiring telephone service, electricity, and a more urban appearance. Masons and carpenters

produced splendid Queen Anne–style residences and fine buildings of locally made materials, such as the Pony School and the Morris State Bank. Mining waned after 1910, and Pony's economy shifted to serve the surrounding agricultural community. The Pony Historic District and nearby Strawberry Mine Historic District are listed in the National Register. Elevation: 5,482 ft. Location: Madison County

Poplar 1131 *map 8 D-1*

The area around Poplar began attracting residents as early as 1860, when Charles Larpenteur built a trading post at the confluence of the Poplar and Missouri rivers. The U.S. Army constructed Camp Poplar here in the 1870s to oversee the Fort Peck Indian Reservation. Poplar was designated reservation headquarters after the military abandoned the camp in 1893. The federal government opened the reservation to settlement through a lottery system in 1913. The Fort Peck Agency in Poplar is listed in the National Register. Elevation: 1,993 ft. Location: Roosevelt County

Poplar River 1129 *map 8 C-1*

French fur traders named this river La Riviere aux Trembles, "Trembling aspen river," for the trees along its banks. Lewis and Clark renamed it the Porcupine on May 3, 1805, for the spiny animal they encountered here. The date it became known as the Poplar River is unknown. The Poplar's headwaters are in Saskatchewan; it flows 155 miles to its confluence with the Missouri River near the town of Poplar. The river is part of the Woody Mountain Trail, a thoroughfare used by the Sioux during their retreat into Canada in the late 1870s.

Porcupine Butte 801 *map 12 E-4*

The origin of this name is not known, but from afar this hill does resemble a porcupine. Crow chief Plenty Coups seasonally camped on the butte. Elevation: 7,010 ft. Location: Sweet Grass County

Porphyry Peak 623 *map 12 C-2*

Porphyry Peak is on the line between Meagher and Cascade counties at the top of the Showdown Montana ski area. The original fire lookout on the peak was built in 1937 and replaced in 1960. The peak is a small, 50-million-year-old igneous intrusion of porphyritic ores. Elevation: 8,192 ft. Location: Meagher County

Portage 934 *map 4 E-1*

When the Lewis and Clark Expedition reached the rapids below the Great Falls of the Missouri River on June 20, 1805, they recognized that they would have to portage their boats around the falls. The drainage across the river from where they began the portage was named "portage creek" by the expedition. When the Great Northern Railway built tracks here in 1887, railroad officials named the station Portage. A town with the same name was established in 1904. Elevation: 3,386 ft. Location: Cascade County

Porters Corner 329 *map 10 D-3*

It is possible that Porters Corner is named for Aleck, Charles, and George Porter, who homesteaded along the East Fork of Rock Creek, near the Skalkaho Road, about 10 miles west of Porters Corner. Elevation: 5,407 ft. Location: Granite County

Port of Scobey 1108 *map 7 A-4*

The Port of Scobey was established as a border crossing in the mid-1960s when MT 13 was routed from Whitetail to Scobey. Before that time, the border was open, and in the early 1900s cattle rustling was common. During the 1920s, bootleggers smuggled liquor across the border, and Canadian farmers hauled wheat to the

Scobey elevator to take advantage of the higher U.S. prices. In 1996, the port became a voice-activated crossing. Americans and Canadians registered to use the system are able to open the border gate by entering an identification number and saying a predetermined phrase. Elevation: 2,443 ft. Location: Daniels County

Potomac 256 *map 10 C-3*
In 1884, Robert S. Ashby named this town located at the convergence of Camas and Union creeks after the Potomac River of his native Virginia. Potomac was a supply point for miners, lumberjacks, and ranchers. Elevation: 3,620 ft. Location: Missoula County

Shepherd and flock, Powder River, c. 1886
L. A. Huffman, photographer, MHS 981-682

Powder River 1162 *map 15 C-4*
The Powder River derives its name from the Sioux word *yela*, "powdery," an apt adjective for the consistency of the river bottom and banks. Capt. William Clark described the Powder River on July 30, 1806: "This river is Shallow and the water very muddy and the color of the banks a darkish brown." In Prince Maximilian's treatise on his travels of 1832–34, he referred to the river as La Riviere a la Poudre. The familiar Montana expression "Powder River, let 'er buck" began with southeastern Montana cowboys; the 91st Division took it up as a battle cry during World War I. The Powder flows 320 miles, from Wyoming to the Yellowstone River near Terry.

Powder River County 1210 *map 23 B-4*
The Montana legislature created Powder River County in 1919 from the southern part of Custer County; Broadus won the county seat in the election of 1920. The county takes its name from the Powder River, which flows diagonally across it.

During World War I, American doughboys from the area used "Powder River, let 'er buck" as their battle cry. Local lore suggests that the phrase originated during a roundup when one enthusiastic cowboy, after being warned about a nasty bronc, stated, "I'm from Powder River, let 'er buck!" The county covers 3,337 square miles of badlands, flatlands, and forests.

Powderville 1223 *map 24 A-1*
In 1883, Ben Mason opened a store and post office across the Powder River from Elkhorn, a telegraph and stage station between Fort Meade and Fort Keogh. The town is named for the river. The post office closed in 1983. Elevation: 2,828 ft. Location: Powder River County

Powell County 312 *map 11 C-1*
The Montana legislature created Powell County in 1901 from part of Deer Lodge County, naming Deer Lodge (the former county seat of Deer Lodge County) as the county seat. The county's name is taken from 10,168-foot Mount Powell, the highest peak in the Flint Creek Range, named

for John W. Powell, an area pioneer and the first Euro-American to ascend the mountain.

Power 343 *map 3 F-4*
In 1886, Frank and Guy Steele established a stage station in eastern Montana near what later became the town of Power. Thomas C. Power, Montana businessman and U.S. senator, bought the Steele's land and in 1910 platted the townsite. Power remained active in the town's businesses, among them the Boorman-Power Lumber & Implement Co., the Power State Bank, and the Power Morgan Company. Elevation: 3,694 ft. Location: Teton County

Prairie County 1160 *map 15 B-3*
The Montana legislature created Prairie County in 1915 from Custer, Dawson, and Fallon counties, with Terry as the county seat. A. W. Morrill of Mildred won a contest to select the new county's name, which reflects the region's landscape. One notable event in Prairie County history was the derailment of a westbound Milwaukee Road train after a rainstorm washed out the Custer Creek bridge near Saugus on June 19, 1938. In the horrific crash, Prairie County's greatest tragedy, 47 people died and another 75 were injured.

Pray 849 *map 20 B-3*
The Pray post office opened in 1909 along the Northern Pacific Railway's branch line from Livingston to Gardiner and Yellowstone National Park. It was named for Charles N. Pray, a Montana congressman from 1906 to 1911 who went on to a distinguished 33-year career as a federal judge in Montana. In 1976, the postal service moved the Pray post office 3 miles east of the railroad line. Elevation: 5,004 ft. Location: Park County

Prickly Pear Creek 458 *map 11 C-3*
On July 19, 1805, Capt. William Clark and his party entered the valley he named for Sgt. Nathaniel Pryor. In his journal, Clark described the stream he named Pryor Creek as "a butifull creek . . . which meanders thro a butifull Vallie of great extent." By the 1869s, it was known as Prickly Pear Creek for the cactus that grows plentifully in the valley. Prickly Pear Creek's headwaters are in the Elkhorn Mountains. It flows southeast before emptying into Lake Helena and the Missouri River. Agriculture expanded during the 1910s with development of the Prickly Pear Valley Irrigation Project, and expanded again during the 1950s with irrigation water pumped into the Helena Regulating Reservoir from the Missouri River. More than 10,000 acres in the Prickly Pear Valley are irrigated. Location: Jefferson and Lewis and Clark counties

Priest Butte Lake 295 *map 3 F-3*
Visible for miles, Priest Butte directed travelers to the first St. Peter's Mission on the Teton River, established in 1859. The small lake nearby took this name much later. Elevation: 3,762 ft. Location: Teton County

Priest Pass 412 *map 11 D-2*
In 1879, Valentine T. Priest hired a crew of Chinese laborers to construct a toll road over a pass that lay just north of MacDonald Pass. Priest's crew finished construction on the road in 8 months. About 300 feet lower than the toll road over MacDonald Pass, the new road proved very successful, forcing Alexander MacDonald to sell his toll road over MacDonald Pass in 1885. However, because Priest never chartered the toll road, Lewis and Clark County and Deer Lodge County took control of the road when Montana became a state in 1889. In 1915, the Priest Pass Road was designated a portion of the Great White

Wild horse roundup near Lodge Grass,
Pryor Mountains, 1925
MHS PAc 95-27.3

Way, the route connecting Yellowstone and Glacier national parks. Elevation: 5,994 ft. Location: Lewis and Clark County

Princeton 356 *map 10 D-4*

Today a ghost town on Boulder Creek, Princeton, formally established in 1880, was named for miner Dick Prince, who had prospected in the area since 1868. The Nonpareil Mine, developed at Princeton by a French company in the 1880s, was followed by several other silver, gold, and lead mines. Mining dwindled through the 1920s and '30s and ceased altogether about 1942. Elevation: 5,411 ft. Location: Granite County

Proctor 108 *map 2 D-1*

The Kootenais moved to the area between Lake Mary Ronan and Flathead Lake in 1869, prompting the federal government to open a commissary near what later became Proctor. The Kootenai referred to the area as Fish Trap. Clarence E. Proctor arrived in the area in 1883 and established a ranch and store. Originally called Dayton, the town prospered, but in 1910, with the opening of the Flathead Indian Reservation to non-Indian homesteaders, the residents realized a location on Flathead Lake would be better for business and moved the town 2 miles to the lakeshore. With it went the name of the town. Residents of the old town petitioned and received approval to open a new post office and rename their town Proctor, after its most prominent citizen. Elevation: 3,175 ft. Location: Lake County

Pryor 1028 *map 21 B-4*

On July 25, 1805, Capt. William Clark noted the "small river" that he named for Sgt. Nathanial Pryor. The community of Pryor sits on the banks of this stream. The first post office opened in 1892 with Emma C. Stoeckel as postmaster. The Chicago, Burlington & Quincy Railroad built a line through the valley in 1900, and in conjunction, the federal government instituted a farming program on the Crow Indian Reservation that resulted in construction of a flour mill at Pryor. The railroad discontinued service through the area in 1910, and the mill closed a few years later. Today the town serves area ranchers and farmers. Elevation: 4,071 ft. Location: Big Horn County

Pryor Creek 1016 *map 22 A-1*

Known to the Crows as Alu'utaashe, "Arrow river," this creek was named by Capt. William Clark in honor of Sgt. Nathaniel Pryor on July 25, 1806. In about 1860, a large battle between the Sioux and Crows took place along the creek, instigated by a Sioux incursion into Crow territory to avenge the death of a warrior killed by a Crow party. Location: Big Horn and Yellowstone counties

Pryor Mountains 1041 *map 21 C-4*

This range of limestone peaks and mesas on the Crow Indian Reservation extends 35 miles between the Clarks Fork of the Yellowstone and the Bighorn rivers. The mountains are named after Pryor Creek, which was named in 1806 for Sgt. Nathaniel Pryor of the Lewis and Clark Expedition. The Crows knew the mountains as Alu'utalaho, "Arrow mountains," a sacred place and source of spiritual renewal tied to the offering of arrows. In 1968, the sec-

retary of the interior established the Pryor Mountain National Wild Horse Range to protect the herd of mustangs that lives here. Limestone caves are found throughout the Pryor Mountains. Big Pryor Mountain is the highest peak at 8,786 feet.

Pumpkin Creek 1161 *map 15 E-4*

Pumpkin Creek is allegedly named because an observation party attached to Lt. Col. George Armstrong Custer's command saw an image of the word *pumpkin* from the top of a butte 60 miles up the creek. In 1928, Congress created the first grazing district on public land, the Mizpah–Pumpkin Creek Grazing District, which ultimately led to passage of the Taylor Grazing Act of 1934. Location: Custer County

Purcell Mountains 3 *map 1 B-2*

Two states and one province (Montana 64 percent, Idaho 18 percent, and British Columbia 19 percent) share the Purcell Mountains. The name Purcell Mountains (also spelled Percell) appeared first on the 1857–59 map of the Palliser Expedition (formally the British North American Exploring Expedition 1857–60) in British Columbia. John Palliser petitioned the Royal Geographic Society to explore a route from the Red River Colony (Winnipeg, Manitoba) through the Rocky Mountains along the international border. The Royal Geographic Society approved the expedition but added a scientific component to it as well. The 1859, 1860, and 1863 reports from the expedition and the comprehensive map published in 1865 proved a major source of information regarding the area. The highest peak in Montana's Purcells is 7,705-foot Northwest Peak.

Surveyors at Quigley, 1905
Malcom Bowden, photographer, MHS

Aerial view of Hebgen-area quake slide, August 22–23, 1959,
that created Quake Lake on the Madison River.

MHS, PAc 86-15, 124-G

Quake Lake 867 *map 19 D-4*

On August 17, 1959, just before midnight, a powerful earthquake shook this area, causing half of a 7,600-foot-high mountain (38–50 million cubic yards of rock) to crash into the Madison Canyon in less than a minute. The landslide buried parts of a popular campground, killed 28 people, and injured 300. The slide dammed the Madison River, forming a new body of water now called Quake Lake (the official USGS name is Earthquake Lake). Elevation: 6,392 ft. Location: Madison and Gallatin counties

Quartz 179 *map 9 B-4*

Originally called Quartz Creek, the town of Quartz takes its name from the vast amount of quartz mined in the area begin-

ning in the 1870s. By May 1871, Quartz Creek had a post office, and 200 mining claims had been filed in the area. In October 1882, the town shortened its name to Quartz. By 1916, mining had ceased, and Quartz gradually faded into obscurity. Elevation: 2,871 ft. Location: Mineral County

Quigg Peak 304 *map 10 D-3*

This mountain is named for Winfield S. Quigley, a Wilmington, Delaware, investor with interests in gold and silver mines west of Philipsburg. In 1896, the town of Quigley grew up around the Golden Sceptre Mine, along with a concentrator and sawmill, but the town was short-lived. Elevation: 8,419 ft. Location: Granite County

IOOF Hall (Independent Order of Odd Fellows), Radersburg, 1970
Detail, Peter Meloy, photographer, MHS 950-492

Rainbow Dam, powerhouse, and falls, Great Falls, 1918
G. V. Barker, photographer, MHS 949-595

Racetrack Creek 426 *map 11 D-1*

The area around Racetrack Creek was known in the 1860s as Racetrack Prairie because its wide, flat terrain was popular among both Indians and settlers for racing their horses.

Racetrack Peak 372 *map 10 D-4*

The name Race Track, or Racetrack, is used for a peak, a lake, a pass, a creek, and a town, none of them in very close proximity. The town and creek are in Powell County; the peak and lake, in Granite County. The region around the town was known as Racetrack Prairie because the area was so wide and flat that the local Indians and pioneers liked to test the speed of their horses there. The region around Racetrack Peak was known as the Race Track Mining District. It was placer mined by Benjamin Daniels in the 1890s and early 1900s. Elevation: 9,522 ft. Location: Granite County

Radersburg 595 *map 11 E-4*

Located almost exactly halfway between Bozeman and Helena, Radersburg was established in 1865 when gold was discovered there. It is named for Reuben Rader, a Virginian who ranched and prospected in the area. Radersburg was soon a center of transportation, a layover point for the government mail stage, and a stopping place for travelers. By 1866, it was home to a wide variety of businesses, including a livery, saloon, general mercantile, barbershop, drugstore, and shoemaker. It had a population of 1,000 in 1869, when it became the county seat of Jefferson County. The seat of government was lost in 1883 to Boulder, and most of the businesses and population moved to Townsend to follow the railroad. Leading lady of stage and screen Myrna Loy (1905–93) was born in Radersburg. Elevation: 4,316 ft. Location: Broadwater County

Rainbow Dam 437 *map 12 A-1*

The Great Falls Water Power & Townsite Company built Rainbow Dam between 1908 and 1910 at the site of Rainbow Falls and Crooked Falls. It provided a more secure source of power for the Anaconda Company, as well as power for several cities. The original dam was constructed of timber cribs filled with rock and concrete. Between 1987 and 1990, workers replaced the timber dam with a concrete one. Elevation: 3,230 ft. Location: Cascade County

Ramsay 509 *map 11 E-1*

During World War I, E. I. DuPont de Nemours and Company built the Ramsay dynamite manufacturing plant to supply the booming copper mines at Butte, and simultaneously constructed a planned community for its workers. The company called the new community Ramsay, in honor of chief engineer William G. Ramsay, who died during construction of the plant and town. The post office opened in 1916. In 1921, DuPont closed the plant and laid off all the workers, leaving the town with 2 residents; 3 years later, it sold the townsite. Ramsay has since grown back into a viable community. In 2004, Rhodia Corporation of France was fined $16.2 million for illegally storing hazardous waste in a defunct phosphorus plant at Ramsay. Elevation: 5,338 ft. Location: Silver Bow County

Ramshorn Peak 840 *map 20 C-1*

Ramshorn Peak, at the southern end of the Gallatin Range just north of Yellowstone National Park, takes its name from the bighorn sheep that frequent the area. At the base of the peak, near the head of Tom Miner Basin, is a petrified forest, which includes many upright petrified trees—part of the Yellowstone Petrified Forests. Elevation: 10,289 ft. Location: Gallatin County

Rankin Ranch NHL 552 *map 11 D-4*

Attorney Wellington Rankin purchased this property in 1923, but the ranch was more often home to Wellington's famous sister. Progressive Jeannette Rankin, the first woman elected to the nation's House of Representatives (1917–19), rose to prominence not only as the first woman to sit in Congress but also because her vote against entry into World War I created a sensation. Elected to Congress a second time (1941–43), she also voted against involvement in World War II. Hers was the only opposing vote; she remained an active peace advocate her entire life. From 1923 to 1956, Jeannette often maintained a summer residence on this ranch in Avalanche Gulch. A landowner with one of the largest private holdings in Montana, Wellington was an influential force in Montana politics. He served terms as state attorney general, as associate justice of the Supreme Court, and as a Republican national committeeman. Wellington hired managers to operate the cattle ranch, but he and his sister spent holidays and leisure time in the home. It was designated a NHL in 1976. Elevation: 4,167 ft. Location: Broadwater County

Rapelje 906 *map 21 A-2*

Rapelje (pronounced RAP-el-jay) replaced the town of Lake Basin, which was a short distance to the east. In 1917, it was surveyed, platted, and named for John M. Rapelje, general manager and vice president of the Northern Pacific Railway and previously a train master in Glendive. Situated at the end of a Northern Pacific branch line from the main line west of Laurel, Rapelje today is a large grain-shipping center, with several elevators and other businesses. Elevation: 4,067 ft. Location: Stillwater County

Rattlesnake Wilderness 229 *map 10 B-2*

Rattlesnake Creek (one of several), the Rattlesnake Mountains, and the Rattlesnake Wilderness are all just north of

Homesteaders in Ravalli when the Flathead Indian Reservation was opened to non-Indian settlement, c. 1912

Herman Schnitzmeyer, photographer, MHS 950-561

Missoula. The creek already had this name when the Stevens survey came through in 1853–54. An earlier name for the creek was Inelkie, a Salish word meaning "Stream of many salmon trout." Congress created the Rattlesnake Wilderness in 1980, protecting 32,000 acres of rugged mountains and pristine lakes, and at the same time added a contiguous 22,000-acre NRA. The Confederated Salish and Kootenai Tribes set aside a 36,000-acre primitive area to the north, open only to tribal members. The proximity to an urban area makes this wilderness unique in Montana.

Ravalli 180   *map 10 A-1*

Residents changed the name of this town from Selish to Ravalli to honor Father Anthony Ravalli, a Jesuit missionary who served the Salish people in the area. Father Ravalli died in 1884, and 3 years later a post office was established in his name. The arrival of the Northern Pacific Railroad made Ravalli an important shipping hub between the Mission and Flathead valleys. In 1890, 200 teams moved rail freight from Ravalli to Polson for distribution to Kalispell, Somers, and points between. Elevation: 2,739 ft. Location: Lake County

Ravalli County 347   *map 10 E-2*

The Montana legislature created Ravalli County in 1893 from Missoula County. Residents named the county after Jesuit missionary Father Anthony Ravalli, who had arrived in the Bitterroot Valley in 1845 and took up residence at St. Mary's Mission. Stevensville served as the county seat for 5 years but lost its bid for permanent county seat to Hamilton, which Copper King Marcus Daly backed during the election of 1898. The county abuts the Montana-Idaho state line, in southwestern Montana.

Raymond 1166   *map 8 A-2*

Originally called Riba, for lumber merchant Adolph Riba, the town changed its name in 1915 in honor of homesteader Joe Raymond, on whose land the railroad siding and townsite were located. One of the

Minneapolis, St. Paul & Sault Ste. Marie Railway towns in Sheridan County, Raymond boasted a small depot, a coal and lumber mercantile, and one of the area's most popular dance halls. The post office opened in 1914. Henry Hill, early businessman and resident of Raymond, observed that, because of the remoteness of the area and the fact that Raymond never incorporated, the people who tended to gravitate to the area showed a certain disdain for "cops and sheriffs." Elevation: 2,289 ft. Location: Sheridan County

Raynesford 562 *map 12 B-2*

Raynesford's history began with the arrival of Edmund R. Huggins and his family in 1889. Huggins purchased several hundred acres of land east of Armington. The Great Northern Railway surveyed a route between Armington Junction and Laurel in 1906 and began construction a year later. Railroad officials acquired a right-of-way from Huggins to build a water tower. He also agreed to sell them 40 acres for a townsite if they named the new town after his youngest daughter, Henrietta Raynesford Huggins. They agreed, and the town of Raynesford was born in 1907. A year later, the railroad established a depot, pumping station, duplex section house, and bunkhouse. The town boasted 2 baseball teams in 1916—the Rocky Ridge Ramblers and the Town Team. The town's boom years were closely aligned with the fortunes of the railroad. With the establishment of paved roads, area residents began traveling by car and truck beyond Raynesford for supplies and services. Elevation: 4,050 ft. Location: Judith Basin County

Red Lodge 991 *map 21 C-2*

Red Lodge, county seat of Carbon County (so named for its rich and numerous coal deposits), was established as a coal-mining community to fuel Northern Pacific Railroad

Rocky Fork Coal Mines, Red Lodge
MHS 950-573

locomotives after 1883. The name is derived from the Red Lodge clan of Crows who inhabited the valley at the time of Euro-American settlement. In 1889, the Northern Pacific built a branch line from Laurel to serve the new coal mines and the growing community. Dr. J. M. Fox, a friend of Northern Pacific president Henry Villard, ran the first mine, and by 1903 the town boasted a population of 3,000. By the mid-1930s, it was famous as a stopping point along the Red Lodge–Cooke City highway. Red Lodge has 2 historic districts listed in the National Register: the Hi Bug and the Red Lodge Commercial District. Elevation: 5,567 ft. Location: Carbon County

Red Lodge Creek 980   *map 21 B-3*

Red Lodge Creek drains the foothills above Cooney Reservoir, joining Rock Creek near Joliet to flow east into the Yellowstone River. The name is derived from a Crow clan who painted their lodges red. Location: Carbon County

Red Mountain 298   *map 11 B-1*

Red Mountain, in the Scapegoat Wilderness, is named for its outcrop of red sediments composed of argillites, siltites, and quartzite. Also exposed are lighter-colored limestones. This is one of 3 Red Mountains in Lewis and Clark County, and 11 statewide. Elevation: 9,411 ft. Location: Lewis and Clark County

Red Rock Lakes NWR 873   *map 19 D-3*

This 40,300-acre NWR in southwestern Montana was established in 1935 to help conserve rare trumpeter swans, whose populations have since rebounded. The 32,350-acre Red Rock Wilderness is one of the few marshland wilderness areas in the nation. Lower Red Rock Lake is the headwaters of the 60-mile-long Red Rock River that flows into Clark Canyon Reservoir. The town of Red Rock, north of the refuge, served as a stage stop for the Redrock & Salmon River Stage Company, which transported gold seekers and then tourists between the Salmon River country in Idaho and Montana and Yellowstone National Park.

Red Rock River 723   *map 19 D-1*

This southwestern Montana river likely takes its name from the outcrops of Cretaceous clays and brick-red sandstone along the banks. The first settlement in the area began in 1864; Joseph Shineberger established the Red Rock Ranch in the 1870s. Unsubstantiated speculation suggests that Shineberger named the river and town. In the 1880s, the town, situated on the Great Beaverhead Wagon Road, saw 8 daily stages between Red Rock and Salmon, Idaho, and Red Rock served as a stage stop for the Redrock & Salmon River Stage Company. The town boasted the most accommodations between Butte and Salt Lake City before the Gilmore & Pittsburgh Railroad arrived in 1910, but it has since disappeared into obscurity.

Redstone 1136   *map 8 B-1*

The town of Redstone emerged to provide services to homesteaders who began arriving in the area as early as 1900. When Olaf Bergh opened a store and post office in 1903, his wife, Mary, suggested the name Redstone, for the large quantity of red shale found nearby. Bergh also opened a coal mine that operated until the 1940s. Like other Montana towns, Redstone wandered a bit before settling down near the confluence of the Muddy River and Eagle Creek, along the Great Northern Railway's branch line constructed through Sheridan County in 1913. The railroad built a long siding near Redstone so they could split the trains for the 10-mile pull uphill to Flaxville. The Great Depression wreaked havoc on the small town, as homesteaders and residents moved away looking for

Reed Point's first school
Detail, MHS 950-591

greener pastures. Elevation: 2,105 ft. Location: Sheridan County

Redwater River 1132 *map 7 D-4*
On May 3, 1805, members of the Lewis and Clark Expedition camped near the area where the Redwater River empties into the Missouri River. Since the site lay some 2,000 miles from the mouth of the Missouri, they named this stream 2,000 Mile Creek. The origin of the current name is not known. In December 1876, en route to Canada after the Battle of the Little Bighorn, Sitting Bull and his band encountered the U.S. Cavalry along the Redwater River. During the 1910s, the Milwaukee Road promoted the Redwater Valley to homesteaders as prime farmland.

Reed Point 908 *map 21 A-1*
The town of Reed Point grew out of the Northern Pacific station known simply as Reed, for the landowner whose property the right-of-way crossed. Lewis Guthrie settled near here and by 1901 had established a store and post office known as Reed. The name of the post office changed to Reed Point in 1906. When dryland farmers started arriving, the community began to grow, and Lewis's brother, Bob Guthrie, platted the townsite in 1911. A new bridge spanned the Yellowstone River in 1911, and Reed Point grew from 4 farms and a few businesses to a community of 300 families. Elevation: 3,748 ft. Location: Stillwater County

Reserve 1181 *map 8 B-2*
Located along the Great Northern Railway's branch line between Culbertson and Flaxville, the town of Wakea was platted in 1911. *Wakea* is a Siouan word for "shelter." However, establishment of the post office in 1912 prompted a name change to Reserve, due to its proximity to the Fort Peck Indian Reservation. Elevation: 1,957 ft. Location: Sheridan County

Rexford 10 *map 1 A-3*
Rexford—named by George M. Stannard and William Ambrose to commemorate Kings Crossing in their native Ireland—

began with the construction of the Great Northern Railway's branch line from Jennings to Fernie, British Columbia, in 1901. Two years later, the railroad built a new depot 1 mile north, to accommodate the new main line and Fernie branch line. Rexford incorporated in 1966 in order to negotiate with the U.S. Army Corps of Engineers during construction of the Libby Dam. The creation of 90-mile-long Lake Koocanusa inundated the old townsite, but not before several old-timers scouted a new location for the town on a bench above the old one. The Corps of Engineers helped build the infrastructure for the new Rexford, but the move was not without some bitter feelings. One resident of the town stated: "We've lived here all our lives . . . The emotional and sentimental value is something you can't wrap up and pack off." Elevation: 2,545 ft. Location: Lincoln County

Riceville 534   *map 12 B-2*
Named for David Rice, the town's first resident, Riceville was established as a station stop on the Great Northern Railway; the post office opened under that name in 1890. Rice, who moved to Montana Territory in 1882 from Leadville, Colorado, built charcoal kilns at Barker to fuel nearby smelters. He then moved to Neihart, where he purchased silver mines. Rice served as Cascade County tax assessor and took up ranching in his later years. Elevation: 4,195 ft. Location: Cascade County

Richey 1154   *map 8 E-1*
Homesteaders began arriving in northern Dawson County after a Great Northern Railway crew surveyed a route through the area in 1909. By 1912, homesteaders had laid claim to everything except the badlands. Businesses began opening in anticipation of the railroad's arrival. Homesteader Clyde Richey recognized the need for a post office and submitted an application in 1911. Local businessmen and residents made a mad scramble to move when the Great Northern platted a townsite just west of "Squatter Town" and began selling lots on August 17, 1916. Residents commemorated the arrival of the railroad branch line on December 2, 1916, as "Steel Day." The railroad named the new town after postmaster Richey. Elevation: 2,504 ft. Location: Dawson County

Richland 1058   *map 7 B-2*
During the homestead boom of the early 1910s, promoters hoping to attract settlers named their community Richland. The town had a post office from 1913 to 1919. In 1926, Richland moved about 15 miles southeast to a location along a branch line of the Great Northern Railway that extended from Flaxville to Opheim. Elevation: 2,697 ft. Location: Valley County

Richland County 1190   *map 8 D-3*
The Montana legislature created Richland County in 1914 from Dawson County. Boosters initially put Gate forward as the name for the new county, but they soon opted for Richland instead, as a means of enticing new settlers to the region. Sidney won the contested county seat election, outdistancing its closest rival, Lambert, by more than 400 votes. Situated on the Montana–North Dakota state line, Richland is the only Montana county with both the Missouri and Yellowstone rivers running through it. Today it is at the center of renewed oil and gas development.

Ridge 1244   *map 24 C-2*
The community of Ridge nestles between the Little Missouri River and the Little Powder River. At one time consisting of a post office, store, and roadhouse, Ridge's claim to fame came in 1918 when war dispatches from the front quoted local cowboy Jess Hurley, upon his arrival on the

banks of the Rhine River, as saying he would "swim into Germany if he had his cow pony." Elevation: 3,964 ft. Location: Carter County

Rimini 459 *map 11 D-2*

Miners began developing ore deposits in the Rimini area as early as 1867, when John Caplice established a claim he called the Lee Mountain Mine. As miners poured into the area, most of them Irish, the camp came to be known as Young Ireland. Seeking support from Territorial Governor (John) Schuyler Crosby to establish a post office named Lee Mountain, several residents traveled to Helena in the summer of 1883. The petitioners found Crosby attending the play *Francesca da Rimini* at the Ming Theater. Crosby informed the visitors that postal officials did not like names of more than one word, but, inspired by the play, the governor suggested the name Rimini. The application was approved, and the name became official in 1884. In 1886, the Northern Pacific Railroad constructed the Rimini–Red Mountain branch line to haul silver, lead, and zinc ore to the smelter at East Helena. Area mines generated about $7 million (1864–1928), but the town's fortunes waned as mining tapered off. In 1942 the U.S. Army established the War Dog Reception and Training Center at Rimini to train sled dogs to support the 10th Mountain Division's proposed invasion of Norway. When the military scrapped the Norway invasion, Camp Rimini became a training center for dogsled teams of the Air Transport Command's Arctic Search and Rescue Units. The U.S. Army closed Camp Rimini in 1944. Elevation: 5,214 ft. Location: Lewis and Clark County

Rimini, c. 1924
Leslie Lyle, photographer, MHS 950-606

Rimrocks 996 *map 21 A-4*

This name refers to the sandstone rimrock cliffs (rims) that stretch from Columbus to the northern edge of Billings. The Rims are part of the Eagle sandstone formation, over 70 million years old. They range in elevation from 200 to 500 feet above the valley floor. During the 1860s, Native Americans purportedly used the Rims for scaffold burials. A glacial plateau spans the area between the Yellowstone River at the Rimrocks and the Musselshell River to the north. Elevation: 3,502 ft. Location: Yellowstone County

Ringling 697 *map 12 E-2*

Ringling had 3 names—Old Dorsey (post office established 1898), New Dorsey, and Leader—and 2 locations before it arrived at its present name and site, both acquired from John T. Ringling. Ringling, of the Ringling Brothers Circus, arrived in Meagher County about 1910 looking for a cattle ranch and dreaming of building a railroad to connect Glacier and Yellowstone national parks. In the end, however, he only managed to build a 23-mile-long line called the White Sulphur Springs & Yellowstone Park Railway Company, which connected Leader with White Sulphur Springs. To honor the man, the railroad changed the station name from Leader to Ringling. Ringling prospered during Montana's homestead boom of the 1910s, and the railroad served as a shipping point for Smith Valley livestock and wheat, operating until 1980 when the Milwaukee Road officially closed. It is widely thought that the circus had some association with Ringling; however the Ringlings never summered their circus or planned to establish their headquarters here. The town did achieve immortality in the Jimmy Buffett song "Ringling, Ringling," which includes the refrain, "Ringling, Ringling, it's a dying town." Despite the lyrics, however, Ringling is still on the map. Elevation: 5,296 ft. Location: Meagher County

Rivulet 192   *map 9 B-4*
In 1890, the Northern Pacific Railroad founded Rivulet as a water and coal stop for steam engines pulling freight between the Coeur d'Alene Mining District and Missoula. Rivulet gained its name from the numerous little streams in the area. Rail workers and their families made up most of the town's population. Rivulet's primary structures were a post office (1903–54), coal dock, school, water pump and tower, and lumber mill. The town's demise came in 1967 after adoption of the diesel engine allowed trains to go over Lookout Pass without taking on coal and water. Elevation: 2,923 ft. Location: Mineral County

Robbers Roost 699   *map 19 B-2*
According to the reminiscence of Orlin Fitzgerald Gammell, who helped procure the logs that built Robbers Roost, ranch owner Pete Daly built the structure in the winter of 1866–67. It served as an inn and stage station along the busy road between

Bannack and Virginia City. Because the 1863–64 events supposedly connected to "road agents" occurred near the Daly ranch, Robbers Roost became the object of legend and lore. Although it never served as a gathering place for Henry Plummer and his suspected gang, and no early-day murders occurred here, the inn is historically important, both as a link between the 2 territorial capitals and as one of the few surviving log stage stations of this early period. Mrs. Daly was caring for Alder Gulch discoverer Bill Fairweather when he died, destitute, at the inn in 1875. Elevation: 4,996 ft. Location: Madison County

Roberts 982   *map 21 B-2*
Originally named Merritt, Roberts began as a Northern Pacific Railroad siding in 1893. The town was platted in 1902, at which time residents adopted the name Roberts. Two stories explain its naming. One says that the town was named for Northern Pacific surveyor W. Milnor Roberts, who promoted the Yellowstone River route for the railroad. The more accepted story among locals is that it was named for Frank Roberts, the railroad express manager between Billings and Red Lodge at the turn of the twentieth century. Elevation: 4,576 ft. Location: Carbon County

Rock Creek (Carbon) 993
map 21 B-3
The Crows referred to Rock Creek as the Swiftwater, and the settlers who arrived in Red Lodge in the 1880s called this fast-flowing stream the Rocky Fork. Shortly thereafter, the creek's name was shortened to Rock Creek. Location: Carbon County

Rock Creek (Granite) 270   *map 10 C-2*
Rock Creek is not a unique name for a Montana waterway, but this Rock Creek was the site of a gold boom that in 1895 brought hundreds of miners to a new town

on its banks, named Quigley. Bankruptcy closed the Golden Sceptre Mine in 1897, turning Quigley into a ghost town. In 1915, Montana Lieutenant Governor William W. McDowell (1912–21) began purchasing land along Rock Creek, which became the 3,500-acre Valley of the Moon Ranch. Today Rock Creek is widely known as a blue-ribbon trout stream. The Welcome Creek Wilderness protects 28,135 acres in the Rock Creek drainage. Location: Granite County

Rocker 516 *map 11 E-1*
Named for the wooden box, or "rocker," used by placer miners to separate gravel from gold in the sluicing process, a settlement first started here about 1865. Described as a "lively, short-lived camp," Rocker was home to some of the richest placer mines in Silver Bow County. The post office officially opened in 1887. The Panic of 1893 caused the closure of the Blue Bird Mine. However, with the construction of the Butte, Anaconda & Pacific Railway through the area, and Rocker's selection as a division point that same year, the community managed to survive the mine's closure. In 1910, the Anaconda Company established a timber framing and treatment plant at Rocker, served by the railway. Elevation: 5,421 ft. Location: Silver Bow County

Rock Springs 1258 *map 15 C-2*
This community is named for Rock Springs Creek, which flows about a mile north of town. The post office was established in 1911 with Joseph G. Langdalen as postmaster. During the 1910s, the town had a general store and 2 doctors. Elevation: 2,946 ft. Location: Rosebud County

Rockvale 988 *map 21 B-3*
Established in 1893, Rockvale derives its name from its location in the Rock Creek Valley, situated at the confluence of Rock Creek and the Clarks Fork of the Yellowstone River. Originally a stop on the Northern Pacific Railroad, it boasted a post office from 1894 to 1914. Elevation: 3,478 ft. Location: Carbon County

Rocky Boy 633 *map 5 D-1*
In 1885, Chippewas, Crees, and Métis, refugees of the failed Riel Rebellion, entered the United States from Canada. Joined by Chief Little Shell's band, who had left their North Dakota reservation, these fragmented bands, referred to as "landless Indians," wandered Montana, appearing in Havre, Chinook, Helena, and Butte. Some established a settlement called Hill 57 near Great Falls. With the assistance of Frank Linderman, Charlie Russell, and others, Chief Stone Child, a Chippewa, led a coalition that successfully lobbied the federal government for a reservation for the Chippewa-Cree. The government established the reservation on part of the abandoned Fort Assinniboine military reserve in 1916. Due to a mistranslation of Stone Child's name, it was named Rocky Boy's Indian Reservation. The town is named for him as well. The post office operated from 1919 until 1943. Elevation: 3,689 ft. Location: Hill County

Rocky Boy's Indian Reservation 619
map 5 D-1
Rocky Boy's Indian Reservation, home to Chippewas and Crees, is named for Chippewa leader Stone Child, whose name was mistranslated as Rocky Boy. Some of these people were refugees of the failed Riel Rebellion in Canada (1885), while others had fled the harsh conditions of their reservation in North Dakota. Led by Stone Child and Chief Little Shell, the bands formed a coalition and, with the assistance of Frank Linderman, Charlie Russell, and others, successfully lobbied the federal government to establish their own reservation.

President Woodrow Wilson created it in 1916 by executive order, designating part of the abandoned Fort Assinniboine military reservation in northern Montana. The federal government officially recognized the reservation in 1934 as part of the Indian Reorganization Act. Tribal headquarters, as well as Stone Child College, are located at Box Elder. Among the enterprises on the reservation are wheat farming, post and pole production, and a ski area.

Rocky Fork Mines 992 *map 21 C-2*

Production of coal from the Rocky Fork Mines began in 1887, although Yankee Jim George is credited with making coal deposit discoveries in the area as early as 1866. Development was slow because the miners were illegally on the Crow Indian Reservation until the reservation boundary was moved in 1890. The Rocky Fork Coal Company tapped the abundant coal seams surrounding present-day Red Lodge to produce coal for the Northern Pacific Railroad. The railroad constructed a line between Red Lodge and Laurel in 1889 to access the coal for its own use as well as to ship surplus to the smelters owned by the Anaconda Company. The Rocky Fork Mines produced coal until their closure in 1932. Elevation: 5,668 ft. Location: Carbon County

Rocky Mountain Front 220 *map 3 D-1*

The Rocky Mountain Front is a 100-mile-long range of spectacular limestone reefs stretching from Marias Pass on the north to Rogers Pass on the south. The headwaters of the Sun, Dearborn, and Teton rivers are in the Front. Its highest summit is 9,392-foot Rocky Mountain. The Old North Trail, an ancient travel route stretching from the Yukon to Central America, is situated along the east side of the Front.

Rocky Mountain Laboratory 317 *map 10 D-1*

Rocky Mountain spotted fever, or "black measles," fatal in 80 percent of adult cases, plagued early settlers in the Bitterroot Valley. In 1906, Howard T. Ricketts identified ticks as carriers of this disease, and in 1921 the U.S. Public Health Service agreed to fund a vaccine development program. In an abandoned schoolhouse near Hamilton, doctors developed an effective Rocky Mountain spotted fever vaccine. Its manufacture required large-scale tick rearing under makeshift conditions, which resulted in tick-related illnesses among the technicians and 2 deaths. In 1927, the Montana legislature authorized construction of a new research facility. Despite local opposition, the Rocky Mountain Laboratory opened in 1928. An improved method for vaccine production eliminated the need for live ticks in 1938, and by 1940 research had expanded to include the study of other insect-borne diseases. During World War II, the lab manufactured typhus and yellow fever vaccines for the military. After the war, the need for the vaccines diminished with the development of broad-spectrum antibiotics. Today the Rocky Mountain Laboratory, listed in the National Register, continues to research immunologic, allergic, and infectious diseases. Elevation: 3,575 ft. Location: Ravalli County

Rogers Pass 333 *map 11 B-2*

Rogers Pass was named for Maj. A. B. Rogers, who surveyed the area in 1887 as a potential route across the Continental Divide for the Great Northern Railway's transcontinental line. Hill, however, selected Marias Pass as the main route, because of its lower elevation. By 1921, the Montana State Highway Commission began constructing the Central Montana Highway, a major east–west thoroughfare across the state. That route used Rogers Pass to cross the Continental Divide, connecting Simms and Bonner in 1938. On

January 20, 1954, the lowest temperature ever recorded in the continental United States registered –70°F on Rogers Pass. Elevation: 5,610 ft. Location: Lewis and Clark County

Rollins 116 *map 2 D-1*
Rollins, just north of the Flathead Indian Reservation on the west shore of Flathead Lake, began in the 1880s as the community of Bay View. At the turn of the twentieth century, the homestead boom hit the town and it underwent a name change. Area residents favored the name Bay View, but the post office application was returned in 1904 with the name Rollins. It was likely not a coincidence; Col. Rehenault A. Rollins, a Civil War veteran and survivor of the Andersonville prisoner-of-war camp, had submitted the application. The town officially became Rollins; it prospered with the growing timber industry and apple and cherry orchards. The Rollins Commercial Club touted the area's potential for orchards in an undated promotional pamphlet, cautioning, however, that "those who sojourn here become so healthy and acquire an appetite so vigorous that the culinary department of every household is kept working overtime to appease the voracious demands made upon it." Elevation: 2,983 ft. Location: Lake County

Ronan 164 *map 10 A-2*
Originally settled by Salish residents in 1883, this town was called Spring Creek for the local warm springs that flow into the nearby Flathead River. Residents changed the name to Ronan Springs in 1893 as a tribute to Maj. Peter Ronan, who served as the Flathead Indian Reservation agent from 1877 until his death in 1893. The town received the nickname "Center City" in 1909 because of its central location in the valley. Ronan experienced a sudden boom when the federal government opened the Flathead Indian Reservation to non-Indian

homesteading in 1910. Two years later, the town incorporated. With the creation of Lake County in 1923, Ronan vied with Polson for the coveted county seat, under the rallying cry, "It was the land that supported us, not the lake." Despite Ronan's claim as the geographic center of the new county, Polson won the election by a wide margin. Elevation: 3,047 ft. Location: Lake County

Roosevelt County 1139 *map 7 C-4*
The Montana legislature created Roosevelt County in 1919 from Sheridan County. Officials named this new county in northeastern Montana in honor of former president Theodore Roosevelt, who had died in January of that year. Roosevelt had spent time in the area during his 1880s ranching days in the Dakotas. After several months of vigorous debate, residents of Roosevelt County finally chose Wolf Point as the county seat.

Roscoe 954 *map 21 C-2*
Roscoe was originally named Morris on its 1901 post office application, but the name was changed to Roscoe in 1905 to alleviate confusion resulting from mail destined for the Norris in Madison County. The story goes that local resident Nancy Morris renamed the town Roscoe after her horse. Elevation: 5,002 ft. Location: Carbon County

Rosebud 1112 *map 15 E-2*
In 1878, Rosebud began as a small post office referred to as Beeman, on the Fort Keogh–Bozeman Stage Line. The Northern Pacific Railroad arrived in 1882 and established a siding near the Beeman post office. The railroad called the station Rosebud, and the name became official on the post office application in 1884. The town soon was home to a general mercantile and several saloons. The area later became part of the Hathaway Irrigation Project, which

Snowden Bridge, Missouri River, connecting Roosevelt and Richland counties
Detail, Jet Lowe, photographer, HAER

diverted water from the nearby Yellowstone River. Elevation: 2,483 ft. Location: Rosebud County

Rosebud Battlefield State Park 1128
map 22 C-4

In spring 1876, Sioux and Northern Cheyennes who fled the Great Sioux Reservation gathered in this area. On June 17, some 750 warriors under Crazy Horse attacked Gen. George Crook and his 1,300 men in one of the largest Indian battles waged in the United States. The Indians withdrew after the 6-hour battle, with a loss of 13 warriors to the army's approximately 70 casualties, setting the stage for the Indian victory 8 days later at the Little Bighorn. The site, which became a state park in 1978, has been approved for designation as a NHL, and confirmation is pending. It. Elevation: 4,600 ft. Location: Big Horn County

Rosebud County 1095 *map 15 D-2*

The Montana legislature created Rosebud County in 1901 from Custer County. This county in southeastern Montana takes its name from Rosebud Creek, named for the abundant wild roses growing along its banks. The county seat of Forsyth was historically dominated by the Northern Pacific Railroad and the Milwaukee Road. Approximately half of the Northern Cheyenne Indian Reservation lies in Rosebud County.

Rosebud Creek 1111 *map 15 E-2*

Named for the wild roses growing prolifically along its banks, Rosebud Creek was known to the Crows as Bichkapaashe, "Rosehip river." In his journal entry of July 28, 1806, Capt. William Clark indicated that the Indians referred to this stream as the Little Big Horn River. The American Fur Company established Fort Van Buren, a trading post, near the confluence of the creek and the Yellowstone River. It operated from 1835 to 1843. During the 1860s and '70s, more than 40,000 buffalo hides were taken from along the creek. On June 17, 1876, Gen. George Crook's column encountered a combined force of Sioux and Northern Cheyennes near the stream, north of present-day Decker. In what is referred to as the Battle of the Rosebud, the Indians forced Crook to abandon his northward march. Just 8 days later, this same force encountered Lt. Col. George Armstrong Custer's vaunted 7th U.S. Calvary at the Little Bighorn. Location: Rosebud County

Ross Fork 742 *map 13 B-1*
Ross Fork is named for the Ross family, who homesteaded here around 1910, at the fork of the Judith River near Rock Creek. The site became a station stop on the Great Northern Railway's spur line between Moccasin and Lewistown in 1912; the post office opened the following year. Elevation: 3,799 ft. Location: Fergus County

Roundup 935 *map 13 D-4*
During the 1880s, area ranches held an annual roundup of open-range cattle at the site of present-day Roundup. In 1882, buffalo hunter James McMillan and his wife established the first Roundup, operating a saloon, store, and dance hall at the confluence of Half Breed Creek and the Musselshell River. The post office opened in 1883. In 1907, the Milwaukee Road reached Roundup, and the new town of Roundup developed a short distance north of the old town. The first coal mine opened that same year, and others followed, to supply the railroad with coal. Roundup is also notable as the home town of Tony Boyle, president of the United Mine Workers of America from 1963 to 1972. Elevation: 3,224 ft. Location: Musselshell County

Roy 817 *map 13 A-3*
Rancher Walter H. Peck established a post office on his ranch in 1892. He intended to call it Ray after a relative, but the post office returned the approved application with the name Roy. When homesteaders began arriving in the area in 1910, the Milwaukee Road started planning a feeder line. The Milwaukee Land Company platted the townsite in 1913 and began selling

lots; the first train arrived on April 27, 1914, and by May, 2 trains per day were stopping at Roy. Roy's population peaked at 400 people in 1917. The railroad closed the line in 1970. Elevation: 3,500 ft. Location: Fergus County

Ruby Range 710 *map 19 C-2*
The Ruby Range gained its name from the bright red garnets mistaken by early prospectors for rubies. Gem-quality garnets can still be found in this 25-mile-long range east of Dillon.

Ruby River 649 *map 19 B-2*
Capt. Meriwether Lewis named this river Philanthropy on August 6, 1805, after one of the cardinal virtues of his mentor, President Thomas Jefferson. The Shoshones knew this river as Passamari, "Water of the cottonwood groves." Stories vary on why early miners called it the Stinking Water, one suggesting it was because of the odor emitted by nearby sulphur springs. The other explanation comes from artist A. E. Mathews, who indicated in 1867 that miners found odoriferous decaying buffalo near the river. The name changed for the final time in 1877, to Ruby River, for the garnets miners panned from the river in their search for gold.

Ruby River Reservoir 727 *map 19 C-3*
The Bannock band of the Shoshone tribe called today's Ruby River Passamari, "Water of the cottonwood groves," according to Robert Dempsey, one of the valley's earliest Euro-American settlers. The miners who traveled along the river referred to it as the Stinking Water—either because of the nearby sulphur springs or the decaying buffalo carcasses discovered near the river in 1867. It became the Ruby River in 1877, named for the garnets miners panned from its waters in their search for gold. In 1936, the State Water Conservation Board

Ryan Dam and powerhouse, Missouri River, Great Falls
MHS 949-577

authorized construction of a dam on the Ruby River designed to impound 1,000 acres of water, enough to irrigate 30,000 acres of land. Completed in 1938 at a cost of $600,000, the Ruby Reservoir still irrigates hay fields in the Ruby Valley. Elevation: 5,396 ft. Location: Madison County

Rudyard 484 *map 4 C-3*
Established as a switching station on the Great Northern Railway, Rudyard was named by a railroad employee for English writer Rudyard Kipling. The post office opened in 1910. With 2 grain elevators by 1914, Rudyard quickly became a grain-shipping center; it shipped more wheat in 1914 than any other High Line community between Havre and Shelby. Elevation: 3,112 ft. Location: Hill County

Ryan Dam 454 *map 12 A-1*
Originally called the Volta Dam, this concrete hydroelectric dam began operating in 1915. Constructed on the crest of the Great Falls of the Missouri River by the Charles T. Main Company, for the Montana Power

Company, the dam created a 7-mile-long reservoir. In 1940, it was renamed Ryan Dam to honor John D. Ryan, longtime Anaconda Company president and Montana Power director. Elevation: 3,005 ft. Location: Cascade County

Ryegate 879 *map 13 E-2*
The Milwaukee Road established Ryegate in 1908 as a depot and station stop; a railroad official named the town for the surrounding rye fields. Within 3 years, the town boasted a bank, hotel, mercantile, bakery, barber, livery, physician, and church. In 1920, after citizens successfully petitioned the legislature to create Golden Valley County, Ryegate became the county seat. Elevation: 3,650 ft. Location: Golden Valley County

St. Ignatius Chapel, St. Ignatius, 1884
Detail, F. Jay Haynes, photographer, MHS H-1346

Sacagawea Peak 733 *map 20 A-2*

Sacagawea Peak, named after the Shoshone woman who accompanied the Lewis and Clark Expedition, is the highest peak in the Bridger Range, northeast of Bozeman. Her name is frequently spelled "Sacajawea" in Montana place names and "Sakakawea" in North Dakota. Elevation: 9,665 ft. Location: Gallatin County

Sacagawea River 925 *map 14 A-1*

Traveling up the Missouri River on May 20, 1805, Capt. Meriwether Lewis wrote the following entry in his journal: "About five miles above the mouth of shell river [Musselshell River] a handsome river of about fifty yards in width discharged itself into the shell river on the Stard. or upper side; this stream we called Sâh-câ-gar me-âh or bird woman's River, after our interpreter the Snake [Shoshone] woman." Later arrivals to the area named the stream Crooked Creek. The U.S. Board of Geographic Names changed the name back to Sacagawea River in 1979.

Sacajawea Hotel 660 *map 19 A-4*

Arrival of the Milwaukee Road in 1908 prompted Three Forks residents to move a mile upriver from their original 1863 townsite. Seeing the immediate need for a hotel, the railroad's purchasing agent, John Q. Adams, put the 1862 Madison House on log rollers and moved it from "Old Town." It was later split into 2 parts that formed the opposite ends of the Sacajawea Hotel; Bozeman architect Fred Willson designed the lobby and hotel rooms in 1910. With the depot across the street, the hotel did a brisk business and served as the area's social center. In 1927, the railroad extended its line to Gallatin Gateway, and the hotel lost much of its tourist business to the Gallatin Gateway Inn. The Sacajawea, however, withstood hard times. Beautifully renovated in the 1990s, and listed in the National Register, today the Arts and Crafts–style interior is warmly informal and inviting. Elevation: 4,071 ft. Location: Gallatin County

Saco 957 *map 6 C-3*

One of many stories about the town's name says that Saco is a contraction of "Sacajawea." The more accepted version is that, like so many other High Line station stops, this one was named by a Great Northern Railway official putting a finger to a spinning globe, which this time landed on Saco, Maine. In 1999, Saco residents broke a Guinness world record by making the world's largest hamburger, using beef from 17 cattle to form a 6,040-pound burger. The chefs cooked on a 24-foot pan built especially for the occasion, and the burger took 1 hour and 40 minutes to cook. (Unfortunately, the town held its record for only 2 years; the previous record holders in Seymour, Wisconsin, reclaimed the title with an 8,266-pound burger.) The local museum is in the Huntley School, named for news anchor Chet Huntley, who had attended school there. The H. Earl Clack Service Station and Saco Mercantile are listed in the National Register. Elevation: 2,183 ft. Location: Phillips County

Sage Creek 589 *map 4 C-4*

Named for the ubiquitous shrub found throughout the Northern Plains, this creek flows out of the Sweet Grass Hills. Reports of a Sage Creek near present-day Gilford appear in fur trappers' journals in the 1850s. Dayton was the first settlement along the banks of Sage Creek, established in the 1890s. Location: Liberty and Hill counties

Salish Mountains 111 *map 1 C-4*

The Salish Mountains take their name from the Salish tribe. The name originates with the people who spoke languages from the interior Columbia Plateau Salish language group. They called their northwest-

Saltese, 1908
MHS 950-824

ern Montana brethren the Sa'lix, referring to the tribes that made their homes in and around Flathead Lake. The highest elevation is 7,464 feet, atop Baldy Mountain.

Salmon Lake 243 *map 10 B-3*

Salmon Lake's most famous resident was Copper King William A. Clark's son, William Clark Jr., who built the Mowitza Lodge in 1915 as a summer retreat for the Clark family. Construction involved hauling building materials from Missoula, 40 miles away, and rafting them across Salmon Lake. The lodge included a shooting gallery, bowling alley, and mountaintop teahouse. In the 1940s, the resort was donated to the Catholic Diocese of Helena for use as a youth camp. It still operates as a youth camp under the name Legendary Lodge. Salmon Lake State Park lies on the lakeshore. Elevation: 3,908 ft. Location: Missoula County

Saltese 113 *map 9 A-2*

Originally called Silver City because of nearby silver mines, town residents renamed their community Saltese in 1891 for Nez Perce chief Seltisse. The post office opened in 1892. Trappers, prospectors, and packers all traditionally referred to the area as Packer's Meadow, because prior to construction of the Mullan Road, it served as a convenient campsite before attempting the journey over the mountains. Saltese is located along the Northern Pacific's branch line to Wallace, Idaho; in 1908, the Milwaukee Road also came through. Elevation: 3,387 ft. Location: Mineral County

Sand Coulee 475 *map 12 A-1*

Named Giffen in 1881, after Nat McGiffen, the town's name changed to Sand Coulee when the McGiffens left the area. Eugene Willis, an African American, in 1883 established the first coal-mining company, Sand

Coulee Coal Company. Recognizing the potential, James J. Hill purchased the company and renamed it Cottonwood Coal Company. Hill's Montana Central Railway reached Sand Coulee in 1888, helping spur a boom. Sand Coulee produced 600,000 tons of coal annually between 1891 and 1896, and its bituminous coal powered the smelters at Great Falls, Butte, and East Helena, as well as the steam engines of the Great Northern Railway. As it grew, the town developed 3 distinct sections: Shacktown, where many of the miners lived; Middletown or Finn Town, named for the large Finnish population; and Downtown, where the majority of the businesses located. Sand Coulee reached its height in 1891–97 and slowly withered when the railroad switched to diesel engines in the 1930s and natural gas became more prevalent for home heating. Elevation: 3,474 ft. Location: Cascade County

Sand Springs 1002 *map 14 B-3*

During the era of large cattle ranches, range riders and travelers used an old trader's cabin on the plains as a stopover in the 1880s. An intrepid individual added a saloon to the old cabin a decade later,

Charles E. Stone family and their general store, Sand Springs, 1951
Austin Wilson, photographer, MHS PAc 93-12

providing refreshments to the occasional visitor. Not until 1909 and the arrival of Fred Allen, however, did the town of Sand Springs develop. Allen worked tirelessly, establishing a store, post office, and dance hall. With the creation of Garfield County in 1919, Sand Springs vied for the county seat. Jordan edged out the other contenders, prompting the editor of the *Sand Springs Star* to suggest that Montana should become 2 states—East Montana and West Montana—in which case Sand Springs would become the geographic center of East Montana. Elevation: 3,214 ft. Location: Garfield County

Sanders 1065 *map 14 E-4*

With the construction of the Northern Pacific Railroad's transcontinental line through Montana in the 1880s, the railroad developed a station as well as a pumping plant at this site to provide water for their steam engines. The post office opened in 1904 as Sanders, named for prominent Montana jurist and politician Wilbur Fisk Sanders. The town developed in conjunction with the sugar beet industry along the Yellowstone River. The Sanders School District, established in 1907, closed in 1950, and Sanders's students were bused to Hysham. The front gate and 2-hole privy are all that remain. Sanders residents, among them descendants of area homesteaders, have carefully refurbished the gymnasium/community hall, which is listed in the National Register. Elevation: 2,603 ft. Location: Treasure County

Sanders County 76 *map 1 E-4*

The Montana legislature created Sanders County in 1905 from Missoula County. The petition for the new county along the Clark Fork River proposed the name Paradise. However, one civic-minded individual reminded the legislative assembly of the practice of naming new counties after the "greats" of Montana—and who exemplified that greatness more than former U.S. Senator Wilbur Fisk Sanders, the nephew of Montana's first Territorial Governor, Sidney Edgerton? Sanders was also the successful prosecutor for the Vigilantes in their bid to rid the territory of its lawless element. By unanimous decision, the legislators created Sanders County. Thompson Falls won the coveted county seat.

Santa Rita 218 *map 3 B-2*
The Santa Rita post office opened in 1937, 6 miles north of Cut Bank. The origin of the name remains a mystery. Elevation: 3,808 ft. Location: Glacier County

Sapphire Mountains 346 *map 10 E-2*
This mountain range east of the Bitterroot Valley was named for the precious gem found in its Precambrian sedimentary rocks. Sapphires for industrial purposes, such as abrasives and bearings, were mined commercially near Skalkaho Pass between 1892 and 1943. At Gem Mountain, a roadside tourist site in the area, would-be prospectors can still try their luck. The highest elevation is 8,998-foot Kent Peak.

Sapphire Village 689 *map 12 C-3*
Named for nearby sapphire mines on the eastern edge of the Little Belt Mountains, this town began as a community of miners and their families at the start of the twentieth century. Elevation: 4,914 ft. Location: Judith Basin County

Sarpy 1100 *map 22 A-4*
In 1896, Frank and Ellsworth Clark established the first homestead claims near Sarpy Creek, which takes its name from John B. Sarpy, an American Fur Company trader

during the 1850s. Homesteaders began arriving in the area after the turn of the twentieth century, either from Hardin or by traveling cross country from the Northern Pacific Railroad at Forsyth. Although the area seemed particularly inhospitable to some, according to those who stayed it was good land, but survival demanded endurance. Homesteader Lila Neidig's description in 1915 paints a romantic picture: "Here I am back in God's country where the delicious sleep is only interrupted by an occasional coyote howl, which has a tendency to make one stay closer to the covers." The Sarpy post office opened in 1907 and closed in 1943. Elevation: 3,533 ft. Location: Big Horn County

Sarpy Creek 1060 *map 14 E-4*
The Crows called this creek Ark-tar-ha. On July 27, 1806, Capt. William Clark named the stream "Labeichs River," after expedition member François Labiche. In 1850, the American Fur Company built a fort where the creek empties into the Yellowstone River and named it for company fur trader John B. Sarpy. In the 1880s, a Vermont firm, the Green Mountain Stock Ranching Company, claimed the FUF brand and established a ranch headquarters on Sarpy Creek. One of Montana's most famous cowboys of that era, Teddy Blue Abbott, worked for this outfit. Location: Treasure and Big Horn counties

Sarpy Creek Mine 1094 *map 22 A-4*
The Sarpy Creek Mine (also known as the Absaloka Mine) opened in 1974. It is owned by Westmoreland Resources and operated by the Washington Group International, Inc. Under this management, the massive strip-mining operation produces 6–7 million tons of coal annually, according to a 2006 Dept. of Interior BIA environmental impact statement. Elevation: 3,554 ft. Location: Big Horn County

Savage 1211 *map 16 A-3*

Savage was established along the Yellow-stone River in 1910, by some accounts receiving its name from H. M. Savage, a U.S. Reclamation Service supervising engineer who worked on the "Big Ditch" (the canal) to provide irrigation along the lower Yellowstone River. However, another naming story states that the community takes its name from Patrick B. Savage, who either worked for the railroad or settled the area as a homesteader. The Missouri River Railway laid track to Savage in 1911; it later became a lateral north/south line between the Northern Pacific Railway and the Great Northern Railway. President Ronald Reagan wrote the residents of Savage a congratulatory letter on June 28, 1985, in recognition of the town's Diamond Jubilee, commemorating its 75th year. Today the community continues to provide services for area grain and sugar beet farmers. Elevation: 1,983 ft. Location: Richland County

Savoy 811 *map 5 C-4*

As with a number of Montana towns, stories differ on how Savoy received its name. One suggests that it is named for the nearby creek, while the second indicates that Great Northern Railway officials named the Savoy railroad station in 1909 for a region in France. Savoy's post office opened that same year. In 1916, residents platted a townsite and built a school, teacherage, and store. Elevation: 2,339 ft. Location: Blaine County

Scapegoat Wilderness 266 *map 11 B-1*

In 1962, Lincoln store owner Cecil Garland organized the Lincoln Back Country Protection Association in response to threats of road development and timber harvesting in the national forest north of Lincoln. Appeals to the Montana congressional delegation and public petitions for wildlands protection ultimately reversed the USFS's plans. On August 20, 1972, Congress designated 240,000 acres of these national forest lands as wilderness, creating a contiguous protected area of 1.5 million acres of forest, meadows, and towering peaks that stretch from the Great Bear Wilderness in the north through the Bob Marshall and into the Scapegoat to the south. The name Scapegoat comes from the name of the mountain located in this area.

Scherlie Homestead 821 *map 5 A-4*

The Enlarged Homestead Act of 1909 brought settlers to Montana and to this area called the "Big Flat." Neil J. Scherlie was among the first to file a homestead claim; over the course of 4 years, his 3 sisters and 2 brothers made claims nearby. Thirty-two-year-old Anna Scherlie arrived in 1913, becoming part of a long tradition of women homesteaders in Montana. By 1916, Anna had 40 acres planted in wheat, oats, and flax. Droughts, the Great Depression, and 2 world wars passed. Anna remained on the homestead long after her neighbors had built modern homes, insisting that she was "too old for modern conveniences." The spartan lifestyle seems to have been Anna's preference. When she died in 1973, an estate of more than $100,000 was divided among 18 nieces and nephews; her ashes were scattered on the property. Scherlie Homestead is listed in the National Register. Elevation: 2,971 ft. Location: Blaine County

Sciuchetti Place 512 *map 19 A-1*

In 1951, Frank Sciuchetti, a miner employed by the Anaconda Company, purchased this property from the Northern Pacific Railway, which had held the land patent since 1864. Elevation: 6,316 ft. Location: Silver Bow County

Scobey 1109 *map 7 B-4*

The seat of Daniels County, Scobey is named for Maj. Charles Richardson Anderson Scobey, a cattleman in the Glendive area in 1883 who served as a territorial legislator and an Indian agent at Fort Peck and Poplar. The town of Scobey is on the old Woody Mountain Trail used by the Sioux, including Sitting Bull, as they moved back and forth across the Canadian border. In 1900, local rancher Mansfield Daniels (for whom the county was named in 1920) asked Maj. Scobey to help secure a post office for the new settlement, which Daniels named Scobey in 1901. The Great Northern Railway refused to put a station in the community, instead choosing a site on the other side of the Poplar River about 1.5 miles farther west, so in the summer of 1913 most of the residents moved to the new spot. The first train arrived on Thanksgiving Day that year. Scobey incorporated in 1916. Scobey's false-fronted wooden courthouse, built at the turn of the twentieth century as the Commercial Hotel, is listed in the National Register. Elevation: 2,469 ft. Location: Daniels County

Daniels County Courthouse, Scobey
Ernie Smith, photographer, MHS 950-886

Scratchgravel Hills 434 *map 11 C-3*

The Scratchgravel Hills are named for the gold mining that occurred in these dry hills in the 1860s. Since there was no water available for sluicing or dredging, placer gold was dug up by scratching in the gravel. Later, some lode mining took place here. Mining was abandoned during World War II and never resumed on any scale. Elevation: 5,158 ft. Location: Lewis and Clark County

Sedan 738 *map 20 A-2*

Referred to on occasion as the "stepchild of Gallatin County," Sedan is east of Flathead Pass in the north end of the Bridger Range. At times, residents have threatened to secede and ally with Park County, since access to Livingston is easier than to Bozeman. The community takes its name from Sedan, Kansas, where John Maddox and his family lived before settling here in 1884. The post office opened in 1891 and closed in 1915. The sense of separation residents experienced created a spirit of self-reliance, as indicated by the 25 townspeople establishing the East Flathead Telephone Company in 1905—stringing lines between their homes to connect members of the cooperative. They also made optimal use of town structures for business and pleasure. Leo and Al Meyer opened the Shields Valley Cheese Factory in Sedan in 1914, providing local dairy farmers with a market for their milk. With the cheese factory on the first floor, members of the Yeoman's Lodge met on the second to socialize, play cards, and listen to Swiss cheesemaker Walter Boegli yodel while he worked. Elevation: 5,553 ft. Location: Gallatin County

Seeley Lake 223 *map 10 B-3*

Seeley Lake and the community of Seeley Lake are named for Jasper B. Seely, who worked as a timber cruiser for Hammond

Lumber Company and built a cabin on what was in 1881 known as Clearwater Lake. The extra *e* in Seeley was added by the early surveyors of the lake. Seely served as the first ranger in the area from 1899 to 1900, on the Lewis and Clark Forest Reserve, which encompassed 3 million acres, taking in the Clearwater and Swan valleys, as well as the present-day Bob Marshall, Scapegoat, and Great Bear wilderness areas. He worked for the USFS as a forest supervisor until 1927. The first road to Seeley Lake came in 1895. The Big Blackfoot Milling Company purchased Seely's land in 1906 and for the next 5 years moved logs from Seeley Lake down the Clearwater and Blackfoot rivers to the mill at Bonner. The Anaconda Company purchased the land and mill a few years later. After World War II, timber companies such as the Bockmier Lumber Company began operations in the vicinity. Pyramid Mountain Lumber started logging the area in 1950 and built a sawmill. Thereafter, the town began to grow, acquiring electricity in 1952 and telephones in 1961. With the paving of MT 83, the town became a popular tourist destination. Located on the southeast end of Seeley Lake, the community remains a draw for tourists in the winter and summer months. Elevation: 4,023 ft. Location: Missoula County

Selway-Bitterroot Wilderness 338
map 9 E-4
In February 1963, Secretary of Agriculture Orville Freeman designated a new wilderness area, the Selway-Bitterroot, comprising some 1.2 million acres in southwestern Montana and eastern Idaho. Boundaries were drawn from a much larger primitive area established by the USFS in 1936. The name Selway comes from Thomas Selway, who ran sheep in Idaho's Selway River country during the late 1890s. Bitterroot is derived from the mountain range in Montana.

Sevenmile Creek 1249 *map 24 C-3*
This Sevenmile Creek, one of several in Montana so named, derives its name from being 7 miles from the Montana-Wyoming state line, running through Carter County's arid grasslands and badlands. Location: Carter County

Sex Peak 58 *map 1 E-1*
The name of this mountain at the headwaters of White Pine and Big Beaver creeks can be traced to a crew of USFS surveyors in the 1920s who spent the day hiking to the head of the South Fork of Trout Creek to shoot the peak for mapping purposes. They thought it appropriate to name the peak for their conversation on the hike up the mountain. The USFS later constructed a lookout on the peak. Elevation: 5,777 ft. Location: Sanders County

Shawmut 852 *map 13 D-1*
The town of Shawmut had the earliest post office in what is now Wheatland County. Originally established in 1885, it was discontinued in 1887 and reestablished in 1888. The original postmaster was Francis E. Shaw, a local rancher. According to local lore, he was from Boston and named the post office Shawmut, both after his own name and after the original Algonquin name for Boston, translated as "Living waters." During the height of its prosperity, the town boasted a hotel, store, restaurant, lumberyard, hardware store, and grain elevator. Elevation: 3,855 ft. Location: Wheatland County

Sheep Mountain 161 *map 9 B-3*
Sheep Mountain, presumably named for the bighorn sheep that still frequent its slopes, was home to a fire lookout from 1929 to 1946. This substantial cabin in the Bitterroot Range west of Superior was built directly on a rock foundation. The lookout was destroyed by fire in 1952. Elevation: 6,735 ft. Location: Mineral County

Sheffield (Custer) 1259 *map 15 D-2*

Sheffield was originally named Lock, after the first postmaster Christine Lockie, a native of Scotland who, with her husband, established a ranch in the area in the 1890s. When the Milwaukee Road was built through Lock in 1909, the station house and post office were renamed Calabar, possibly for the ancient city of Calabar in Nigeria. In 1929, the town was renamed Sheffield in honor of B. B. Sheffield, a nearby rancher. Elevation: 2,418 ft. Location: Custer County

Ringside, Dempsey-Gibbons fight, Shelby, July 4, 1923
Detail, MHS 950-440

Shelby 278 *map 3 C-4*

Shelby is named for Peter P. Shelby, employee of the Great Northern Railway and later general manager of the Montana Central Railway. A railroad station was established here about 1892, at the junction of the Great Northern Railway and the Great Falls & Canada Railway. The latter company became the Montana & Great Northern Railway Company in 1901 and merged with the Great Northern Railway in 1907. The station had a post office and, within a few years, hotels, saloons, general stores, and other businesses. Shelby is probably best known for the heavyweight boxing match held between Jack Dempsey and Tommy Gibbons (which Dempsey won) on July 4, 1923. Elevation: 3,295 ft. Location: Toole County

Shepherd 1004 *map 22 A-1*

The town of Shepherd is named for Russell E. Shepherd, a New York native who arrived in Billings in 1906 and quickly organized the Billings Land and Irrigation Company on the bench east of Billings. Two years later, he helped organize the Merchants National Bank. The post office opened in 1915. As a financial partner in the Billings Bench Water Association, Shepherd and other investors provided money to construct a 65-mile canal to transport irrigation water from the Yellowstone River to the farming community of Shepherd. Elevation: 3,107 ft. Location: Yellowstone County

Sheridan 678 *map 19 B-2*

Sheridan traces its beginnings to the construction of a sawmill on Mill Creek by James Gammell in 1863. As placer mining developed, other residents began building in the vicinity. Discussion turned to a name for the budding town when Rozelle Bateman, regarded as the "Father of Sheridan," decided to apply for a post office. Stories vary on the origins of the town's name in 1866. The most interesting centers around "Sheridan's Ride," a poem by Thomas B. Read about the 1864 Battle of Winchester in the Shenandoah Valley of Virginia. According to the poem, Union general Philip Sheridan begins the day 20 miles from the battlefield and, in a heroic ride, makes it back in time to rally his forces to victory. Today Sheridan is a bustling ranch town in the Ruby Valley. Elevation: 5,121 ft. Location: Madison County

Sheridan County 1173 *map 8 B-2*

In 1913, veteran county splitter Daniel McKay successfully lobbied the Montana legislature to create Sheridan County from Dawson and Valley counties. Residents named the new northeastern Montana county after Gen. Philip Sheridan, who had served with distinction during the Civil War and retired as commanding general of the U.S. Army. Plentywood won the county seat election over Medicine Lake by a mere 42 votes. During the 1920s and '30s, Sheridan County was a hotbed of Socialist and Communist sentiment, and home to a radical newspaper, the *Producers News*, published in Plentywood.

Shields River 814 *map 20 A-3*

Capt. William Clark named this river on July 15, 1806, after expedition blacksmith John Shields. The river's headwaters are in the Crazy Mountains.

Shonkin 546 *map 12 A-3*

Speculation suggests that the town's name either originates from the Blackfeet name for the Highwood Mountains or is derived from that of early settler John Shonk. Shonkin was established in the 1870s when ranchers pushed their cattle onto the open range. By June 1880, the town had 170 residents. A year later, the Shonkin Stock Association organized to protect livestock from rustlers and Indians. The post office opened in 1886; homesteaders began arriving in 1910. Elevation: 3,181 ft. Location: Chouteau County

Sidney 1215 *map 8 E-3*

Residents submitted an application for a post office in 1888 under the name Eureka. Upon learning that one Eureka, Montana, already existed, Judge Hiram Otis decided to reapply, using the name Sidney for 6-year-old Sidney Walter, whose parents were living with the judge. Construction on the Lower Yellowstone Irrigation Project began in 1905, with the intent to irrigate 60,000 acres in the Yellowstone Valley. Completion of the Northern Pacific Railway's branch line from Glendive to Sidney in 1912 ensured the town's role in the ongoing development of the valley. Sidney incorporated on April 21, 1911, electing Thomas Gardner as the first mayor. The town received a boost in 1924 when the Holly Sugar Company opened up a sugar refinery in Sidney to process locally grown sugar beets. Sidney's economy boomed with oil discoveries in the vicinity during the 1970s. Elevation: 1,888 ft. Location: Richland County

Silesia 987 *map 21 B-3*

The town of Silesia and nearby Silesia Springs were named by Julius Lehrkind for the Silesia region of central Europe that is now part of Poland, the Czech Republic, and Germany. Lehrkind, originally from Silesia, started a brewery here about 1900. Charles Buzzetti opened the post office at the junction of the Northern Pacific Railway's main line and its branch line to Red Lodge and Bridger. Elevation: 3,396 ft. Location: Carbon County

Silver Bow County 533 *map 19 A-1*

The Montana legislature created Silver Bow County from Deer Lodge County in 1881, with Butte as the county seat. The county takes its name from Silver Bow Creek, so named by 3 prospectors in 1864 for the illusion of a silvery bow reflected from its surface. Although Silver Bow is the state's smallest county in land area, during the heyday of Butte's copper mines it boasted the largest population. Today Silver Bow County is part of the largest Superfund site in the nation. Butte and Silver Bow consolidated government structures in 1977.

Silver Bow Creek 470 *map 11 E-1*

On a January evening in 1864, 3 gold prospectors searching for "color" in a creek west of Butte named it Silver Bow after the clouds parted and the sun shone on the water, illuminating it in the shape of a drawn bow. Recently, Silver Bow Creek achieved notoriety as part of one of the nation's largest Superfund cleanup sites, which stretches from Butte to Missoula. Location: Silver Bow County

Silver Creek 453 *map 11 C-3*

This Silver Creek originates near the town of Marysville and flows generally eastward until it empties into Lake Helena. It was named by early prospectors for the high percentage of silver mixed in with the placer-gold deposits along the creek. Silver City, on the creek, was the first county seat of Edgerton County, which later became Lewis and Clark County.

Silver Gate 952 *map 20 D-4*

John L. Taylor, born in North Carolina but raised in Park and Gallatin counties, founded Silver Gate in 1932 with partner J. J. White. The town takes its name from its "gateway" position at the entrance to Yellowstone National Park, and from the silver cast of the mountains. Today 30 residents live in the town year-round, but during the summer thousands of tourists pass through on their way to the park. Local building codes of the original townsite required frontier architecture and log construction for community businesses and dwellings, which adds to the town's rustic atmosphere. Elevation: 7,390 ft. Location: Park County

Silver Lake 400 *map 10 E-4*

Silver Lake, a natural lake west of Anaconda, provided a critical element of the elaborate water delivery system developed by the Anaconda Company to operate its concentrators and smelters. The system collects water from Storm, Twin, and Georgetown lakes and transports it via ditches and flumes to pumping stations. The Anaconda Company first diverted water into Silver Lake in 1901; in 1902 and 1918, it constructed dams at either end to increase storage capacity. Today the elaborate water system still provides millions of gallons of water for Butte's industrial operations. Elevation: 6,438 ft. Location: Deer Lodge County

Silver Run Peak 973 *map 21 C-1*

Silver Run is the fifth-highest peak in Montana. It was named in 1896 by A. Lee Corey, the first forest ranger in the Beartooth Range. Elevation: 12,542 ft. Location: Carbon County

Silver Star 622 *map 19 A-2*

Green Campbell made the first gold discovery in this area in 1866. The community was named for the Silver Star mining claim, discovered by George and Bill Boyer in the 1860s. The post office opened in 1869. Miners in the area lived in 2 main camps. At the suggestion of the Boyers, one camp was named Silver Star and the other Rag Town. Rag Town eventually became Iron Rod. Local legend claims that in 1878, Edward, Prince of Wales, traveled through the area and stayed in the Silver Star Hotel for 3 days. Of special interest in Silver Star is the private collection of large mining machinery that sits alongside the highway. Elevation: 4,563 ft. Location: Madison County

Simms 335 *map 11 A-3*

The town of Simms began as part of the Sun River Irrigation Project in 1906. S. B. Robbins, an engineer on the project, purportedly named the town after an early trapper who lived in the area. Elevation: 3,566 ft. Location: Cascade County

"Jawbone Railroad," Sixteenmile Canyon, between Ringling and Lombard

Ralph DeCamp, photographer, MHS 951-076

Sixteen **677** *map 12 E-2*

Sixteen, established in 1890, is named for Sixteenmile Creek, which flows through a 16-mile-long canyon, from the town to the Missouri River at Lombard. Between 1894 and 1897, the Montana Railway Company ("Jawbone Railroad") built its line through the canyon, ending the isolation the town had previously suffered during the winter; this route later became part of the Milwaukee Road. Elevation: 4,982 ft. Location: Meagher County

Sixteenmile Creek **643** *map 11 E-4*

On July 26, 1805, Lewis and Clark named this Howard's Creek for expedition member Thomas P. Howard. The current name emerged during the 1895 construction of the Montana Railway ("Jawbone Rail-

road") along Sixteenmile Creek. The name represents the distance from the headwaters to the mouth of the creek at the Missouri River. In 1910, the Milwaukee Road purchased the "Jawbone Railroad," rebuilding the line and constructing 5 tunnels in Sixteenmile Canyon, which a 1914 Milwaukee Road promotional brochure refers to as "Montana Canyon." Location: Gallatin and Meagher counties

Skalkaho Creek and Pass **337** *map 10 D-2*

The name Skalkaho is derived from the Salish words *skalen* and *kalalko*, meaning "beaver" and "green wood," or "Place of beaver." On Walter W. DeLacy's 1865 map of Montana Territory, the creek appears as Ska-ka-ke. In 1924, the State of Montana and the USFS constructed a road over 7,260-foot Skalkaho Pass, connecting Hamilton with Philipsburg and Anaconda. Location: Ravalli and Granite counties

Sleeping Buffalo Rock 923 *map 6 C-2*

A nearby ridge overlooking the Cree Crossing on the Milk River was the original resting place of this ancient rock, which resembles a bull buffalo lying down. Since late prehistoric times, native peoples have revered the Sleeping Buffalo's spiritual power. Highway construction necessitated relocating the Sleeping Buffalo, first to Trafton Park in Malta, and then elsewhere, before it was moved to this site in 1967. The rock is listed in the National Register. Sleeping Buffalo Hot Springs, named for the revered rock, was discovered in 1922 when a man exploring for oil encountered a tremendous flow of hot mineral water. The 3 pools range from 90° to 106°F. Elevation: 2,293 ft. Location: Phillips County

Sleeping Child Creek 353 *map 10 E-2*

At the time of the Stevens survey in 1853–54, Sleeping Child Creek was named Fabulous or Weeping Child Creek. One version of the legend says that a child had been abandoned here at the hot springs by its mother when her tribe was being pursued by settlers. The settlers, hearing the baby cry, named the springs Weeping Child Springs. Other stories give the origin of the name as Snetetse, a Salish word meaning "Place of the sleeping child." A commercial hot springs appeared here as early as 1894. Location: Ravalli County

Sluice Boxes State Park 536 *map 12 B-2*

Sluice Boxes State Park was designated in the early 1970s to protect and provide access to a spectacular limestone canyon on Belt Creek. In 1891, the Montana Central Railway built a branch line to Monarch and Neihart through the canyon, constructing a series of trestles and a tunnel.

The railroad ran Sunday "fishing trains" from Great Falls to the canyon, from 1914 until they closed the line in the 1940s. The limestone quarries and kilns at Albright in mid-canyon provided fluxing limestone to the Anaconda Company's smelter at Great Falls. Elevation: 4,345 ft. Location: Cascade County

Smith Mine 1007 *map 21 C-2*

Elijah Smith and Phillip Gallaher first developed the Smith Mine east of Red Lodge in 1897. The mine later became the property of the Montana Coal & Iron Company. During World War II, the company greatly increased coal production at the mine. On February 27, 1943, an explosion rocked the mine, killing 74 miners. This disaster and the competition of cheaper strip-mined coal led to the eventual end of coal mining in the Red Lodge area. Elevation: 4,841 ft. Location: Carbon County

Smith River 407 *map 11 A-4*

On July 15, 1805, Capt. Meriwether Lewis wrote: "We passed the river near where we dined and just above the entrance of a beautifull river 80 yards wide which falls in on the Lard. Side which in honour of Mr. Robert Smith the Secretary of the Navy we called Smith's River." The Smith River rises near, but not in, the Castle Mountains and then runs through a steep canyon between the Big Belt and Little Belt mountains before joining the Missouri River at Ulm. The scenic canyon is popular with recreational floaters and anglers. Montana Fish, Wildlife & Parks manages 6 sites along the river, including Camp Baker, Eden Bridge, and Smith River state parks.

Snider 147 *map 1 E-3*

The Snider post office opened on January 1, 1949, named in honor of Dave Snider, a native of New Brunswick, Canada, who came to the Thompson Falls region in 1909. He was a forest ranger, miner, Thompson River Valley rancher, deputy sheriff, and owner of the Union Café in Thompson Falls. Snider was a longtime proponent of developing the Thompson River Valley. During the 1930s, the town provided a headquarters for a CCC camp. A number of the CCC buildings remain today, along with several houses on the Thompson River. Snider died in 1961; the Snider post office closed in 1969. Elevation: 2,503 ft. Location: Sanders County

Snowcrest Range 803 *map 19 D-2*
The Snowcrest Range is presumably named for its snow-covered peaks. The range straddles the line between Madison and Beaverhead counties, north of the Centennial Valley. Its highest peaks are Sunset Peak (10,548 feet), Hogback Mountain (10,572 feet), and Antone Peak (10,573 feet).

Snowshoe Peak 23 *map 1 C-2*
Prospector B. Parmenter, who broke a pair of snowshoes while hunting mountain goats above Leigh Lake, named Snowshoe Peak. It is in the Cabinet Wilderness, near Snowshoe Creek. Elevation: 8,738 ft. Location: Lincoln County

Snowy Mountains 836 *map 13 C-2*
The Big and Little Snowy Mountains rise 8,500 feet from the surrounding prairie and cover a 10-by-24-mile area south of Lewistown. This limestone formation is characterized by a lodgepole-fir forest on the north and dry, rocky terrain on the south. It is dominated by 2 rocky summits: Greathouse Peak (8,655 feet) and Old Baldy (8,684 feet). At the head of Blake Creek sits Big Ice Cave, a cool getaway during summers when temperatures can reach into the 90s.

Somers 88 *map 2 D-1*
Great Northern Railway magnate James J. Hill contracted with John O'Brien to

Somers dock, steamboat Klondike, *Flathead Lake, c. 1915*
Detail, MHS 951-123

build a sawmill on the north end of Flathead Lake in 1900, with the provision that the John O'Brien Lumber Company would supply the Great Northern with 600,000 railroad ties per year for 20 years. The lumber company owned 122 homes in this company town and furnished water and electricity to its workers. The company floated logs down the Whitefish, Stillwater, Swan, and Flathead rivers and across Flathead Lake to the mill at Somers, where they were milled into railroad ties and lumber. The mill added a tie treatment plant in 1901, and the railroad purchased the entire operation a few years later. The Great Northern Railway closed the lumber mill in 1948 but continued to operate the tie plant until its closure in 1986 by the Burlington Northern Railroad. The origin of the name Somers is uncertain. Elevation: 2,914 ft. Location: Flathead County

Sonnette 1197 *map 23 B-3*

Charles Oscar Mason is credited with establishing this community in 1880, known as Selway. The town, located near the head of Pumpkin Creek, reached its peak population of 152 residents in 1919. In 1926, for unknown reasons, the townspeople selected the name Sonnette for their new post office. The post office closed in 1967. Elevation: 3,737 ft. Location: Powder River County

Southern Cross 391 *map 10 E-4*

Established in 1868 as a mining camp on Cable Mountain, overlooking Georgetown Lake, Southern Cross operated as a company town until the gold mines shut down in 1941. It then saw a long period of decline. The tiny ghost town came to national attention in 1998 when *People* magazine ran a story about the townsite's new owners evicting local residents. These "squatters" eventually lost their homes; the town and all its buildings remain in private

hands. Elevation: 6,996 ft. Location: Deer Lodge County

South Willow Creek 948 *map 13 D-4*

South Willow Creek flows out of the Little Snowy Mountains and into the Musselshell River just east of Roundup. It is significant as the location of the Northfield Ranch Company, established in 1881 by Englishman James Harrison Hightower, who shipped in a herd of 1,200 cattle. North Willow Creek flows into the Musselshell River south of Mosby. Location: Fergus and Musselshell counties

Spanish Peaks 779 *map 19 B-4*

According to an account left by Lt. James Bradley, an early veteran of the Montana military frontier, the name Spanish Peaks comes from a Crow legend about a camp of Spanish trappers in the Gallatin Canyon around 1836. The highest points in this portion of the Madison Range, which is directly north of Big Sky, include Jumbo Mountain (10,416 feet) and Wilson Peak (10,700 feet).

Sperry Glacier 96 *map 2 B-3*

Lyman B. Sperry, a professor of geology and zoology from Minnesota, arrived at Lake McDonald in 1894 to survey the tourist potential of the area for the Great Northern Railway. On a return trip the following summer, his group, accompanied by an unnamed Great Northern photographer, explored Avalanche Basin and found several glaciers, including one subsequently named for Sperry. Elevation: 8,045 ft. Location: Glacier National Park

Sphinx Mountain 805 *map 19 C-4*

Like its Egyptian namesake, this Montana mountain resembles a reclining lion with a human head, especially when viewed from the southwest. The Sphinx is one of southwestern Montana's most distinctive landmarks, jutting off the Madison Range. Elevation: 10,876 ft. Location: Madison County

Spring Meadow Lake State Park 456
map 11 C-3

This state park began its life as a gravel pit in 1929, after a devastating fire in downtown Helena renewed demand for building materials. Helena Sand & Gravel, while digging the pit which became a lake fed by underground springs, expanded in 1946 with the purchase of a Saurman dragline and its 120-foot boom. Gravel operations shut down in 1964. Willows sprouted along the shore, and a wide variety of birds (more than 100 species recorded), fish, beavers, muskrats, and painted turtles took up residence. In 1981, Montana Fish, Wildlife & Parks established a 56-acre state park, which attracts more than 40,000 visitors annually for boating, picnicking, swimming, and bird watching. Elevation: 3,920 ft. Location: Lewis and Clark County

Springdale 843 *map 20 A-3*

Cyrus B. Mendenhall founded a ranch in the area in 1882 and called it Springdale, for the numerous underground springs on the property. In 1883, the Northern Pacific Railroad laid tracks through Springdale and established a depot. Mendenhall also purchased Hunter's Hot Springs in 1885. He constructed a hotel at the springs after the winter of 1886–87 wiped out his cattle herd; he operated the hotel for a number of years before selling it to Jim Murray. Many people who journeyed to Hunter's Hot Springs found out about the resort through advertisements in the Northern Pacific timetables. Elevation: 4,227 ft. Location: Park County

Sprole 1140 *map 8 D-1*

In 1910, this town was platted on the north side of the Great Northern Railway tracks and named for Lt. Col. Henry W. Sprole, an agent on the Fort Peck Indian Reservation from 1893 to 1898. Like many eastern Montana towns, Sprole experienced a short burst of growth as a result of the railroad's arrival with homesteaders, and then it declined. Sprole enjoyed a brief resurgence after the discovery of oil near the Murphy Corporation's East Poplar Field in 1951. Elevation: 1,982 ft. Location: Roosevelt County

Square Butte (Cascade) 364
map 11 A-4

A volcanic formation called Square Butte rises up from the Sun River Valley approximately 1,000 feet, making it a prominent landmark. Capt. Meriwether Lewis passed beneath the butte in 1806 and christened it Fort Mountain. The butte appears in numerous Charlie Russell paintings, most significantly *Charles M. Russell and His Friends*. In the 1920s, a homesteader named Shelton constructed a house on top of the butte and staked a claim to a portion of the 1,200 acres of grasslands. Elevation: 4,797 ft. Location: Cascade County

Square Butte (Chouteau) 616 *map 12 A-4*

An igneous intrusion that geologists call a laccolith, this Square Butte is a landmark that was familiar to early explorers. Lewis and Clark mentioned the butte in their journals in 1805, and in 1853 railroad surveyor Isaac I. Stevens called the formation Square Hill. The butte appears in several Charlie Russell paintings. In 1971, the BLM designated 1,947 acres on top of the butte as a natural area. Elevation: 5,703 ft. Location: Chouteau County

Square Butte (town) 620 *map 12 A-4*

Named for the nearby geographic feature of the same shape and name, Square Butte was a station stop on the Milwaukee Road beginning in 1913, the same year that the Milwaukee Land Company laid out the town's neat, now-tree-lined streets. Strategically placed between Lewistown and Great Falls, Square Butte was important for a time because it offered an abundant supply of mineral-free water (from a freshwater spring) and coal for the locomotives. In 1915, residents concerned about an "oversupply of tramps, beggars and vagabonds" petitioned the Chouteau County commissioners to appoint a justice of the peace. The commissioners complied, and the following year hired the Harrington Granite Works to build a county jail at Square Butte. Intended as an interim holding facility, the jail on Salsbury Avenue, listed in the National Register, was constructed on the property of rancher-businessman William P. Sullivan. Sullivan may have meant it to deter his 15 or so cowhands from Saturday night mischief. Perhaps his ploy was effective; there is no evidence that the jail was ever actually used for prisoners. The jail did, however, later serve as road crew housing, a bachelor's residence, and a granary. It also provided local children with a unique clubhouse. The unusual construction of granite blocks quarried nearby illustrates the local importance of this stone, which was shipped to distant cities by the trainload between 1914 and 1922. Ownership of the Sullivan Ranch passed to Dean and Donna Strand, who donated the jail to the Geraldine Historical Committee in 1997. Elevation: 3,141 ft. Location: Chouteau County

Squaw Peak/Ch-paa-qn Peak 189
map 10 B-1

The earliest known name for this peak was Skiotah Peak, which was trans-lated from the Salish as "Squaw's tit." That name was used until 1921, when it was renamed Squaw Peak to avoid vulgarity. It has recently been renamed again, as a result of the 1999 Montana legislature's decision to remove the word *squaw* from geographic features. It is now Ch-paa-qn Peak, Salish for "Shining peak." Elevation: 7,805 ft. Location: Missoula County

St. Helena Cathedral and School 473
map 11 D-3

Patterning it after the Votive Cathedral of the Sacred Heart in Vienna, Austrian-born Albert O. Von Herbulis designed this Helena centerpiece, which was built at a cost of $645,590. The twin spires rise 230 feet, and the stained-glass windows, crafted in Munich by the famous F. X. Zettler, include 11,696 square feet of art glass. Although officials laid the cornerstone in 1908 and the congregation celebrated the first mass in 1914, the cathedral was not completely finished until 1924. Von Herbulis also designed the St. Helena School

Métis camp with Red River Colony carts and Square Butte, Chouteau County, 1880

Detail, H. Jay Haynes, photographer, MHS H-371

in 1908, which used to sit adjacent to the cathedral. The Sisters of Charity of Leavenworth, Kansas, taught elementary students here from 1909 to 1936, when it became Cathedral High School, which operated until 1969. St. Helena Cathedral is listed in the National Register; the school was torn down in 2008. Elevation: 4,105 ft. Location: Lewis and Clark County

St. Ignatius 181 *map 10 A-2*
St. Ignatius takes its name from the priest who established the Society of Jesus, Saint Ignatius of Loyola. In 1840, Jesuit missionaries Father Pierre-Jean De Smet and Father Adrian Hoecken first saw the valley where St. Ignatius would stand. Their Salish guides told them they called the place Snielemen, the "Meeting place." At the request of the Indians, in 1854 Father Hoecken oversaw the relocation of the first St. Ignatius mission—which had been established by Father De Smet near the town of Cusick in Washington Territory—to the Mission Valley. Located near Fort Connah, a Hudson's Bay Company post established in 1847, the mission grew and by 1864 boasted a flour mill, sawmill, and church. The Sisters of Providence established a school for girls and a hospital named St. Julian. A new brick church was begun in 1891. The mission reached its peak between 1890 and 1896, with over 300 students attending the school the Ursuline nuns had established in 1884. The town continued to grow when the federal government opened the Flathead Indian Reservation to non-Indian homesteading in 1910. Today it is still a popular destination for those who wish to see the oldest town on the reservation and its beautiful church. Elevation: 2,942 ft. Location: Lake County

St. Ignatius Mission 182 *map 10 A-1*
The St. Ignatius Mission, named for Saint Ignatius of Loyola, dates to 1854. From 1875 to 1900, the Jesuit mission operated a lumber mill, an agricultural and industrial school for boys, and a boarding school for girls, as well as a printing press from which they produced narratives from the Holy Scripture in the Kalispel language and a Kalispel dictionary. The Jesuits laid the cornerstone of the present mission church in 1891. When it was finished, Brother Joseph Carignano, a cook with no formal art training, covered the church walls and ceilings with 61 paintings. Next to the mission is a museum and gift shop that displays mission and Indian artifacts and sells religious items. The log home that was the original residence of the Sisters of Providence still remains. St. Ignatius Mission is listed in the National Register. Elevation: 2,913 ft. Location: Lake County

St. Joseph's Catholic Mission Church 573 *map 11 D-4*
Settlements like the small town of Canton sprang up in the 1860s to serve upper Missouri River Valley ranchers and farmers. By 1872, Canton boasted a mercantile, post office, saloon and dance hall, doctor, and hotel. In 1875, area residents came together to construct this simple, elegant Colonial-style church. Paid for with community donations and built by 90 volunteers, the church was dedicated on October 22, 1876. It is the state's oldest standing Catholic church not built by a religious order. The style, rarely found in Montana, reflects the roots of the many settlers who hailed from Canton, New York, and elsewhere back east. Arched windows with decorative moldings and a fan light over the original 4-panel entry doors (now enclosed in the vestibule) are elements of this style. In 1952, before the waters of Canyon Ferry Lake swallowed the original site, St. Joseph's was moved 2.5 miles to its present location. The church, now National Register listed and near St. Joseph's Cemetery, where many of its founding members rest, became a focal point for the displaced community. The Canton Church Project, organized in 1996

with the help of the Catholic Diocese of Helena, today maintains the church. Elevation: 3,802 ft. Location: Broadwater County

St. Marie 1075 *map 7 C-1*
The Glasgow Air Force Base trained U.S. airmen from 1955 until it closed in 1968. The town of St. Marie was built to house 7,200 airmen and their families. The origin of its name is not known. There are still blocks of empty streets and abandoned buildings, but the town is now a growing retirement community where nearly 200 people live. The 1960s vintage housing units are for sale as condominiums, and the St. Marie Village Association maintains the grounds. Elevation: 2,750 ft. Location: Valley County

St. Mary 134 *map 2 B-4*
This town near the shores of St. Mary Lake had a wild start, boasting 7 saloons in the 1890s. The post office opened in 1898. It is assumed that the community takes its name from the lake. There were sporadic logging operations around the lake before the establishment of Glacier National Park in 1910. After designation of the park, St. Mary served as an eastern entrance. Hugh and Margaret Black recognized the tourist potential of the community and constructed one-room cabins, a restaurant, and a gas station, adding 2 motels during the 1940s and completing the St. Mary Lodge in 1952. Elevation: 4,561 ft. Location: Glacier County

St. Mary Lake 133 *map 2 B-3*
These 2 lakes have had a variety of Indian names. The Kootenai call them Old Woman Lakes, and at various times the Blackfeet have referred to them as Pahtomahxí kimi, "Inside big water," and Natóaki-Omahxíkimi, "Holy lady big water." In 1854, Lt. James Doty of the Isaac I. Stevens 1853 railroad survey named the lower lake

Chief Mountain Lake and the upper lake Bow Lake. The origin of the name St. Mary is unknown. Elevation: 4,484 ft. Location: Glacier National Park

St. Mary's Mission 279 *map 10 D-1*
In response to a request from the Salish for "Black Robes," in 1841 Jesuit priests Pierre-Jean De Smet, Nicholas Point, and Gregory Mengarini founded the first Catholic mission in what would later become Montana Territory. The original mission was located between the present sites of Fort Owen and Stevensville, in the Bitterroot Valley. The founding date of September 24 coincidentally fell on the day the Catholic Church honors the Blessed Mother, and so the priests named the mission and the nearby river St. Mary's. They established a school and cultivated the fields. Father Anthony Ravalli arrived in 1845, and, with his help, the priests built grist and flour mills and a sawmill. Relations soured between the priests and the Salish when the priests began to expand their ministry and spread their religion to the Blackfeet. In 1850, John Owen purchased the property from the Jesuits and opened a trading post. In 1854, the Jesuits renewed their missionary efforts by establishing St. Ignatius Mission to serve the Salish and others south of Flathead Lake. In 1866, they returned to the Bitterroot, where Father Joseph Giorda, Father Ravalli, and Brother William Claessens reestablished St. Mary's in its present location near Stevensville. Father Ravalli, for whom Ravalli County was named in 1893, was an artist, sculptor, physician, pharmacist, architect, and carpenter. He is buried in the small mission cemetery. The mission closed in 1891 when Chief Charlo and the Salish people left the Bitterroot Valley for the Jocko Reservation. Listed in the National Register, the historic mission is maintained by the nonprofit Historic St. Mary's, Inc. Elevation: 3,311 ft. Location: Ravalli County

St. Marys Lake 198 *map 10 A-2*

St. Marys Lake lies at the foot of the Mission Range at the mouth of Dry Lake Creek. The lake is named for St. Mary's Mission, established by Jesuit priests Pierre-Jean De Smet, Gregory Mengarini, and Nicholas Point in 1841 in the Bitterroot Valley. Elevation: 4,014 ft. Location: Lake County

St. Peter's Mission Church and Cemetery 360 *map 11 A-3*

St. Peter's began in 1859 on the Teton River, near present-day Choteau, as a ministry to the Blackfeet. The site of the present church was the mission's fourth location, established in 1866. Soon after, Indians killed a mission herder, forcing the priests to abandon this site. They returned in 1874 to build the small log church that stands today, and the mission developed into a school. Louis Riel, leader of the Northwest Rebellion in Canada, was a lay teacher at the school in 1883. Catholic Ursuline sisters came in 1884 to establish the first local school for both Indian and white children. The sisters stressed music and the arts, and an opera house, built in 1896, held an auditorium for concerts and performances given by students and visiting artists. The boys' school closed in 1896, and in 1908 fire destroyed the boys' school buildings. In 1912, the Ursuline nuns and the school moved to Great Falls, but Indian girls were still educated here until 1918, when fire destroyed the convent and school. From 1885 to 1938, St. Peter's had its own post office. St. Peter's Mission Church (on private property) and Cemetery are listed in the National Register. Elevation: 4,188 ft. Location: Cascade County

St. Phillip 1230 *map 16 B-4*

At the start of the twentieth century, this area at the eastern edge of Montana attracted a sizeable population of Polish farmers, and in 1910 they erected St. Phillip's Catholic Church, named for benefactor and parishioner Philip Wicka. Wicka donated a statue of Saint Philip to grace the church's interior, and the town adopted the name of the saint, although they added an extra *l* in Phillip. Elevation: 2,986 ft. Location: Wibaux County

St. Regis 146 *map 9 A-3*

St. Regis takes its name from the St. Regis River, named St. Regis De Borgia by Jesuit priest Pierre-Jean De Smet, after a fellow priest in the Jesuit order. Settlers began arriving in this area after completion of the Mullan Road from Fort Benton to Walla Walla, Washington, in 1860. The post office opened in 1896. In 1897–98, the Blackfoot Milling Company constructed the Big Blackfoot Lumber Mill near St. Regis. The Northern Pacific Railroad finished laying tracks through the town in 1890, and by 1909, with the completion of the Milwaukee Road, the town was flourishing. Prosperity came to a halt in 1910 when a fire ravaged the area; the lumber mill was shuttered in 1914, and the county seat moved to Superior that same year. The town's population dwindled for the next 80 years. Today St. Regis is a tourist stop along I-90, providing services as well as access to nearby alpine forests and lakes. Elevation: 2,642 ft. Location: Mineral County

St. Regis River 149 *map 9 A-3*

Jesuit priest Pierre-Jean De Smet named the St. Regis River in 1841 for Saint Regis De Borgia, a priest who belonged to the same Jesuit order. The river flows into the Clark Fork River at the town of St. Regis in northwestern Montana.

St. Regis, c. 1903
Detail, MHS 950-796

St. Xavier Mission Church and Rectory 1074 *map 22 B-2*

In 1886, Jesuit priests Urban Grassi and Peter Paul Prando visited the Crow tribe to select a site for a permanent mission. They returned the following year, cleared a 9-by-12-foot patch of snow, and pitched a tent, where they lived for 8 months. They named the mission after Saint Francis Xavier, sixteenth-century cofounder of the Jesuits. The "Black Robes" had a significant influence on the Crow people, who were at that time in transition from a hunting and gathering existence to an agrarian way of life on the reservation. In 1887, the simple frame school was completed. Ursuline sisters arrived, and by Christmas 50 students were attending the school. The simple wood-frame mission church dates to 1888 and is still in use. The 1889 rectory was moved 38 feet, onto a new foundation, in 1970. The little complex of buildings, listed in the National Register, continues to serve as the Catholic mission on the Crow Indian Reservation. Elevation: 3,067 ft. Location: Big Horn County

Stanford 652 *map 12 B-4*

Stanford began with the establishment of a trading post by Thomas C. Power in 1875, about 3 miles from its present location. Three stories explain how Stanford acquired its name. One is that, in 1880, Joseph and George Bower named the town after Stanfordville, New York, and simply abbreviated the name. Another says that when the town applied for a post office, which the people wanted to name Antelope Butte Springs, the postmaster general declared the name too long and substituted the name Stanford in recognition of U. S. Senator Leland Stanford of California. A third explanation states that the town takes its name from a Great Falls man, Maj. James T. Stanford. The railroad survey crew of the Great Northern Railway's Billings and Northern branch line routed the new line outside of Stanford by about 3 miles, so after 28 years in one location, in 1908 the town picked up and moved to the railroad. Elevation: 4,278 ft. Location: Judith Basin County

St. Mary's Mission, Stevensville, c. 1880
MHS 950-742

Starr School 1254 *map 2 B-4*

This small community of fewer than 250 residents on the Blackfeet Indian Reservation, near Browning, takes its name from the school located there. One of the reservation's first established schools, today it is an immersion school where children learn traditional cultural practices. Resident families preserve these traditions. Although Starr School has no businesses, tourists occasionally visit. Elevation: 4,685 ft. Location: Glacier County

Stemple Pass 344 *map 11 C-2*

Stemple Pass is named for a West Virginia native, John A. Stemple, who prospected around Virginia City before staking a claim at the head of Silver Creek, near Marysville, in 1874. A small town by the same name emerged near the Homestake Mine, with a post office, store, and stage stop. Elevation: 6,376 ft. Location: Lewis and Clark County

Stevensville 280 *map 10 D-1*

Stevensville takes its name from Isaac I. Stevens, who in 1853 led an expedition across Montana to survey the feasibility of a northern railroad route across the continent. Stevens also served as Washington Territory's first governor. The town's origins go back to St. Mary's Mission, founded nearby by Fathers Pierre-Jean De Smet, Nicolas Point, and Gregory Mengarini in 1841. The Jesuits sold the mission in 1850 to Maj. John Owen, who for 22 years operated a trading post named Fort Owen. When John R. Winslett and J. K. Houk left the Emigrant Road (typically referred to as the Oregon, California, and Mormon trails—wagon routes used to cross the continent) with packhorses and merchandise to trade in the Bitterroot Valley, they met with opposition from Fort Owen. As a result, they constructed a store a few miles south of the trading post in 1863. By the following year, the new location sported another store, a saloon, and a blacksmith shop. With the community growing, residents decided to name their settlement Stevensville in honor of Isaac I. Stevens. G. A. Kellogg platted the townsite in 1879. With the creation of Ravalli County in 1893, Stevensville became the county seat. The town lost a hotly contested election for the permanent Ravalli County seat in 1898 to Hamilton, in part due to the influence of Copper King Marcus Daly. Stevensville's economy has revolved around agriculture through most of its history. Other area industries included a lumber mill, a flour mill, and some mining. Stevensville has more than 40 National Register properties, among them St. Mary's Church and Pharmacy. Elevation: 3,326 ft. Location: Ravalli County

Stillwater County 924 *map 21 A-3*

The Montana legislature created Stillwater County in 1913 from Carbon, Sweet Grass, and Yellowstone counties. This south-central Montana county takes its name from the Stillwater River. At one time, it was part of the Crow Indian Reservation. The famed Yellowstone Trail bisected the county. This route, active from 1912 to 1930, served as the first transcontinental road running from Massachusetts to Washington, through the northern tier of the continental United States. The Yellowstone Trail did not construct highways, but encouraged towns to volunteer labor for road repairs and improvements along the route. Columbus serves as the county seat.

Stillwater Ranger Station Historic District
40 *map 2 B-1*
The Stillwater Forest and its ranger station mark a milestone in the history of Montana forestry. Through the efforts of state forester Robert McLaughlin, the first log structure at Stillwater Ranger Station was built in 1922. At McLaughlin's urging, the 1925 legislature designated the Stillwater Forest a managed site. After 40,000 timbered acres burned in 1926, the Stillwater Ranger Station became a year-round facility for timber management and fire protection. It was the only major ranger station in the state system until 1954. Ranger Pete De Groat built the main log residence in 1928, and CCC forestry crews added several more buildings in the 1930s. Maurice Cusick, supervisor from 1936 to 1967, built 4 others. Today these historic log buildings constructed of local materials are National Register listed and a tribute to Montana's early forestry and conservation efforts. Elevation: 3,161 ft. Location: Flathead County

Stillwater River 942 *map 21 B-2*
Capt. William Clark named the Stillwater River "Rose bud river" on July 19, 1806. In the 1860s, John Bozeman named it Stillwater River because there was a quiet, sandy ford across the river near where it exits the mountains. The Crow tribe referred to the river as Itch-kep-pe, mean-

ing "Quiet water," derived from a legend about a young man's vain attempt to save his lover from the raging river; both their bodies washed into a quiet pool, which was named in their honor. Eventually, the entire river became known by the name for this quiet pool.

Stockett 483 *map 12 A-1*
The Great Northern Railway moved its coal mining operations from Sand Coulee to Cottonwood Coulee in 1898. This company town was named Stockett, for Cottonwood Coal Company manager Lewis Stockett. Stockett reached its peak in the 1920s with 1,500 residents. The mines stopped operating after diesel for railroad engines and natural gas for home heating were introduced. Stockett now serves area ranchers and farmers but is also a bedroom community for commuters to Great Falls. Elevation: 3,643 ft. Location: Cascade County

Stryker 28 *map 1 B-4*
Stryker takes its name from early homesteaders David and Frank Stryker. David filed for his homestead in 1898; he later operated a stage station on the Kalispell–Fort Steele (British Columbia) trail. When the Great Northern Railway rerouted its main line from Columbia Falls to Rexford, it passed close to the Stryker stage stop. With the completion of the line, the railroad constructed a depot at Stryker, and Frank opened a store and post office nearby. A forest fire swept through the town in 1926, destroying most of the buildings, but the community survived. Stryker became a prominent stopping point for the railroad, not because of the scenic beauty but rather for the fresh fish. The eastbound Oriental slowed to a stop at Stryker each day to pick up a package of fresh trout from a local hatchery, destined for hungry travelers in the dining car. Stryker's depot closed when construction of Libby

Dam precipitated a change in the railroad route during the 1970s, but the town still endures. Elevation: 3,314 ft. Location: Lincoln County

Stryker Peak 31 *map 1 B-4*

Stryker Peak is the high point of Stryker Ridge. It is named for David Stryker, a native of Indiana who homesteaded in Stryker Meadow in the 1890s. He was a freighter, stage driver, hotel owner, and storyteller. The USFS built a fire lookout on the peak in 1935, which was used until 1955. Elevation: 7,338 ft. Location: Lincoln County

Suffolk 754 *map 13 A-2*

C. A. Goodno, assistant to the president of the Milwaukee Road, in 1913 named Suffolk after a town in New England. The population topped out at 100 residents. Elevation: 3,383 ft. Location: Fergus County

Sula 410 *map 18 A-1*

Located in Ross's Hole (*hole* being another word for *valley*), Sula has seen its share of travelers. Native Americans had traversed the Bitterroot Valley and crossed today's Lost Trail and Gibbons passes for generations before the arrival of Euro-Americans. The first recorded American presence was on September 4, 1805, when the Lewis and Clark Expedition stumbled out of the mountains, hungry and exhausted from their journey over Lost Trail Pass. Capt. William Clark wrote in his journal that day: "We met a part of the Flat head [Salish] nation . . . & found them friendly." At the end of the entry, Clark noted that he was the first "white man who ever wer on the waters of this river [Bitterroot River]." Ross Hole received its name from Alexander Ross, a Hudson's Bay Company fur trader who had traveled through the area in spring 1824. Wood "Longhaired"

Thompson arrived in the valley in 1887 and bought out ranchers who called it quits after the devastating winter of 1886–87. In 1889, settlers named the post office after Thompson's daughter, Ursula (Sula for short), purportedly the first non-Indian child born in Ross's Hole. Elevation: 4,411 ft. Location: Ravalli County

Sumatra 1023 *map 14 C-3*

Now a ghost town, Sumatra was established in 1905 as a station stop, called Summit, on the Milwaukee Road. Apparently, when the town applied for a post office in 1910, the name was changed to Sumatra, after an Indonesian island, to avoid confusion with the several other Summits already in Montana. Elevation: 3,208 ft. Location: Rosebud County

Sun River 418 *map 12 A-2*

Known to the Blackfeet as Nat-to'-se, "Medicine river," the Sun River was an important path for commerce between native peoples and American fur traders. The origin of the name is unknown, but it was called the Sun River as early as 1853 during the Isaac I. Stevens survey expedition. In 1866, the Jesuits established St. Peter's Mission between the Dearborn and Smith rivers, and the U.S. military established Fort Shaw in 1867 as the primary military post bordering Blackfeet country. Fort Shaw also served as the regimental headquarters for the Military District of Montana Territory. Beginning in 1869, Robert Ford trailed cattle into the Sun River Valley, followed by Robert Vaughn and Conrad Kohrs in the 1880s, and by sheepmen Thomas C. Power and Dan Floweree in the succeeding decades. Large U.S. Reclamation Service projects, such as the Fort Shaw Irrigation Project's construction of canals, diversions, and dams, facilitated homesteading in the valley, beginning in the 1890s and concluding during the homestead boom in the 1910s.

Sun River (town) 359 *map 11 A-4*

Sun River was established in 1867 by John Largent, who laid out the town, sold lots, and opened a store and post office. Largent and Joe Healy also built a toll bridge across the Sun River to profit from the Mullan Road traffic between Fort Benton and the new gold mines to the south. The bridge replaced Healy's ferry over the historic Sun River Crossing, a natural ford of the river that Native Americans had used for centuries. Elevation: 3,412 ft. Location: Cascade County

Sun River WMA 260 *map 11 A-1*

Originally called the Sun River Game Range, the Sun River WMA was established in 1948 as winter range for the area's elk herd. At the time, the Montana Fish and Game Dept. lacked the funds to purchase ranchland in the area they deemed critical to the Sun River elk herd. As a result, concerned citizens Tom Meselt and Carl Malone made the down payment, holding the land until the state could purchase it outright. Over the course of the next several years, 9 additional land purchases were made, the last in 1974. The range covers some 20,000 acres along the Rocky Mountain Front and allows elk to migrate from their summer range in the mountains to the prairies, where they can find adequate winter feed. Elevation: 4,885 ft. Location: Lewis and Clark County

Sunburst 265 *map 3 B-3*

In 1907, W. G. Davis moved from his ranch in southern Alberta to an area just west of the Sweet Grass Hills. One morning, while tending his sheep, Davis saw the sun burst out of the clouds, illuminating the plains below. He named his ranch the Sunburst Ranch. Six years later, Davis and 2 other ranchers platted the townsite, and the town of Sunburst grew up along the Great Northern Railway's branch line to Canada. The discovery of oil at the Kevin-

Sunburst field in 1922 prompted construction of the International Oil Refinery that year. Sunburst incorporated in 1924. The population peaked at 1,000 residents sometime between 1924 and 1930. For many years, the town commemorated the oil discoveries with an annual Refinery Day, which became an official holiday for the community. The Texas Company closed the refinery in 1959. Elevation: 3,361 ft. Location: Toole County

Sundance Mountain 972
map 21 C-1

Sundance Mountain was named by a group of fishing enthusiasts from Camp Senia, a nearby dude ranch, that in 1919 attempted to introduce trout to the nearby lake. They named this Beartooth Range mountain and lake for the way the sunlight sparkled off the water. Elevation: 12,272 ft. Location: Carbon County

Sunday Creek 1144 *map 15 D-3*

The usual story about the origin of the name is that Capt. William Clark named it in honor of Sunday, July 29, 1806, the day the expedition had to pull their boats through the Missouri River's Buffalo Rapids near the mouth of this eastern Montana creek. Location: Rosebud and Custer counties

Superior 165 *map 9 A-4*

Originally known as Superior City, Superior received its name from a former resident of Superior, Wisconsin. Residents started settling near Cedar Creek in 1869, and a fledgling town emerged in 1870. The town established a post office in 1871 under postmaster Silas R. Smith. Four years later, the post office moved to the A. P. Johnston Ranch, and in 1889 the government requested that Johnston move the post office west to the area near Flat Creek, which became the permanent location

Charette Hotel, Superior, c. 1915
MHS 951-237

Swamp Creek 24 *map 1 B-4*

The swamp for which Swamp Creek is named lies at the point where the creek empties into Fortine Creek, in northwestern Montana. The Swamp Creek School opened in 1912, with Georgina Emard as teacher, and continued to operate until about 1944. Location: Lincoln County

Swan Lake (town) 148 *map 2 D-2*

Local lore suggests 2 possibilities for the name of the community. In one, the name recalls early settler Emmett Swan. The other suggests that the name comes from the swans that frequent the nearby lake. The community began to develop sometime around 1905. The Somers Lumber Company, a subsidiary of the Great Northern Railway, purchased approximately 85 million board-feet of timber from the Flathead National Forest near Swan Lake in 1914. The town of Swan Lake developed as the railhead for that timber. The company decked the logs nearby, until high water allowed their transportation to the mill at Somers, via the Swan River and Flathead Lake. Swan Lake is a popular summer recreation area today. Elevation: 3,116 ft. Location: Lake County

of Superior. Missoula County, the Iron Mountain Mine, and private funds paid for construction of a bridge across the Clark Fork River to facilitate transportation of zinc and lead ore from local mines. In 1908, the Superior Hotel became the first place in the nation where the Gideons International group placed Bibles—a plan hatched at their 1908 convention to place the Bible in every hotel room in America. Six years later, Superior became the county seat of newly created Mineral County. Logging and mining continued to shape Superior's history well into the late twentieth century. Elevation: 2,757 ft. Location: Mineral County

Sutherland Creek Bay 1024 *map 6 E-4*

This tributary of the Missouri River was called Gibson's Creek by Lewis and Clark, after expedition member George Gibson, when they passed through the area on May 14, 1805. It is unknown how or when the name changed to Sutherland Creek. It now enters a bay created by Fort Peck Reservoir. Elevation: 2,250 ft. Location: Valley County

Swan Range, Swan Lake, and Swan River 151 *map 2 D-2*

On an 1884 Rand McNally map, the Swan River and Swan Lake are referred to as the Sweatinghouse River and the Sweatinghouse Lake. However, by 1895, most maps had adopted Swan, a name apparently proposed by early English hunters in the area and acknowledged by the locals, according to Ken Wolf's 1980 *Montana Magazine* article "History of the Swan Valley." During the 1890s, the Big Blackfoot Milling Company sent its agents into the valley to harvest virgin forests of tamarack and ponderosa pine to feed their mill at Bonner. The Swan Valley abuts 2 large wilderness areas, the Bob Marshall and the tribally administered Mission Mountains Tribal Wilderness. The Swan River NWR was established in 1973 to protect 1,568 acres of wildlife habitat. The range's highest summit is 9,356-foot Holland Peak.

Sweet Grass County 866   map 20 A-4
The Montana legislature created Sweet Grass County in 1895 from Park, Meagher, and Yellowstone counties. Helen Van Cleve put forth the name Sweet Grass for this south-central Montana county because of the abundant native grass, *Hierochloe odorata*, that grew around her home near Melville. Big Timber is the county seat.

Sweet Grass Creek 880   map 21 A-1
This creek derives its name from the spicy, vanilla-smelling grass *Hierochloe odorata*, which is burned in native purification ceremonies. The stream rises in the Crazy Mountains and empties into the Yellowstone River above Greycliff. The fertile land along its banks was settled primarily by Norwegian sheep and cattle ranchers. Location: Sweet Grass County

Sweet Grass Hills 327   map 4 B-1
The Sweet Grass Hills have been known by many names over the years: the Blackfeet referred to this island range as Kato-yi-six, "Sweet pine hills"; Peter Pond, a partner in the North West Company in Canada, referred to them as the Three Sugar Loaf Mounts in 1785; the Hudson's Bay Company called them the Three Paps in 1802; Capt. Meriwether Lewis called them the Tower Mountains in 1806. The current name, Sweet Grass Hills, refers to *Hierochloe odorata*, a native grass abundant in the area, used for ceremonial purposes. The Sweet Grass Hills, comprised of 6,983-foot West Butte, plus Gold Butte, Mount Royal, and Mount Brown, maintain a religious and cultural significance to the Blackfeet people and other tribes. During the 1890s and again in the 1930s, several small gold mines operated in these hills, and some of those claims remain viable today. The Blackfeet tribe, local farmers, and environmentalists have successfully resisted proposals for open-pit gold mining. Location: Toole and Liberty counties

Swift Reservoir 204   map 3 D-1
Built by the Valier Land and Water Company as part of the Pondera County Canal and Reservoir Company, and authorized by the Carey Land Act Board, Swift Reservoir was formed with the construction of Swift Dam in 1911–14. Both were named for chief engineer William Swift. The dam was a large, arched, rock-filled structure unusual for the time. In June 1964, floodwaters running at 33,000 cubic feet per second destroyed the dam, wreaking havoc on downstream homes, farms, and livestock; 29 people lost their lives as a result of the dam's failure. The U.S. Bureau of Reclamation built a new dam at the site in 1967. The current dam measures 205 feet high and 573 feet long and is capable of storing 29,975 acre-feet of water. Elevation: 4,884 ft. Location: Pondera County

Swimming Woman Creek 870   map 13 D-2
According to local legend, Swimming Woman Creek takes its name from an Indian woman who swam across the flooded creek during a storm to save her baby. The creek originates in the Snowy Mountains and flows south for about 40 miles to its confluence with Careless Creek, west of Franklin. Location: Golden Valley County

Homestead at Marsh, northeast of Terry, 1911
Detail, Evelyn Cameron, photographer, PAc 90-87.42-7

Tamarack Creek 142 *map 9 A-3*

Mineral County's Tamarack Creek is one of 6 creeks around the state named for the tamarack, also called larch, a tree common to the mountains of western Montana. The word *tamarack* is a version of the Abenaki word *hackmatack*. The wood from this tree was used especially by the Chippewa and Cree tribes for making snowshoes. There was a ranger station on this Tamarack Creek around 1913, but it was consolidated into another station by 1917. Location: Mineral County

Tampico 1020 *map 6 C-4*

Located along the Great Northern Railway's main line, Tampico traces its development to an 1890s railroad siding and water tank constructed to replenish the steam engines. The railroad also constructed a depot and section house. The post office opened in 1908 under the name Tampico—named by railroad officials for Tampico, Mexico. George and John Lohr established the townsite, and by 1910 the large numbers of homesteaders in the vicinity led to the formation of a community that offered a variety of services. The post office closed in 1973. Elevation: 2,152 ft. Location: Valley County

Targhee Pass 896 *map 20 E-1*

Targhee Pass, named for Bannock chief Targhee, already had this name when Ferdinand V. Hayden, with the assistance of a $40,000 congressional appropriation, led an expedition to Yellowstone in 1871. When the Nez Perces approached Yellowstone National Park during their flight in 1877, Chief Joseph led his people across Targhee Pass on August 22, thus staying several days ahead of Gen. O. O. Howard's forces. Howard did not catch up until the battle in the Bears Paw Mountains in early October. Elevation: 7,072 ft. Location: Gallatin County

Tarkio 190 *map 9 B-4*

The Tarkio region contained abundant grass and water and boasted one of Mineral County's earliest farming areas. The area around Tarkio received its name from a group of Milwaukee Road construction workers from Tarkio, Missouri, in 1907. The railroad built an electrical substation here in 1915 for electrification of the line between Harlowton and Avery, Idaho. The Anaconda Company established a logging camp in the Tarkio area in the 1920s. Today Tarkio's economy relies on its panoramic views, fishing, and hunting. Elevation: 3,034 ft. Location: Mineral County

Taylor Creek 848 *map 20 C-1*

Taylor Creek, also known as Taylor Fork and Dodge Creek, is a tributary of the Gallatin River. It is named for John Taylor, who settled on the river in the 1860s and continued as a trapper in the area into the 1880s. His cabin was located where the Nine Quarter Circle Ranch now is. Location: Gallatin County

Teigen 889 *map 13 B-4*

In 1884, Mons Teigen established a sheep ranch in the area with Knute and Ole Opheim; Teigen acquired sole ownership in 1897. He married Elsie Borsden of Helena and built a log cabin on the ranch. In 1912, the Milwaukee Road and the Great Northern Railway conducted surveys in this central Montana region. The Milwaukee Land Company platted the Teigen townsite in 1914; the post office opened the same year. Homesteaders poured into the area between 1913 and 1916, despite the fact that the Milwaukee Road did not lay track to Teigen until 1917. By 1918, there were 2 general stores, a blacksmith shop, and a lumber and grain company. After the 1920 oil discovery in the Cat Creek fields east of Teigen, near the Musselshell River, many speculators drilled in the Teigen area as well, with no success. Teigen fell victim to the drought of the 1920s and the following Great Depression. All that marks the existence of the town now is the hotel that Mons Teigen built in 1917. Elevation: 3,195 ft. Location: Petroleum County

Tendoy Mountains 780 *map 19 D-1*

This small range in southwestern Montana extends 25 miles west of the Red Rock River. It is named for Shoshone chief Tendoy, who led the Lemhi band from 1863 until his death in 1907. Lemhi County, Idaho, residents erected a monument on his grave that same year. Members of the Society of Montana Pioneers commemorating his judicious leadership during the maelstrom of Montana's early gold rush period contributed $25 toward purchasing the monument. It is unknown when or by whom the mountain range was named. The highest elevation is 9,688-foot Ellis Peak. Location: Beaverhead County

Tenth Street Bridge 422 *map 12 A-1*

When this critical link between Great Falls and Black Eagle opened in 1920, the *Great Falls Tribune* described the Tenth Street Bridge as "a carved monument above the water." Voters approved more than $224,000 for bridge construction in 1918, but when bids exceeded available funds, county commissioners held a design competition. Spokane structural engineer Ralph Adams and Great Falls architect George Shanley collaborated on the winning plans, which cost less to implement. Engineer Evarts Blakeslee supervised construction. Crews built a railroad trestle across the river and used handcars to transport the mixed concrete to wooden forms for the cast-in-place arches. Construction of the access to the south end of the bridge proved a major financial problem for the city. The county completed the north approach as part of a federally aided project. The imposing finished structure of 8 sweeping arches spans 1,130 feet across

the Missouri River, reflecting the pride and optimism of the community and the vision of city founder Paris Gibson. Listed in the National Register, it is Montana's longest and oldest reinforced-concrete, open-spandrel, ribbed-arch bridge. Elevation: 3,313 ft. Location: Cascade County

Terry 1165 *map 15 C-4*

Terry was originally called Joubert's Landing, for the man who provided wood to riverboats traveling on the Yellowstone River. J. W. Montague, who arrived in 1877, built a supply point for freighters traveling from Bismarck, Dakota Territory, to Miles City, Montana Territory. When the Northern Pacific Railroad arrived in 1881, the town was named for Gen. Alfred H. Terry, commander of the 6-year military operation against the Sioux. At one time, Terry was the largest stock-shipping point in the Northwest. It also had a large wool warehouse. Photographer Evelyn Cameron and her husband, Ewen, settled near Terry in 1893; Evelyn purchased her first camera in 1894. Her photographs of eastern Montana residents and landscapes portray a life less than glamorous in a land less than hospitable. Evelyn Cameron died in 1928 and is buried at Terry. Elevation: 2,251 ft. Location: Prairie County

Teton County 272 *map 3 D-2*

The Montana legislature created Teton County in 1893 from Chouteau County. The county takes its name from the Teton River and Teton Peak. Fur trade lore suggests that French fur trappers and traders used the word *teton* for geographic features supposedly shaped like a woman's breast. However, in a report to the Smithsonian Institution, Maj. John Wesley Powell stated that *titon* or *teton* derives from the Indian word *titan*, which translates as "at or on land without trees"—referring to those Indian tribes living on the prairie. Choteau is the county seat.

Teton River 527 *map 4 E-3*

The origin of the name Teton for the river, mountains, and county is a combination, and possibly intentional confusion, of 2 root words. The Sioux name Teton came from the word, *thi'thuNwaN* (pronounced "TEE-too-wah"), meaning "village," combined with the word *thiN'ta*, meaning "prairie." This word sounds similar to the French *teton*, for "breast," which was frequently used to describe mountains.

Therriault Lakes 19 *map 1 A-4*

Big Therriault Lake and Little Therriault Lake, just east and northeast, respectively, of St. Clair Peak, are named for brothers Antoine, Charles, and Michel Therriault, natives of New Brunswick, Canada, who arrived in the Flathead Valley in the late 1880s and established homesteads, sawmills, and other enterprises. There are USFS campgrounds at both lakes. Elevation: 5,602 ft. Location: Lincoln County

Thoeny 994 *map 6 B-4*

Thoeny was named for its first postmaster, Jacob M. Thoeny, in 1915. By 1918, the community had a newspaper, 2 general stores, a blacksmith shop, and several other businesses, all without the benefit of being located on or near a railroad. Elevation: 2,477 ft. Location: Valley County

Thompson Falls 80 *map 1 E-2*

North West Company trader and explorer David Thompson established a trading post named Saleesh House in this area in 1809. The town was founded in 1882 in anticipation of the Northern Pacific Railroad's arrival the following year. The post office operated under the name Thompson until 1912, when postal officials changed the name to Thompson Falls to match the name of the railroad station. Enthusiastic about their town's potential, Thompson residents even boarded trains to persuade newcomers to settle there instead of at archrival Belknap, farther northwest. Ten thousand hopeful miners wintered here in 1883 on their way to gold diggings in Idaho. The Northwestern Development Company constructed a concrete dam across the Clark Fork River at Thompson Falls and by 1917 had 6 hydroelectric generators in place. The Montana Power Company acquired the dam and reservoir in 1929. The Thompson Falls Multiple Resource Area, listed in the National Register, includes homes, the county jail, several hotels, and the Northern Pacific warehouse. Thompson Falls State Park lies just south of town. Elevation: 2,564 ft. Location: Sanders County

Thompson Falls Dam 82 *map 1 E-2*

Between 1905 and 1909, the Northwestern Development Company acquired water rights on the Clark Fork River and, in the 1910s, began constructing a concrete dam across the Clark Fork at Thompson Falls. By 1917, 6 hydroelectric generators were in place. The Montana Power Company acquired the dam and reservoir in 1929. The falls are named for North West Company trader and explorer David Thompson, who established Saleesh House, a fur trading post, in this area in 1809. Elevation: 2,394 ft. Location: Sanders County

Thompson Chain of Lakes 43 *map 1 D-3*

North West Company trader and explorer David Thompson, for whom these lakes are named, mapped this northwestern corner of Montana between 1808 and 1812, providing a detailed map of the region for exclusive use by the British fur companies operating out of Canada. Upper, Middle, and Lower Thompson lakes are now part of the Thompson Chain of Lakes, consisting of 18 lakes and dozens of campgrounds, including those at Logan State Park on Middle Thompson Lake. Elevation: 3,331 ft. Location: Lincoln County

Missouri River headwaters, near Three Forks
Albert Schlechten, photographer, MHS 951-281

Thompson River 87   *map 1   E-3*

This river in northwestern Montana bears the name of famous North West Company fur trader, explorer, and cartographer David Thompson, who in November 1809 built a fur trading post called Saleesh House, 3 miles southwest of here the Thompson River flows into the Clark Fork River.

Three Forks 661   *map 19   A-4*

In 1810, Pierre Menard and Andrew Henry, working as partners in the St. Louis Missouri Fur Company, sought to establish a trading post at the spot where the Gallatin, Madison, and Jefferson rivers (the "three forks" of the town's name) come together to form the Missouri. Pressure from the Blackfeet forced them to abandon the post that same year, and no further attempts to settle the area arose until Gallatin City, the first county seat of newly created Gallatin County, was established near the conflu-

ence in 1862. In February 1865, the town moved across the river. By 1871, James Shedd had constructed a series of toll bridges that bypassed this second Gallatin City, resulting in the establishment of the community of Bridgeville by 1881. Two years later, the Northern Pacific Railroad constructed its main line within 2 miles of Bridgeville. A group of Englishmen purchased the townsite in 1882 and named the community Three Forks (later called Old Town). None of the existing communities moved to the Northern Pacific rail line, and when John Q. Adams arrived in 1908, representing the Milwaukee Land Company and Milwaukee Road, he platted a new townsite 1 mile south, naming this new community Three Forks as well. The new town incorporated in 1909 and experienced a booming start when it became a division point for the Milwaukee Road. However, with the 1915 electrification of the Milwaukee Road between

Harlowton and Avery, Idaho, Three Forks lost its roundhouse, car yard, and dispatcher's office. The Milwaukee Road closed its line in 1980. Three Forks, however, had found new life with the completion of the interstate highway, as well as the designation of Missouri Headwaters State Park in 1957. Parker Homestead State Park, which features a sod-roofed cabin built in the early 1900s, lies 8 miles west. Elevation: 4,073 ft. Location: Gallatin County

Three Forks of the Missouri NHL 656
map 19 A-4
On July 27, 1805, with a difficult portage behind him, Capt. Meriwether Lewis stood atop a limestone cliff observing "three noble streams" in a sweeping view of a vast basin ringed by snowcapped mountains. Lewis and Clark named these 3 rivers the Jefferson, Gallatin, and Madison, after 3 politicians who had played key roles in the Louisiana Purchase and the organization of their expedition. Lewis understood immediately that the Three Forks of the Missouri was "an essential point in the geography of this western part of the Continent." A few years after the expedition, John Potts and George Drouillard returned to the Three Forks, where they were killed in separate incidents with the Blackfeet. Near the Three Forks, a naked John Colter began the legendary run for his life, with scores of Blackfeet warriors in pursuit. Three Forks of the Missouri NHL, designated in 1960, remains central to the 560-acre Missouri Headwaters State Park created 3 years earlier. Elevation: 4,037 ft. Location: Gallatin County

Thurlow 1260 *map 15 D-2*
This small community, located on an abandoned Burlington Northern Railroad siding, established a post office in 1915. The origin of its name is unknown. Elevation: 2,464 ft. Location: Rosebud County

Tiber Dam and Lake Elwell 383 *map 4 C-1*
As early as 1910, the newspaper in Chester trumpeted the irrigation potential of the Marias River. After numerous private and federal surveys, ground was broken in 1952 for the world's largest rolled earth–fill dam. President Harry Truman attended the groundbreaking ceremony for the $21 million construction project, which was completed in 1956 and named for a river in Italy. Tiber Dam impounds more than 1.4 million acre-feet of water, designed to irrigate some 127,000 acres of cropland. The reservoir, Lake Elwell, is named for local judge and reclamation advocate Charles B. Elwell. In 2003, a 5.5 mW hydroelectric plant took shape at the dam, producing enough electricity to power 5,000 homes. Elevation: 3,019 ft. Location: Liberty County

Tobacco River and Plains 12 *map 1 A-3*
In April 1808, David Thompson left Kootenay House in British Columbia, a North West Company trading post he had established the year before, and traveled south along the Kootenai River. He arrived at a "beautiful meadow" that he called Tobacco Meadows because of stories he had heard about the Kootenais growing tobacco here. Father Pierre-Jean De Smet traveled through this area in 1845 and referred to the plain as Prairie du Tabac. It is assumed that the plains and river are so named because of the cultivation of this native tobacco by the Kootenais, who ceremonially smoked before hunting. David Thompson called the river Fine Meadow River. However, early settlers referred to it as Grave Creek, recalling the drowning of a miner in the 1860s. The Tobacco River begins at the confluence of Fortine and Grave creeks and empties into Lake Koocanusa.

Tobacco Root Mountains 683 *map 19 B-3*
According to the story, John R. Edwards of Flint Creek named the Tobacco Root

Mountains in 1860 for a species of mullein that grew in the mountains. Old-timers smoked this mullein (a member of the snapdragon family) when tobacco was scarce. The Tobacco Root's most noted (and tallest) feature is 10,604-foot Hollowtop Mountain, named for the peculiar bowl-shaped aspect the mountain presents when viewed from the north or northeast; other high peaks are Potosi, Ward, and Granite. Numerous mines pocked the range, with ore processing centered at the town of Pony. The largest producer was the Bismarck Mine, which produced copper ore.

Tongue River 1137 *map 15 D-3*
The Tongue River originates in the Bighorn Mountains of Wyoming and flows some 180 miles northeast to its confluence with the Yellowstone River at Miles City. The name comes from a translation of the Crow name for the river, De'eshaashe, referring to a Sun Dance held at the headwaters where 100 buffalo tongues were offered as a sacrifice.

Tongue River Dam 1149 *map 23 C-1*
The federal Public Works Administration and the State Water Conservation Board built the Tongue River Dam in the 1930s as a joint project. Completed in 1940, the dam stands 91 feet high and 1,824 feet wide, providing flood protection, irrigation, and recreation opportunities to residents of the Tongue River Valley. Tongue River Reservoir State Park, created in January 1983, is a popular fishing destination. Elevation: 3,411 ft. Location: Big Horn County

Toole County 294 *map 3 B-4*
The Montana legislature created Toole County in 1914 from Hill and Teton counties. This north-central Montana county takes its name from Joseph K. Toole, first governor of the state of Montana. The county boomed with the discovery of the

Kevin-Sunburst Oil Field in 1922. Shelby, the county seat, hosted the 1923 world heavyweight championship boxing match between Jack Dempsey and Tommy Gibbons, which Dempsey won.

Torrey Mountain 603 *map 18 B-4*
According to George Metlen of Dillon, Torrey Mountain is named for a member of the USGS crew who mapped the East Pioneers in the late nineteenth century. Elevation: 11,147 ft. Location: Beaverhead County

Toston 630 *map 11 E-4*
Thomas Toston settled in the area in 1871, establishing a ferry across the Missouri River that same year and a post office in 1882. The Northern Pacific Railroad arrived a year later, prompting construction of the Toston Smeltering Company smelter, which processed gold and silver ore until its closure in 1899. Toston at one time boasted 2 newspapers, the *Toston Times* and the *Toston Sun*. When the smelter closed, the town continued to prosper as an agricultural center, but earthquakes in 1923 and 1925, along with a devastating fire (also in 1925), crippled the once-thriving community. Elevation: 3,924 ft. Location: Broadwater County

Tower Rock State Park 388 *map 11 B-3*
Rugged and weathered, with a few scrub firs and junipers around its base, this geological feature rises almost perpendicular to the Missouri River. There is little doubt that Tower Rock is the "Tower" Lewis and Clark described in their journals on July 16, 1805. Capt. Meriwether Lewis ascended the rock with some difficulty and enjoyed the sweeping view, noting "immense herds of buffaloe in the plains below." Tower Rock is listed in the National Register; the site became a state park in 2004. Elevation: 3,931 ft. Location: Cascade County

Townsend 591 *map 11 D-4*

Townsend, the seat of Broadwater County, was a railroad town created in 1883 when the Northern Pacific Railroad completed its transcontinental line. Not only did the company plat the townsite, it also supplied the name—after Alma Townsend, the wife of former Northern Pacific president Charles B. Wright. The railroad was not the only industry contributing to the health of the community. Farmers, ranchers, and the timber industry kept the town alive through the drought of the 1920s and the Great Depression. Elevation: 3,831 ft. Location: Broadwater County

Tracy 479 *map 12 A-1*

Nat McGiffen discovered coal in the area in 1882; Don Tracy took over the mines with the departure of McGiffen and his family. The community took its name from Tracy. Like Stockett and Sand Coulee, this mining town attracted miners from many countries. With the switch to natural gas at the Anaconda Company smelter in Great Falls in the 1920s, the Tracy mines closed. The 1930s and '40s saw the majority of Tracy's homes moved to Great Falls. Elevation: 3,437 ft. Location: Cascade County

Trapper Peak 373 *map 10 E-1*

Trapper Peak is the highest point in the Selway-Bitterroot Wilderness. It is thought to have been a favorite area for trappers. Elevation: 10,157 ft. Location: Ravalli County

Travelers' Rest State Park and NHL 247 *map 10 C-1*

Lewis and Clark stopped at this site in 1805 on their way to the Pacific Ocean, and again on their return in 1806. Located at a historic crossroads where generations of native people paused in their travels, Travelers' Rest is the only documented Lewis and Clark campsite in Montana, and one of few in the nation. In 2002, archaeologists uncovered several hearths and a latrine that proved without a doubt that the Corps of Discovery had used the site. Montana Fish, Wildlife & Parks owns the site of Travelers' Rest NHL; it became a state park in 2001. The Travelers' Rest Preservation and Heritage Association manages the site. Elevation: 3,184 ft. Location: Missoula County

Treasure County 1055 *map 14 D-3*

The first fur trading fort in what would become Montana was constructed in present-day Treasure County at the confluence of the Yellowstone and Bighorn rivers, by Manuel Lisa in 1807. He named it Fort Raymond (Ramón) after his son, though many referred to it as Fort Manuel Lisa. In 1919, county promoters chose the name Treasure as a strategy to draw settlers to this new county created from Rosebud County. Hysham became the county seat.

Saloon, Toston, c. 1915
MHS 944-655

Trego 26 *map 1 B-4*

Along with the construction of the Great Northern Railway's main line from White-fish through Eureka in 1903, the railroad built a depot south of Eureka. Railroad officials named the town after Anna Trego Hogeland, wife of chief engineer A. H. Hogeland. An early mainstay for earning a living in Trego was providing railroad ties to the Great Northern. Known as tie hacks, the average man could make about 35 ties in a 10-hour day. Legend has it that Big Ole Knudson of Trego could hand-hew 100 ties a day. Elevation: 3,096 ft. Location: Lincoln County

Trident 658 *map 19 A-4*

The limestone deposits Capt. Meriwether Lewis mentioned in his journal entry of July 27, 1805, remained undeveloped until 1907, when Daniel A. Morrison redis-covered them. Construction of the Three Forks Portland Cement Company's plant began in 1908 and was completed in 1910. Intending to call his community Three Forks, Morrison discovered that he had been scooped with the incorporation of nearby Three Forks in 1909. Left without a name for his growing town, Morrison chose Trident, since it has essentially the same meaning—"three prongs." Ethnic tensions marred the town's early develop-ment; American-born workers did not like living in close proximity to immigrants from Austria and Italy, who settled apart from the mainstream community in an area known derisively as "Woptown." The Ideal Cement Company purchased the Three Forks Portland Cement Company in 1914. In 1990, Holnam, Inc., purchased the Ideal Cement Company, and the plant became part of Holcim Ltd.'s holdings in 2001. Although the community is gone, the cement plant continues to be an eco-nomic mainstay for the surrounding area. Elevation: 4,037 ft. Location: Gallatin County

Trout Creek 47 *map 1 D-2*

Established as a station stop in February 1883 by the Northern Pacific Railroad, this town takes its name from the nearby stream. The post office opened under the same name in 1885. In 1910, the townsite was moved downstream to the opposite side of the creek, on a timbered area newly cleared by Jim Hylent. The town experi-enced an economic boost with construc-tion of the Noxon Rapids Dam (1955–56), upstream near Noxon. Elevation: 2,366 ft. Location: Sanders County

Troy 8 *map 1 B-1*

There are several stories about how Troy received its name. One states that E. L. Preston, a Great Northern Railway sur-veyor who helped lay out the townsite, named the town after Troy Morrow, the son of the family he boarded with at the time. According to another, the town received its name from the Troy system of units, used to measure gold, silver, and other pre-cious metals. A third has the name com-ing from a Great Northern civil engineer. As railroad construction began in the area in 1891, the town of Lake City came into existence. When the construction crews moved on, the camp declined. Residents hoping to salvage its existence changed the name to Troy in 1892. That fall, the Great Northern established a freight divi-sion point nearby, giving rise to West Troy. The original residents abandoned old Troy for the new townsite. Eventually, the name West Troy was shortened to Troy. The town draws economic support from the timber and mining industries. Elevation: 1,888 ft. Location: Lincoln County

Tullock Creek 1045 *map 14 E-3*

Tullock Creek is named for Samuel Tull-ock, a fur trader with the American Fur Company. In 1832, Tullock built Fort Cass, also known as Tullock's Fort, 3 miles below the mouth of the Bighorn River. The company abandoned the fort in 1835 because of Sioux opposition; Tullock built Fort Van Buren farther down the Yellowstone River that same year. Charles Larpenteur destroyed the fort in 1842 to prevent another company from gaining use of it. Location: Treasure and Big Horn counties

ern Railway came through the "Big Flat" in 1928 with its new line between Saco and Hogeland, it missed Turner. Undeterred, the citizens packed up their buildings and belongings and moved the town 2 miles to its present location along the railroad tracks. Elevation: 3,043 ft. Location: Blaine County

Turah 250 *map 10 C-2*

Turah, established in 1883, takes its name from Keturah, the daughter of N. C. Thrall, an assistant vice president of the Northern Pacific Railroad. Turah operated as both a stage station on the Mullan Road and a station on the Northern Pacific. Elevation: 3,323 ft. Location: Missoula County

Turner 820 *map 5 B-4*

In 1912, Henry Turner built a store on the east bank of Buckley Coulee and opened a post office later that year. The community of Turner was born. When the Great North-

Turquoise Lake 195 *map 10 A-2*

Turquoise Lake, at the headwaters of Glacier Creek in the Mission Mountains Wilderness, is named for the color produced by the glacial deposits in the lake. Elevation: 6,428 ft. Location: Missoula County

Tweedy Mountain 597 *map 18 B-4*

The highest peak in the eastern part of the Pioneer Mountains is Tweedy Mountain, named for Frank Tweedy, a USGS geologist who mapped the area in 1887. Elevation: 11,154 ft. Location: Beaverhead County

Daily coaches on the Whitehall to Dillon route, Stark Hotel, Twin Bridges, 1897
MHS 951-354

Twin Bridges 646 *map 19 B-2*

Brothers Mortimer H. and John T. Lott arrived in the Ruby Valley in 1864 and established themselves near the confluence of the Big Hole, Beaverhead, and Ruby rivers. After a year in the area, they realized that 4 Indian trails converged at a natural ford of the Beaverhead River. Recognizing that the area could become a logical transportation hub, they built toll bridges across the Beaverhead and Big Hole rivers, as well as constructed and improved existing roads. Originally referred to as the Bridges, Twin Bridges seemed a natural evolution of the name. Agriculture and mining supported early development of the community, although dryland farming suffered from what one resident referred to as "some killer years" that forced many families to abandon their homesteads. The Montana State Orphans Home operated in Twin Bridges from 1892 to 1975. Elevation: 4,633 ft. Location: Madison County

Twin Lakes 417 *map 10 E-4*

The Twin Lakes, only a few hundred yards apart, are in the Anaconda Range. Paralleling the access road is a flume, built in 1901 to bring water to Silver Lake. The flume eventually became part of the Butte Water Company's system that collected water from Storm Lake, Twin Lakes, and Georgetown Lake for use in the ore reduction operations of the Anaconda Company. Elevation: 7,630 ft. Location: Deer Lodge County

Two Dot 768 *map 12 D-4*

Two Dot, also spelled Twodot, is named for the "Two Dot" brand of local rancher H. J. Wilson. In 1900, Richard A. Harlow's Montana Railway ("Jawbone Railroad") reached the town, and the Two Dot post office opened. At the height of its prosperity in the 1910s, the town boasted a bank, newspaper, hotel, haberdashery, hardware store, and several other businesses. Cur-rently the town's only business is the Two Dot Bar. Elevation: 4,440 ft. Location: Wheatland County

Two Medicine fight site 214 *map 3 C-2*

Capt. Meriwether Lewis and 3 members of the expedition explored this area on their return from the Pacific Coast. On July 26, 1806, the group met 8 Blackfeet who camped with them on the Two Medicine River. Lewis mistakenly thought that these men were Gros Ventres. Next morning, Lewis caught the Blackfeet attempting to steal their guns and horses. A fight ensued, and 2 Blackfeet were killed. This incident was the only encounter with Native Americans during the expedition that ended in tragedy. Elevation: 3,641 ft. Location: Pondera County

Two Medicine River 238 *map 3 C-3*

Two interpretations circulate about the origin of the name Two Medicine—one cooperative, the other antagonistic. The cooperative interpretation describes 2 bands of Blackfeet planning medicine lodge ceremonies along this river in north-central Montana. When they realized they were there for a common purpose, they camped together. In the other interpretation, 2 factions developed after they camped, and so they split into 2 camps and held 2 medicine lodge ceremonies. The Blackfeet word for the river is Naht-oh-kee-oh-kahss-o-moch-sich-i-mee.

Main Hall, University of Montana, Missoula
MHS 951-452

Uall Creek 1091 *map 15 B-2*

Uall Creek, also You All Creek, was originally known as Elwell Creek, named in the
1870s for Captain Elwell of the 11th U.S.
Cavalry. In the 1880s, southern cowboys
driving cattle up to open range in east-
central Montana mispronounced it "You
All Creek," and the name stuck. Location:
Garfield County

UL Bend NWR 921 *map 14 A-2*

Early steamboat travelers often got off and
walked across this narrow spit of land to
stretch their legs, but the dramatic bend
in the Missouri River that now is part of
the UL Bend NWR was probably named
for the UL Ranch, established in 1902 by
the U. L. Cattle Company of Great Falls.
The company was founded by William M.
McGinnis, Frank Klepetko, Charles Goo-
dale, and others. The UL Bend NWR was
established in 1967 to protect migratory
bird habitat; it's also a reintroduction site
for the endangered black-footed ferret. UL
Bend is a "refuge within a refuge" as part
of the Charles M. Russell NWR. In 1976,
Congress designated 20,819 acres of the
UL Bend as wilderness. Location: Phillips
County

Ulm 403 *map 11 A-4*

William "Billy" Ulm was a cattle rancher
from Indiana who settled in this area with
his brothers Wilson and Lake Ulm in the
early 1880s. The post office opened in 1883,
and in 1887 Ulm became a stop on Col.
Charles Broadwater's Montana Central
Railway (later part of the Great Northern
Railway) as it progressed north from Butte
and Helena. The town took on new life in
1914 when the U. S. Bridge Company built
a bridge across the Missouri River, providing easy access for farmers to bring grain to
the Ulm elevators. The bridge remained in
use until 1983, when it was replaced. Elevation: 3,345 ft. Location: Cascade County

Unionville 428 *map 11 D-3*

The rich strike at Last Chance Gulch
in July 1864 drew hundreds to this area,
including James Whitlatch, the discoverer
of Helena's first quartz lode in September 1864. The town of Unionville sprang
from his Whitlatch-Union Mine, named
for the discoverer and the Union army he
served during the Civil War. The camp
included stores, saloons, a Chinese laundry, boardinghouses, and a school, as well
as an extensive complex of stamp mills
and warehouses. The largest producer of
gold bullion in the United States by the
early 1870s, the Unionville district was
prolific until 1897, when the gold-bearing
lode in the Whitlatch-Union Mine disappeared under a fault. Efforts to relocate it
failed, and the mine closed. Other mines
in the district survived for a time before
they also closed. By the early twentieth
century, fewer than 100 people remained
in Unionville. Although it never regained
prominence as a mining camp, Unionville
today thrives as a bedroom community for
Helena, its mining heritage still evident.
Elevation: 4,918 ft. Location: Lewis and
Clark County

University of Montana 230
map 10 C-2

The Montana legislature created this university in 1893. Fifty students enrolled in
the first classes, held in 1895 in a refurbished schoolhouse donated by the Missoula community. Between 1897 and 1908,
A. J. Gibson designed the first campus
buildings, which were constructed on 40
donated acres. The new campus opened
in 1899. George Carsley and his New York
mentor, Cass Gilbert, designed a new
campus master plan in 1918 that allowed
orderly expansion after World War I. Federal grants financed 5 additional buildings
on the Missoula campus between 1935
and 1939. Originally called Montana State
University, its name has undergone several
changes. It became the State University of

Montana (1913–35), then was again Montana State University (1935–65), and finally the University of Montana (since 1965). It is listed in the National Register. Enrollment in 2006 was nearly 14,000 students, in 15 schools and colleges and more than 70 departments. *Rolling Stone* magazine called the University of Montana the "most scenic campus in America." There are 4 affiliated campuses: Montana Tech at Butte, the College of Technology at Helena, Western Montana College at Dillon, and the College of Technology at Missoula. Elevation: 3,220 ft. Location: Missoula County

University of Montana–Western
694 *map 19 C-1*
In 1893, the Montana legislature chartered the state's original 4 educational units of higher learning, at Bozeman, Missoula, Butte, and Dillon. The State Normal School was established at Dillon to train Montana's schoolteachers. Construction on the first campus building, Main Hall, began in 1896, and it was completed in time for the first day of classes on September 7, 1897. Over the years, the school has undergone several name changes: State Normal School (1897–1903), State Normal College (1903–1949), Western Montana College of Education (1949–1965), Western Montana College (1965–1988), Western Montana College of the University of Montana (1988–2001). Now known officially as the University of Montana–Western, the college continues its principal role of training Montana's teachers. Main Hall remains the focal point of the National Register–listed historic campus. Elevation: 5,120 ft. Location: Beaverhead County

University of Montana Biological Station
135 *map 2 D-2*
Founded by University of Montana biologist Morton Elrod in 1899, the University of Montana Biological Station is the nation's oldest active biological research

station. The 160-acre site on Flathead Lake's Yellow Bay is home year-round to students and researchers with an interest in the aquatic ecology of Flathead Lake and its river system. It has grown from a single brick building in 1915 to 60 buildings with a state-of-the-art limnological lab built in 1988. Yellow Bay is named for the yellow outcrop of rock, part of the Algonkian Formation, above the bay. Elevation: 2,916 ft. Location: Lake County

Upper Missouri River Breaks National Monument 1008 *map 5 E-2*
The area that now comprises the Upper Missouri River Breaks National Monument in central Montana has witnessed events of critical importance in the history of the state. Lewis and Clark spent 3 weeks during May and June 1805 within the present boundaries of the monument. The American Fur Company maintained several trading posts in the area from 1831 to 1845. At the mouth of the Judith River, Father Pierre-Jean De Smet and Father Nicholas Point celebrated mass with members of the Blackfeet and Salish tribes in 1846, in an attempt to bring peace between them. In 1855, Isaac I. Stevens conducted treaty negotiations with several tribes to establish hunting boundaries and to obtain access for military roads, railroads, and telegraph lines across northern Montana. Steamboats plied the river through the monument from 1859 to 1890, transporting furs down the river and bringing mining equipment and other goods up the river. Several large ranches, including the PN and the DHS, were in the area. The monument was established by presidential proclamation on January 17, 2001, during the last days of the Bill Clinton administration, for the purpose of preserving the area's scenic, wildlife, historical, and cultural values.

Upper Waterton Lake 69 *map 2 A-2*

Capt. Thomas W. Blakiston, a member of the Palliser Expedition, named this lake for British naturalist Charles Waterton in 1858. Supported by the Royal Geographic Society, the Palliser Expedition (1857–60), led by John Palliser, undertook the task of exploring a route along the international border from the Red River Colony (Winnipeg, Manitoba) through the Rocky Mountains. In a report of the International Border Survey of 1878, Waterton Lake is referred to as Chief Mountain Lake. Elevation: 4,200 ft. Location: Glacier National Park

Upsata Lake 257 *map 10 B-4*

This prairie pothole lake is named for Ole Opsata, an early settler in the area. Over time, the name was transcribed as Upsata. Elevation: 4,136 ft. Location: Powell County

Ursuline Academy 430 *map 12 A-1*

The sisters of the Order of St. Ursula came to Montana in 1884 to establish schools for Indians. When the homestead movement created a need for additional urban educational facilities, the Great Falls Townsite Company offered the sisters any 2 city blocks. They chose this site that overlooks the city but is removed from the bustle of the city's center, for its tranquility. In 1912, the Ursuline Academy opened its doors to day and boarding students of all denominations. The campus grounds hold the academy, a detached gymnasium, and 2 shrines. Iconography by Sister Raphael Schweda graces the academy's interior. Great Falls architect George Shanley chose the Collegiate Gothic style to reflect the academy's commitment to learning and its ecclesiastical associations, but the building also represents the culmination of the Ursulines' mission to bring education and culture to Montana's youth. The sisters continued their teaching mission at the National Register–listed Ursuline Academy until it became the Ursuline Centre in 1971. They still serve the community and graciously open their home to ecumenical activities. Elevation: 3,438 ft. Location: Cascade County

Ursuline Convent of the Sacred Heart 1141 *map 15 D-3*

The first Ursuline convent in Montana opened in Miles City on January 18, 1884. Six teaching sisters of the Order of St. Ursula from Toledo, Ohio, came to Montana, invited by Father Eli Lindesmith, the chaplain of Fort Keogh. Bishop John B. Brondel requested that 3 of the sisters settle in Miles City. The 3 remaining "Lady Black Robes" traveled south, led by Superior Mother Amadeus Dunne, to establish St. Labre's Mission among the Northern Cheyennes. The Convent of the Sacred Heart enrolled sons and daughters of settlers from all over eastern Montana. Twenty dollars a month paid for their "board, tuition and washing." In 1897, fire destroyed the convent. Local ranchers and merchants donated land, and prominent Helena architect Charles S. Haire was commissioned to design a new academy. The 3-story brick and stone structure, listed in the National Register, was completed in 1902. Dominican sisters of Everett, Washington, and Presentation sisters of Aberdeen, South Dakota, taught at the convent until 1978. From 1978 to the 1990s, the building housed the Miles City Mental Health Center, and it currently houses a community center. Elevation: 2,376 ft. Location: Custer County

Utica 701 *map 12 C-4*

Jack Waite, P. W. Korell, Jack Murphy, S. S. Hobson, and Joseph Cutting spent a cold Christmas Eve in a cabin at the foothills of the Little Belt Mountains in 1880. Legend has it that, in jest, one of them suggested they establish a town, to which one of his companions replied, "Anyone who would start a town here is crazy." The idea, however, took hold, and they agreed to name the new town Utica in honor of Utica, New York, home of that state's insane asylum. Perhaps a more plausible version of the story tells that Cutting, Murphy, and Korell arrived in the area and named the new town after their home town in New York. In 1881, Cutting started several businesses along the Judith River west of Hobson, running a saloon, express office, store, post office, and hotel from one building. Guests spending the night enjoyed the comfort of the floor and the warmth of their bedroll. The new town prospered with the development of mining in nearby Yogo Canyon as well as the establishment of the stage line between Great Falls and Billings. Montana artist Charlie Russell immortalized the tiny community in 1907 with his painting *A Quiet Day in Utica,* also known as *Tin Canning a Dog,* commissioned by store owner Charles Lehman. Elevation: 4,467 ft. Location: Judith Basin County

Chinese merchant Chung Own, Virginia City, c. 1900
MHS 956-176

Valier 246 *map 3 C-2*

In 1908, Charley and W. G. Conrad sold their 200,000-acre 7 Block Ranch to W. G. Cargill, of La Crosse, Wisconsin, for $1 million. The following year, Cargill and Peter Valier, a railroad construction engineer also from La Crosse, incorporated the Valier Townsite Company to build a town on the shores of the newly made Lake Frances. This reservoir is named for Frances Conrad, the wife of W. G. Conrad. Cargill applied to the State of Montana under the Carey Land Act for an irrigation project that, in 1927, resulted in Swift Dam, built in the mountains west of Valier. It impounded 5,600 acres of water and created Birch Creek Reservoir, which is 6 miles long and 3 miles wide. North of Valier is a place known as "Rock City," where wind and water have eroded the Marias River Canyon into an unusual grouping of rock formations along the cliffs. The Valier Public School is listed in the National Register. Elevation: 3,812 ft. Location: Pondera County

Valley County 1029 *map 6 D-4*

The Montana legislature created Valley County in 1893 from Dawson County. This northeastern Montana county takes its name from the topography of the Milk River and Missouri River valleys, now subsumed by Fort Peck Reservoir. One of Montana's largest counties in area, it encompasses part of the Fort Peck Indian Reservation. Glasgow is the county seat.

Vananda 1067 *map 14 D-4*

Vananda was established as a station stop on the Milwaukee Road in 1910, but by the 1920s it began to lose population due to drought. The origin of the name remains a mystery. Elevation: 2,717 ft. Location: Rosebud County

Vance Lodge 44 *map 2 B-1*

Outdoorsman and adventurer Andrew Vance came to Montana from Iowa in 1880. He found work hunting buffalo in the Yellowstone Valley to feed Northern Pacific Railroad crews. In the ensuing decades, Vance guided visitors in Yellowstone National Park

Vananda, 1921
MHS 951-551

and participated in the Klondike gold rush in the Yukon. In 1914, he, his wife, Ella, and daughters, Maud and May, staked a 160-acre homestead claim here among the aspen groves and meadows near the North Fork of the Flathead River. Andy worked on a trail crew in Glacier National Park, ran a sawmill, and hunted and trapped for food, while Ella kept an extensive garden. In 1920, he began building a 2-story lodge of square-notched logs to replace their original cabin. Ben Hensen scored all the logs, Jack Reuter hewed the timbers, and a man named McBlair did the finish work. The lodge comfortably accommodated family as well as guests, whom Andy guided into the wilds of northern Montana and Canada; the lodge also became a regular site for hosting social gatherings of the scattered residents of the remote North Fork community. Andy died in 1924 when he was hit by a train near Belton, and Ella died in 1929. Daughter May married Ben Hensen, who had helped build the lodge. Hensen became postmaster, and the ranch served as post office for a time during the 1930s. Since 1937, it has been a seasonal home to members of the Hensen family. Elevation: 3,554 ft. Location: Flathead County

Vandalia 1011 *map 6 C-4*

One explanation of the name Vandalia is that a band of vandals or beggars raided the camp of an early Great Northern Railway survey party. More likely it was named by James J. Hill for Vandalia, Illinois. Situated on a siding of the Great Northern Railway's main line, Vandalia later served a dispersed ranching community. In 1905, Glasgow businessmen and others in the region began lobbying President Theodore Roosevelt for federal funding to construct an irrigation project using water from the Milk River. As a result of their successful efforts, the Milk River Irrigation Project was born. Vandalia Diversion Dam, a major dam on the river, was completed in 1921. Elevation: 2,125 ft. Location: Valley County

Vandalia South Canal 1034 *map 7 D-1*

The U.S. Reclamation Service built the Vandalia South Canal in 1915–17 as part of the Milk River Irrigation Project. The canal ran 46 miles, from the Vandalia Diversion Dam to the vicinity of Nashua in Valley County.

Vaughn 375 *map 11 A-4*

In 1869, Robert Vaughn homesteaded in the Sun River valley near "the Leavings," a Mullan Road stage station. A narrow-gauge railroad, the Great Falls & Canada Railway, dubbed the "Turkey Trail," entered the area just short of the Vaughn ranch in 1890, carrying coal and passengers between Great Falls and Lethbridge, Alberta. The tracks were rebuilt in 1903 to standard gauge, and the Great Northern Railway purchased the line in 1907. Homesteaders in the valley picked up their supplies at this end-of-the-track community. Capt. Tom Couch, general manager of the Boston & Montana Consolidated Copper and Silver Mining Company of Great Falls, purchased the ranch from Vaughn in 1889. Couch platted the townsite at the end of the railroad line in 1910, and Thomas C. Power built the Sunnyside Mercantile Store in Vaughn the same year. Elevation: 3,364 ft. Location: Cascade County

Vaux Reservoirs 1212 *map 8 E-3*

Vaux Reservoirs, on Lone Tree Creek, are actually 2 piggy-backed reservoirs. Augustus Vaux, a native of Minnesota, had settled in the area about 1906 and opened a lumber business in Sidney. Vaux served as Sidney's mayor from 1913 to 1916 and was active in the Sidney Chamber of Commerce. Vaux, who owned the Lone Tree Ranch, built Vaux Dam No. 1 in 1916 to provide a swimming spot for Sidney residents; he later added a dance pavilion. The chamber of commerce built 2 bathhouses at the reservoir in 1924. Elevation: 2,064 ft. Location: Richland County

Vermiculite Mountain 17   *map 1   C-2*

The name of this mountain in the Purcell Range refers to vermiculite, a mineral that exfoliates under heat, making it useful in construction, agriculture, and horticulture, but primarily as insulation and in fire-proofing. It is unknown who named the mountain. The word *vermiculite* comes from the Latin word *vermiculus,* "little worms," which aptly describes the physical reaction vermiculite undergoes when exposed quickly to heat: it expands by exfoliation and creates wormlike pieces. Edward N. Alley discovered the Rainy Creek vermiculite deposit during World War I while looking for vanadium. According to the story, the flame from his candle came into contact with the mica on the mine tunnel's wall, causing it to swell. Alley worked to develop a market for vermiculite under the name Zonolite. He sold his company in 1934 to the Zonolite Company, which merged with the Universal Zonolite Insulation Company in 1939. They shortened the name to Zonolite Company in 1948. Demand for the mineral during World War II expanded mining operations, and in 1963 W. R. Grace purchased the mine on Vermiculite Mountain and the mill located at the confluence of Rainy Creek and the Kootenai River. By 1980, W. R. Grace employed 200 people. The high concentration of tremolite asbestos in the vermiculite resulted in a public health crisis for workers as well as other residents in the town of Libby. The EPA is currently conducting a massive cleanup at the old mine and mill site, and at contaminated areas in and around Libby. Elevation: 4,241 ft. Location: Lincoln County

Vermilion River 48   *map 1   D-2*

Gold prospectors began placer mining near the mouth of the Vermilion River in 1867, resulting in the brief emergence of a mining camp. The camp was short-lived, however, and the origin of the river's name remains unknown, though it might relate to the red color of the rock along the river. The Vermillion Mine, spelled with 2 *l*'s, operated sporadically from the 1890s to the 1940s, primarily as a silver-lead property under a variety of owners and lessees, before closing. A post office served the area from 1889 to 1905. About 13 miles up the river is Vermilion Falls, which cascades down through a narrow gorge in the Cabinet Mountains. Also in the area are Vermilion Peak and Vermilion Pass, as was, for a brief time, the town of Vermilion.

Veseth Reservoir 886   *map 6   E-1*

Veseth Reservoir is named for the Olaf and Einar Veseth families, Norwegian immigrants who established the Veseth sheep ranch along Little Warm Creek and Beaver Creek. Ole and Einar settled in Montana in the 1880s, and some of their descendants, especially Mons Veseth, developed the ranch into a large sheep operation. Elevation: 2,699 ft. Location: Phillips County

Victor 291   *map 10   D-1*

Located on the west side of the Bitterroot River, 4 miles east of the mouth of Sweat House Canyon, Victor began as a community named Sweat House, after the cleansing sweathouses the Salish built along the creek. Frank Woody platted the townsite in 1881 and called it Garfield, after President James Garfield. James Garfield had actually traveled to the Bitterroot Valley in 1872 to negotiate the removal of the Salish from the valley. However, that name was already taken as a post office. Ironically, at a public meeting the name was changed to Victor, to honor Salish chief Victor, who had served as a leader of the Bitterroot Salish from 1842 to 1870. Woody and other Missoula-area businessmen were interested in developing the valley, due to recent silver strikes on Big Creek, Bear Creek, and Gash Creek. A. B. Hammond was instrumental in funding and constructing a branch line called the Bitter Root Valley Railroad, running from the Northern Pacific Railroad's line south into the Bitterroot Valley, to tap into the mining districts created from these silver ore deposits. Victor made an unsuccessful bid for the contested Ravalli County seat in 1898, losing out to Stevensville, which in turn lost to Hamilton. Repeal of the Sherman Silver Purchase Act in 1893 hit Victor hard, forcing many of the local mines to close and the town's economy to nosedive. The town's fortunes reversed in the middle to late 1890s with the growth of the timber industry and agricultural enterprises. The lumber mills in the Bitterroot Valley found a steady market in the Butte mines. Although the timber industry has faded in economic importance, farming and ranching continue to sustain Victor's economy. Elevation: 3,413 ft. Location: Ravalli County

Vida 1120 *map 7 E-4*

When August C. Nefzger opened a post office in 1911, he named it for his daughter Vida, who had just married Orville Todd. In 1919, the town of Vida ran for county seat of McCone County but lost to Circle in a narrow election. In 1951, Vida moved west, to the site of the small town of Presserville, to take advantage of its location on MT 13. Elevation: 2,370 ft. Location: McCone County

Virgelle 566 *map 4 D-3*

Virgelle derives its name from Virgil and Ella Blankenbaker, who were among the first to homestead this area when former Blackfeet Indian Reservation lands along the Missouri River were opened to non-Indian settlement in 1889. Blankenbaker's large sheep ranch prompted the Great Northern Railway to build a siding to this site near his home in 1900. The Virgelle post office opened in 1902. The Enlarged Homestead Act of 1909 brought farmers to the region, and in 1912 Blankenbaker built a large, well-designed mercantile

that offered upstairs lodgings for railroad crews. In 1913, he established a ferry across the river; a free ferry still operates here. At the end of the decade, a bank, lumberyard, and 2 grain elevators lined Virgelle's streets, though even at its peak the town had a population of only about 30. Blankenbaker died in 1936 while serving a second term in the legislature. The mercantile continued to serve the local population until the 1960s. It then stood empty until owner-outfitter Don Sorensen reopened it in 1975. The Virgelle mercantile and bank are listed in the National Register. Elevation: 2,574 ft. Location: Chouteau County

Virgelle Ferry 568 *map 4 D-3*

The ferry is located at Virgelle, just upstream of Coal Banks Landing, where steamboats took on coal during their voyages up and down the Missouri River, and where they offloaded passengers and cargo when low water prevented them from reaching Fort Benton. Fort Benton's newspaper, the *River Press*, reported that the ferry would be "a great accommodation to the traveling public in that part of Chouteau County." John C. Meyers built the ferry for $1,050 in 1913. Virgil Blankenbaker operated it for many years, until Chouteau County purchased it. The county paid ferrymen $80 per month and provided the ferry operator's family with a residence on the north side of the river. It upgraded the old ferryboat with an International tractor engine around 1950 and replaced the original boat in the early 1960s. The ferry, still in operation today, runs from March to November. Elevation: 2,510 ft. Location: Chouteau County

Virginia City NHL 734 *map 19 C-3*

Prospectors found placer gold along an alder-choked streambed in this area in spring 1863. Thousands came to work claims, and others came to mine the miners. Confederate sympathizers named the townsite Varina, after the wife of Confederate president Jefferson Davis, but Union supporter Dr. G. G. Bissell changed the name to Virginia when he filed the official townsite documents. A brief period of lawlessness and vigilante justice ended with the creation of Montana Territory in spring 1864. Virginia City quickly rose to be territorial capital (1865–75), but the placer gold soon played out. Bypassed on the railroad route in the 1880s, the town was saved from abandonment by gold dredging operations from the 1890s to the 1940s. Great Falls legislator Charles Bovey and his wife, Sue, began buying the dilapidated gold rush–era buildings in the 1940s. Virginia City became one of the first major preservation efforts in the West and was designated a NHL in 1961. It is the Madison County seat. In 1997, the State of Montana purchased the Bovey properties, which now mix with privately owned homes and businesses. Elevation: 5,775 ft. Location: Madison County

Volborg 1186 *map 23 A-4*
In 1912, Tillie Volborg Osmenson Allen and her husband, Charles M. "Curlew" Allen, were the first homesteaders to file their homestead claim on Pumpkin Creek, establishing a post office the same year. Today Volborg is still little more than a post office and country store. Elevation: 2,993 ft. Location: Custer County

City Hotel, Windham, 1920
MHS 951-803

Wagner 878 *map 6 C-1*

Andrew Davidson platted this town in 1910, near the Great Northern Railway's main line west of Malta. The town soon boasted 150 residents as well as a general store, blacksmith shop, and lumberyard. The Great Northern owned a coal chute here as well. The community's prosperity, however, faded during the drought of the 1920s. The origin of the name remains unknown. Elevation: 2,299 ft. Location: Phillips County

Wahkpa Chu'gn Buffalo Jump
631 *map 5 C-1*

As many as 30 million buffalo once roamed the North American prairies, migrating seasonally in herds of 25 to 300. Knowing the habits of these animals allowed communal hunting, and Indians gathered at this place where the rolling prairie suddenly gives way to steep river valley walls, to drive hundreds of buffalo over the precipice. At the cliff's base, tribal members dispatched injured animals, and butchering began at once. Discovered in the 1950s, the site has been under the protection of Hill County since 1964; Wahkpa Chu'gn, pronounced "walk-paw-chew-gun," is the Assiniboine term for "Milk River." Archaeological investigation at Wahkpa Chu'gn reveals that native peoples used this site extensively for at least 2,000 years. Although more buffalo jumps have been found in Montana than in any other Northern Plains area, most are poorly preserved; at Wahkpa Chu'gn, an exceptional level of preservation provides a unique and visually stunning chronology of use over time. The site is listed in the National Register. Elevation: 2,604 ft. Location: Hill County

Walkerville 517 *map 11 E-1*

Walkerville claims the title as the highest incorporated town in Montana, at elevation 6,309 feet. The town is named for Joseph R. Walker, one of the 4 Salt Lake City brothers who financed Marcus Daly's $25,000 purchase of the Alice Mine in 1875. The Alice Mine, discovered by Rollo Butcher on January 2, 1875, proved an economic mainstay for Walkerville. While Butcher is credited with constructing the first dwelling in 1877, the main street is named for Marcus Daly, who managed the Alice Mine until 1880. Walkerville incorporated in 1890. Although silver mining began declining in the 1890s, copper mines such as the Belle of Butte, Minnie Healy, and Gray Rock ensured the town's survival. The community reached a peak population of 4,000. During World War II, 247 men served in the armed forces, representing one tenth of the town's population. When the Anaconda Company began open-pit mining, they sought to expand the Alice Pit in 1960. However, the residents of Walkerville, along with mayor Jimmy Shea, squared off against the powerful company, halting the expansion and saving the community from extinction. It is now part of the Butte–Anaconda Historic District. Although Walkerville may seem like an extension of Butte, it retains its own identity and strong sense of community. Elevation: 6,309 ft. Location: Silver Bow County

War Horse NWR 888 *map 13 B-4*

According to a Petroleum County history and a newspaper article published in the *Helena Independent Record* in 1979, Walter Winnett originally named this landform in central Montana War Horse Butte. According to the county history, Winnett named the butte for its resemblance to Native American war tipis. However, according to Ruth Hoffman, the original name of War House was corrupted to War Horse. In the news article she stated that during the 1800s, both the Crows and Blackfeet claimed the territory and "had war houses—stone walls which they hid behind to watch their enemies—on the butte." She further claimed that remnants of these war houses existed in the 1940s. In 1912, the Winnett Irrigation Company began constructing a dam on Fords Creek and a canal to bring water 6 miles to War Horse Lake (named after the butte), to irrigate both sides of the Buffalo Creek Valley and supply its 55 miles of ditches. The company applied to the State Water Conservation Board to renovate the intake ditches and dam in 1935, and between 1935 and 1937 the CCC worked on the project, installing a massive reinforced concrete headgate structure. War Horse NWR has 3 units—War Horse Lake, Wild Horse Lake, and Yellow Water Reservoir—all administered by the Charles M. Russell NWR. Elevation: 3,138 ft. Location: Petroleum County

Ward Peak 705 *map 19 B-3*
Ward Peak, at the head of Washington Creek in the Tobacco Root Mountains, is named for Henry Ward, a University of Rochester professor of geology who began mining in the area in 1865. Ward later gathered one of the finest meteorite collections in the nation. Elevation: 10,267 ft. Location: Madison County

Warm Springs 448 *map 11 E-1*
Louis Belanger found these warm springs in 1865. Issuing from the top of the "Mound," the springs' temperature ranged from 130° to 170°F. He purchased the land around the springs and later was instrumental in developing a hotel and bathhouses to serve the public, who visited for medicinal purposes. The post office opened in 1871. Drs. A. H. Mitchell and Charles F. Mussigbrod then purchased the facility and, at the behest of Territorial Governor Benjamin Potts, established a privately operated mental hospital at the site. Warm Springs became a "resort for the sick" as well as a recreational facility. The State of Montana purchased the hospital in 1912 and renamed it Warm Springs State Hospital

in 1965. The patient population peaked at 1,954 in 1980; it was designated a mental health facility in 1983. Warm Springs State Hospital underwent major renovations in 1997 at the cost of $16.5 million. Elevation: 4,815 ft. Location: Deer Lodge County

Warm Springs Creek 450 *map 10 E-4*
A tributary of the Clark Fork River, flowing out of the Flint Creek Range, this creek was a source of water for early smelting operations in Anaconda. Warm Springs Creek derives its name for its close proximity to the hot springs just west of where the creek enters the Clark Fork, the site of Warm Springs State Hospital. Location: Deer Lodge County

Warm Springs Mound 447 *map 11 E-1*
A curious sedimentary cone with a thermal spring bubbling inside rises nearly 40 feet high from the Deer Lodge Valley floor. On cold, clear days, with steam issuing from the mound, it resembles a large Indian lodge with smoke curling out the top. Thick grasses at the base and the saline deposits attracted hundreds of white-tailed deer. The Shoshones knew the cone as It Soo'-Ke-En Car'-Ne. The French translated the Shoshone name as La Loge du Chevreuil, "Lodge of the white-tailed deer." The French name eventually denoted not just the mound but the valley as well, and settlers later shortened the French translation to Deer Lodge. Elevation: 4,828 ft. Location: Deer Lodge County

Warm Springs Ponds 462 *map 11 E-1*
In 1911, the Anaconda Company attempted to curtail the amount of tailings washing downstream from Butte, carried by Silver Bow Creek to the Clark Fork River. The company constructed a 20-foot-high tailings dam on the creek at Warm Springs, called Pond No. 1. Five years later, they constructed a second dam upstream, Pond

No. 2. In 1959, the company finished a 28-foot dam farther upstream, Pond No. 3, which eight years later was converted into a treatment pond where they injected lime, intended to precipitate out heavy metals by raising the pH level of the creek. Atlantic Richfield Company (ARCO) acquired the Anaconda Company in 1977. Complying with Superfund requirements, ARCO reconstructed the pond system and bypass at a cost of $45 million, to improve water quality and the Clark Fork River system fishery. Currently, Montana Fish, Wildlife & Parks leases the ponds and surrounding area for management as a wildlife conservation area and to provide public recreation access to the ponds. Elevation: 4,859 ft. Location: Deer Lodge County

Warren 1038   *map 21 C-4*
Originally a stop on the Chicago, Burlington & Quincy Railroad, Warren was a shipping point for the Big Horn Calcium Company, whose limestone quarry in the nearby Pryor Mountains supplied many western sugar refineries. Although the origin of the name is unknown, a post office operated here from 1911 to 1953. Elevation: 4,419 ft. Location: Carbon County

Warrick 668   *map 5 D-1*
Warrick grew out of the frustration of one man, ranch manager Dan Arnold, of the NL Horse Ranch on Birch Creek, who tired of sending a cowboy to Big Sandy to fetch the mail. In 1890, he petitioned for a post office at the ranch headquarters. Arnold, a Texan, named the new post office Warrick, his wife's maiden name, and Mowny Arnold became postmaster. The post office continued operation until 1957. Elevation: 3,984 ft. Location: Chouteau County

Washoe 999   *map 21 C-2*
The Anaconda Company created, named, and owned the company town of Washoe. Founded in 1907, the town supplied coal for the smelters in Anaconda until cheaper hydroelectric power slowed the demand for coal. The name Washoe is derived from the town and county of the same name in Nevada, where Anaconda also had interests. The company's smelter in the town of Anaconda was also named Washoe. Elevation: 5,002 ft. Location: Carbon County

Wassweiler Hotel and Bath Houses 457
map 11 D-3
Ferdinand and Caroline Wassweiler settled here in 1865 on 160 acres and operated a small hotel and bathhouse. They gained title to the land and 2 hot springs near Tenmile Creek in 1869. The mineral water offered area miners a welcome respite from the dusty gold-mining camp at Last Chance Gulch. In 1874, the Wassweilers sold the east half of their property and water rights to Col. Charles Broadwater. In 1883, the Wassweilers built this hotel and attendant bathhouses on their remaining acreage. Broadwater built the grand Broadwater Hotel and Natatorium, which opened in 1889, on his property. The Wassweiler Hotel and Bath Houses continued to operate here until 1904. Broadwater's hotel, however, never attracted the clientele he had envisioned, and it began to deteriorate. The far-famed natatorium closed after it sustained earthquake damage in 1935. The Broadwater Hotel was razed in 1976. Some of the landscaping and a portion of the billiard hall remain. The Wassweiler Hotel and Bath Houses, listed in the National Register, are the only hot springs hotel structures now left in the Helena area. Elevation: 3,978 ft. Location: Lewis and Clark County

Wassweiler Hotel and Bath Houses, near Helena, c. 1870
Detail, MHS 951-609

Waterloo 628 *map 19 A-2*

Waterloo traces its origins to the arrival of gold miners along the Jefferson River in 1864. According to one story, residents named the town after the Battle of Waterloo due to friction over the location of the post office, which opened in 1900. Among the interesting stories of the area in the Madison County history, *Pioneer Trails and Trials,* is one about Emily Foster and a trapper named Welsh who went into business selling soft soap to area residents; the trapper supplied the beaver fat and Mrs. Foster did the rest. The community store and post office closed in 1971. Elevation: 4,463 ft. Location: Madison County

Weigand Reservoir 838 *map 5 D-4*

Weigand Reservoir is named for the Weigand (Albert and Katherine) family who resided on the Fort Belknap Indian Reservation around 1913. Although sources remain vague on the exact date, Lone Tree Dam was constructed around 1948 as part of the Fort Belknap Irrigation Project, impounding water from Mud Creek.

Elevation: 2,540 ft. Location: Blaine and Phillips counties

West Blacktail Creek 1051 *map 14 D-4*

This Rosebud County creek is named for the black-tailed deer found along its banks.

West Butte (Toole) 305 *map 3 A-4*

The westernmost of the Sweet Grass Hills buttes, West Butte is the tallest of the trio. Native American people, including the Blackfeet, Plains Crees, Assiniboines, Salish, Kootenais, and Gros Ventres, all attach spiritual and cultural significance to this island range. Elevation: 6,983 ft. Location: Toole County

West Glacier 74 *map 2 C-2*

Located south of Lake McDonald, the town of Belton began in 1892. Great Northern Railway officials named it Bell's Town, or Belton, for Daniel Webster Bell, who had a mining claim nearby. He had cut ties for the railroad and had been a camp cook for the survey crews in 1890. With the creation of Glacier National Park in 1910, the community became the west entrance to the park. To promote its tourism potential, in 1949 residents changed the name to West Glacier. Elevation: 3,196 ft. Location: Flathead County

West Goat Peak 431 *map 10 E-3*

West Goat Peak is the highest peak in the Anaconda-Pintler Wilderness. It is named, along with East Goat Peak, for the mountain goats that frequent the area. Elevation: 10,793 ft. Location: Deer Lodge County

West Quincy Granite Quarry 613
map 12 A-3

Volcanic activity eons ago laid down this substantial granite deposit, known as the Shonkin Sag laccolith. In 1914, I. E. Jenkins and W. H. Guyor began formal quarrying, naming their company after their home town of West Quincy, Massachusetts, the nation's "granite capital." Brothers J. Arthur and Paul Rudin, along with Carl Johnson, all natives of Sweden by way of Massachusetts, leased the West Quincy Quarry in 1916. They marketed their stone as "Lone Tree Granite," named after the nearby ranch and former stage stop. These 2 companies quarried granite from the 2 tiers of the outcropping, employing 27 workers at their peak. In 1928, the Tanners, Lone Tree ranchers, purchased the quarry land and then leased it to the Rudin brothers. Rudin Bros. Granite Company supplied the stone for buildings, monuments, and engraved markers across Montana, including the boulder that marks cowboy artist Charlie Russell's grave. After Art Rudin's death in 1939, Johnson and Rudin's 2 sons operated the quarry. Johnson purchased the business in 1943, operating it into the 1960s. The quarry is listed in the National Register. Elevation: 3,164 ft. Location: Chouteau County

West Yellowstone 905 *map 20 E-1*

Hoping to tap into the growing tourist trade of Yellowstone National Park, the Union Pacific constructed an extension of the Oregon Short Line branch from Ashton, Idaho, to the west side of park. The first train arrived on June 11, 1908, at this community originally referred to as Riverside. The town's name as well as the post office designation changed to Yellowstone in 1909. The community received a boost in 1910 when James Moore blazed a trail from Taylor Fork, connecting the Gallatin Valley to the west entrance of Yellowstone National Park. Work to build a better road through the Gallatin Canyon to the park began in 1919, and by 1927 tourists poured through the canyon by rail and motorcar. The town changed its name to West Yellowstone in 1920 and incorporated in 1966. Train service to West Yellowstone ended in 1960. Today the community thrives as a service center for park visitors. Elevation: 6,664 ft. Location: Gallatin County

West Yellowstone Oregon Short Line Terminus 907 *map 20 E-1*

In 1905, Union Pacific officials began constructing a branch line in the pine-forested wilderness from Ashton, Idaho, to the western edge of Yellowstone National Park. As the company laid the final tracks in 1907, Samuel P. Eagle, Alex Stuart, Charles Arnet, and L. A. Murray applied for commercial leases, prompting the USFS to survey and plat a townsite. West Yellowstone became a thriving permanent settlement, dominated by the beautiful 1909 Union Pacific depot. Designed by the Union Pacific engineering office, it combines Richardsonian elements with rustic exposed wood and hoodlike roofs. In 1925, Gilbert Stanley Underwood, later noted for his imaginative resort designs and railway passenger stations, drew up the plans for the new dining lodge and employee dormitories. Welded tuff that was gathered along the railroad line enhances the

Main Street, Westby, c. 1920
MHS 951-612

rustic appearance of foundations, walls, colossal chimneys, and massive fireplaces, complementing the log construction. This collection of railroad buildings constructed between 1905 and 1927 has withstood severe weather, major fires, rebuilding, and expansion. The district, listed in the National Register, stands today as a rare reminder of early park tourism and a tribute to a fine architect. Elevation: 6,669 ft. Location: Gallatin County

Westby 1207 *map 8 A-3*

The most northeasterly town in Montana actually began its life in North Dakota. Like many towns in the region, Westby came into being when homesteaders began to filter in from 1903 to 1908. Because many Danes settled in the area, when it came time to choose a name, they picked Westby—"West" because the town was the farthest west in North Dakota and "by" (pronounced "bee"), Danish for "town." The post office opened in 1910. When the Minneapolis, St. Paul & Sault Ste. Marie Railway came through the area in 1913, res-

idents looked on with consternation as the railroad bypassed their community. Undeterred, in 1914 they moved the town to the Montana–North Dakota state line and set up along the railroad tracks. With North Dakota a state where the sale of alcohol was illegal, and Montana a state where it was legal, Westby residents, as one wag put it, "split the town with the business 'improper' on one side of the line and the business 'proper' on the other side." The *Great Falls Tribune* reported in February 1990 that Westby was exploring different ideas about enterprises to boost its economy—these ran the gamut from harvesting wild baby's breath flowers to raising potbelly pigs and fainting goats. Elevation: 2,107 ft. Location: Sheridan County

Wheatland County 796 *map 13 D-2*

The Montana legislature created Wheatland County from Meagher and Sweet Grass counties in 1917, with Harlowton as the county seat. The county's name reflects the area's agricultural mainstay.

Whitcomb Lake 915 *map 6 D-2*

Whitcomb Lake is named for Charles Whitcomb, born in Wisconsin in 1865. Upon his arrival to the Malta area in 1897, Whitcomb partnered with Samuel Dennison to purchase a 2,000-acre ranch along Beaver Creek, south of Malta. Whitcomb also constructed a cyanide mill in Ruby Gulch, near Zortman, that produced large quantities of gold through the 1930s. Elevation: 2,487 ft. Location: Phillips County

White Cliffs 640 *map 4 E-4*

The White Cliffs are a limestone formation along both sides of the National Wild and Scenic River portion of the Missouri River. Although the Lewis and Clark Expedition did not name the cliffs, expedition member Patrick Gass, when camped at Eagle Creek in the area on May 31, 1805, said of them: "They seems as if built by the hand of man, and are so numerous that they appear like the ruins of an ancient city." In 1833, self-taught naturalist Prince Maximilian of Weid traveled up the Missouri River with the American Fur Company. He described the cliffs in expansive terms: "Here the most strange forms are seen, and you may fancy that you see, colonnades, small round pillers with large globes or a flat slabe at the top, little towers, pulpits, organs with their pipes, old ruins, fortresses, castles, churches with pointed towers." Elevation: 2,677 ft. Location: Chouteau County

White Pine 59 *map 1 E-2*

The town of White Pine was platted along the Northern Pacific Railroad's main line in 1883 and named for a large stand of white pine trees that surrounded the community. When the post office closed in 1965, the Montana Highway Dept. removed the community's road sign, but it remains a small community. Elevation: 2,570 ft. Location: Sanders County

White Sulphur Springs 638 *map 12 D-2*

White Sulphur Springs was originally called Brewers Springs, after James Scott Brewer, who laid claim to the thermal springs in 1866. In 1876, postmaster Henry Brainerd requested that postal officials change the name to White Sulphur Springs, for the white deposits found around the springs. Brewer sold the springs in 1877 to Dr. William Parberry, who laid out the townsite a year later, and in 1880 White Sulphur Springs won the Meagher County seat from Diamond City. Mining boomed in the nearby Castle Mountains during the 1880s, but tapered off in the 1890s, when the timber industry began to develop. According to *Mountains of Gold, Hills of Grass,* 3,000 residents lived in White Sulphur Springs during the peak of the timber industry. Still, some realized that this boom would not last; as one area rancher cautioned: "We were here before you and we will be here after you are gone." This prophecy bears witness today in the form of an abandoned tipi burner (for burning waste wood) that stands on the west side of town. Ranching remains an economic mainstay for the community as well as the county. Elevation: 5,049 ft. Location: Meagher County

Whitefish 56 *map 2 C-1*

Whitefish takes its name, so the story goes, from area trappers in the mid-1850s who found plentiful native whitefish in nearby Whitefish Lake. During the late 1880s, lumbermen began harvesting timber around the lake, to be processed in Kalispell's mills. The logs were transported to the mills via Whitefish Lake, the Whitefish River, and the Flathead River. Although a community began to develop between 1890 and 1892, the town was not platted until 1903, when the Great Northern Railway decided to reroute its main line from Columbia Falls to Rexford, bypassing Kalispell. The new town of Whitefish became a division point.

Winter Carnival parade, Central Avenue, Whitefish, c. 1965
Lacy Studios, photographer, MHS 951-732

Clearing the wooded townsite left a number of stumps, prompting the nickname "Stump Town." Whitefish incorporated in 1905. Timber and farming were Whitefish's primary industries for its first half century. Today the nearby Whitefish Mountain Resort, formerly called Big Mountain Ski Resort, begun in 1947, is a mainstay of the area's economy. Elevation: 3,029 ft. Location: Flathead County

Whitefish Lake 50 *map 2 C-1*
Whitefish Lake was named in the 1850s for the abundant whitefish harvested there. Whitefish Lake State Park, established in 1960, is on the southwest edge of the lake. Elevation: 2,999 ft. Location: Flathead County

Whitefish Range 33 *map 2 B-1*
The Whitefish Range, just south of the international border, is named for the town and lake of the same name. The highest peak in the range is Nasukoin Mountain (8,086 feet). Whitefish Mountain Resort, formerly Big Mountain Ski Resort, is located on the south end of the range.

Whitehall 605 *map 19 A-3*
Edward G. Brooke is credited with naming the town of Whitehall, although 2 stories tell how he chose the name. The first states that he named the town after the old Gilmer & Salisbury Stage Company station on Whitetail Creek, a mile or so from the current town. In 1867, the station consisted of a 2-story, white, wood-framed house—the only structure painted white between Alder Gulch and Last Chance Gulch. According to the other story, when the post office moved from the Milk Ranch

to the stage station, Brooke did not like the name "Milk Ranch" and so, in 1869, renamed the post office for Whitehall, Illinois. The Northern Pacific Railroad laid track through Whitehall in 1889 as part of the Garrison to Logan branch line. The townsite was platted in 1889, and again in 1890, by U.S. deputy surveyor James M. Page. The Utah-Idaho Sugar Company constructed a sugar beet–processing plant here in 1918. It never operated, but the brick smokestack still stands. Elevation: 4,360 ft. Location: Jefferson County

Whitetail and Whitetail Creek 1122
map 7 A-4

Both the town and creek are named after the prolific white-tailed deer that populate the creek bottoms. A dam along the creek forms Whitetail Reservoir, one of 4 so named in Montana. The town started when Gus Wahl and Esther Wahl Davidson opened the first store in 1912. The following year, the town moved south, to the end of the Minneapolis, St. Paul & Sault Ste. Marie Railway. Whitetail grew quickly when homesteaders arrived and developed businesses. Because of the town's proximity to the Canadian border, a customs office opened in a railroad car in 1915; the immigration office followed in 1931. Area agriculture dwindled in the 1920s and 1930s as a result of drought and the Great Depression. Elevation: 2,502 ft. Location: Daniels County

Whitetail Peak 975 *map 21 C-1*

Whitetail Peak in the Beartooth Range is the fourth-highest summit in Montana. According to local legend, it was named by Ben Greenough for the white-tailed deer he claimed to have shot on the flanks of the mountain. Greenough, a prominent resident of Red Lodge, worked as a hunting guide in the Beartooths during the early years of the twentieth century. Elevation: 12,548 ft. Location: Carbon County

Whitetail Reservoir 538 *map 11 E-2*

This Whitetail Reservoir, one of 4 so named in Montana, was built in 1921–22. It takes its name from Whitetail Deer Creek. Elevation: 7,247 ft. Location: Jefferson County

Whitewater 917 *map 6 B-2*

Whitewater takes its name from the stream that flows through the town—Whitewater Creek, so called for its cloudy appearance. In 1927, the Great Northern Railway built a branch line 7 miles west of Whitewater, prompting N. J. Brandt to move his store and the post office to this new location. Elevation: 2,325 ft. Location: Phillips County

Whitlash 339 *map 4 B-1*

Whitlash owes its name to a typographical error. Local ranchers and homesteaders in the Sweet Grass Hills applied for a post office in 1892 under the name Whiplash. When the approved application was returned, it read "Whitlash," and Whitlash it remained. The post office moved 6 times, until Alfred and Tom Strode laid out a townsite on Half Breed Creek in 1905, the same year Alfred was appointed as postmaster. Frank Henry and Malvin Matteson discovered natural gas nearby in 1914 while drilling for water. Sixteen years later, a pipeline supplied Great Falls with gas, and a second line pumped crude oil to the refinery at Cut Bank. U.S. Customs operated out of the town from 1933 until 1969, when it was moved to the actual border. Elevation: 3,939 ft. Location: Liberty County

Wibaux 1227 *map 16 B-3*

Wibaux (pronounced "WEE-bow")derives its name from a French cattleman, Pierre Wibaux, who first arrived in Montana in 1884. After the brutal winter of 1886–87, Wibaux bought up the stock of less

Charcoal kiln, Wickes, 1970
Detail, Peter Meloy, photographer, MHS 951-799

for cattleman Pierre Wibaux. Only 3 towns appear in Wibaux County on the Montana highway map.

Wickes 507 *map 11 D-3*

Wickes owes its existence to the 1869 discovery and development of silver deposits south of Helena. The original owners of the Alta Mine, one of the territory's richest silver mines, sold their interests to a group of New York investors in 1876. The cartel, headed by William W. Wickes, immediately organized the Montana Company and platted the townsite in 1877. The town took Wickes's name. The company initially lagged in developing the silver deposits, until Samuel T. Hauser helped reorganize it into the Alta Montana Company in 1879. The community grew to 400 residents by 1880. A fire destroyed the Alta mill in 1882, forcing Alta Montana to sell out the following year to Hauser. Hauser reorganized the company again, creating the Helena Mining & Reduction Company, which built a new smelter in 1884 and rebuilt the silver mill. Hauser also convinced the Northern Pacific Railroad to build a branch line between Helena and Wickes. As a result, Wickes boomed between 1883 and 1893. By 1893, it had approximately 1,500 residents. The mining company closed its smelter that year after the repeal of the Sherman Silver Purchase Act of 1890, but Wickes struggled on. Sporadic mining kept the community alive into the mid-twentieth century. Elevation: 5,200 ft. Location: Jefferson County

fortunate ranchers and expanded his herd to 75,000 by the 1890s. The Keith post office operated near ranch headquarters between 1882 and 1884; between 1884 and 1895, the post office was known as Mingusville. It was at Mingusville that the Northern Pacific Railroad built a stockyard that allowed Wibaux to ship his cattle to market. By 1893, residents had begun to call the settlement Wibaux, and the post office changed its name to Wibaux in 1895. Wibaux County was formed in 1914, with Wibaux as the county seat. St. Peter's Catholic Church, the Pierre Wibaux House, and the Wibaux Commercial Historic District are listed in the National Register. Elevation: 2,649 ft. Location: Wibaux County

Wibaux County 1225 *map 16 C-3*

The Montana legislature created Wibaux (pronounced "WEE-bow") County in 1914 from Dawson, Fallon, and Richland counties. This county that abuts the Montana–North Dakota state line takes its name from the county seat of Wibaux, named

Wild Horse Island 124 *map 2 D-1*

In 1854, John Mullan, of the Isaac I. Stevens 1853 railroad survey expedition, was one of the first to write about this island in Flathead Lake: "On one of these, called the 'Wild Horse' island, is a band of wild horses that belong to a Pend d'Oreille Indian. Some years ago the father of this man had horses stolen from him by the Blackfeet. In retaliation he stole a number from the Blackfeet, and put them on this island, all of which he intended for the benefit of his children. This is now a band of sixty or seventy horses and only a few days ago they took off a band of forty-five." Raymond Bourke MacDonald bequeathed most of the island for a state park, which was established in 1978. Location: Lake County

Wild Horse Lake 885 *map 13 B-4*

Walter J. Winnett named Wild Horse Lake, which is part of the War Horse NWR. The refuge is attached administratively to the Charles M. Russell NWR. Elevation: 3,035 ft. Location: Petroleum County

Willard 1236 *map 16 D-3*

Homesteader Fred Willard Anderson moved to southeastern Montana from Murdoch, Minnesota, in 1909. He established a post office to which he gave his middle name ("Anderson" was already taken) on the stage road between Baker and Ekalaka in 1910. With only 2 rooms in the house, Anderson put the mailboxes in his bedroom. He sold out to Charles Anderson in 1926, who moved the post office and store 1.5 miles to present-day MT 7 between Baker and Ekalaka. Elevation: 3,328 ft. Location: Fallon County

Willow Creek (town) 663 *map 19 A-4*

The community of Willow Creek takes its name from the nearby stream. On July 31, 1805, Capt. Meriwether Lewis dubbed this stream the Philosophy River, after one of President Thomas Jefferson's cardinal virtues. The settlement here began in 1864 and soon grew due to a mining boom in nearby Norwegian Gulch. The Northern Pacific Railroad arrived at Willow Creek

in 1883; the Milwaukee Road, in 1908. The town received a boost with the homestead boom in the early 1900s, but the dry years in the 1920s forced many homesteaders to move on. Elevation: 4,161 ft. Location: Gallatin County

Willow Creek Reservoir (Lewis and Clark) 281 *map 11 A-2*

The U.S. Reclamation Service constructed this Willow Creek Reservoir, one of 4 so named in Montana, in 1907–11. The Willow Creek Dam is 93 feet high and 650 feet long. The reservoir has a campground, fishing access, and boat ramp. Elevation: 4,150 ft. Location: Lewis and Clark County

Willow Creek Reservoir (Madison) 686 *map 19 A-4*

Montana has 4 reservoirs named Willow Creek. Construction of this Willow Creek Reservoir began in 1936 under the auspices of the State Water Conservation Board. Completed in 1938, the 12,000-acre-feet reservoir provides irrigation water to ranchers and farmers in the Willow Creek Valley, between Pony and Harrison, and is named for Willow Creek, which flows out of the Tobacco Root Mountains. Elevation: 4,731 ft. Location: Madison County

Wilsall 757 *map 12 E-2*

Wilsall takes its name from Will Jordan, of the Jordan-Robertson Company cattle ranch, and his wife, Sally. Will's father, Walter B. Jordan, helped lay out the town, and the Wilsall Townsite Company sold the lots. The Northern Pacific Railway line arrived in December 1909, and the post office opened a year later. In the 1910s, homesteaders poured into the Wilsall area to raise cattle and grow wheat. A major fire in 1916 destroyed much of the town, and the population slowly declined in the 1930s and '40s. The annual lutefisk dinner each December at the local Lutheran church

Main street, Wisdom, c. 1940
MHS 951-812

draws ranch families from miles around. Elevation: 5,051 ft. Location: Park County

Windham 676   map 12   B-4
Windham is named for the Vermont home county of rancher L. H. Hamilton, who began ranching in the Sage Creek area in the 1880s. In 1907, he and others platted this town on the Great Northern Railway's branch line between Lewistown and Great Falls. At one time, 6 passenger trains passed through Windham each day. Supported by the railroad and homesteaders, Windham boomed briefly as a result of the Great Northern Railway Company's subsidiary Cottonwood Coal Company, which operated a coal mine in the area during the 1910s. Elevation: 4,264 ft. Location: Judith Basin County

Winifred 743   map 13   A-2
One story regarding the naming of Winifred involves Milwaukee Road officials Percy Rockefeller and E. D. Sewall. It seems that one or both of these men had daughters named Winifred. When the town was founded in 1913 with the arrival of the Milwaukee Road, the railroad named it Winifred. Elevation: 3,225 ft. Location: Fergus County

Winnett 913   map 14   B-1
Winnett is named for Walter John Winnett, who started his central Montana ranch in 1879. The community began to separate its identity from the ranch in 1909, and the post office opened in 1910. During the homestead boom of the 1910s and oil boom of the early 1920s, Winnett grew rapidly. Its many businesses included

a bank, hotel, and newspaper. In 1925, it became the county seat of the newly established Petroleum County. Drought and the Great Depression, however, destroyed much of Winnett's prosperity. Elevation: 2,953 ft. Location: Petroleum County

Winston 543 *map 11 D-4*
Named for the Winston brothers, contractors from Minneapolis who hauled ore through the area in the 1890s, Winston lay on a siding on the Northern Pacific Railroad's main line southeast of Helena. The post office opened in 1892. Fred Goudy built a saloon there in 1894, which was followed shortly by construction of the Durnens' Hotel. Elevation: 4,352 ft. Location: Broadwater County

Wisdom 522 *map 18 B-3*
On August 6, 1805, Capt. Meriwether Lewis named today's Big Hole River the Wisdom River and today's Ruby River the Philanthropy River. Lewis wrote that the Corps "called the bold rapid an clear stream Wisdom, and the more mild and placid one which flows in from the S.E. Philanthrophy in commemoration of two of those cardinal virtues, which have so eminently marked that deservedly selibrated character [of President Thomas Jefferson] through life." The Wisdom post office opened in 1884 and moved from ranch to ranch until Hattie Noyes laid out a townsite on part of the Noyes Ranch at a place known locally as "the Crossings." Mrs. Noyes decided not to give the new community her family name for fear of confusion with Norris in Madison County, and the name Wisdom became identified with the new town as well as the post office. Elevation: 6,058 ft. Location: Beaverhead County

Wise River 526 *map 18 A-4*
On August 6, 1805, Capt. Meriwether Lewis named today's Big Hole River the Wisdom River in honor of his benefactor President Thomas Jefferson. Early settlers called its tributary the Wise River, a shortened version of Wisdom. The river flows north from the Pioneer Mountains to its confluence with the Big Hole River.

Wise River (town) 530 *map 18 A-4*
This community takes its name from the Wise River, which flows into the Big Hole River nearby. The Wise River post office has operated since 1913, when Ellen Pyle became the first postmaster. Elevation: 5,661 ft. Location: Beaverhead County

Wolf Creek (Roosevelt) 1101 *map 7 D-3*
Montana has more than 2 dozen streams named Wolf Creek. The Lewis and Clark Expedition camped in the vicinity of this particular creek on May 5, 1805, and mentioned sighting a large number of wolves in the area. However, they named the stream Lackwater Creek. Several outfits operated trading posts in the area, including the Hudson's Bay Company, T. C. Power, and Sherman Cogswell. Wolf Creek flows into the Missouri River at Wolf Point, in Roosevelt County.

Wolf Creek (town) 376 *map 11 B-3*
In 1887, the Montana Central Railway built its line through the narrow Prickly Pear Canyon, and the town of Wolf Creek, named for its location along the creek of the same name, grew to serve the railroad. Englishman Charles Forman built a 10-room, 3-story hotel in a simple, no-frills style. Wolf Creek's small collection of buildings and homes included Forman's Wolf Creek Hotel, a livery stable, and a meat company. The hotel catered to the stages that traveled through the canyon during the nineteenth century, and also served railroad travelers on the new railroad. Wolf Creek later served workers building the Holter Dam between 1908

and 1910, gas pipeline laborers in the 1930s, and crews working on the new interstate in the 1960s. Interstate 15 split the town in half, nearly obliterating it. The Wolf Creek Hotel is listed in the National Register. Elevation: 3,630 ft. Location: Lewis and Clark County

Wolf Mountains 1125 *map 22 C-4*

This small range south of the Rosebud Mountains separates the Crow Indian Reservation from the Northern Cheyenne Indian Reservation to the east. The Crow tribe regarded the Cheetiish, or "Wolf teeth mountains," as a sacred place, conducive to dreams and vision quests. The Crow name refers to pinnacle formations south of present-day Forsyth that resemble wolf teeth. On January 8, 1877, Col. Nelson A. Miles, with 400 soldiers of the 5th and 22nd Infantry Regiments operating out of Fort Keogh, encountered a mixed force of approximately 600 Sioux and Cheyenne warriors under the leadership of Crazy Horse. The Battle of the Wolf Mountains occurred south of present-day Birney; some say that the Indians' defeat here influenced Crazy Horse's decision to surrender several months later. From these mountains, on June 25, 1876, Lt. Col. George Armstrong Custer first spotted the Indian encampment on the Little Bighorn River. Rich deposits of coal lie under the mountains, and there has been significant coal development near Decker, just east of the Crow Reservation.

Wolf Point 1103 *map 7 D-3*

Wolf Point began as a trading post in the 1860s, at the confluence of Wolf Creek and the Missouri River. The name resulted from wolfers stacking wolf carcasses like cordwood at the site where the steamboats docked one winter. Farming began in the area as early as 1874. The Great Northern Railway arrived in 1887, its line running a mile north of town. On May 30, 1908,

the federal government allotted the Fort Peck Indian Reservation, with each tribal member receiving 320 acres. In 1913, the surplus land was opened to non-Indian homesteading, and residents decided to move the town to the railroad line. Wolf Point incorporated in 1915 and became the county seat in 1919. Elevation: 1,999 ft. Location: Roosevelt County

Wolf Point Bridge 1113 *map 7 D-4*

Also known as the Lewis and Clark Bridge, the bridge at Wolf Point was the result of many years of intense lobbying of the state and federal governments by local politicians, businesspeople, and promoters of northeastern Montana. Built in 1929–30 by the Missouri Valley Bridge & Iron Company, of Leavenworth, Kansas, the bridge is a 3-span, Pennsylvania through-truss structure, 1,074 feet long. The center 400-foot span is the longest through-truss span in Montana. The bridge served traffic on MT 13 until the late 1990s, when it became obsolete. Preservationists were determined to save the structure. As the nearby replacement bridge neared completion in 1998, the Montana Historical Society agreed to accept ownership of the Wolf Point Bridge. Listed in the National Register, it is now closed to vehicular traffic. Elevation: 1,967 ft. Location: McCone County

Woods Bay 119 *map 2 D-2*

Named for J. C. Wood, who came to the area in 1891 with his wife, Robin, Woods Bay lies at the north end of Flathead Lake. Wood is credited with establishing the first cherry orchards in the area; the family grew bing and royal Anne cherries. They were among the first to market Montana cherries to the East Coast. Apple and plum orchards also were common in this area. Yellow Bay State Park lies south of Woods Bay. Elevation: 2,902 ft. Location: Lake County

Woodside 306 *map 10 D-1*

Lambert L. Wood homesteaded this area in the 1880s, and his home served as a stage stop and post house. When the Northern Pacific Railroad came through in 1890, Wood sold the homestead to the Missoula Mercantile and established a post office, naming the community Woodside. The railroad later deeded the right-of-way to the state, and US 93 was built upon the old grade. Wood's former stage stop was a well known local landmark until it burned in 1958. Elevation: 3,486 ft. Location: Ravalli County

Woodworth 252 *map 10 B-3*

Chauncey Woodworth established the post office in 1889 and named it after himself. Woodworth was one of several timber camps in the area that supplied fuel for the Anaconda Company's smelter works in Anaconda. The camp was especially active during the early 1940s, housing and feeding logging crews. The post office closed in 1945. Elevation: 4,238 ft. Location: Powell County

Worden 1019 *map 22 A-1*

Worden was established in 1882 as a station named Clermont on the Northern Pacific Railroad. It was renamed Worden in 1907. Residents wanted to call the town Dixon, after U.S. Senator Thomas Dixon, but since there was already a Dixon in Montana, the name was not available. At Dixon's request, residents instead named the town for Dixon's wife, Frances, whose father, F. L. Worden, was one of the founders of Missoula. Elevation: 2,962 ft. Location: Yellowstone County

Wyola 1114 *map 22 C-3*

Wyola, a small community on the Crow Indian Reservation, began as a Chicago, Burlington & Quincy Railroad station stop, where the steam locomotives took on water piped from the Little Bighorn River into the trackside water tank. The Crows called this spot Ammoole, "Where they wait," because of the train station. The post office opened in 1911. The Wyotana Mining Company opened a bentonite mill in 1942, which closed after only 10 years because of the bentonite's poor quality. Bentonite is used in drilling (as a water absorbent), geotechnical engineering, and kitty litter. Elevation: 3,724 ft. Location: Big Horn County

Skiing party, Obsidian Cliff, Yellowstone National Park, 1887
Detail, F. Jay Haynes, photographer, MHS H-1849

Yaak 2 *map 1 A-2*

Homesteaders began drifting into the Yaak area, referred to by one visitor as "a wild region of deep canyons, small waterfalls, and snow-capped peaks," shortly after the passage of the Forest Homestead Act of 1906. Aware of the potential for fraud, the USFS examined each 160-acre homestead to certify it as agricultural land, not timberland. Yaak derives its name from the Yaak River. According to local lore, A'ak is a Kootenai name meaning "Arrow." The Kootenai River forms the shape of a drawn bow; its tributary the Yaak River is its arrow. Elevation: 2,983 ft. Location: Lincoln County

Yaak River 7 *map 1 B-1*

This spectacular river in northwestern Montana flows into the Kootenai River and was named A'ak by the Kootenais meaning "Arrow." The river's name is sometimes spelled "Yahk." A gold rush in 1895 brought hundreds of people to the area, resulting in the establishment of the town of Sylvanite, named for the type of ore, a gold-silver telluride, found in the area. Homesteaders followed the miners. A catastrophic fire in 1910 wiped out the town of Sylvanite but opened the heavily timbered Yaak River bottomlands to farming. During the 1970s and '80s, local logging operations harvested timber in the Yaak Valley to supply area sawmills.

Yankee Jim Canyon 858 *map 20 C-2*

Yankee Jim Canyon, on the Yellowstone River, is named for James George (1841–1924), who arrived in Montana in the early 1860s. A native of Vermont (hence the "Yankee"), George was variously a hunter and prospector before squatting on land adjacent to the canyon in 1871. That same year, Bart Henderson and Adam "Horn" Miller built a wagon road through the canyon to provide access to the gold diggings in Cooke City and to Mammoth Hot Springs in what was soon to become Yellowstone National Park. George improved the road in 1873, declaring it the National Park Toll Road, and established a way station and toll booth at his ranch house. The Northern Pacific Railroad built a branch line through the canyon in 1883, and Park County purchased Yankee Jim's toll road in 1893 for $1,000. The road was rerouted in 1912. Today the canyon is popular with kayakers and rafters.

Yellow Water Reservoir 904 *map 13 C-4*

Speculation suggests that a member of the Raynolds Expedition of 1859–60 camped along this creek and noted the color of the water, hence the name. During the summers of 1937 and 1938, CCC laborers built an earthen dam a quarter mile long and 31 feet high, to store water for release into Flatwillow Creek. The Yellow Creek Water Users' Association was formed in 1948 and dug a series of irrigation ditches. In the 1950s, Montana Fish, Wildlife & Parks established the reservoir as a recreation area. Elevation: 3,118 ft. Location: Petroleum County

Yellowstone County 1012 *map 14 E-2*

The Montana legislature created Yellowstone County in 1883 from Gallatin and Custer counties. It takes its name from the Yellowstone River, called La Roche Jaune by French trappers, for the yellow rock, and Iichiilkaashaashe, "Elk river," by the Crows. The Yellowstone Valley supports diverse agriculture, its principal crops being sugar beets, wheat, and soybeans. Billings is the seat of this county in south-central Montana.

Yellowstone National Park 891 *map 20 C-2*

Established on March 1, 1872, Yellowstone National Park is the nation's oldest national park, and the largest in the lower 48 states. Native Americans had used the area for thousands of years prior to trapper John Colter's 1807 excursion into the "wonderland" of hot springs, mud pots, and geysers. Other than verbal reports from fur traders and trappers, however, the area remained largely unknown until the 1860s and '70s. The Hayden Expedition of 1871 scientifically documented the extraordinary natural features and wildlife of the region, while the expedition's artist, Thomas Moran, and photographer, William Jackson, helped publicize the natural wonders of Yellowstone with artwork and photographs. Their efforts helped galvanize Congress to create the park the following year. Millions of tourists now visit the park annually to glimpse buffalo and elk herds and a growing population of gray wolves that were reintroduced to the park in 1995. The northern strip of the park lies within Montana; the remainder is in Wyoming.

Yellowstone River 1218 *map 8 E-3*
French fur trappers named this river La Roche Jaune, "Yellow rock." The Crow tribe called the river Iichiilkaashaashe, "Elk river." The main stem is the longest stretch of river in the continental United States without major impoundments, flowing 670 miles from Yellowstone National Park, through Montana, to its confluence with the Missouri River near the Montana–North Dakota state line. The Yellowstone River Valley supports cattle ranches and large sugar beet farms, as well as Montana's most populated city, Billings.

Yellowstone Trail 903 *map 21 A-1*
Formed in 1912, the Yellowstone Trail Association had as its motto "A Good Road from Plymouth Rock to Puget Sound." Its purpose was to encourage interested towns to volunteer labor to provide repairs and improvements to roads in their areas, which would then be linked to form a paved transcontinental route. The association took off as the number of automobile

owners increased from 350,000 in 1912 to over 1 million in 1915. The route of the Yellowstone Trail as it was pieced together from county and state roads went from Minneapolis to Seattle by way of Aberdeen, South Dakota, and Yellowstone National Park. In Montana, the route paralleled the Milwaukee Road and today's I-90 from Baker to Lookout Pass. As federal, state, and county governments began constructing highways and roads in the 1920s and 1930s, the Yellowstone Trail was subsumed by other highways (US 10, US 12). The Yellowstone Trail Association disbanded in 1930.

Yellowtail Dam 1066 *map 22 C-2*
In 1965, the U.S. Bureau of Reclamation completed Yellowtail Dam, named for longtime Crow leader Robert Yellowtail. The name is ironic: Yellowtail had opposed the government-built dam, lobbying for a lease of property rather than sale. The 525-foot-high, 1,480-foot-long dam generates hydroelectric power from the Bighorn River. The resulting 71-mile-long reservoir called Bighorn Lake provides irrigation water, flood control, and recreation. Elevation: 3,646 ft. Location: Big Horn County

Yogo Creek 682 *map 12 C-3*
The Yogo Mining District in the Little Belt Mountains, famous for its high-quality sapphires, first gained notoriety with the 1879 discovery of gold along Yogo Creek. According to sources, Yogo is an anglicized translation of a Blackfeet word meaning either "to romance" or "blue sky." Population along Yogo Creek peaked at about 1,200 by the early 1880s; the area then was abandoned until 1894, when gold prospectors Jake Hoover and Frank Hobson discovered mysterious blue pebbles in their gold dust. Hobson sent some gold, as well as some of the stones, to a schoolteacher in his home state of Maine. She wrote back, thanking him for the sapphires,

prompting him to ask, "What the hell are sapphires?" The sapphires came from an igneous dike 8 feet wide and 3.5 miles long, the largest deposit of gem-bearing ore in the world outside the South African diamond fields. The New Mine Sapphire Syndicate purchased several of the mines in 1898, and the American Sapphire Company followed suit in 1904. The Montana Dept. of Publicity published an article in *Montana Business Yesterday* (1927) claiming that Montana Yogo sapphires were "among the finest in the world" for their uniform color. This claim made them widely sought after by gemologists and jewelers. Sapphire mining continues in the area today. Location: Judith Basin County

York 487 *map 11 C-4*

With the discovery of gold in the Big Belt Mountains, the town of New York City appeared at the junction of Trout Creek and York Gulch in 1866. It was not long before the name was shortened to simply York. As the town developed, a smaller community, Brooklyn, appeared across the creek. Over a 3-year span (1866–69), the population of York jumped to roughly 7,000 residents. As with most of Montana's mining communities, the population dwindled when placer mining faded by 1874. The Trout Creek Mine Company hydraulically mined York Gulch from 1888 to 1889; the Golden Messenger Mine opened a year later and operated until 1945. Locals boast that the York Bar serves the best hamburger in the county. Elevation: 3,978 ft. Location: Lewis and Clark County

Yorks Islands 604 *map 11 E-4*

On July 24, 1805, Capt. Meriwether Lewis wrote: "We saw many beaver and some otter today; the former dam up the small channels of the river between the islands and compel the river in these parts to make other channels . . . Thus the river in many places among the clusters of islands is constantly changing direction." Capt. William Clark later noted this spot on his map sketches as "Yorks 8 islands." A slave belonging to Capt. William Clark, York served as a member of the expedition and contributed his efforts and skills to its success. When the expedition returned to St. Louis in 1806, York asked Clark for his freedom; Clark released York from slavery several years later. He later reported that York had died of cholera sometime before 1832. In 2001, the Crimson Bluffs chapter of the Lewis and Clark Trail Heritage Foundation successfully petitioned to have this area, formerly called Deepdale, renamed in York's honor. Elevation: 3,854 ft. Location: Broadwater County

Zortman, 1908

Detail, MHS 951-885

Zempel Lake 1057 *map 14 D-4*

Zempel Lake is a private reservoir named for Fred Zempel, a native of North Dakota who homesteaded in the area in 1910. Elevation: 2,691 ft. Location: Rosebud County

Zortman 839 *map 5 E-4*

Zortman takes its name from Oliver Peter Zortman, who discovered gold in the Little Rocky Mountains in the late 1880s. Over time, Zortman extracted $600,000 worth of gold from his Alabama Mine, which he had named for his home state. In 1898, Charles Whitcomb developed the Ruby Gulch Mine (2.5 miles from Zortman), one of the richest mines in the area. Five years later, Whitcomb built the second-largest cyanide mill in the world, with a capacity of 100 tons. Fires in 1912 and 1936 crippled the mine, but the death blow came with the federal government's passage of Order L208, which halted gold mining at the beginning of World War II. The mine was unable to reopen after the war because of the depressed price for gold and high operating costs. With the mine's closure, the town's population dispersed, and by the early 1970s only 21 people lived in Zortman. In 1979, the international Pegasus Gold Corporation, headquartered in Spokane, Washington, bought the Zortman-Landusky gold mines and began mining operations that proved to be environmentally destructive. In 1996, Pegasus Gold agreed to begin a $37 million remediation of the massive cyanide contamination that resulted from their operations. The company's bankruptcy in 1998, however, left the State of Montana to clean up the pollution. In 2002, the Fort Belknap tribes sued the state for damages to the watershed. Elevation: 4,024 ft. Location: Phillips County

Zurich 741 *map 5 C-3*

Sometime around 1887, Great Northern Railway officials named one of their main line sidings Zurich, for the city in Switzerland. It took some time before a community developed at the site. In 1907, rancher John Acher established the first post office about 4 miles east of the present townsite, but it was not until 1913 that Charles Grass platted a townsite near the railroad. Grass established a general mercantile there, and by 1915 the population of Zurich stood at 40. Local businesses included a lumberyard, livery, restaurant and pool hall, grain elevator, and blacksmith shop. The community built the tiny Zurich chapel in 1916. It served several denominations, including Methodists, Mormons, Lutherans, and the American Sunday School Union. Elevation: 2,384 ft. Location: Blaine County

How to Use This Map

This map of Montana is divided into 24 numbered sections. A grid of these numbered sections overlaid with county names appears on the following page.

As discussed in the "How to Use This Book" section on page xxvii, an individual site's description provides two pieces of map information: a locator number (unique to each site) and a map directional, which consists of a map number (one of the 24 individual map sections) and a grid number (for locating a point using the corresponding letters and numbers bordering the map sections).

Here is how to find a specific location on the map. For an example, we will use the same name line explained in the "How to Use This Book" section at the beginning of the book:

Paradise Valley **841** *map 20 B-2*

In this example, **841** is the locator number and *map 20 B-2* is the map directional. In the directional, the individual map number is 20 and the grid number is B-2. To find the Paradise Valley, you would note the locator number and the map directional shown in the name line. You would then turn to map 20 (the map number can be found on the overall map section grid on the following page as well as on the bottom of each individual map section's page). Looking at map 20, you would find the letter B and the number *2* along the map edge and locate the point at which they intersect

inside the map boundary. Find the locator number 841 in this general area, and there you have the Paradise Valley.

On the maps, locator numbers appear as close to a site's actual location as possible without obscuring any wording. The locator numbers for creeks and rivers appear at their confluences. In some cases, a place name shown on the map may differ slightly from the corresponding one in the text (see the introduction for details on the method used for choosing place names).

You will notice that the locator numbers appear in various colors. This is meant to distinguish among particular types of places, as follows:

red ■ towns, cities, and counties

blue ■ geographic features, such as mountain peaks and ranges, rivers, lakes, and glaciers

brown ■ historic sites

green ■ state and federal lands, such as state parks and wilderness areas

orange ■ Indian reservations

fuchsia ■ human-engineered or -altered constructions, such as dams, bridges, and reservoirs (including natural lakes physically altered to provide irrigation).

A color key indicating these distinctions appears at the bottom of each individual map section.

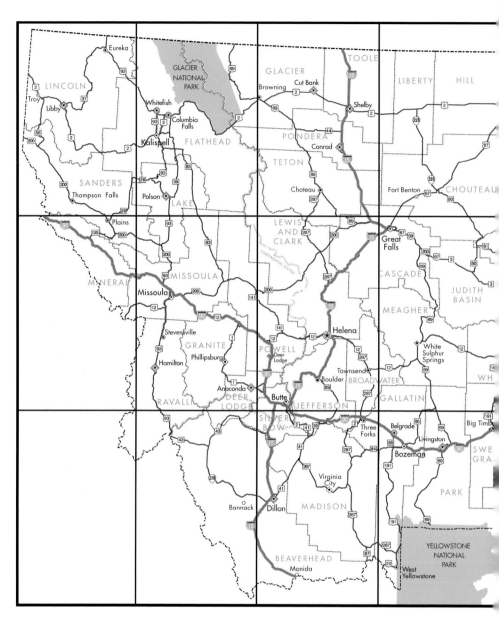

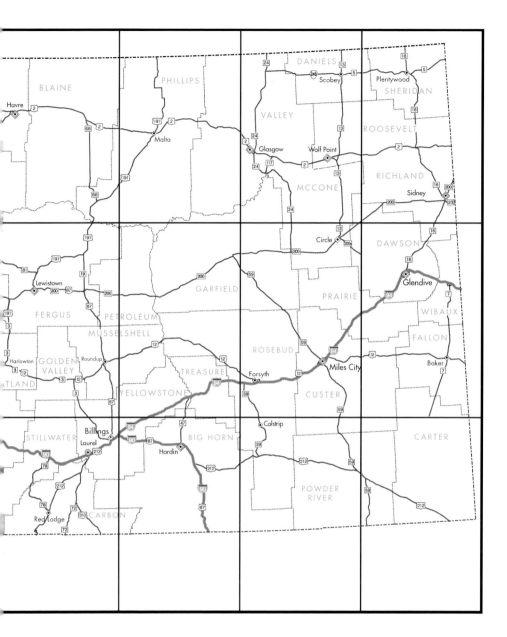

BLAINE

Havre

PHILLIPS

DANIELS
Scobey

SHERIDAN

Plentywood

Malta

VALLEY

Glasgow   Wolf Point

ROOSEVELT

RICHLAND

MCCONE

Sidney

Circle

DAWSON

Lewistown

GARFIELD

PRAIRIE

Glendive

WIBAUX

FERGUS   PETROLEUM

MUSSELSHELL

ROSEBUD

FALLON

Harlowton   GOLDEN   Roundup
VALLEY

TREASURE

Forsyth

Miles City

Baker

CUSTER

Billings

STILLWATER   Laurel

Colstrip

BIG HORN

CARTER

Hardin

POWDER
RIVER

Red Lodge   CARBON

YELLOWSTONE

			5	6	7	8
			13	14	15	16
			21	22	23	24

307

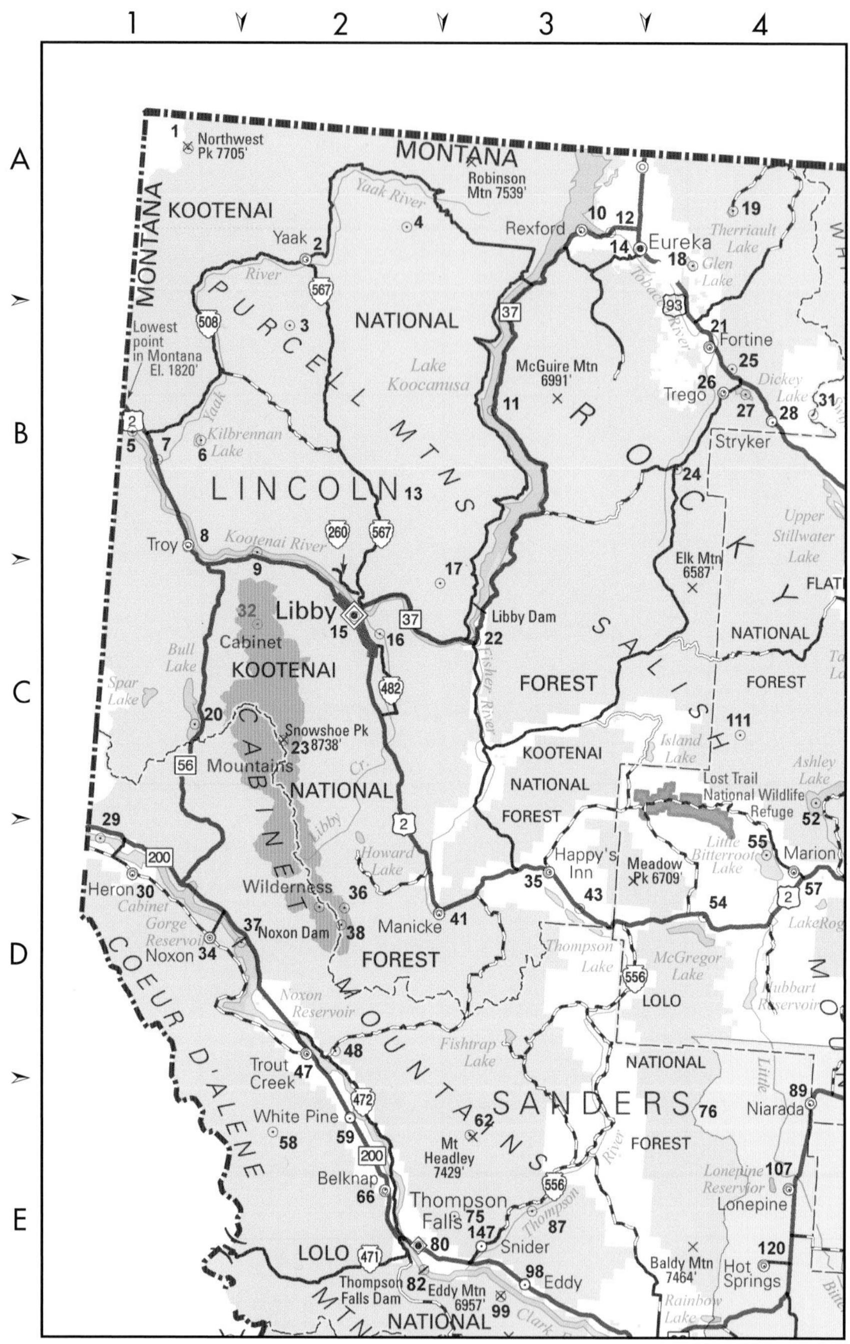

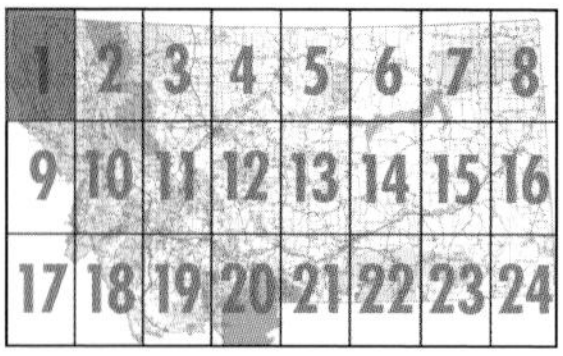

Map 1

1 2 3 4

A
B

MONTANA

1 × Northwest Pk 7705'

KOOTENAI

Yaak 2
River

567

508 3

NATIONAL

Lowest point in Montana El. 1820'

Robinson Mtn 7539'

Rexford
10 12
14 ⊙ Eureka
18 Glen Lake

19

Therriault Lake

93 21 Fortine
25
26
Trego
27 28 31

Lake Koocanusa

McGuire Mtn 6991'
×

11

37

PURCELL MTNS

Kilbrennan Lake

2
5
7
6

LINCOLN 13

Stryker

24

ROCK

Troy 8 260 567
Kootenai River

9

17

Elk Mtn 6587'
×

Upper Stillwater Lake

FLAT

NATIONAL

FOREST

32 Libby
15 16 37
Cabinet

Libby Dam

22

SALISH

KOOTENAI

FOREST

482

111

Bull Lake

Spar Lake

20

Snowshoe Pk 23 8738'

56 Mountains

NATIONAL

KOOTENAI

NATIONAL

FOREST

Island Lake

Lost Trail National Wildlife Refuge

Ashley Lake

52

CABINET

29

200

Heron 30
Cabinet Gorge Reservoir
Noxon 34

37 Noxon Dam 38
Manicke

36

Wilderness

Howard Lake

2

Libby Cr.

41

FOREST

Happy's Inn

35

43

Meadow Pk 6709'
×

54

Little Bitterroot Lake

55 Marion
57
2 LakeRog

MONTANA

Noxon Reservoir

556

McGregor Lake

LOLO

Hubbart Reservoir

Thompson Lake

COEUR D'ALENE

48

Trout 47
Creek 472

White Pine 59
58 200

Belknap
66

Fishtrap Lake

MOUNTAINS

SANDERS 76

NATIONAL

FOREST

62

Mt Headley 7429'

Thompson Falls 75
80 147

556

Thompson River

87 Snider

Little

89 Niarada

Lonepine Reservoir 107
Lonepine

E
LOLO 471

Thompson Falls Dam 82 Eddy Mtn 6957'
99

98 Eddy

Clark

Baldy Mtn 7464'
×

Rainbow Lake

Hot Springs 120

MTN

NATIONAL

Map 1

■ towns/cities/counties
■ geographic features
■ historic sites
■ state and federal lands
■ Indian reservations
■ human-constructed sites

1	2	3	4	5	6	7	8
9	10	11	12	13	14	15	16
17	18	19	20	21	22	23	24

Map 1

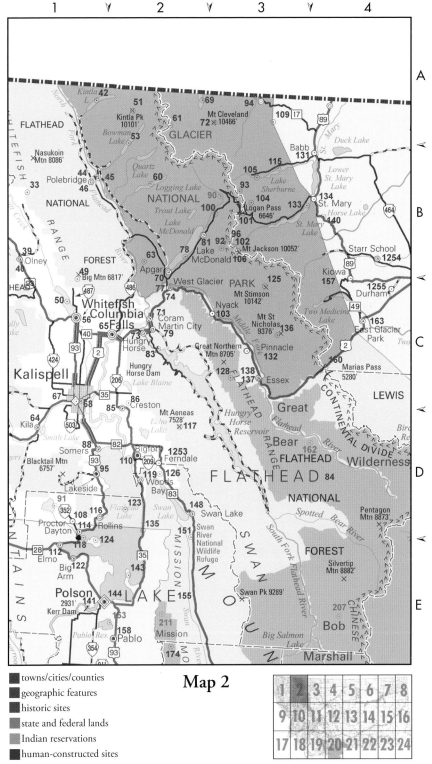

Map 2

■ towns/cities/counties
■ geographic features
■ historic sites
■ state and federal lands
■ Indian reservations
■ human-constructed sites

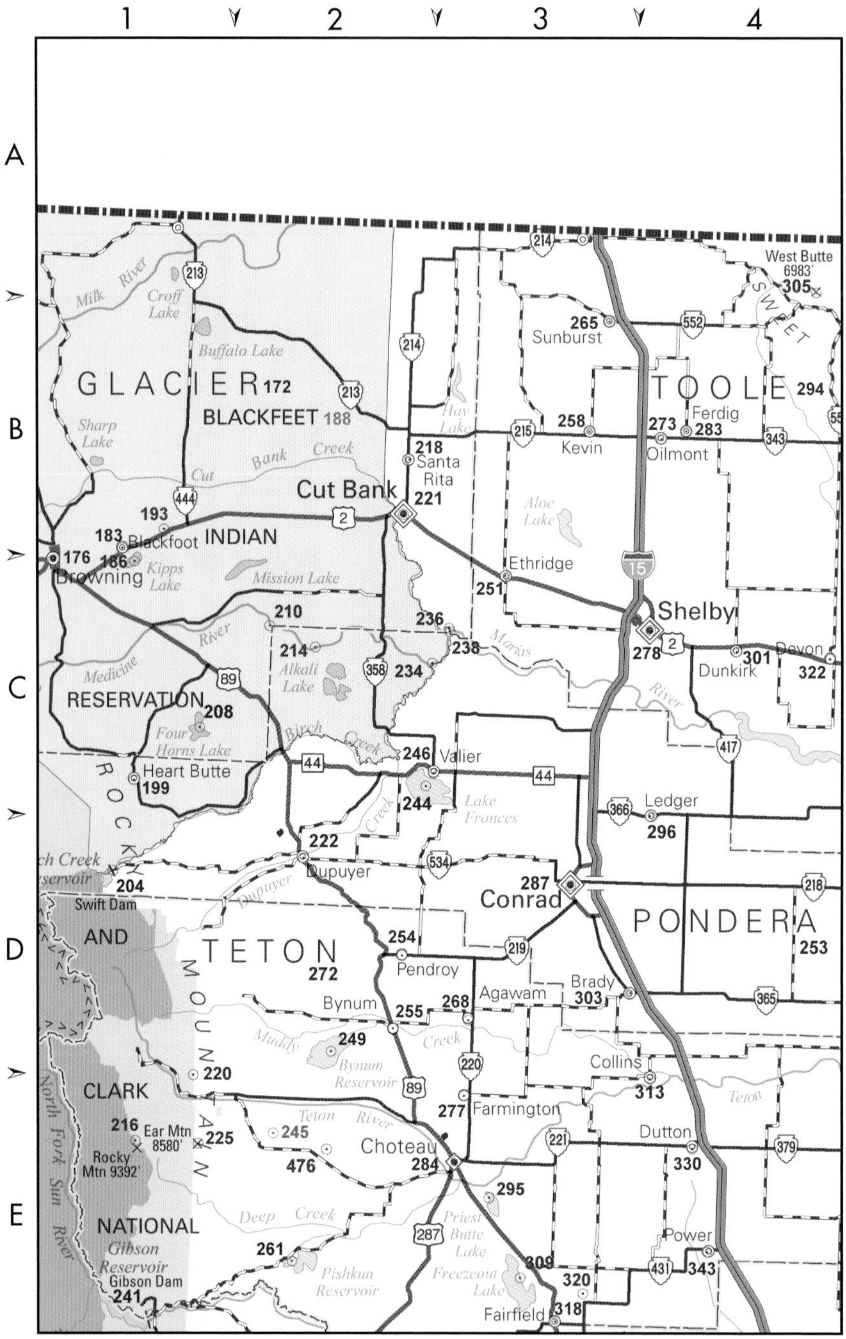

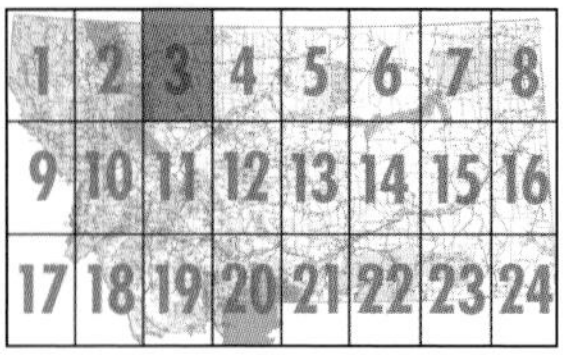

1 2 3 4

A

GLACIER 172

BLACKFEET 188

Milk River

Croff Lake

Buffalo Lake

Sharp Lake

B

Cut Bank Creek

213

193

444

183 Blackfoot INDIAN

176 186
Browning

Kipps Lake

Mission Lake

210

214
Alkali Lake

89

358 234

RESERVATION
208

Four Horns Lake

Heart Butte
199

Medicine River

C

ch Creek servoir

204

Swift Dam

ROCK

AND

TETON

272

MOUNTAIN

220

CLARK

216 Ear Mtn
8580'

Rocky Mtn 9392'

225

245

476

Choteau
284

261

NATIONAL

Gibson Reservoir

Gibson Dam
241

D

Dupuyer

222

Dupuyer

Bynum

255 268

249

Bynum Reservoir

89

277 Farmington

Muddy Creek

220

Teton River

Deep Creek

Pishkun Reservoir

Priest Butte Lake

287

295

309

320
318

Fairfield

Freezeout Lake

E

214 258

265
Sunburst

Hay Lake

218 Santa Rita
221

2

Aloe Lake

251

236

238

246 Valier

244

Lake Frances

44

534

287

Conrad

254

Pendroy

219

Agawam

Brady
303

221

Marias River

258 273 283
Kevin Oilmont

215

Ethridge

15

Shelby

278 2

301 Devon
Dunkirk 322

417

366 Ledger
296

PONDERA

253

365

Collins
313

Dutton

330

379

Power

431 343

TOOLE

West Butte 6983'
305

552

294 55

343

SWEET

218

Teton

Map 3

1 2 3 4 5 6 7 8
9 10 11 12 13 14 15 16
17 18 19 20 21 22 23 24

■ towns/cities/counties
■ geographic features
■ historic sites
■ state and federal lands
■ Indian reservations
■ human-constructed sites

Map 3

310

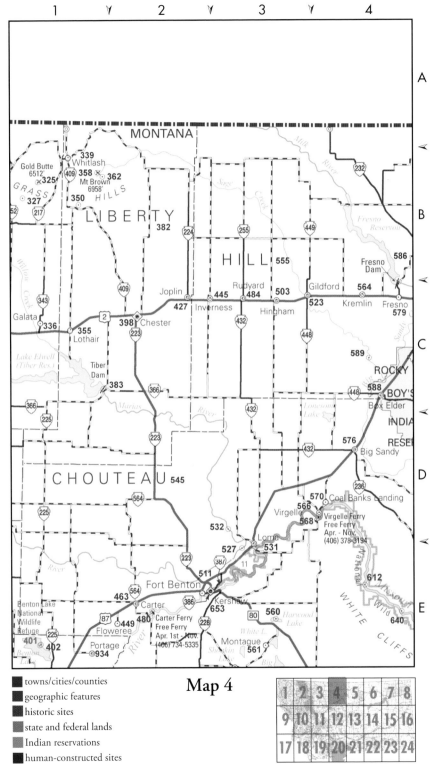

1   2   3   4

A

MONTANA

339
Gold Butte
6512'
Whitlash
409
358 × 362
325
Mt Brown
6958'
350
GRASS
327
52
217
HILLS

LIBERTY

382
224

HILL

555
255
449
586
Fresno
Dam
449
343
409
Joplin
445
Rudyard
484 503
Gildford
564
564
Fresno Dam
427
Inverness
523
Kremlin
Fresno
579
Galata
2
398 Chester
Hingham
432
355
Lothair
223
448
589
ROCKY
Lake Elwell
(Tiber Res.)
Tiber
Dam
383
366
448
588
BOY'S
366
225
432
Box Elder
Marias
River
Lonesome
Lake
INDI
223
576
RESE
432
Big Sandy
CHOUTEAU 545
236
225
564
570 Coal Banks Landing
566
Virgelle
532
568
Virgelle Ferry
Free Ferry
Apr. - Nov.
(406) 378-3194
Loma
527 531
223
387
612
511
11
564
Fort Benton
463
386
Benton Lake
National
Wildlife
Refuge
Carter
Kershaw
653
WHITE
225
87
449 480
Carter Ferry
Free Ferry
Apr. 1st - Nov.
(406) 734-5335
228
80
560 Harwood
Lake
E
640
Floweree
Portage
401 402
934
White L.
Montague
561
CLIFFS

Map 4

towns/cities/counties
geographic features
historic sites
state and federal lands
Indian reservations
human-constructed sites

1	2	3	4	5	6	7	8
9	10	11	12	13	14	15	16
17	18	19	20	21	22	23	24

Map 4

311

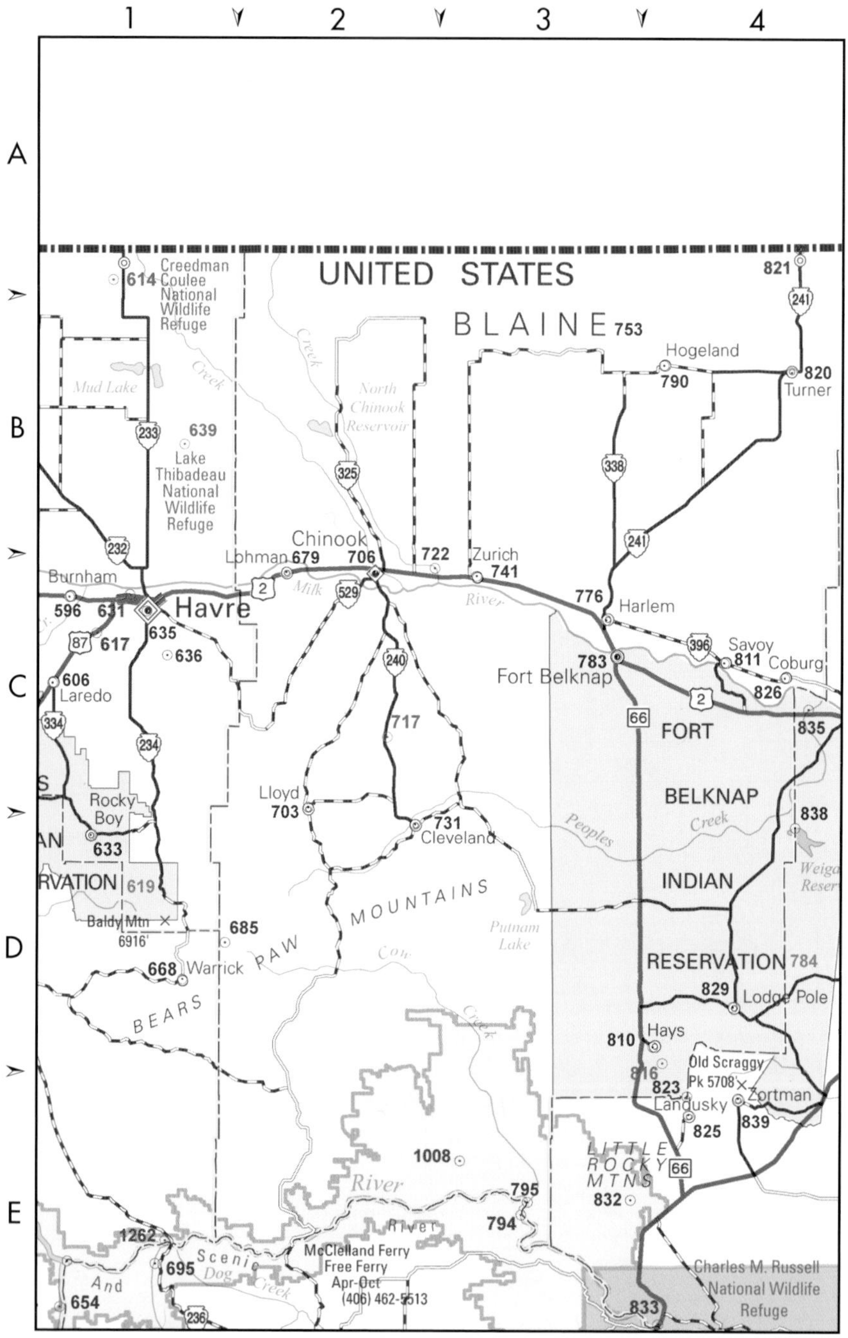

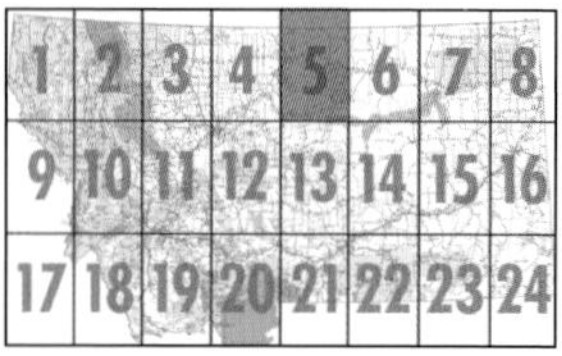

1   2   3   4

A

UNITED STATES

614 Creedman Coulee National Wildlife Refuge

821

241

BLAINE 753

Hogeland

820 Turner

790

Mud Lake

B

233

639

Lake Thibadeau National Wildlife Refuge

North Chinook Reservoir

325

338

232

241

Burnham

Chinook

Lohman 679 706 722 Zurich

2 Milk 529 741 River

776 Harlem

596 631 Havre

87 617 635

606

Laredo

636

240

783 Fort Belknap

396 Savoy

811 Coburg

826

FORT

66

835

C

334

234

717

BELKNAP

838

Rocky Boy

Lloyd

703

731 Cleveland

Peoples Creek

INDIAN

Weiga Reser

633

RVATION 619

Baldy Mtn 6916'

685

BEARS PAW MOUNTAINS

Putnam Lake

RESERVATION 784

829 Lodge Pole

D

668 Warrick

Cow

810 Hays

816

Old Scraggy Pk 5708'

823 Zortman

Landusky 839

825

1008

795

794

LITTLE ROCKY MTNS

832

66

E

1262

River

695

Scenic

654

236

Dog Creek

McClelland Ferry Free Ferry Apr-Oct (406) 462-5513

833

Charles M. Russell National Wildlife Refuge

Map 5

1	2	3	4	5	6	7	8
9	10	11	12	13	14	15	16
17	18	19	20	21	22	23	24

Map 5

towns/cities/counties
geographic features
historic sites
state and federal lands
Indian reservations
human-constructed sites

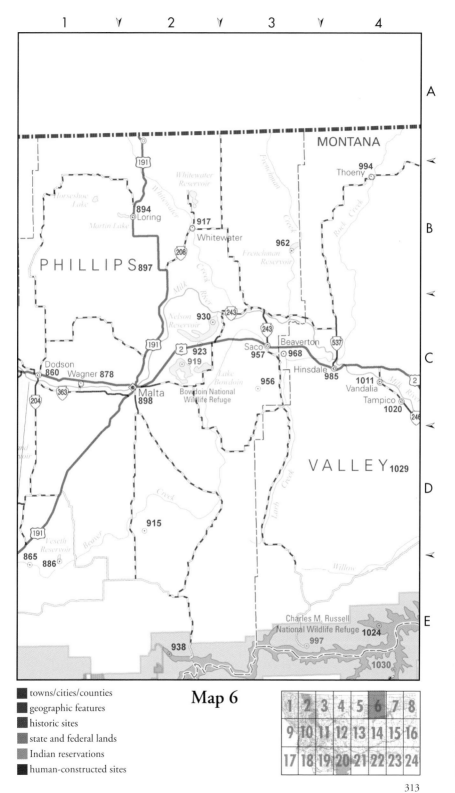

MONTANA

Thoeny 994

PHILLIPS 897

Whitewater
Whitewater Reservoir

917

962

Frenchman Reservoir

894
Loring

Horseshoe Lake

Martin Lake

208

Milk River

Creek River

Rock Creek

Frenchman Creek

191

191

Nelson Reservoir

930

243

243

Saco
957

Beaverton

537

923
919

968

2

Dodson
860

Wagner 878

Lake Bowdoin

Hinsdale
985

956

1011
Vandalia

2

363

Malta
898

Bowdoin National Wildlife Refuge

Tampico
1020

204

191

reservoir

VALLEY 1029

246

915

865

886

Veseth Reservoir

Beaver Creek

Creek

Lash Creek

Willow

Charles M. Russell
National Wildlife Refuge 1024

938

997

1030

Map 6

- ■ towns/cities/counties
- ■ geographic features
- ■ historic sites
- ■ state and federal lands
- ■ Indian reservations
- ■ human-constructed sites

1	2	3	4	5	6	7	8
9	10	11	12	13	14	15	16
17	18	19	20	21	22	23	24

Map 6

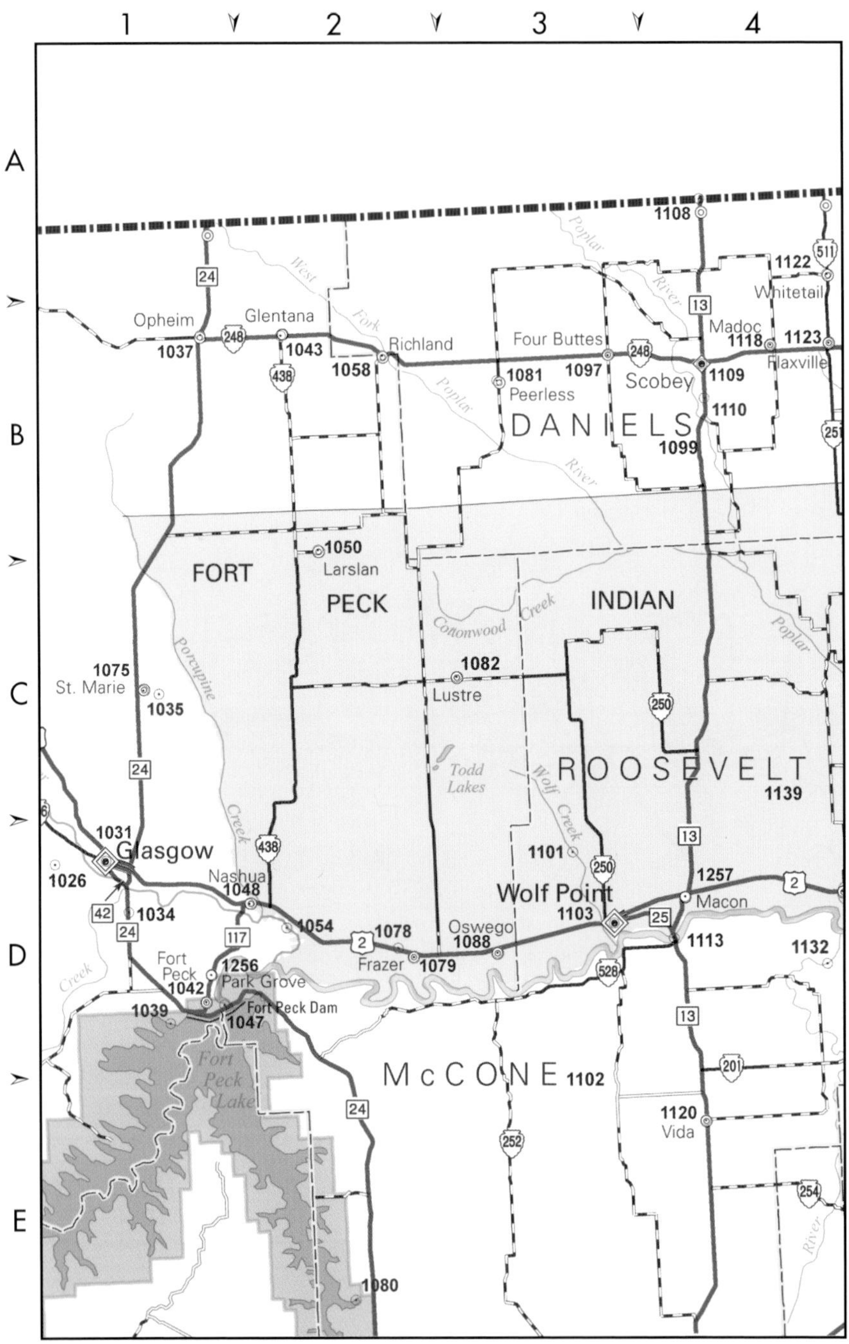

Map 7

Coordinate grid (top): 1 V 2 V 3 V 4

Row labels (left): A, B, C, D, E

Places and labels:

1108
1122
511
24
13
Whitetail
Opheim Glentana Richland Four Buttes 248 Madoc 1118 1123
1037 248 1043 1081 1097 Scobey 1109 Flaxville
438 1058 1058 Peerless 1110
D A N I E L S 1099
251

1050
Larslan
FORT
PECK INDIAN

1075 1082
St. Marie Cottonwood Creek
1035 Lustre 250

Porcupine ROOSEVELT
Todd Wolf Creek 1139
Lakes
1031 6 1101 13
Glasgow 438 250
1026 Nashua 1257
42 1048 1054 Wolf Point 1103 25 Macon 2
24 1034 117 1078 Oswego 1113 1132
Fort 2 1088 528
Peck 1256 1079
1042 Park Grove Frazer
1039 1047 Fort Peck Dam 13

Fort McCONE 1102
Peck
Lake 24 1120
201 Vida

252 254

1080

Legend:
- towns/cities/counties
- geographic features
- historic sites
- state and federal lands
- Indian reservations
- human-constructed sites

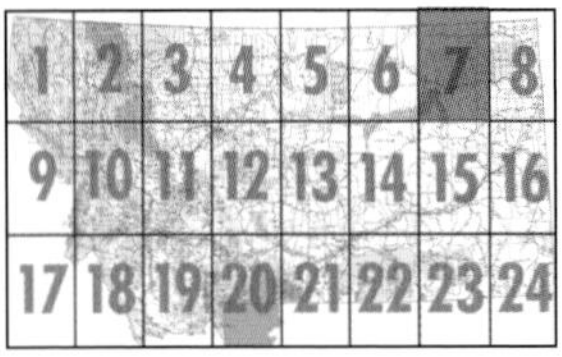

Map index grid:
1 2 3 4 5 6 7 8
9 10 11 12 13 14 15 16
17 18 19 20 21 22 23 24

Map 7

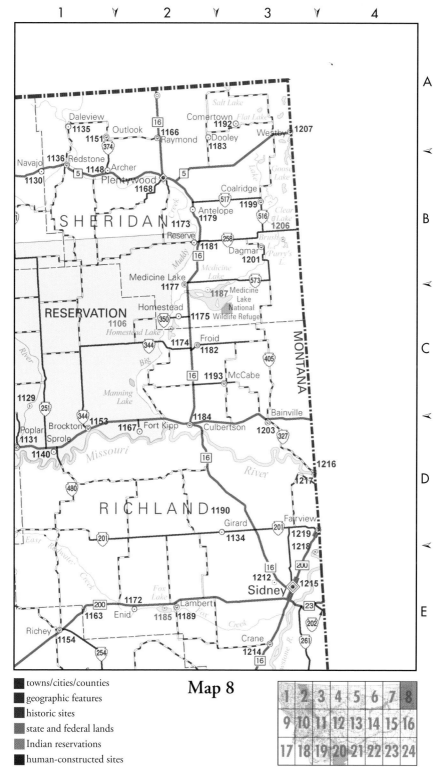

Map 8

■ towns/cities/counties
■ geographic features
■ historic sites
■ state and federal lands
■ Indian reservations
■ human-constructed sites

1	2	3	4	5	6	7	8
9	10	11	12	13	14	15	16
17	18	19	20	21	22	23	24

Map 8

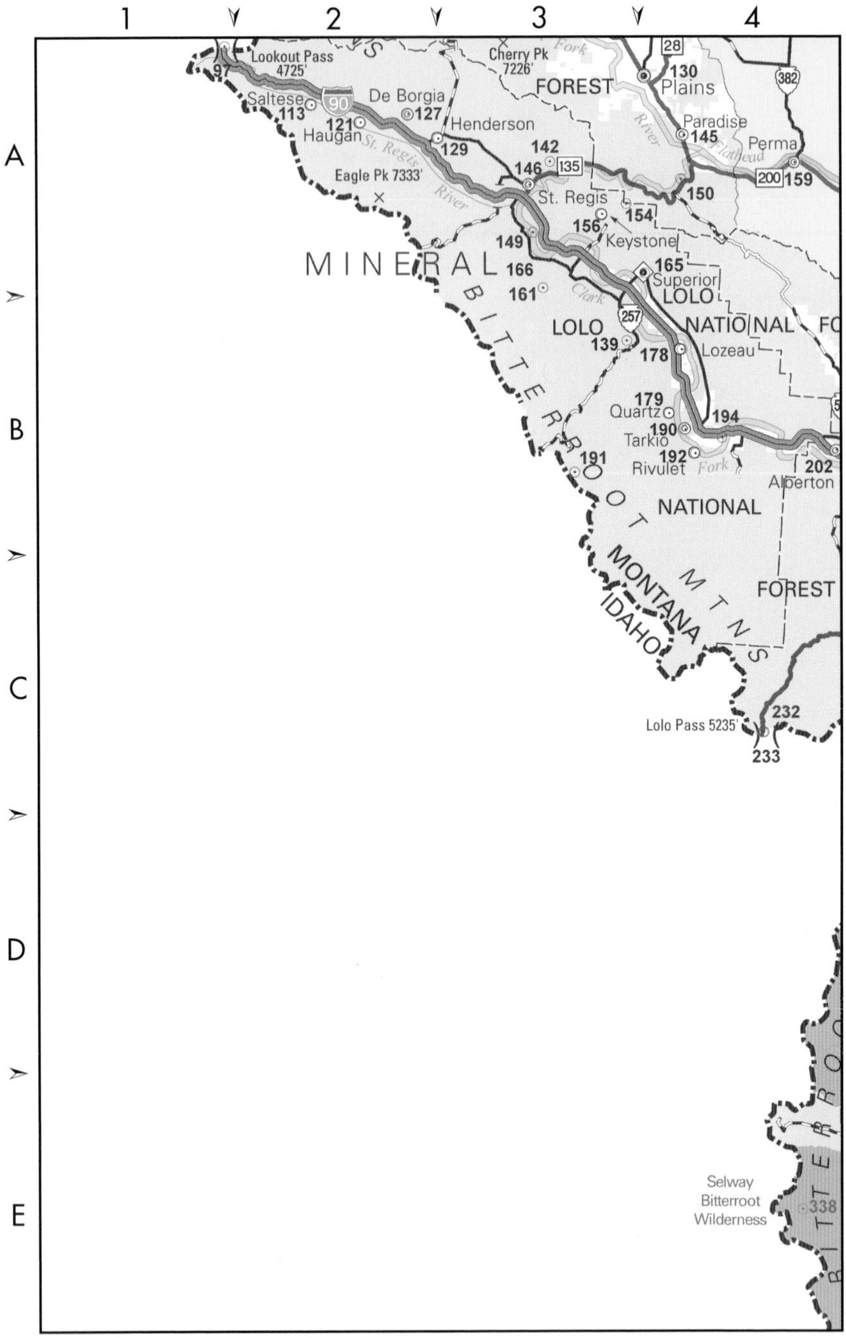

Map 9

1 2 3 4

A

B

C

D

E

97
Lookout Pass
4725'
Saltese
.113
Haugan
121
De Borgia
127
Henderson
129
142
Eagle Pk 7333'
146 135
St. Regis
156 154
149
166
161
MINERAL
139
178
Lozeau
LOLO
LOLO
257
179
Quartz
190 194
Tarkio
191 192 202
Rivulet Alberton
NATIONAL
MONTANA
IDAHO
BITTERROOT MTNS
FOREST
Cherry Pk
7226'
FOREST
28
130
Plains
Paradise
145 Perma
200 159
150
Keystone
165
Superior
NATIONAL FO
St. Regis River
Clark Fork
Fork
Lolo Pass 5235
232
233
Selway
Bitterroot
Wilderness
338
BITTERROO

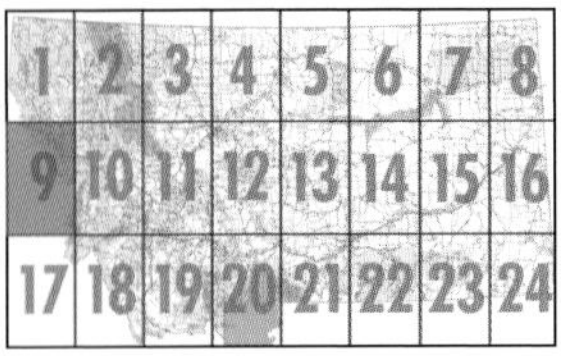

Map 9

towns/cities/counties
geographic features
historic sites
state and federal lands
Indian reservations
human-constructed sites

Map 9

1 2 3 4 5 6 7 8
9 10 11 12 13 14 15 16
17 18 19 20 21 22 23 24

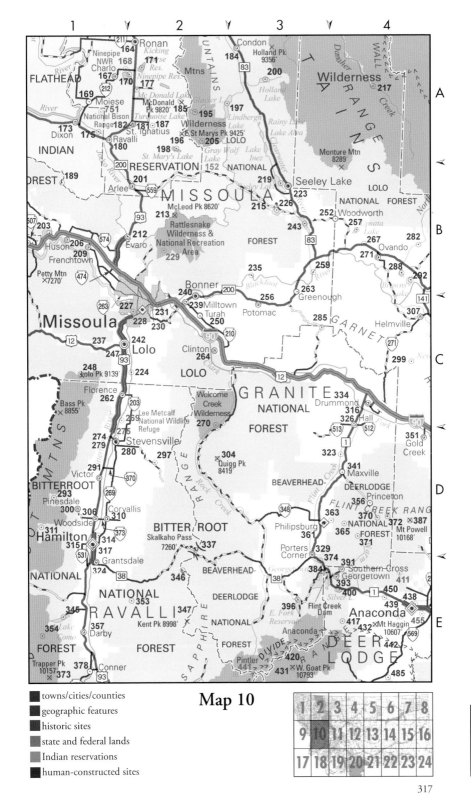

Map 10

Columns: 1, 2, 3, 4 (top) with markers between

Row A
211 • Ronan
164
Kicking
171 Horse
168 Res.
Ninepipe
NWR
Ninepipe Res.
Charlo
167
FLATHEAD
170
177
Mtns
Condon ×
Holland Pk
9356'
184
83
200
Wilderness
217
169
212
Moiese
751
McDonald ×
Pk 9820' 185
195
197
Glacier L.
Holland
Lake
Danaher
WALL

National Bison
Range 182 181 187
173 Dixon 175
 St. Ignatius
180
Ravalli
196
Wilderness
× St Marys Pk 9425'
205 LOLO
Lindbergh
Lake
Rainy Lake
Lake Alva
Clearwater River
RANGE

INDIAN
St. Mary's Lake
Gray Wolf Lake
Lake
Inez
Monture Mtn
8289'
×

200
RESERVATION 152
NATIONAL

FOREST 189
201
Arlee 559
Seeley Lake
219
223
LOLO

Row B
MISSOULA
McLeod Pk 8620'
213 ×
Rattlesnake
Wilderness &
National Recreation
Area
229
215
226
252 Woodworth
257
Lpsata
Lake
267
282
Ovando
271

93
203
574
Huson
206
209
Frenchtown
Petty Mtn
×7270'
474
212
Evaro
FOREST
83
235
259
263
Greenough
288
292

Row C
Missoula
263
227
231
228 230
Bonner
240
239 Milltown
Turah
250
200
256
Potomac
285
307
Helmville
271
GARNET

12
237
242
Lolo
247
93
248
Lolo Pk 9139'
224
90 210
Clinton
264
LOLO
Clark
12
299

Row D
Florence
262
Bass Pk
× 8855'
203
Lee Metcalf
269 National Wildlife
275 Refuge
274
279
Stevensville
280
297
Welcome
Creek
Wilderness
270
GRANITE
NATIONAL
Drummond
334
316
326 Hall
513 512
FOREST
323
341 Maxville
DEERLODGE
Princeton
356
90
351
Gold
Creek
× 304
Quigg Pk
8419
Rock Creek
1
BEAVERHEAD

Row E
291
Victor
370
BITTERROOT
293
300 306
Pinesdale
269
Corvallis
310
311
Woodside
Hamilton
315 317
314
373
531
Grantsdale
324
38
346
353
NATIONAL
345
RAVALLI
347
354
Lake
Como
357
Darby
FOREST
FOREST
BITTER ROOT
Skalkaho Pass
7260'
337
BEAVERHEAD-
DEERLODGE
NATIONAL
FOREST
Kent Pk 8998'
Philipsburg
361
363
365
370
371
372 × 387
Mt Powell
10168'
NATIONAL
FOREST
Porters
Corner
329
374
384
391
393
Southern Cross
Georgetown
411
400
450
438
439
Anaconda
455
569
442
DEER
LODGE
348
Flint Creek
FLINT CREEK RANGE
E. Fork
Reservoir
396
Flint Creek
Dam
Anaconda
417
432 × Mt Haggin
10607'
485
Trapper Pk
10157'
×
378
373
Conner
93
SAPPHIRE MTNS
DIVIDE RANGE
Pintler
441
420
431 × W. Goat Pk
10793'

Legend

- ■ towns/cities/counties
- ■ geographic features
- ■ historic sites
- ■ state and federal lands
- ■ Indian reservations
- ■ human-constructed sites

1	2	3	4	5	6	7	8
9	10	11	12	13	14	15	16
17	18	19	20	21	22	23	24

Map 10

317

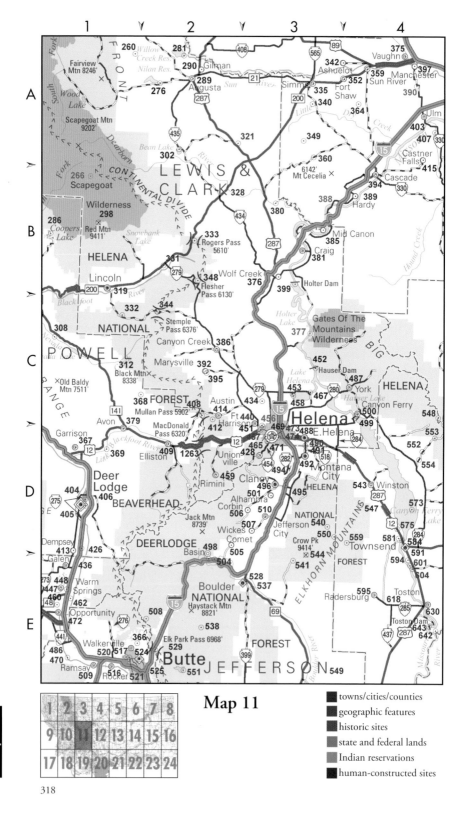

Map 11

- towns/cities/counties
- geographic features
- historic sites
- state and federal lands
- Indian reservations
- human-constructed sites

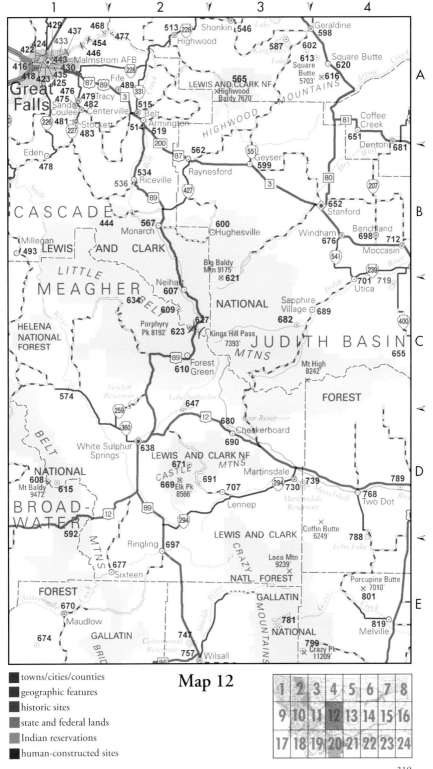

1   Y   2   Y   3   Y   4

429   **437**   **468**
  477
424   **433**   **454**
422   **446**
416   **443** Malmstrom AFB
418 **423** **425** **430**   228
Great **476** **475** 87 89 Fife **489**
Falls **479** Tracy   3 331
Sand **482** **515**
226 Coulee **481** Centerville   Belt
  227 Stockett   **514** Armington **519**
483

513 228 Shonkin **546** Geraldine **598**
Highwood   **587** **602**
  613 Square Butte
  Square **620**
  Butte
LEWIS AND CLARK NF 5703' ×**616**
×Highwood
Baldy 7670'
  HIGHWOOD   MOUNTAINS   Arrow   Creek
  81   Coffee
  Creek
  651
200   **562** **551**   Dry   Wolf   Denton **681**
Eden 87 Geyser
478 Raynesford **599**
  80
534   3 207
536 Riceville
  89 427   **652**
Stanford

C A S C A D E   **567**   **600**   Windham Benchland
444 Monarch Hughesville **676** **698** **712**
Millegan   541 Moccasin
493 LEWIS AND CLARK   Big Baldy
  LITTLE   Mtn 9175'   River
M E A G H E R   Neihart ×**621**   Judith   239
  607   701 **719**
634 **609** NATIONAL   Sapphire Utica
HELENA Porphyry   **627**   Village **689** 400
NATIONAL Pk 8192' **623** Kings Hill Pass **682**
FOREST   7393'   J U D I T H   B A S I N
  89 Forest   MTNS   **655**
610 Green   Mt High
  8242'
574   **647**   FOREST
259 Lake Sutherlin
360 12 **680** Fair Reservoir
  Checkerboard
  690
White Sulphur **638**
Springs LEWIS AND CLARK NF
NATIONAL **671** MTNS Martinsdale   **789**
608 CASTLE **691**   **739**
Mt Baldy **669** Elk Pk **707** 294 **730**   **768**
9472' **615** 8566'   Lennep   Two Dot
B R O A D-   12   Martinsdale
W A T E R   89   Reservoir
592   294   Coffin Butte   **788**
  LEWIS AND CLARK   6249' Echo Lake
  Ringling **697**   Loco Mtn
  677   9239' Porcupine Butte
  Sixteen   CRAZY   ×   × 7010'
FOREST   NATL. FOREST   **801**
670   GALLATIN
Maudlow   **781**   **819**
674 GALLATIN   NATIONAL Melville
  747   **799**
  757 Wilsall   × Crazy Pk
  86   11209'

towns/cities/counties
geographic features   **Map 12**
historic sites
state and federal lands
Indian reservations
human-constructed sites

1	2	3	4	5	6	7	8
9	10	11	**12**	13	14	15	16
17	18	19	20	21	22	23	24

A
B
C
D
E

Map 12

319

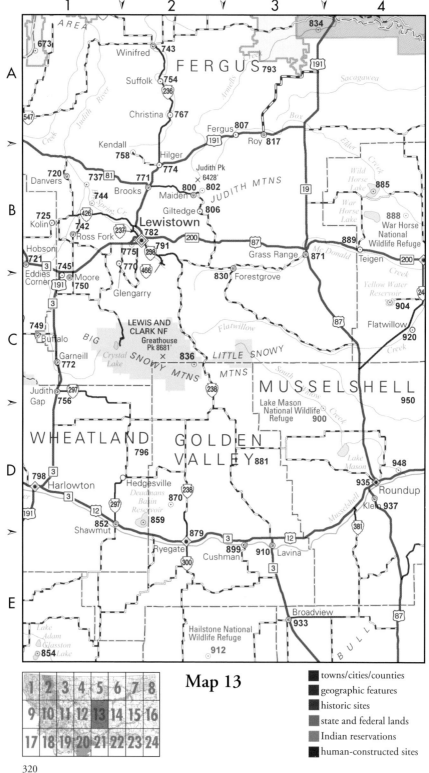

Map 13

	1	2	3	4	5	6	7	8
	9	10	11	12	**13**	14	15	16
	17	18	19	20	21	22	23	24

■ towns/cities/counties
■ geographic features
■ historic sites
■ state and federal lands
■ Indian reservations
■ human-constructed sites

Map 13

320

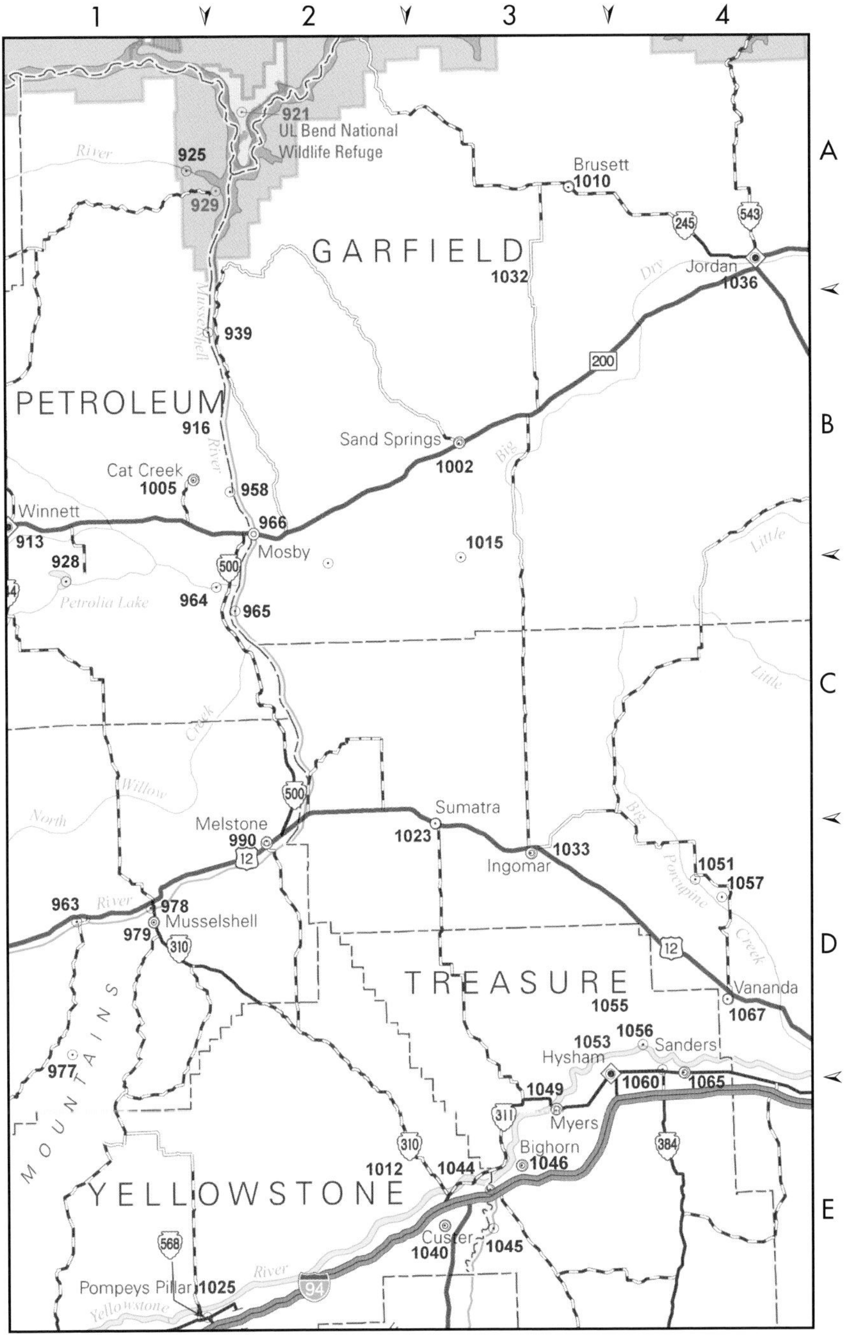

Map 14

Map 14

Legend:
- towns/cities/counties
- geographic features
- historic sites
- state and federal lands
- Indian reservations
- human-constructed sites

Map grid:
1 2 3 4 5 6 7 8
9 10 11 12 13 14 15 16
17 18 19 20 21 22 23 24

Column markers: 1 2 3 4

Row markers: A B C D E

Map labels and features:

GARFIELD
PETROLEUM
TREASURE
YELLOWSTONE
MOUNTAINS

UL Bend National Wildlife Refuge 921
925
929
939
916
1032
Brusett 1010
Jordan 1036
245
543
200
Sand Springs 1002
Cat Creek 1005
958
Winnett 913
928
966
Mosby
500
964
965
1015
1051
1057
500
Melstone 990
12
Sumatra 1023
1033
Ingomar
963
978
979
310
Musselshell
977
1055
1053
1056
Sanders
Hysham
1049
1060
1065
Myers
311
Bighorn 1046
310
1012
1044
384
Vananda 1067
568
Custer 1040
1045
Pompeys Pillar 1025
94
River
Missouri River
Petrolia Lake
North Willow Creek
Yellowstone River
Big Dry
Little
Big Porcupine Creek

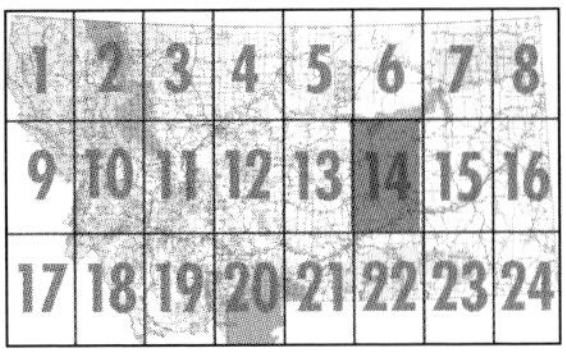

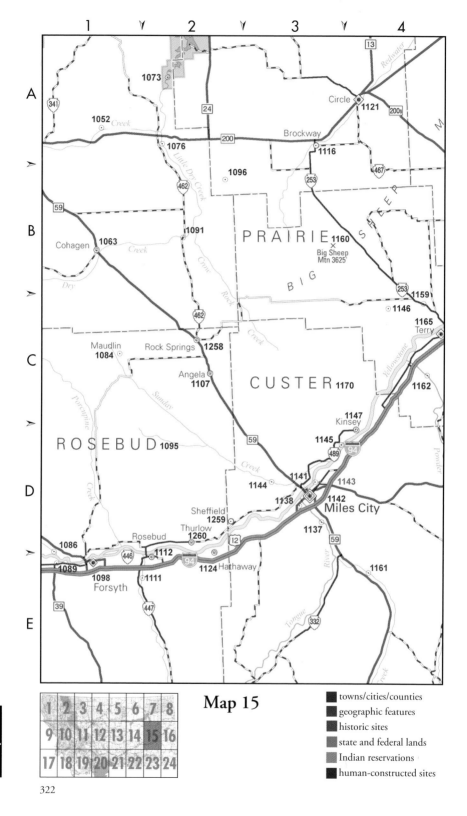

Map 15

Legend:
- towns/cities/counties
- geographic features
- historic sites
- state and federal lands
- Indian reservations
- human-constructed sites

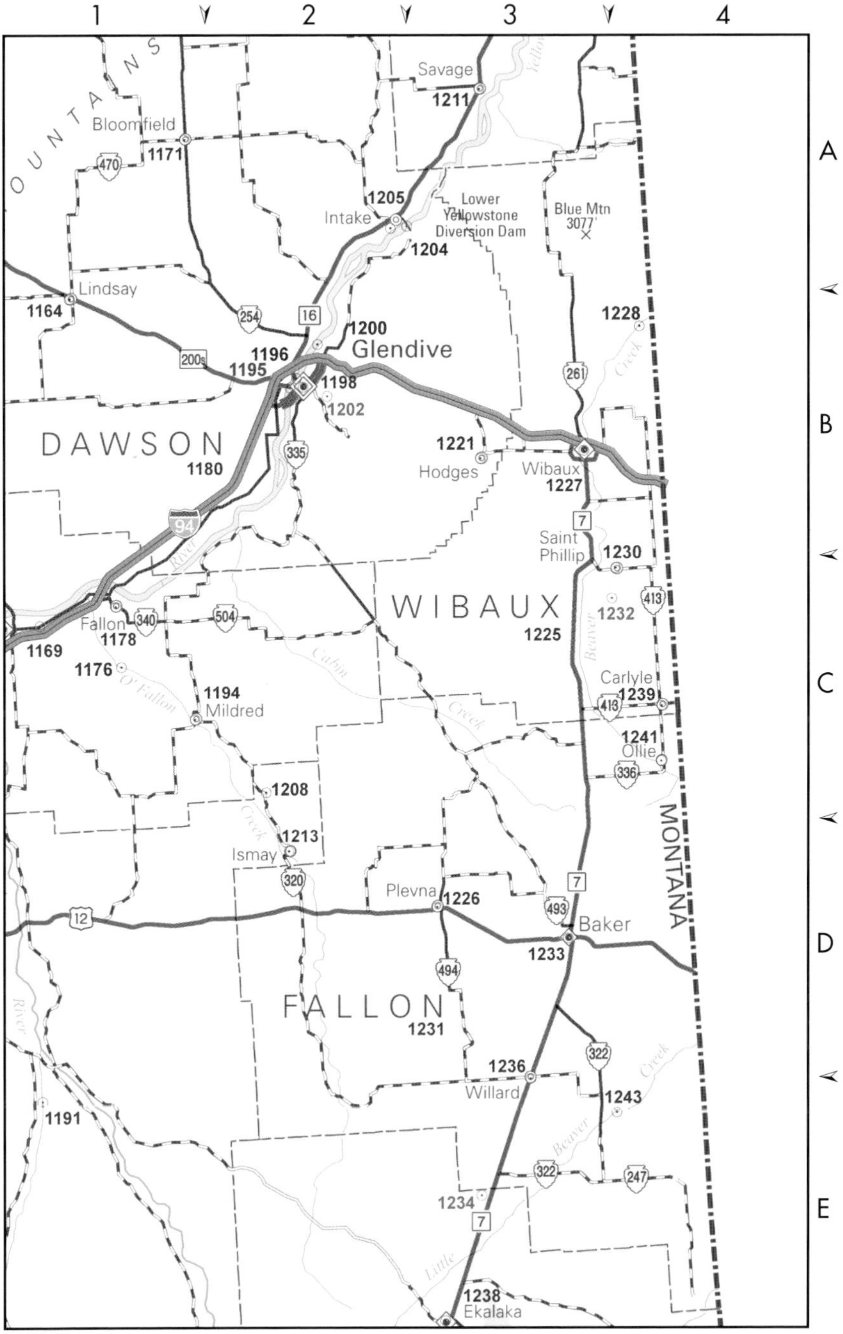

Map 16

Grid coordinates (top): 1 — 2 — 3 — 4
Row labels (right side): A, B, C, D, E

OUNTAINS

Savage
1211

Bloomfield
470 **1171**

1205
Intake
Lower
Yellowstone
Diversion Dam
1204
Blue Mtn
3077'
×
1228

Lindsay
1164
254   16
1200
1196   Glendive
200s   **1195**
1198
1202
261

D A W S O N
1180
335

1221
Hodges
Wibaux
1227

94

Saint
Phillip
7
1230

W I B A U X
1232
413
Fallon 340   504
1178
1169
1225

1176
O'Fallon
Carlyle
Carlyle
1239
413

1194
Mildred
1241
Ollie
336

1208

1213
Ismay
320

M O N T A N A

Plevna **1226**
7
12
1233
493   Baker

1494

F A L L O N
1231

1236   322
Willard   **1243**

1191

322   247

1234
7

1238
Ekalaka

Legend
- towns/cities/counties
- geographic features
- historic sites
- state and federal lands
- Indian reservations
- human-constructed sites

Map 16

Grid index:
1 2 3 4 5 6 7 8
9 10 11 12 13 14 15 **16**
17 18 19 20 21 22 23 24

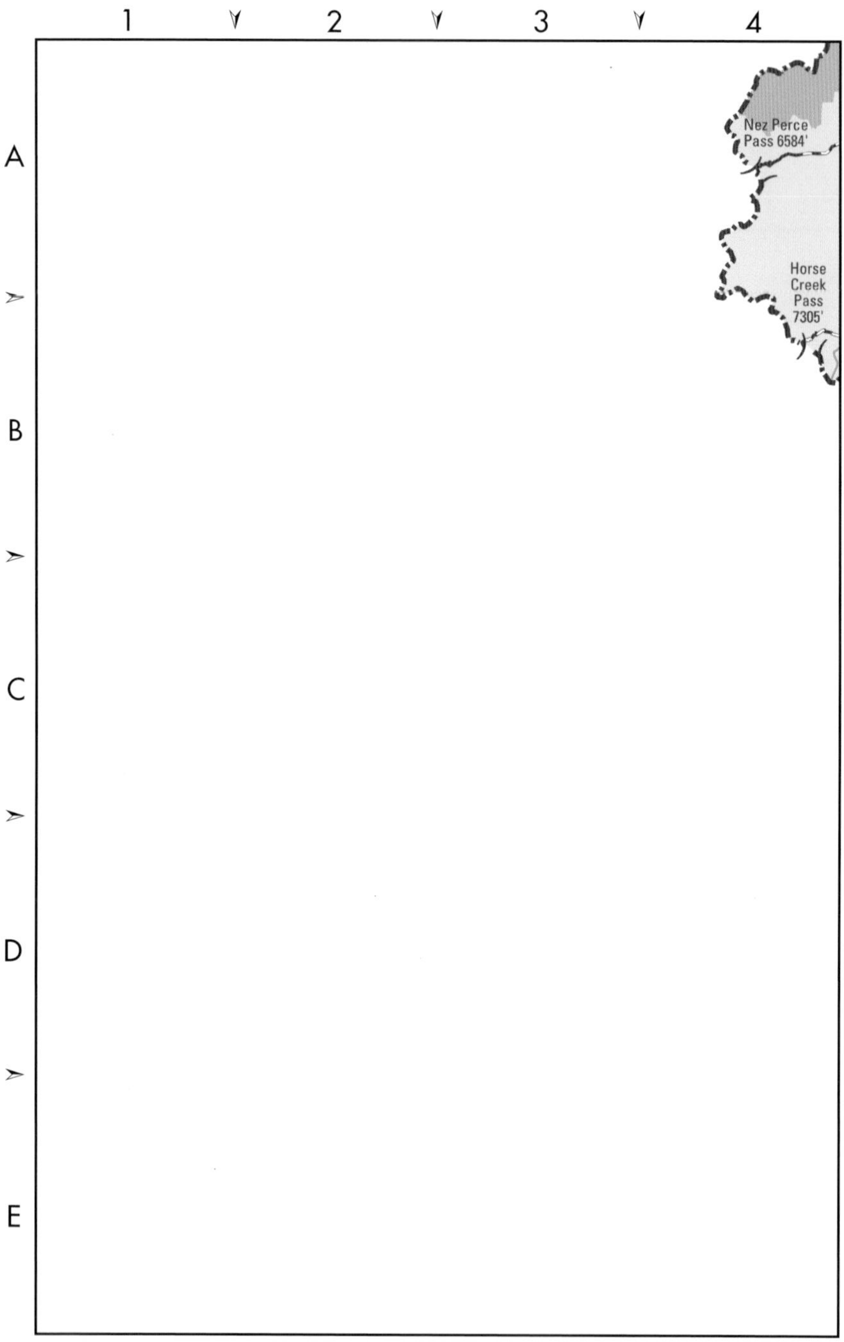

| 1 | ∨ | 2 | ∨ | 3 | ∨ | 4 |

A

Nez Perce
Pass 6584'

Horse
Creek
Pass
7305'

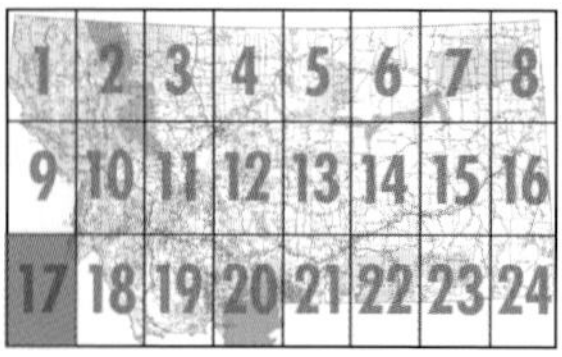

B

C

D

E

1	2	3	4	5	6	7	8
9	10	11	12	13	14	15	16
17	18	19	20	21	22	23	24

Map 17

■ towns/cities/counties
■ geographic features
■ historic sites
■ state and federal lands
■ Indian reservations
■ human-constructed sites

Map 17

324

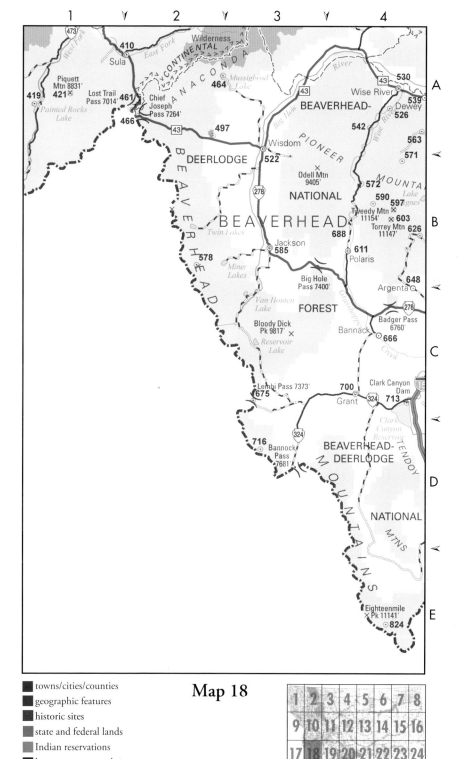

Map 18

towns/cities/counties
geographic features
historic sites
state and federal lands
Indian reservations
human-constructed sites

1	2	3	4	5	6	7	8
9	10	11	12	13	14	15	16
17	18	19	20	21	22	23	24

Map 18

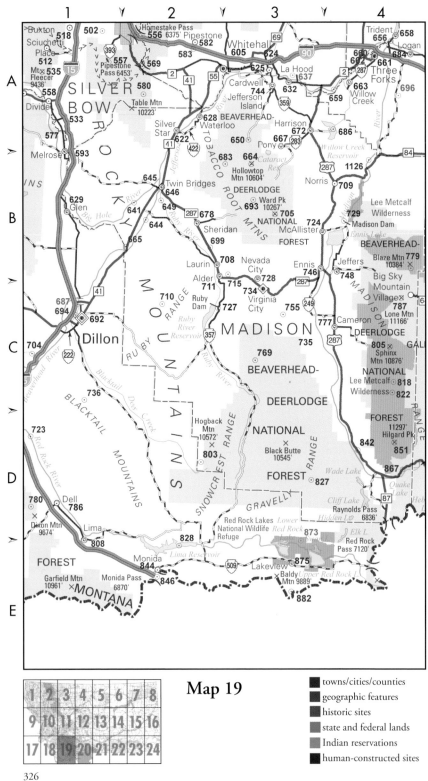

Map 19

- towns/cities/counties
- geographic features
- historic sites
- state and federal lands
- Indian reservations
- human-constructed sites

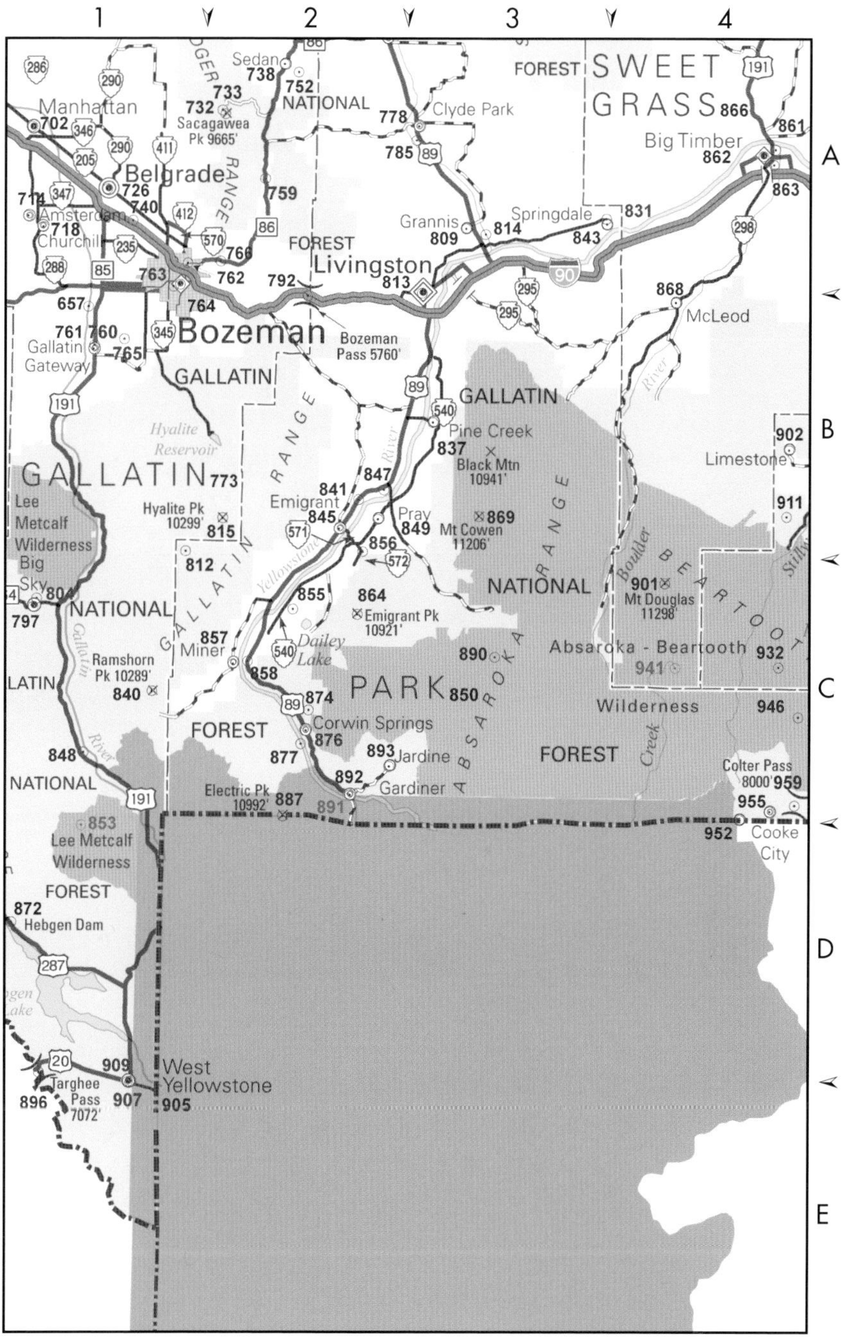

Map 20

1   **2**   **3**   **4**

286

FOREST SWEET
290
Sedan
738
732 733 752 GRASS 866
Manhattan 732 NATIONAL 778 Clyde Park 191
702 346 Sacagawea 862 Big Timber
Pk 9665' 785 831 861
205 411 785 89 862
Belgrade 759 Springdale 863
726 740 Grannis 814 843
711 347 86 809 831 298
718 Amsterdam 412 863
Churchill 235 570 766 FOREST
288 85 763 762 792 Livingston 868
657 764 813 295 McLeod
761 760 813 295
Gallatin 765 Bozeman 345 Bozeman
Gateway Pass 5760'
191 GALLATIN GALLATIN 902
Hyalite GALLATIN 540 Limestone
Reservoir Pine Creek 911
GALLATIN 773 837 Black Mtn
Lee 841 847 10941'
Metcalf Hyalite Pk 845 Emigrant Pray 869
Wilderness 10299' 571 849 Mt Cowen
Big 815 856 11206' 901
Sky 812 572 Mt Douglas BEARTOOTH
804 855 864 NATIONAL 11298'
797 857 Emigrant Pk 941 932
Ramshorn Miner 10921' Absaroka - Beartooth
Pk 10289' 858 Dailey 890 946
840 540 Lake 850 Wilderness
LATIN 874 PARK Colter Pass
848 89 Corwin Springs 8000' 959
FOREST 877 876 FOREST 955
NATIONAL 892 893 Jardine 952 Cooke
191 Electric Pk 887 891 Gardiner City
853 10992'
Lee Metcalf
Wilderness
FOREST
872
Hebgen Dam
287
909 West
896 Targhee 907 Yellowstone
Pass 905
7072'

A B C D E

■ towns/cities/counties
■ geographic features
■ historic sites
■ state and federal lands
■ Indian reservations
■ human-constructed sites

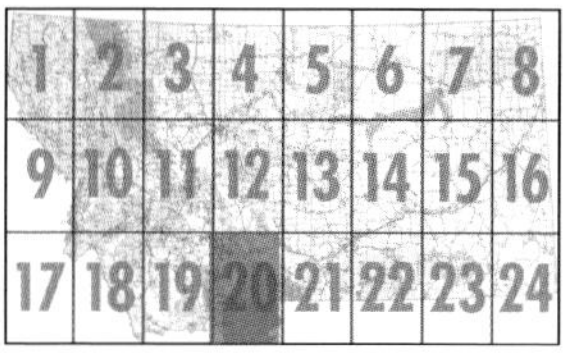

1	2	3	4	5	6	7	8
9	10	11	12	13	14	15	16
17	18	19	20	21	22	23	24

Map 20

327

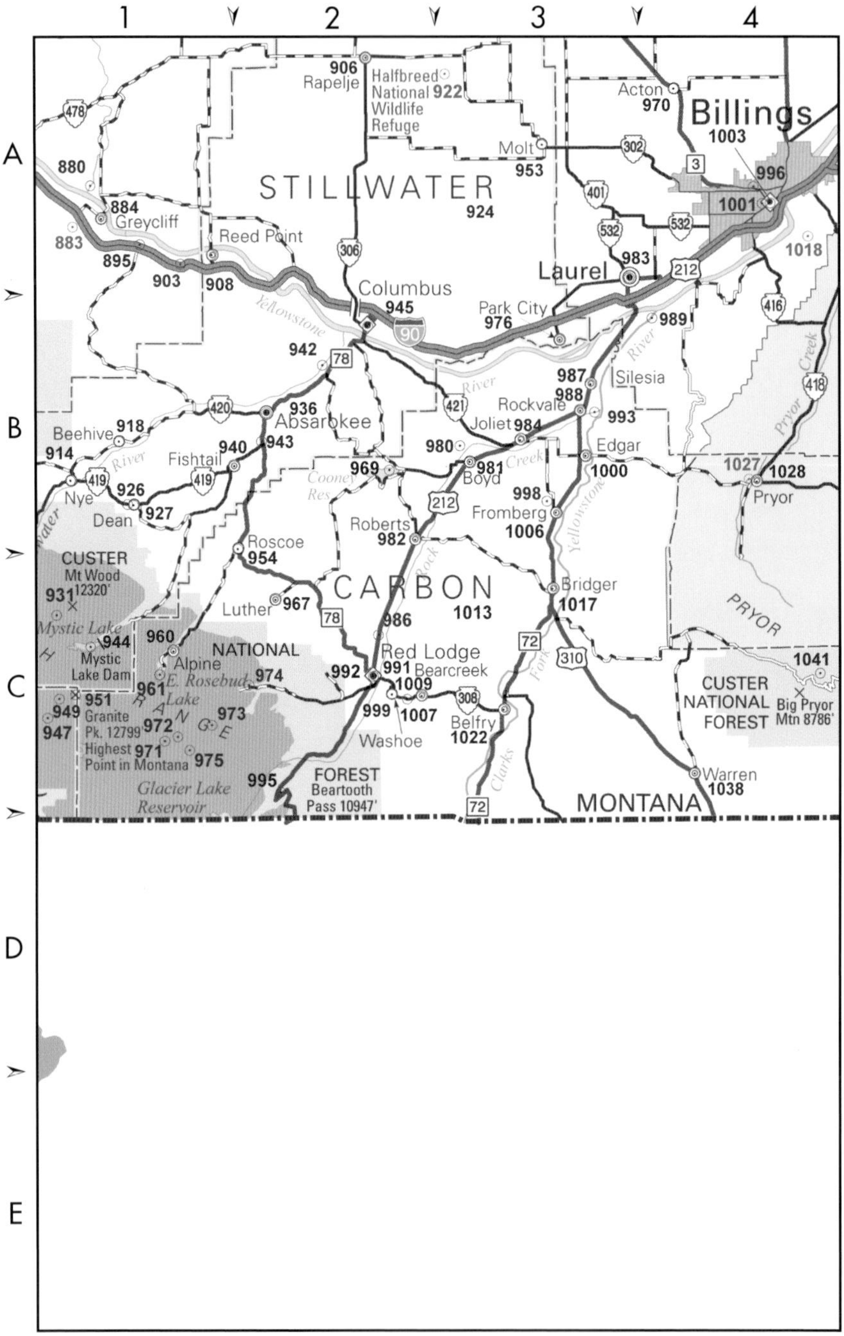

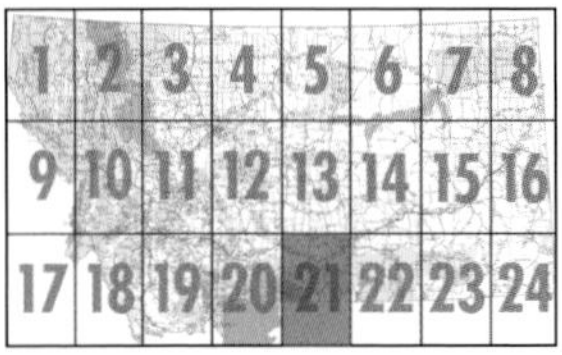

STILLWATER

906 Rapelje
Halfbreed National 922 Wildlife Refuge
Acton 970
Billings 1003

478

Molt 953
302
996

A
880
884 Greycliff
401
3
1001

883
Reed Point
306
532
532
1018

895
903 908
Columbus 945
212
Laurel
983
416

Yellowstone
90
Park City 976
989

942
78
421
987 988
Silesia
418

Beehive 918
420
936 Absarokee 943
Rockvale
Joliet 984
993
Pryor Creek

B
914
River
940
969
980
Edgar
1000
1027 1028

Nye 926
419
419
Boyd 981
998
Pryor

Dean 927
Roberts 982
212
Fromberg 1006

CARBON
Roscoe 954
Bridger 1017

CUSTER
Mt Wood 12320'
931
Luther 967
78
986
1013

Mystic Lake
944 960
NATIONAL
Red Lodge
991 Bearcreek
72
310
PRYOR

C
Mystic Lake Dam
Alpine
E. Rosebud
974
992
1009
308
CUSTER NATIONAL FOREST
1041

951 961
Lake
973
999 1007
Belfry 1022
Big Pryor Mtn 8786'

949 972
G E
975
Washoe
Clarks
Warren 1038

947 971
Highest Point in Montana
995
FOREST
Beartooth Pass 10947'
72
MONTANA

Granite Pk. 12799

Glacier Lake Reservoir

D

E

Map 21

1	2	3	4	5	6	7	8
9	10	11	12	13	14	15	16
17	18	19	20	21	22	23	24

towns/cities/counties
geographic features
historic sites
state and federal lands
Indian reservations
human-constructed sites

Map 21

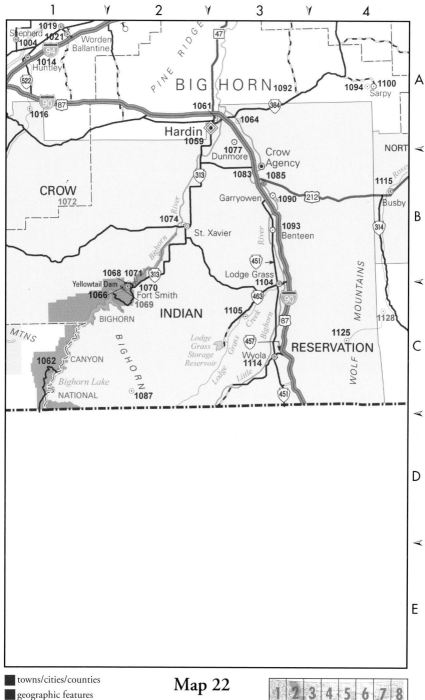

Map 22

towns/cities/counties
geographic features
historic sites
state and federal lands
Indian reservations
human-constructed sites

1	2	3	4	5	6	7	8
9	10	11	12	13	14	15	16
17	18	19	20	21	22	23	24

Map 22

329

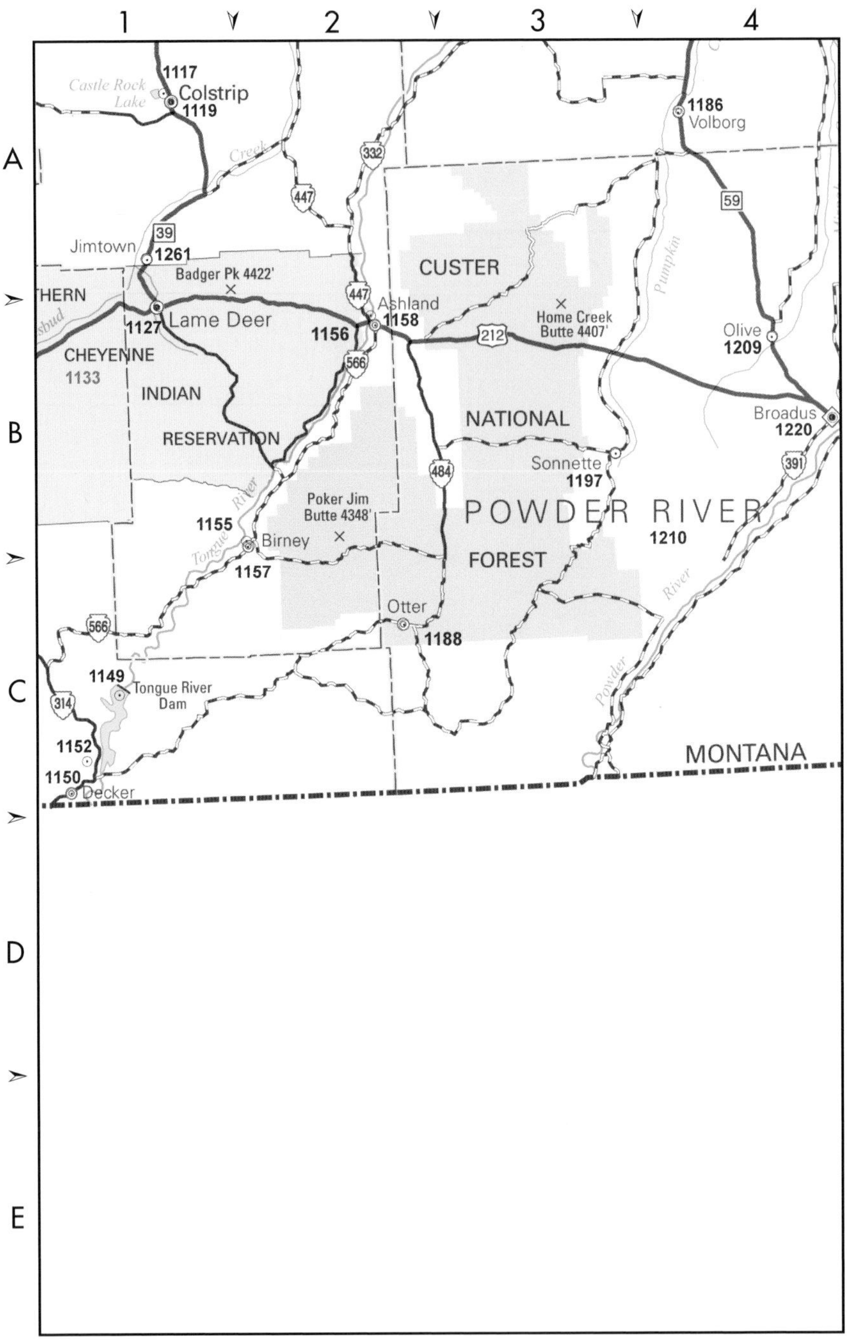

Map 23

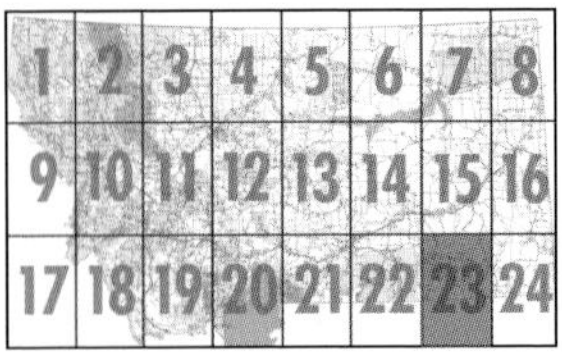

Legend:
- towns/cities/counties
- geographic features
- historic sites
- state and federal lands
- Indian reservations
- human-constructed sites

Map locations shown:

Row A:
- Castle Rock Lake
- 1117 Colstrip 1119
- ___ Creek
- 332 (highway)
- 447 (highway)
- 1186 Volborg
- 59 (highway)

Row A (lower):
- Jimtown 39 1261
- Badger Pk 4422'
- HERN
- CHEYENNE 1133
- 1127 Lame Deer
- 447 1156
- Ashland 1158
- 212
- CUSTER
- Home Creek Butte 4407'
- Olive 1209
- 566

Row B:
- INDIAN
- RESERVATION
- NATIONAL
- Sonnette 1197
- Broadus 1220
- 391
- 484
- POWDER RIVER
- 1210
- 1155
- Poker Jim Butte 4348'
- Birney
- 1157
- FOREST
- Tongue River
- Otter 1188

Row C:
- 1149 Tongue River Dam
- 314
- 566
- 1152
- 1150 Decker
- Powder River
- MONTANA

Row D: (empty)

Row E: (empty)

Map index grid (Map 23):
```
1  2  3  4  5  6  7  8
9  10 11 12 13 14 15 16
17 18 19 20 21 22 23 24
```

Map 23

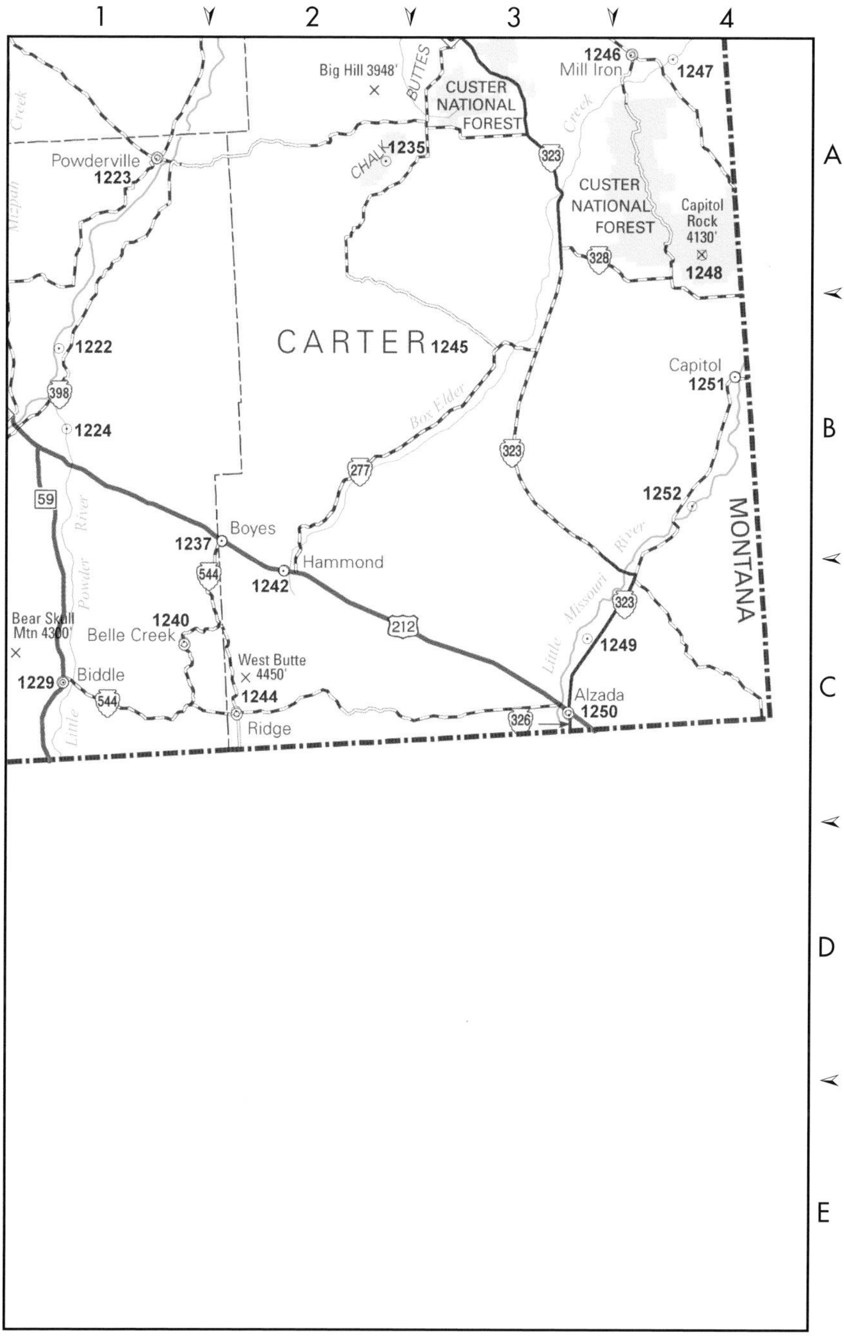

1   2   3   4

Big Hill 3948'
×

CHALK BUTTES

**CUSTER
NATIONAL
FOREST**

1246 ⊙
Mill Iron

1247

1235

323

Powderville ⊙
1223

**CUSTER
NATIONAL
FOREST**

Capitol
Rock
4130'
⊗
1248

328

A

1222 ⊙

CARTER **1245**

Capitol
⊙
1251

Box Elder

398

1224 ⊙

277

323

B

59

Powder River

Boyes ⊙
1237

Hammond ⊙
1242

1252

MONTANA

544

323

Little Missouri River

1249 ⊙

C

212

Bear Skull
Mtn 4300'
×

1240
Belle Creek ⊙
Biddle

West Butte
× 4450'
1244

Alzada ⊙
1250

1229 ⊙

544

Ridge

326

Little

D

E

■ towns/cities/counties
■ geographic features
■ historic sites
■ state and federal lands
■ Indian reservations
■ human-constructed sites

Map 24

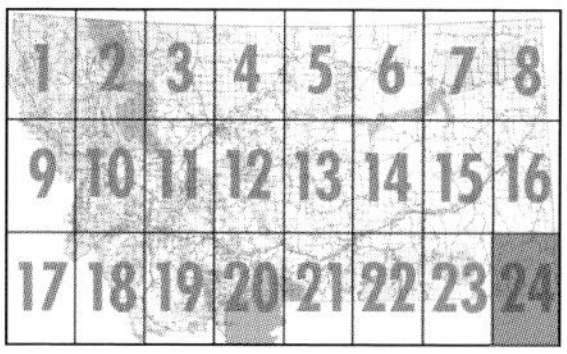

1	2	3	4	5	6	7	8
9	10	11	12	13	14	15	16
17	18	19	20	21	22	23	24

Map 24

Site Listing/Index

INDEX

INDEX

INDEX

INDEX

INDEX

(see above)

INDEX